Utopias and Architecture

Utopias and Architecture is concerned with the enduring central question in architecture of how buildings communicate. Post-modern architecture often fails to create welcoming built environments, yet in this book Nathaniel Coleman shows how a significant contemporary architecture persists as a real possibility. Utopia is examined as fundamental to the invention of a meaningful architecture and Nathaniel Coleman traces the role of utopias for social imagination through architectural theory and history, utopian literature, utopian studies, philosophy, sociology and anthropology.

Comprising an investigation of architectural ideas and works of the 1950s and 1960s, the author focuses on Aldo van Eyck's Amsterdam Orphanage, Louis I. Kahn's Salk Institute and Le Corbusier's La Tourette. These exemplary works, constructed when modernist orthodoxy was faltering, proposed an alternative modernity which revealed pathways to recuperating architectural meaning. Nathaniel Coleman extends his investigation into the present, examining Daniel Libeskind's Berlin Jewish Museum, Tod Williams and Billie Tsien's Neurosciences Institute and Renzo Piano's Tjibaou Cultural Centre, buildings that continue to renew the tradition of modern architecture in distinct ways.

Utopias and Architecture presents an alternative to the predominant current modes of theorizing and practising. No book available on architecture examines utopia with equal depth, or so persuasively challenges conventional readings of the role of utopia for architectural invention, making this work a unique contribution to architectural design methodology, history and theory and utopian studies.

Nathaniel Coleman first studied architecture at the Institute for Architecture and Urban Studies in New York, and continued his education at the Rhode Island School of Design. He practiced in New York and Rome and completed his PhD at the University of Pennsylvania, where Joseph Rykwert was his supervisor. Currently a Senior Lecturer in Architecture and Urban Design and the Director of Architecture and Landscape, Coleman is also a member of the Centre for Tectonic Cultures Research Group at the University of Newcastle upon Tyne. He previously taught in the US.

Utopias and Architecture

Nathaniel Coleman

Routledge
Taylor & Francis Group

LONDON AND NEW YORK

First published 2005
by Routledge
2 Park Square, Milton Park, Abingdon, Oxon OX14 4RN

Simultaneously published in the USA and Canada
by Routledge
270 Madison Ave, New York, NY 10016

Transferred to Digital Printing 2007

Routledge is an imprint of the Taylor & Francis Group, an informa business

Typeset in Univers by Keystroke, Jacaranda Lodge, Wolverhampton
Printed and bound in Great Britain by TJI Digital, Padstow, Cornwall

British Library Cataloguing in Publication Data
A catalogue record for this book is available from the British Library

Library of Congress Cataloging in Publication Data
A catalog record for this book has been requested

ISBN 10: 0-415-70084-1 (hbk)
ISBN 10: 0-415-70085-x (pbk)

ISBN 13: 978-0-415-70084-9 (hbk)
ISBN 13: 978-0-415-70085-6 (pbk)

To the memory of my mother,
Corrine

Contents

Illustration credits

The author and publisher gratefully acknowledge the following for permission to reproduce material in this book. Every effort has been made to contact copyright holders for their permission. The publishers would be grateful to hear from any copyright holder who is not acknowledged here and will undertake to rectify any errors or omissions in future editions of the book.

Centre Culturel Tjibaou – ADCK/Renzo Piano Building Workshop Archietectes and Nathaniel Coleman   13.20, 13.21–31.29

Nathaniel Coleman and FLC/ADAGP, Paris and DACS, London 2004   0.1, 6.1, 6.3–6.5, 6.7, 6.8, 7.10–7.19, 7.23, 7.24, 13.11

FLC/ADAGP, Paris and DACS, London 2004   1.2, 5.3, 5.7, 6.2, 7.3, 7.5–7.9

Florence, Biblioteca Nazionale (National Library)   3.2

Hannie van Eyck   5.8, 10.3, 11.3, 11.4, 11.9

Louis I. Kahn Collection. The Architectural Archives of the University of Pennsylvania   5.4, 5.5, 8.1–8.3, 9.1, 9.2, 13.30

Metropolitan Museum of Art, Robert Lehman Collection   3.1

Philadelphia Museum of Art   9.4–9.6

Photo SCALA, Florence – Courtesy of the Ministero Beni e Att. Culturali, 1990   3.2, 3.3

The New York Public Library, Astor, Lenox and Tilden Foundations   1.1, 2.1, 4.1, 4.2, 5.1, 5.2, 12.1

Venice, Accademia, Photo SCALA, Florence – Courtesy of the Minestero Beni e Att. Culturali, 1990   5.6

Venturi, Scott Brown and Associates, Inc.   5.9

All other photographs are copyright of the current author.

Acknowledgments

My sincere appreciation goes to the individuals who shared their buildings with me. In particular, Antoine Lion at La Tourette, who introduced me to his home and his Order and who shared his interest in Le Corbusier, Thomas More and utopia with me; Bob Lizarraga at the Salk for sharing his long experience with the day-to-day operations of the Institute. Thanks go as well to Yuki Imai for making my visit to the Neurosciences Institute so smooth, and to Einar Gall and Gerald Edelman for helping me to understand their unique research centre, especially its correspondences with and divergences from the Salk. I owe a special debt of gratitude to Alban Bensa who generously met with me at his office in Paris to discuss some nagging questions I had about the Tjibaou Cultural Centre. Acknowledgment is also due to staff at the Amsterdam Orphanage, Jewish Museum Berlin and Tjibaou Cultural Centre for giving me access to their places of work and for permitting me to take photographs. Thanks are due also to Hannie van Eyck, Studio Libeskind, Renzo Piano Building Workshop and Tod Williams Billie Tsien Associates for their expressions of support for the aims of this project when approached for permission to use certain illustrative materials, some of which are included herein.

Substantial early, and unwavering, encouragement for this project came from Joseph Rykwert and David Leatherbarrow. I owe them both a great debt that I hope this book, in some small way, honours. I am also grateful to Caroline Mallinder at Routledge for her ongoing faith in this project. Gratitude is also due to the many students in the US and UK who provided me with innumerable opportunities (in studios, seminars and lectures) to explore the ideas and conclusions developed in this book. Alex Burry, who undertook a careful reading of the entire manuscript, is owed a very special debt of gratitude for his generous effort and thoughtful comments. My wife, Elizabeth, for her patience, love, support, generosity and faith that I would actually complete this book, which of course I could not have done without her. For all these reasons and more, especially her ongoing critical reading of the text as it developed, I owe her the most.

A book of this sort could not have come to fruition without generous institutional support. It is for this that I would like to call special attention to the British Academy, the Graham Foundation for Advanced Studies in the Fine Arts and the Research Committee of the School of Architecture, Planning and Landscape, University of Newcastle, who have each offered partial support for this book.

Utopia has long been another name for the unreal and the impossible. We have set utopia over against the world. As a matter of fact, it is our utopias that make the world tolerable to us.

From *The Story of Utopias* (1922), Lewis Mumford,
Gloucester, MA: Peter Smith, 1959, p. 1

A map of the world that does not include Utopia is not worth even glancing at, for it leaves out the one country at which Humanity is always landing. And when Humanity lands there, it looks out, and seeing a better country sets sail.

From *The Soul of Man Under Socialism* (1891), Oscar Wilde.
Online. Available at http://wilde.thefreelibrary.com/
Soul-of-Man-under Socialism (6 January 2005)

Introduction: utopias and architectures?

> Architecture should embody the invisible, the hopes and dreams in something we live in, we die in and we **remember**.
>
> Daniel Libeskind[1]

Because my main concern in this book may appear to be about a particular type of utopia, expressible at least in architectural terms as 'humane modernism', its title, *Utopias and Architecture*, may be deceptive. If humane modernism is a reasonable category of architectural elaboration, which I think it is, it denotes a reaction to the most reductive aspects of modern (twentieth-century) architecture, which critic and historian Kenneth Frampton calls 'orthodox modern'.

It is architecture based, in large part, on the 'Athens Charter (1933)' of CIAM, a French acronym for what translates in English as the International Congress of Modern Architecture. CIAM was established in 1928 to shepherd the then new architecture from the periphery of culture to its centre, which by the post-World War II years had mostly been accomplished. Its last meeting took place in 1959. Nevertheless, since the late1940s, 'humanist modern' reactions to the ubiquity of 'orthodox modern' architecture have made inroads. Significant examples of this alternative include the later buildings of Le Corbusier (1887–1965), the post-1950s work of Louis I. Kahn (1901–1974) and the buildings of Dutch architect Aldo van Eyck (1918–1999), which is why the theory and practice of these three architects is at the heart of the present discussion.

The Athens Charter, set down by Le Corbusier in 1941, draws on efforts to establish the tenets of the functional city originating more than a decade earlier, which, broadly put, would redress the inefficiencies of outmoded traditional cities. In the functional city, chaos, brought on by the introduction of the machine (modernity/ the automobile) would be eradicated, not by restricting machines but by remaking cities more *rationally* so that they could absorb the consequences of technological advance. To do this, cities would have to become more scientific, less emotionally charged.

Paradoxically, the reformist tone of the 'Charter' reveals not the potential of an enriched city but rather one reduced, rigidly clarified and emptied, as much as possible, of its mysterious contradictions – particularly its complex physical organization and mixed adjacencies of different kinds of occupation. Even though human scale was meant to be the basis for all planning decisions of the functional city, the result suggested is of minimums made into the maximum possibility. By now, the long-standing rigid separation of types of uses, reorganization of street patterns in conformity with the requirements of traffic planners, and a general disciplining of the urban condition according to the logic of a pseudo-scientific rationalism has overwhelmed the traditional city. Although their limitations long ago became known, these characteristics continue in the present day to define the struggle between what makes cities places of wonder (possibility) and the desire to manage them (control).

If there ever was a utopian dimension to the attitude revealed by CIAM in the Athens Charter, it turned on the belief that, 'on both the spiritual and the material planes, the city must ensure individual liberty and the advantages of collective action'.[2] The tension between ample scope for possibility and stultifying control sets the stage for my attempt to reform the concept of utopia, now mostly associated with a desire for order spurred on by supposed rationality taken to irrational extremes. Nevertheless, if utopia seems destined to occlude liberation, realization of liberty's promise depends on social imagination, which in turn relies on utopian dreaming to open up pathways toward its achievement.

Utopia in the plural (the *Utopias* of the title) suggests, first, not one architectural style or another but rather that the concept of utopia can have multiple senses: one recognized by adherents of liberal democracies as pathological; the other, embraced by aspirants for even more than liberal democracies can deliver, as constitutive. The worst excesses of totalitarian states can be part of a utopian project but so can the greatest achievements of social reformers who put their schemes into action, even partially. The potential of utopian imagination and its capacity for terror seem to turn on the permissibility of partiality as opposed to totality. Absoluteness opposes acceptance. Utopia turns mean, pathological, when the model of a superior situation, which it puts forward *must* be fully realized. The 'all or nothing' demand commonly associated with utopian projection taints its constitutive potential.

Between the constitutive potential of utopia and its capacity to turn pathological, there swarm near-infinite expressions of what 'the good life' ought to be and what it must never include. Hence, I am more concerned with how architects invent exemplary buildings than with some fixed notion about the good life and its setting, which, at any rate, might quickly become outdated. In short, the argument elaborated throughout this book is that exemplary architecture is *always* part of some potential whole imagined by its architect, a whole that serves as an organizing model – even if for the realization of only a single building – conceived of as a partial utopia. Moreover, such buildings are primarily expressions of social imagination, meditations on how individuals or groups do, or might, come together upon the stage offered by a particular setting. As I will attempt to show, it is impossible to neglect utopia in the formulation of social imagination (although it is probably easier to acknowledge the crucial role social imagination plays in the invention of exemplary architecture than it is to accept utopia).

An enduring exemplary?

The word exemplary and its association with particular examples of architecture, in this instance Le Corbusier's Convent of Sainte-Marie-de-la-Tourette at Eveux-sur-l'Abresle, France (1953–1960), Louis Kahn's Salk Institute for Biological Studies, La Jolla, California (1959–1965) and Aldo van Eyck's Municipal Orphanage, Amsterdam (1955–1960), might suggest that I am advancing a restrictive view of architectural merit based on personal taste. Alternatively, even more alarming, it could appear as though I am militating for a limited set of forms whose appeal is universal and timeless, based in the elementary forms of archaic habitation, especially pure archetypical geometric shapes, such as circles and squares.

The exemplariness of a building may not be permanent, but within a given culture, it certainly seems enduring. The continuing hold that Solomon's Temple, the Parthenon, the Pantheon, the Hagia Sophia, Chartres Cathedral, St Peter's and the Campidoglio exert over the imagination confirms this. In the middle ground, between the end of the Renaissance and the present, identifying the type of exemplariness the aforementioned buildings embody is more difficult. From the sixteenth through the nineteenth century, a series of extensions, elaborations and revivals confirm the continuing influence of these buildings, all of which had circles and squares in varying degrees of evidence. It is even less easy to say which buildings of modern times, from around the dawn of the twentieth century to the present, will continue to be admired a thousand years from now. However, it is possible to argue that whatever the above listed buildings do not share stylistically they might well share conceptually: primarily a utopian dimension that is emphatically social. With that in mind, it might be possible to learn from earlier (exemplary) buildings without either copying them or rejecting the uniqueness of the present.

0.1
**View from
north-west.
Convent of La
Tourette, Eveux-
sur-l'Abresle,
1953–1960.**
Architect:
Le Corbusier

0.2
**View towards the
Pacific Ocean.
Salk Institute for
Biological Studies,
La Jolla, CA,
1959–1965.**
Architect:
Louis I. Kahn

0.3
**View towards
the north-west.
Amsterdam
Orphanage,
Amstelveenseweg,
Amsterdam,
1955–1960.**
Architect:
Aldo van Eyck

The speed with which fashion and taste now change and the degree to which culture seems unstable (even more plural than utopias) arguably makes any sense of continuity retrogressively nostalgic. Only the conditions of a closed society with a culture that evolves barely at all or at a near glacial pace (in a pre-global warming sense) could assure the continuing appeal or relevance of particular forms. Nevertheless, my argument in favour of utopias' relevance for architectural invention is not predicated on either formalist or stylistic preferences; actually, my objective is to reveal the problems with just such modes of evaluation.

The concepts I develop are hopefully flexible, or supple, enough to be sustainable, even extrinsic to particular forms. My intention is to elaborate on principles without suggesting a presupposed stylistic or formal result; what I propose is far more situational than universal or archetypal. In this, I follow van Eyck's theory in practice. He was preoccupied with parallel historical and cultural traditions, viewed through a lens of relativity, each of which, he believed, could inform the most modern work in the West. It is not so much *geometrical forms* as *forms of conduct* that concern me. Rather, what does concern me is how architects can offer a setting able to contain the continual elaboration and invention of social action, which is the argument I advance in favour of the examples examined herein. If there is a preoccupation with the past, it turns on the degree to which each architect envisions a radically altered future through an idealized imaginary past.

Van Eyck, Kahn and Le Corbusier (as early as the 1930s) may be considered together, not simply because each informed the other and often built with concrete. They had similar aims as well. Chiefly, each sought to enrich orthodox modern architecture beyond its limitations without rejecting it, which van Eyck and Kahn especially imagined as necessary if architects were to have any hope of touching the emotions of the people for whom they build. Throughout their lives, these architects were preoccupied with institutions and the social lives of individuals, especially the settings architects provide to house the first for the elaboration of the second. Such commonalities are touched on throughout the work, particularly in those chapters specifically dedicated to a study of their theories and practices.

Optimistic architecture[3]

My consideration of an optimistic architecture (of the *ought*) begins where architectural treatises and literary utopias intersect: where individual propositions of the right principles of architecture meet individual propositions of the principles of right societies. While literary Utopias are key to my research, it is the imagining and making of architecture that is the focus, and it is my desire to begin revealing those aspects of architectural thinking and doing that are analogous to utopian projection. To that end, I consider imagination as a process that works upon content, and utopia as a part of this process. And because utopia is one of the very few survivors of holistic thinking to persist from the origins of the modern through the earliest questioning of it into the present, it has much to offer present day architectural practice, especially as a pathway toward recollecting its orienting objective.

Ultimately, my objective is to elaborate on a sorely neglected dimension of utopian influence on architecture. Considerations of utopia tend to overlook its positive dimension because utopia and architecture too often pair up with questionable results. Most negatively, this includes a conception of utopia as proposing exclusively totalizing projects for absolute application. In contradistinction to the common view of utopia as absolute and therefore impossible, the dimension of utopian influence on architecture I explore is the underexamined potential of utopias to contribute to a continuing renewal of architecture. Something utopias can do by encouraging recollection of the architect's capacity to invent settings for the social.

Reforming utopia

My overarching aim here is to reposition utopia as a positive informing model, rather than as an absolute, restrictive and impossible one. As such, I advance a redefinition of utopia that links it to desires for wholeness that need not be fully realized to remain valid or valuable. Familiar understandings of the utopian concept are introduced, which, by contrast, highlight my reconceptualization of utopia as an idea in the plural (utopias), a multidimensional concept with positive and negative potential and far-reaching consequences. Development of the relationship between utopia and architecture proceeds alongside emphatic affirmation of the social dimension of both. In my effort to identify utopian potential, I will show how distinguishing the concept of utopia from science fiction, futurology and technological utopianism, with which it is often confused, is necessary for an understanding of architecture and utopia.

Throughout, I will argue that architectural invention is akin to utopian projection and that utopia harbours the potential to rescue architecture from aimlessness, obsessive matter-of-factness, or a non-critical embrace of global capitalism. Correspondingly, utopia is revealed as a more supple (open, rather than closed) concept than familiar understandings of it permit, which extends ideas of utopia while demonstrating its relevance to current debates surrounding the objectives of architecture.

In the chapters that follow, I elaborate on the concepts of utopia in general and on the idea of a 'humanist utopia' in particular. These chapters elaborate on how utopia is conceptualized, particularly by challenging contemporary obsession with novelty. In the penultimate chapter, utopia is reintroduced as a content of the imagination made tolerable by being unspoken, while remaining necessary for invention of an exemplary architecture. In the final chapter, I examine the concepts developed through consideration of recent architecture (completed during the 1990s), which will reveal the continuing relevance of the conclusions I advance, regardless of apparent architectural style.

Present future

If Aldo van Eyck had a failing, it was his inability to identify any present-day architects as fellow travellers. Consequently, right up until his death in 1999, he dismissed most recent architecture, much of it for good reason. Just as my argument in favour of utopia emphasizes partial completion over total application, there must have been one or two architects doing worthy work, even in the 1990s. Sadly, for all his sophistication and cultural depth, van Eyck's stubborn diaspproval of most post-war architecture makes it all too easy to dismiss his resistance as reductive and simplistic, no matter how untimely that would be. I have attempted to be less partisan and perhaps more balanced than van Eyck might have been, hopefully without overly diluting my polemic.

Arguing for the value of utopia as social imagination in the invention of architecture may not be particularly fashionable, especially when done through a glance backwards to the future by way of ideas and buildings from the 1950s and 1960s. Nonetheless, the promise of contemporary architecture is my primary concern. Toward that end, in the final chapter I will consider the work of three architects currently practising, who are stylistically and formally distant from Le Corbusier, Kahn and van Eyck, but whose work (and theories) can contain and support the concepts I develop nonetheless. These architects and their buildings include the Jewish Museum, Berlin (1989–1999) by Daniel Libeskind, The Neurosciences Institute, La Jolla, California (1992–1995) by Tod Williams and Billie Tsien, and the Jean-Marie Tjibaou Cultural Centre, Nouméa, New Caledonia (1991–1998) by Renzo Piano.

Part 1

Conceptualizing utopias

Chapter 1

Architecture and orientation

It will, indeed, be long before the world has been all colonized, and all its deserts brought under cultivation. But the radical question is, not how much habitable land is in the world, but how many human beings ought to be maintained on a given space of habitable land.

Observe, I say *ought* to be, not how many *can* be.[1]

John Ruskin

Architecture, which is ever the result of constructive activity is nearly always preoccupied with some *ought*; yet much contemporary architectural theory and practice is obsessed with expression of how the world *is*.[2] Examples of this include the populism of stylistic post-modernism and the disorienting objectives of stylistic deconstructivism. Such work, because it is self-consciously uncritical of present conditions, must remain forever captive of what *is*.

Throughout this book, the focus is on architects who imagine and attempt to construct an ought; that is, architects who set locations for human practices that are diverse and contradictory but whose buildings nonetheless fulfil the orienting objective of architecture by addressing the persistent human desire for place identification.[3] Determinate settings for social life include individual rooms, buildings, complexes of buildings, quarters of cities and even whole towns.

The present in the past

The work of architecture is imaginative. Architects invent what is not there and yet must always begin with an idea of something located somewhere. This paradoxical situation suggests that all future projects have a past, just as present and previous ones do. Understood in this way, imagination is less epiphanic than it is a process. Architects' inventions do not spring full-blown from (or within) their heads but rather are worked on by the imagination. Conceptualized in this way, imagination is intentional rather than fanciful. Ultimately, whatever the imagination works on refers to things beyond both itself (as a process) and its contents (the things it works upon). As a result, imagination – as a process – cannot be exclusive. What is unique about individual creation thus derives from what is unique about the individual, but also from the depth and breadth of references which a creative individual's imagination can draw upon as it works on the referential content it manipulates.

Creativity can thus be understood as an elaboration on identity that is empirical and structural. Owing something to the ideas of *novice* and *expert* developed by cognitive scientists, this conception of creativity shed light on how even ill-defined, or ill-structured problems are solved. Such problems – akin to the ones posed to architecture – have a multiplicity of equally good possible solutions rather than just one. The difference between a novice and an expert is that the former sees the world and its possibilities as unrelated bits of information whereas the latter looks at the same information and is able to discern patterns of interrelationship, which are directly related to a unique individual's knowledge and experience.

Cognitive science accounts for cogent responses to ill-defined and ill-structured problems as the result of recursive attempts to accomplish an end. Efforts of this sort start out with careful preparation that depends upon mental schemas to order the information collected and generated. Cognitive scientists also acknowledge that ill-defined problems are insoluble without rhetoric. Because there may be any number of equally right answers, the best response will be identifiable only if it is persuasive.[4] Patterns, or mental schemas, provide experts with an added capacity to think through difficulties because they can see in the parts a potential whole; in the whole, they see a collection of interrelated parts.[5] Ideas on creative invention, such as these, inform the practical conception of utopia developed here.

Architecture and renewal

The usefulness, then, of utopia for thinking through architectural problems is that it provides architects with a place from which it is possible to consider and invent wholes (utopias of a sort) even though these are not intended for total realization. Because the distant location of utopias suggests limits even as it encourages an expanded horizon of potential for projects, envisioning projects in this way could have a positive benefit for architecture, especially by returning the social dimension of utopia to architectural thinking, which it shed when the excesses of positivist orthodox modernist theories and practices became anathema.

My conceptualization of utopia owes more to social theorist Karl Mannheim than to philosopher Karl Popper.[6] Popper feared utopia as a permanent threat to liberty whereas Mannheim argued for it as the lifeblood of social imagination. Philosopher Paul Ricoeur, in turn, elaborates on Mannheim's ideas by arguing that utopia is a concept (even a force) with both a positive and a negative dimension, each counterbalanced by ideology, which itself has positive and negative dimensions counterbalanced by utopia. In general, according to Ricoeur, utopia is progressive while ideology is conservative. The constitutive dimension of either utopia or ideology counterbalances the pathological dimension of the other. For my purposes, Ricoeur's most important insight is that utopia can be constitutive. With this in mind, the relation between utopia as constitutive – suggesting comprehensible patterns of social life – and architecture, as an arrangement of configurative patterns, reveals that the potential for complex order in architecture has a utopian character.

Architecture was first described as a configurative discipline – a kind of utopic pattern making – in the writing of Italian architect and theorist Leon Battista Alberti (1404–1472), and it appears again in the writing and architecture of Dutch architect and theorist Aldo van Eyck (1918–1999), especially in their shared ideas regarding the reciprocity of city and house and house and city.[7] It is with patterns made up of interdependent parts, and the potential of these for making comprehensible wholes, that optimism and utopia begin to illuminate something about the nature of exemplary architecture that genius alone cannot explain. Across this trajectory of associations, exemplary architecture is revealed as being as much a product of genius as the result of a mind conditioned by optimism to see a small contribution (a single building, for example) as a part *within a potential whole* that begins to form it. Although he does not call it utopia, this view of architecture – room, building and city – as parts within a potential whole borrows from David Leatherbarrow's idea that each architectural invention ought to learn from past efforts in order to surpass them, and that each building ought to be envisioned as the partial completion of a potential whole.[8]

The idea of a whole (or its potential) guides the creation of each part in such a way that, even though limited in scope, conception of such parts does not occur in isolation. The conviction that exemplary architecture is a part within a potential whole implies a critical appraisal of contemporary practice as mostly not exemplary. During the last half-century or more, the vast majority of buildings have been constructed as radically isolated from one another and thus cannot be conceived of as elements contributing to a comprehensive built environment. Cities now mirror the preponderance of detached homes that reflects a post-urban attitude toward domestic, social and commercial life. Rather than establishing a comprehensible human environment, contemporary building practice often fuels individual fears of isolation by emphasizing disconnection in a habitat of fragments deployed according to the unsettling logic of business, irony or perversity. But not always.

Envisioning each element of the human habitat as a part within a potential whole is as much an outgrowth of optimism as it is of utopia. Only reform (or renewal) can confirm the potential of parts, wholes, utopias and optimism required to make a more compassionate human habitat. After all, utopia and exemplary architecture are ever the result of a belief that *what could be*, or *ought to be*, is superior to *what is*. What may surprise is how frequently visions of potential have their roots in an exemplary past (distant in time and space). Indeed, it is fair to say that there can be no utopia, and no exemplary architecture for that matter, without some golden age to draw upon for ideas about transfiguring the future. This is the case despite the pervasive confusion of futurology with utopia, especially when it comes to architecture. Ultimately, response to what *is*, with convictions about what *ought* to be, requires a past, even a mythical one, to discover its potential.

Renewal and reform always depend on a capacity for going backwards to go forward. Key to this process is a search within one's own mind for a model according to which reformed practice can be organized. Architects have long appealed to a primitive hut as just such a model. It is a structure thought to provide access as close to the first principles of architecture as it is possible to get, yet traces of this structure exist nowhere other than in the mind's eye of the architect searching for it. Nonetheless, absence of the primitive hut from physical reality does little to diminish its importance for the renewal of present practices. If a desired (or required) thing resides in paradise, and no current map indicates its location, getting to it will only be possible via dreams and wishes. Reconstructions of it will necessarily be interpretations based on resemblances modelled after a non-existent object forever beyond our reach. Even though it is impossible to get there, returning to paradise nonetheless remains a reasonable destination for the memory, still able, by way of example, to fulfil its promise to the here and now.

Necessary periodic renewal of practice confronts architects with a standing challenge to reclaim and recall a place that historians *must* disavow because they cannot locate it. If one can travel in his or her mind to paradise for a visit to the primitive hut, renewing practice, and thus any architect's architecture, becomes possible by grounding it on first principles – first because they are the closest to origins. It does not matter that these principles are rules not based on rules; what does matter is that they form a part of the architectural conscience that guides efforts and provides criteria for evaluating buildings. Utopian perspectives can encourage

1.1
**Laugier,
Marc-Antoine,
*Essai sur
L'architecture*,
N.-B. Duchesne,
1755.
Frontispiece**
Source: Art and
Architecture
Collection, Miriam
and Ira D. Wallach
Division of Art,
Prints and
Photographs, The
New York Public
Library, Astor,
Lenox and Tilden
Foundations

renewal by facilitating playful engagement with imaginary pasts. In this way, history becomes memory. By returning a sense of wonder to practice, utopias can contribute to the reform of it in the present.[9]

Positive and arbitrary

Even with primitive huts to guide renewal, architectural practice is no longer organized by shared principles bound by disciplinary faith in Vitruvius's *Ten Books on Architecture* or the venerability of the Classical orders. The long-term fallout from having the foundations of architectural knowledge shaken is shown in the present-day architect's overzealous preoccupation with the surface (or visual aspects of building), which reveals an even further reduction of French theorist-architect Claude Perrault's (1613–1688) conception of 'positive and arbitrary beauty'. Positive beauty, that which is measurable, is determined, or so it might now seem, by developers and the construction industry. That which the architect still has control over is, accordingly, the arbitrary, the decoration of predetermined sheds, just as Robert Venturi suspected.[10]

Perrault's conviction was that positive beauty, because it is verifiable, is not subject to the whim of fancy. On the other hand, because there are no absolute rules for architecture, such as proportion previously appeared to provide, architects had to develop criteria for judging their own works and by which others could judge them. Taste, for Perrault, provided just such a criterion of judgment. He argued that taste, which lends itself to cultivation because it is an agreed upon social construction, is the only sure way to protect architecture from fancy. A crucial facet of Perrault's construct – what separates it from later developments – was his conviction that, because of its venerability, a classical language of architecture would persist indefinitely as the vehicle by which buildings would continue to communicate. Even though the character of contemporary practice may originate with Perrault's split between positive and arbitrary beauty, institutionalization of them into objective (construction) and subjective (an architect's decoration of construction) seriously reduces his intent, largely depriving architects of both their social value and their purpose.

In the shadow of such developments, architects have mostly forgotten that, traditionally, their special competence was a capacity to give *form* to social environments. Recollection of such ability could be a carrier of renewal for architecture and the disalienation of architects. Although architects now typically neglect social forms in their architecture, social scientists and anthropologists continue to study them for clues to how individuals and groups occupy spaces and relate to artefacts. The ongoing patterns of life that link past and future with tradition and innovation form an intelligible web that individuals and collectives both make and find themselves within. Architects once gave tangible form to these settings, but with the shift of architectural concern to a nearly exclusive preoccupation with arbitrary beauty, the appeal of such problems has diminished to the point of nearly withering away.[11]

In the present day, novelty so preoccupies producers and consumers of buildings that it might actually be a commercial liability for an architect to explore architecture as a discipline primarily distinguished by its ability to give tangible form to the social settings that structure the human environment. However, this is precisely what architects must do if their work is again to have a place within the fabric of society, which demands more than making interesting things or decorating exteriors. Utopia, which is social imagination, is preoccupied with social forms and how to house them. Architects who think architecture through utopia are able, almost by a force of will, to return an enriching social dimension to their work.

Utopias and towns

Towns lend themselves to consideration according to the same themes of renewal introduced above. Bodies, buildings and cities come together in the physical manifestation of social space. Towns and cities are figurative human artefacts; they refer to and present citizens with conditions of *situatedness* that the environment can render comprehensible to the body at the moment of experience. This kind of configured environment is an ancient possibility no longer open to us because of the uncertainty with which we occupy the planet and experience our social relations.[12] Architects estranged from their primitive hut to guide them, their social role to give them purpose, and from the configuration of traditional cities to situate them are hard pressed to envision a method of working able to effectively counter their marginalized position as decorators of exteriors or product designers of isolated and unrelated *objects*. The account of architecture's present situation sketched out here carries an implied dimension too often missed. Possibility and hopefulness are necessary correlates of stories of development and decline – out of present failings, the past may offer possibilities of renewal, such as those that utopian imagination encourages and permits.

Bodies and utopias

A paramount concern for an interplay between individual and collective, and between house and city, effectively links towns and utopias. Like towns, utopias are attempts to pattern places and behaviours (comportment) into a configured arrangement. For architects to move in from the margins of the social sphere, as something other than purveyors of excess value alone, they must reclaim such associations. Human bodies suggest how such disalienation might begin. People present themselves as configured wholes through individual sentient bodies made up of constitutional inheritance and physical structure; procreation passes both along from one generation to the next. Accordingly, the body is a microcosm of society; buildings that analogize both can become settings for individual and collective human potential.

Such a view of society, bodies and buildings comes close to anthropologist Mary Douglas's conviction that social bodies are analogous to physical bodies, especially because both share a whole made up of interrelated and interdependent parts.[13] The *self* consequently presents architects with a model of social and physical order originating with a reference – the body – that all human beings share. In turn, examination of this bodily reference – through analogy rather than representation – provides architects with a guide for how to recollect their social role.

Bodies are referents that architecture has analogized in the past that could again suggest a ground of relative certainty that remains open to architects. Moreover, because every individual's constitution is both unique and an inheritance, everybody is always linked to what lies beyond (or before) them in time and space (even if subjectivity, paradoxically, appears the only possible certainty). Because a genetic past joins each individual to the family or group from which he or she springs, an inherent relation exists between single individuals (particular groups as well) and other members of the human race. Furthermore, instinctual inheritances, preoccupied with species survival, link *all* human beings. In this way, planetary existence models how the local and universal can find room for coexistence.

The skeleton, organs and skin of each person are unique and general for many of the same reasons that constitution is; beyond that, there is an architectonic dimension to human structure. The structure of human persons was a model of order that ancient Greeks ardently examined in their philosophy and politics (especially during the sixth to fourth centuries BC). Their architecture corresponded to this structure, especially through development of the column orders, temples and temple precincts: the whole is immanent in the part; in the individual column and in the individual person. In turn, Augustan architect and theorist Vitruvius enthusiastically elaborated on these ideas, particularly in his consideration of eurhythmy.[14]

Human beings, as a collection of eurhythmically interrelated parts, present architects and anthropologists with a link to the origins of human desire for order and harmony. Mary Douglas, for example, developed this cosmological idea in her book *Natural Symbols* (1996). She posited the body as a unity, as an integral whole, and as the model of human social order and of individual and social conceptions of cosmos. Thought of in this way, unity is a desire that begins with the body: a unitary whole and ever-present model *of* and *for* harmony. In sum, because individual parts make up the body, it forms a unity comprehensible as made up from diversity, also understandable as a harmonious interrelationship of parts to whole.

About 14 centuries after Vitruvius, Alberti coined the term *concinnitas* to convey his belief that beauty, as a product of wholeness, emerges out of a correspondence among *separate* parts that make up a whole *body*. Nature, according to Alberti, is the supreme example and presentation of this consonance. *Concinnitas*, though rare, is not capricious: it is a law that dictates a definite number, outline and position of parts within a body:

> It is the task and aim of *concinnitas* to compose parts that are quite
> separate from each other by their nature, according to some precise rule,
> so that they correspond to one another in appearance . . . Neither in the
> whole body nor in its parts does *concinnitas* flourish as much as in nature
> . . . If this is accepted, let us conclude as follows. Beauty is a form
> of sympathy and consonance of parts within a body, according to definite
> number, outline, and position, as dictated by *concinnitas*, the absolute
> and fundamental rule in Nature. This is the main object of the art of
> building, and the source of her dignity, charm, authority, and worth.[15]

Alberti's *concinnitas* carries within it a sense of *concordia discontinuum*, which describes a resultant harmony that occurs across and through discontinuous parts whose diversity creates a web of relationships that establishes consonance. These two ideas suggest that an orienting harmony, based on nature and the human body as a model, remains a possibility even in a climate of apparent discord. The sort of unity out of diversity indicated by these ideas of harmony, or consonance, corresponds with utopias.

The whole person (made up of constitution and body) is comprehensible as both interiority and presentation. As part and whole, and as a model of wholeness, the body is consequently the intersection where utopia and architecture meet; it is also the *site* of both. Moreover, architecture and utopias both refer to bodies by seeking to establish harmony across and through discontinuous parts; for example, through buildings and societies whose collected diversity forms a web of relationships that establishes accord, or at least its potential.

Kahn, Le Corbusier and Aldo van Eyck

Throughout the present study, I elaborate on concepts of utopia by exploring the writings and buildings of three architects who, I argue, exemplify the relationship of utopian imagination to the invention of exemplary architectures. These architects, Le Corbusier (1887–1965), Louis I. Kahn (1901–1974) and Aldo van Eyck (1918–1999), imagined their efforts within a spatio-temporal context that is broader than much modernist work. This context allows for a social content not restricted or defined by either the ephemeral nature of style or by adherence to determinist precepts conditioned by limited views of possibility. These particular architects sought to represent an ideal content through their works. In addition, they imagined they could make the communal and social present by inventing works that provide a setting for the elaboration of both. In this way, their ideas (the thought content and imagination that their constructed buildings express) are arguably utopian.

The focus of this study is on social institutions because they hold implications for houses in one direction and cities in the other. Furthermore, architecture, when it claims a social purpose, is best suited to the configuration of institutions. Institutions are significant because they provide communities sharing common purposes a means by which to orient themselves through formation of centres that establish places of self-acknowledgment. The key factor that determined selection of the three architects listed above is a general recognition of their works as superlative over a long duration.

Le Corbusier was the most potent architect of the twentieth century, sufficiently so to remain a powerful figure at the beginning of the twenty-first century. Influential architectural historian Sigfried Giedion believed that Le Corbusier could justifiably occupy this position, considering him and his work to be exemplary. He evaluated La Tourette as a particularly complete presentation of Le Corbusier's architectural virtues, which includes a uniquely close connection 'to the Eternal Present which lives in the creative artifacts of all periods'.[16] This closeness, according to Giedion, is characterized by 'an urge to probe into the elemental, the irrational, the sources of symbolic expression' that 'emerges . . . not in the adoption of shapes but in the expression of inner affinities'.[17] Characteristics disclosed by the Priory of La Tourette as an interpretation of, 'French monasteries of the twelfth century [whose] spirit continues to live' in Le Corbusier's invention.[18]

16

One such French monastery was Le Thoronet in Provence, which Le Corbusier visited before starting work on La Tourette. Giedion also argued that what makes Le Corbusier and his work exemplary is his encounter with the past, especially notable because 'his search for inner similarities had nothing to do with art history: it embraced the entire architectural development'.[19]

In large part, Le Corbusier established the ground upon which Kahn and van Eyck elaborated their own exemplary work. Kahn, for example, acknowledged this when he said 'Every man has . . . a figure in his work he feels answerable to. I often say, often say to myself, "How'm I doing, Corbusier?" You see, Corbusier was my teacher. I say, Paul Cret was my teacher and Corbusier was my teacher.'[20] Furthermore, Kahn also recognized Le Corbusier's contribution to architecture and architects in general:

> If you copy Le Corbusier's designs you are somewhat of a thief. But if you take that which is in essence architectural from him, you take it very freely, because it does not belong to him either. It belongs to the realm of architecture. The fact that he discovered it is very fortunate for us, but it does not belong to him.[21]

The uniqueness of Kahn's work, especially compared to most post-World War II architecture in the US, stems, in no small part, from his ability to learn from Le Corbusier and from his conviction that it is the job of the architect to establish institutions by articulating a compelling form for them. Consequently, the record of his achievement continues to model an exemplary frame of mind and manner of working for architects. For example, Kahn believed that his responsibility to his clients lay in deconstructing the briefs they brought him in order to reveal the *sum and substance* that programme statements often hide. This process led to the embodiment of what he uncovered in the constructed building.

Kahn acknowledged Le Corbusier as a teacher; in turn, when he first met van Eyck in 1959, the two recognized each other as fellow travellers with shared concerns. According to Francis Strauven, van Eyck's biographer:

> Both of them, quite independently, had been developing a strongly similar approach since 1954. They had both aimed at the essence of architecture, to the essence of every brief, and they both strove for the establishment of a polycentric reality on the basis of articulated geometric patterns. Like Aldo van Eyck, Kahn appealed both to an archaic essence and to classical tradition . . . and expressed himself in elementary, archetypal forms.[22]

What ultimately separates van Eyck and Kahn is their divergent conception of institutions. The essence of an institution that Kahn sought was not revealed in order to transform it, but rather to present it at as close a point to its ideal original state as was possible, which he believed would redeem it. Van Eyck, on the other hand, sought to reveal the unforeseen potential of institutions by opening them up to challenges that could humanize and perfect them through reinvention. Because of this, Kahn's conception of monumentality was far more fixed than van Eyck's, and it often veiled the degree to which both were concerned with monuments as markers that configure the human landscape by making institutions (and, potentially, the city) memorable. Kahn could be thought of as having been concerned mostly with a monumentality of scale, whereas the modesty of van Eyck's architecture could appear not to be monumental at all.

The effect of Le Corbusier's discoveries on Kahn and van Eyck's development is attested to by Kahn's statements above and by van Eyck's admiration of Le Corbusier as a true artist. In turn, van Eyck's thought and architecture provided models Le Corbusier would turn to in one of his final projects. Guillaume Jullian de la Fuente, who collaborated with Le Corbusier, writes:

> Since 1963 with the Olivetti project we began to pose the question of how to structure the spatial parts without using 'la promenade architecturale' as the means to connect the whole. Aldo van Eyck's orphanage and his writings in *Forum* were one of the issues of focus of attention at the moment. The idea of a project as a small city/part of a city was confronted with the Hospital of Venice project.[23]

The Venice Hospital project by Le Corbusier remains unbuilt, yet it is a testament to the degree to which adoption of his discoveries, in the manner suggested by Kahn, belong not only to him but to the realm of architecture. Because of this, the consequences of Le Corbusier's own discoveries could later return to him, interpreted and transformed by younger architects such as van Eyck, to become examples of new avenues of research that he and others could pursue.

These three architects and the examples of their work also facilitate investigation of the transformations occurring within the modern movement during the post-World War II years. It was during these years, but especially by the mid-

1.2
**Model – Venice
Hospital project of
Le Corbusier**

1950s, that modernist orthodoxy was beginning to be subjected to a high degree of negative criticism concerning its aims as much as its results. Construction of the three buildings considered here took place during the period 1953–1965, which is significant because it makes of each an example of a reconceptualization of modernism that was evolutionary in aim at the very moment when modernist architecture was beginning to be dismissed.

Le Corbusier, Kahn and van Eyck never envisioned the abandonment of the modernist enterprise. The success of their efforts to extend and deepen modern architecture turns on a recollection of a capacity to see the part in the whole and the whole in the part. The wrapping of structures determined by the imperatives of real estate development, or the production of commodities meant to distinguish a position in the marketplace, was not their primary concern.

Comprehensive utopias

Because utopian thought considers the part in the whole and the whole in the part of the social bodies that it describes, it is able to consider questions that go beyond immediate problems or *matter-of-fact* responses to them. The work of the three architects noted above benefited from just such a mental tuning. In fact, the exemplary architecture they designed not only benefits from the kind of picture of the whole that utopias provide, but would have been impossible without it. Nevertheless, since the end of World War II, architects have been working in a climate where faith in progress is so shaken that the ensuing loss of confidence in modernity has for some time begged a rethinking of modernity as it has evolved since the Reformation, especially during the post-Enlightenment period.

Without the kind of organizing social structures that existed during the pre-modern period and that survived until the eighteenth century, modern architects have found themselves adrift in a diminished domain. Yet, these three architects and their buildings demonstrate an awareness that human beings, even in an age of uncertainty, long for a stability that analogizes the same order most find within their own bodies.

Each of the projects examined here is an essay concerning the problem of individual and social identity, particularly as established by the constructed presentation of institutions. Aldo van Eyck in particular, who was a member of Team X, the breakaway group from CIAM (Congrès International d'Architecture Moderne), sought to investigate problems of identity as a search for structural principles. On the other hand, architects like Robert Venturi were primarily concerned with the appearance of things, as demonstrated, for example, in his *Complexity and Contradiction* (1966).[24] The former did not require a stylistic post-modernism; the latter demanded it.

These opposing viewpoints revolve around an ongoing debate about how to reconcile the reality of modernity with an awareness of its limitations and failings. Modernity, understood as faith in unending progress as its own objective, certainly ran its course during the first half of the twentieth century. Technological advance and unlimited power in the hands of human beings, free of any clear and limiting ethical framework, continues to fan the possibility of nearly unfathomable catastrophe. Yet, modernity is a reality, which makes outright rejection of it impossible.

1.3
**Torre Velasca,
Milan, 1957–1960.
Architects:
L. B. Belgiojosa,
E. Peresutti and
E. N. Rogers**

This conflict entered architecture as a debate between inventive reconsideration of the past and an imitation of it.

A relevant example of this debate is Ernesto Rogers's presentation of his Torre Velasca building in Milan at the CIAM conference of 1959 held in Otterlo. Rogers courted controversy by suggesting that his building's appearance – similar to an oversized ersatz medieval tower, really had nothing to do with his intention.

His concern, Rogers argued, was with 'the intimate value of our culture' but he stubbornly resisted acknowledging that his building *looks* like a medieval tower enlarged to the scale of a modern city. According to him, the reasons his Torre Velasco reminds viewers of a medieval tower have little to do with his intentions for it, either expressionistically or technically. This implies that the tower arrived at its present form quite naturally, as an organic outcome of emotional and rational investigation, which inevitably lead to its appearance. In a curious way, this argument aligns Rogers's vision with Le Corbusier's, Kahn's and van Eyck's.

If Rogers is taken at his word, he was seeking a reconciliation similar to that of the three architects examined here: all four wanted to reconcile past and future by inventing an architecture in the present contiguous with cultural inheritance but not imitative of past forms or appearances. Even if past cultural feelings may indeed persist in the present, the present is also significantly different from the past. Thus, to engage the past, one must go backwards and forwards at the same time without regressing into it, which Le Corbusier, Louis I. Kahn and Aldo van Eyck were able to do, but Rogers, despite his protestations to the contrary, could not.

Because of its physical appearance and Rogers's questionable defence of it, a number of the conference participants soundly attacked his Velasca Tower. British architect Peter Smithson argued that it was 'dangerous', adding that he thought it 'a bad model to give because there are things that can be so easily distorted and become not only ethically wrong but also aesthetically wrong'. Smithson continued his attack, stating that the tower's 'formal plastic vocabulary is so shot through with overtones of former plastic vocabulary, that it does not represent a model of a moral sort but of an immoral sort'. He also challenged Rogers's building as being out of step with contemporary conditions: 'Now your building I suggest does not live in the same world as the artefacts of our day because the plastic language it speaks is of another time.'[25]

Dutch architect Jacob Bakema elaborated on Smithson's position, arguing, 'I think that form is communication about life, and I don't recognize in this building a communication about life in our time. You are resisting contemporary life.'[26] At the close of the conference, Bakema made a clear presentation of what he saw as the crucial difference between the 'Italian Group' of which Ernesto Rogers was a part, and 'Team X' of which Peter Smithson was a member. According to him, Rogers's group was 'escapist fatalist'. On the other hand, Smithson's group, of which van Eyck was also a member, presented a 'Utopian View'.[27]

Configuring the discipline

In the period beginning with van Eyck's attempt at a *Configurative Discipline* (mid-1950s) and concluding with the exceptional popularity of Venturi's *Gentle Manifesto* (mid-1960s), the fate of architecture as currently practised was in large part fought out and decided (for the moment, at least). Aldo van Eyck's attempts are efforts at reason and sensation, whereas Venturi seeks pleasure alone. This is a propensity Venturi inherited from theorists of architectural sensuality such as Geoffrey Scott, who argued, in opposition to John Ruskin's emphasis on the ethical function of art, that

> [t]he spaces, masses and lines of architecture, as perceived, are appearances. We may infer from them further facts about a building which are not perceived; facts about history or society. But the art of architecture is concerned with their immediate aspect; it is concerned with them as appearances.[28]

Following Scott, Venturi's preoccupation is chiefly with spectators engaging in aesthetic appreciation of building surfaces, whereas for van Eyck, actor and spectator are one and the demands of the first give rise to the experience of the second.

However, given the pervasive hedonism of contemporary life, it is no wonder that, with its basis in formal play and novelty, the apparent ease of Venturi's *Gentle Manifesto* has been a guiding light for much post-1960s practice, while the difficult complexity of van Eyck's search for structural principles extrinsic to form has been less influential. With these considerations in mind, my choice of which projects to consider was ultimately determined by the degree to which each exemplifies the conviction that architecture is the setting of human communities based upon principles extrinsic to form that nonetheless depend on form to render them comprehensible.

By examining the writing and buildings of Le Corbusier, Louis Kahn and Aldo van Eyck, I hope to show how each conceived his projects within a utopian framework without attempting to establish a utopia. In this, I am proposing that La Tourette, the Salk Institute and the Amsterdam Orphanage are exemplary of the finest architecture. These projects demonstrate that it is possible to imagine and produce such work even in the absence of any accepted universal truth. Through its establishment, work of this sort proposes a new and situational truth that demands to be proven again with every new project and at each new location.

Furthermore, the structures by Le Corbusier, Kahn and van Eyck examined here also confirm that it is possible to invent and construct built works that fulfil the orienting objective of architecture even under difficult cultural and economic conditions. My intention is not to present an absolute or to encourage the direct replication of these respective architects' methods or works. Rather, it is to call attention to what they share and to suggest that each presents a *possibility* for architecture yet to be exhausted; the approach and mental tuning demonstrated by each remains applicable and exemplary.

Postscript: the autonomy project

Influenced by post-structuralism and in response to the failures of architects' flirtations with positivist social science, a new, post-1968 generation of architects set for themselves the task of 'thinking architecture back into its own'. Free of social obligation and unfettered by the habits of culture, such theorizing and practising, which to varying degrees now underpins the mainstream of architectural thought and practice, continues to elaborate on what theorist K. Michael Hays has called the 'autonomy project'.[29] If it is possible to argue, as I do, that Le Corbusier, van Eyck and Kahn's works harbour a utopian dimension characterized by a preoccupation with architecture as a setting of the social, then the architects of the post-1968 generation are post-utopian, if not downright anti-utopian. (Architects of the post-1968, post-utopian generation are a part of this generation less because of their actual age than according to when they came to artistic maturity.)

Hays's reading, which appears to be generally accurate, suggests that architects as divergent as Aldo Rossi and Peter Eisenman, or Benard Tschumi and Rem Koolhaas inhabit a domain of shared suspicion for the architectural authenticity that Aldo van Eyck remained committed to until his death in 1999. Therefore, if I appear to end this study too soon, by not accounting for current-day utopian architects, it is because there is a paucity of architects currently theorizing or practising (or who have been doing so since 1968), who would acknowledge utopia as playing any part in architectural imagination. In fact, most would vehemently reject such a possibility, a state of affairs I elaborate on in subsequent chapters. Even so, I do consider three projects completed during the latter half of the 1990s, by three architects whose work, nonetheless, does appear to harbour a utopian dimension.

Briefly stated, each of these newer projects pairs, in direct and less direct ways, with the three earlier projects at the centre of this study: Daniel Libeskind's Jewish Museum Berlin pairs with Le Corbusier's La Tourette in at least two ways, both structures are dedicated to inward contemplation, ideally revealing the transformative potential of hope. Moreover, the manner of construction demon-strated by both hints at fallibility as a crucial humanizing characteristic, reserving perfection for the unknown or unknowable.

Tod Williams and Billie Tsien's Neurosciences Institute, La Jolla, California, pairs with Kahn's Salk Institute, most obviously by being a research centre located just up the road from the earlier research centre, which established La Jolla as a prime location for such institutions. Both buildings make extensive use of concrete; both also engage in a significant dialogue with the land.

Renzo Piano's Jean-Marie Tjibaou Cultural Centre, Nouméa, New Caledonia, pairs with van Eyck's Orphanage in more surprising ways. Whereas van Eyck introduced traditional and foreign sources to his building in an effort to expand the scope of the institution while humanizing it, Piano's building introduces the height of sophisticated European building methods, materials and services to a local institution infused throughout by interpretations of indigenous building techniques and forms. Each of the buildings introduced above is elaborated on in the final chapter of this book.

Chapter 2

Situating utopias

The disappearance of utopia brings about a static state of affairs in which man himself becomes no more than a thing. We would be faced then with the greatest paradox imaginable, namely that man, who has achieved the highest degree of rational mastery of existence, left without any ideals, becomes a mere creature of impulses.[1]

Karl Mannheim, *Ideology and Utopia*, 1936

Contemporary studies of utopia are reluctant to advance any but the broadest definitions of it.[2] Explanations of utopia as *longing* so frequently lack specificity that most encounters with it are confusing. Consequently, each application begs for a contextualized definition of it to clarify the author's intent. For example, because the concern of this study is architecture, development of a useful definition of utopia must emphasize those aspects that foster invention of an exemplary architecture. A provisional definition of utopia emphasizing its generative potential might be: utopias articulate possibilities intended to clarify work toward their realization under existing conditions. So defined, a utopia is a clarifying model that suggests the kinds of conduct that might lead to its eventual fulfilment.

Models of this sort are established in terms of current conditions but are highly critical of them. Utopias theorize transformation. In comparison to a persuasive utopian model, the present will appear inadequate. Although forward looking, utopias are impossible to invent without a past, which is why utopias seem always to reconcile paradise, as elsewhere in space, with an age of gold, as elsewhere in time. The combination of these two longings into one concept provides a shelter for classical learning (ideas of the age of gold) and religious feeling (ideas of paradise), allowing both to survive, often unrecognized, into the modern secular epoch.

Thus, utopias propose, even if on a limited scale, a basic transformation of some part of the human condition. *Some* is crucial, which is why sociologist Karl Mannheim argued that *relative* utopias could be realizable whereas *absolute* ones are not. His proposition suggests that an individual building, as a limited (partial or relative) utopia, could reasonably be a location for testing out a utopia. An individual building might be a tryout of utopian plans in the present for transformed application elsewhere or at another scale. Similarly, projects so large as to be *absolutist utopias*, because they stubbornly resist realization, may nevertheless contain possibilities for application as more limited utopias. Le Corbusier's totalizing urban schemes, for example, were so vast in scope as to guarantee they would remain forever unrealizable, even though they influenced his thinking through of smaller projects, one such example of which is La Tourette.

The golden age of utopia

Hesiod's *Theogony* includes one of the earliest Western descriptions of human origin as an age of gold. His story begins with a plea to the muses for a description of how the world was born. He imagined that this knowledge could help to better orient him within the order of things. The muses responded with a detailed account of creation, emphasizing the original emergence of cosmos out of chaos.[3] A number of human ages followed creation; the first was golden. In *Works and Days* (1995), Hesiod describes this age as exemplary, during which a 'golden race' occupied the nourishing world: a time of original bliss still dreamed of long after its passing.[4] Four successive generations followed the golden first age. The second age was silver, not fallen but lesser than the first. The third age was bronze, inferior to the second and degenerate compared with the first.

The fourth generation was god-like but still not as golden as the first, although it was superior to the second and third ages before it, and the fifth age following it. This noble fourth generation was a 'god-like race of hero men . . . called demi-gods'. Nevertheless, they were nearly wiped out in battle. Zeus moved the survivors to 'an abode apart from men [where he] made them dwell at the ends of [the] earth'. They lived well enough in this other place, remaining 'untouched by sorrow in the islands of the blessed along the shore of deep swirling Ocean, happy heroes for whom the grain-giving earth bears honey-sweet fruit flourishing thrice a year'.[5] Might Hesiod's island-bound fourth generation be a model for Sir Thomas More's Utopians and other idealized island dwellers?

A fifth generation followed the fourth: it was an age of iron, fallen once and for all. Its members would forever gaze toward the island home of the hero-gods. Dreaming backwards toward the fourth generation, the fifth pined after the first golden age – or the promise of some future generation akin to it. Upon reflection, Hesiod's fifth generation seems strikingly close to descriptions of human struggle outside Paradise as a Fallen race whose dreams of a golden age go unanswered:

> Would that I were not among the men of the fifth generation, but either had died before or had been born afterwards. For now is truly a race of iron, and men never rest from labour and sorrow by day and from perishing at night; and the gods shall lay sore trouble upon them . . . and bitter sorrows will be left for mortal men, and there will be no help against evil.[6]

For Hesiod, the most distant past, closest to origins, remained ever incorruptible. The future, because unknowable, was full of promise. Only the present could be certain, but it all too often came up short. By revealing the persistence of human longing for orientation in the world, historian of religion Mircea Eliade explained the ageless appeal of Hesiod's story. In terms indicating an interrelationship of the age of gold, paradise and utopia, he suggested that yearning to be orientated

> shows up very clearly a specific condition of man in the cosmos – what we may call 'the nostalgia for Paradise'. I mean by this the desire to be always, effortlessly, at the heart of the world, of reality, of the sacred, and briefly, to transcend, by natural means, the human condition and regain a divine state of affairs: what a Christian would call the state of man before the Fall.[7]

Although only paradise is mentioned, utopia and an age of gold are clearly implied. Of particular interest is Eliade's linkage of nostalgia with orientation, which situates individuals within the cosmos. By engaging in a sort of psychology of desire for *numinous* contact, Eliade hints that utopia, bound as it is to paradise and an age of gold, might be a transformation of *sacred history* into *secular possibility*. In terms of content and context, Plato's *Republic* and More's *Utopia* bear this out. Each is a scheme for organizing desire toward realization of a common good.

Searching for paradise, yearning for the age of gold, and the attempt to fulfil both aspirations through utopia are a sort of nostalgia that can orient thought and desire. Nostalgia, however, is a knotty emotion, whose description derives from the Greek *nostos*, a return, combined with the Greek *algos*, pain, and *algien*, to feel pain. Nostalgia is also akin to the Swiss-German *heimweh* homesickness, which is the original meaning of nostalgia.[8] 'In addition to homesickness in the narrower sense, nostalgia has come to mean a longing for what is past, a painful yearning for what has gone by.'[9] Taken together, these terms denote an intense longing for (a) home. Constructed homes can be as much the locus of nostalgia as is the land of their location. Home and land are idealized through the longing for them.[10]

Nostalgia can also be a longing for some thing or place distant in space and/or time that represents happy circumstances imagined as continuing to exist just out of reach. In this sense, before the emergence of utopian projection, nostalgia was common to speculation about the location of Paradise. Utopia's eventual dominance over Paradise arose concurrently with extensive European ocean-going exploration and discovery, events marked by a reorientation of maps. Most importantly, North came to replace East at the top of maps, which had long denoted the location of Paradise (a switch probably resulting from the North Star's usefulness for navigation). Ideas about geography were also transformed at this time; it went from a practice of sacred mapping to being an empirical discipline. Because of these changes, Paradise eventually disappeared as a place depicted as real on maps of the world.[11] In time, the promise of North America and other destinations became the focus of longings previously reserved for paradise and an age of gold.

The backward glance of nostalgia is analogous to gazing toward paradise or back to the age of gold; all three can organize thought about future action, or that action itself. The critical locus of these *elsewheres* provides a *place* for addressing current conditions, which is something each shares with the principal function of utopia.

Age of gold + paradise = utopia

In response to the age of discovery and voyages to the New World during the later fifteenth century, longing for an age of gold – as a past condition – and search for paradise – as a lost location – were reconciled into utopian speculation. The New World appeared to promise a far-away place of boundless potential that many Europeans believed was inhabited by Adamic natives. With discovery of a pristine land populated by a race supposedly uncorrupted by culture, regaining paradise became conceivable. This other place was as much good place (*eutopia*), as no place (*outopia*) – the first reflecting an assumption of its potential goodness, the second a consequence of extreme spatio-temporal distance. As coined by Sir Thomas More, the word utopia conjoins temporal and spatial distance. His location of an ideal commonwealth on the *New Island of Utopia* calls attention to its paradisaical distance, while its pre-Christian population calls attention to its golden age goodness.

With the New World providing an *actual* model of a better time and place, and More's book articulating a hypothesis about its potential, the possibility of replicating both in Europe became a serious prospect.[12] As reconciliation and not replacement, utopia *contains* paradise and the golden age as much as it presents a third possibility.[13]

Because utopian proposals for transformed future conditions so often include characteristics of both paradise and an age of gold, it is possible to observe *retrospective* and *prospective* dimensions coexisting in utopias. Paradise, located elsewhere in *space*, and the age of gold, located elsewhere in *time*, are retrospective: the first is some other place, the second an earlier epoch. In this way, the location of models for future action lie in the past, which counterbalances the common view that utopia is exclusively prospective. Since utopias envision improved conditions intended to replace existing ones, their concern is as much with the past and present as with the future. Linked to past events and places and to the present as a response to it, utopia is more complex than the conventional view of it as simply an invention of novel approaches *ex nuovo*.

Latent in Mannheim's conception is his conviction that for a utopia to be one it must have the potential for at least partial realization (of which more later). Inasmuch as no new condition – whether a society or a building – emerges from nothing or out of nowhere, both past and present provide source material for potentially realizable utopias. What is more, because they think ideal futures through exemplary pasts, utopias are as traditional and bound to memory as they are forward looking.

As a conjunction of paradise and an age of gold, utopia is a kind of speculative nostalgia. The future ideals of utopias redescribe paradise and an age of gold in an effort to reanimate the second while bringing the first closer. Some past, interpreted as a model for present reform, is a primary content that remains the foundation for possible future action. In their most constitutive manifestation, utopias result less in a strict timetable for reform than in the potential for it. In this way, a promised golden age, or paradise, or the two combined as a utopia, need not become a dictate; rather, they can give form to potential, a possibility disclosed by E. M. Cioran:

> Let it be said that we substitute one ghost for another, that the fables of the golden age are well worth the eternal present we dream of, and that the original ego, basis of our hopes, evokes the void and ultimately reduces itself to it. . . . Yet a void that affords plenitude, a fulfilling void – does it not contain more reality than all history possesses from beginning to end?[14]

Cioran's quarrel with history turned on his sense of it as a burden, precisely because its idealization 'of knowledge and action' too often annihilates hope.[15] As the handmaiden of progress, history idealizes activity at the expense of an *eternal present* that paradise and a golden age reveal as places outside time. Cioran believed that an unflinching adherence to an eternal present could have prevented history from becoming 'synonymous with burden and torment'.[16] He went so far as to argue that 'even to breathe would be torture without the memory or anticipation of paradise, supreme – and yet unconscious – object of our desires, unformulated essence of our memory and expectation'.[17]

Nevertheless, Cioran was ambivalent about utopias. Even though he identified paradise as an anticipation, he believed utopias seek 'to reconcile the eternal present with history', and do so by combining progress with the golden age. In short, utopia attempts 'to remake Eden with Instruments of the Fall'.[18] For him, then, paradise and the golden age must remain emotional compensations for an eternal present conquered by time (history and progress). Cioran's argument, though, raises the possibility that emphasizing utopias' backward glance, rather than their apparent obligation to history, could temper their propensity for progress – for locating a golden age in the future.

Whole parts and part wholes

Cioran's estimation that 'fables of a golden age [are] a fulfilling void' is double-edged; stories of originary wholeness may be feebly compensatory, but it is just such compensations that make life tolerable, even filling it with hope. One such compensation plays a prominent role in Plato's *Symposium*, in which Aristophanes makes a peculiar speech that is a fascinating expression of human desire. In it he describes a longing for originary wholeness that ascribes a spherical shape to the earliest human beings. These beings were of three kinds: men/men, women/women and men/women. Men were sun, women earth, those who were men and women together had something of the moon, which allowed them to combine male (sun) and female (earth). Because of their combined strengths, these beings attacked the gods. In response, Zeus decided to slice them through the middle, decreasing their force while letting them live. Thus split, the halved beings felt incomplete and each began a search for its complement and wholeness:

> So you see how ancient is the mutual love implanted in mankind, bring-
> ing together the parts of the original body, and trying to make one out of
> two, and to heal the natural structure of man. . . . So the desire for the
> whole and the pursuit of it is named love.[19]

Though a myth, Aristophanes' speech nonetheless demonstrates how powerful
human longing for wholeness and orientation can be. Identification of just such
a longing as central to human desire gives an inkling of the characteristics that
alternative conceptualizations of utopia might take on. Utopia's constitutive dimension, which participates in envisioning wholeness, no matter how provisional,
encourages a habit of holistic thinking that could be vital for the imagination of
architectural projects ready to receive unknown varieties of human action and
inhabitation.

Although buildings as constructed, and societies in practice, rarely match
exactly the drawings or schemes from which they spring, plans and utopias are of a
dual nature. They can be either fixed prescriptions intended for unmediated
application to reality or presentations of ideas about potentiality. Even a blueprint can
be generative; *as-built* conditions rarely exactly match earlier drawn versions of
projects – design drawings can only approximate an architect's vision. As-built
drawings are as close to an exact presentation of constructed reality as architectural
representation can come, and this only because they are made after the fact.
Discrepancy between plans and buildings illustrates how transformations can and do
occur during the shift from theoretical model to actuality, from design to constructed
building. Such transformation suggests that, from conception to realization, patterns
are established and returned to during a process that moves from idea through to
construction.

The strength of an architectural idea depends more on the degree to
which original patterns (of thought) remain intelligible after construction rather than
on the exactness of realization. An initiating idea and its development through
application organizes and orients efforts toward realization. The result may capture
this process within itself. If it has, existing and initiating patterns will continuously
present themselves through physical occupation and mental consideration. A
conception of utopia as *pattern*, rather than as *prescription*, could form the other side
of a negative utopia, revealing what Paul Ricoeur calls utopia's *constitutive* dimension.
Both Plato and More suggest how utopian projection might establish patterns rather
than prescriptions. In the *Timaeus* (1977), Plato quotes Timaeus as saying:

> Whenever . . . the maker of anything keeps his eye on the unchanging
> and uses it as his pattern for the form and function of his product the
> result must be good; whenever he looks to something that has come to
> be and uses a model that has come to be, the result is not good.[20]

Authors of utopias also interpret patterns that they believe are unchanging. Enduring
patterns, though, remain as out of reach for utopians as they did for Plato (or
Timaeus). Thus, even though an unchanging pattern may be permanent it forever
resists materialization. Moreover, resistance to capture is a crucial source of an

unchanging pattern's endurance. Yet, like the primitive hut that shadowed architectural theories at least from Vitruvius to Le Corbusier, Plato's unchanging pattern promised good results precisely because it was not a model in his sense; direct replication of an existing model would actually place good results at a distance, whereas interpretations of unchanging patterns bring them closer to hand. Accordingly, unchanging patterns are something of a golden age. Replicating them is not possible but returning to them always is, though only as reservoirs of ideas about the 'good life'. An unchanging pattern is a source that models completeness. In so being, it is both beautiful and perfect – a result of its wholeness, a condition Plato elaborated on when he had Timaeus describe the world as made by the Creator:

> Nothing was taken from it or added to it, for there was nothing that could be; for it was designed to supply its own nourishment from its own decay and to comprise and call all processes, as its creator thought that it was better for it to be self-sufficient than dependent on anything else.[21]

Timaeus emphasized the link between perfection and completeness, whereas Renaissance architect/theorist Leon Battista Alberti defined beauty in terms of completeness. Similarly to Timaeus's description of perfection, Alberti proposed the following:

> Beauty is that reasoned harmony of all the parts within a body, so that nothing may be added, taken away, or altered, but for the worse. It is a great and holy matter; all our resources of skill and ingenuity will be taxed in achieving it; and rarely is it granted, even to Nature herself, to produce anything that is entirely complete and perfect in every respect.[22]

As a self-sustaining world, planet Earth is a model of Nature's great creation that Alberti referred to. His belief that harmony within a body is the best indicator of beauty is applicable at all scales. It is part of a web of analogies that relate the individual, as part of a social whole, to the parts of a building that make it complete. Alberti proposes this pattern of associations as an ideal, an objective, presented to human beings through the perfection of the living world as a harmonious entity (Nature as a presentation of God's genius). Along these lines, a just society is a social whole, represented as much by the buildings that shore it up as by the human beings who make it, inhabiting its buildings and cities as settings for their ongoing patterns of life. Alberti was quite specific about the value of intelligible patterns made up of harmoniously interrelated parts at all scales:

> If (as the philosophers maintain) the city is like some large house and the house in turn like some small city, cannot the varied parts of the house . . . be considered miniature buildings? Could anything be omitted from these, through inattention and neglect, without detracting from the dignity of the whole work? The greatest care and attention, then, should be paid to studying these elements, which contribute to the whole work, so as to ensure that even the most insignificant parts appear to have been formed according to the rules of art.[23]

For Alberti, interrelation among parts was an indicator of beauty as much as of perfection. He applied this idea of completeness to the world, Nature, society, buildings and individuals, as well as to the relationship of each to the other, and of each part of a thing to the other parts that form it. The best world would be the one most complete, or whole, reflecting the harmonious relationships among *all* of its parts. Although unachievable, the rich web of associations that preoccupied Alberti approaches the kinds of harmony utopias propose.

Alberti also explicitly considered the projection of ideal cities. He proposed such a city as an objective, akin to beauty, that although rarely granted or achieved ought to be attempted nonetheless. His conception reiterates the ideal, or utopia, as a pattern rather than as a prescription:

> It would be worthwhile therefore to follow the example of Plato, who when asked where the city which he had dreamed up could be found, replied, 'That does not concern us; we are more interested in what type of city should be considered best. Above all others you should prefer that city which most closely resembles this ideal.' We too should project a city by way of example, which the learned may judge commodious in every respect, yet which will nonetheless conform to the requirements of time and necessity. In this we should follow Socrates' advice, that something that can only be altered for the worse can be held to be perfect.[24]

By referencing Socrates, Alberti links his own definition of beauty to Plato's presentation of perfection, an idea that, by way of wholeness, concerns cities, individuals and collectives. In his discussion of beauty, Alberti also argued that although perfection is always the *aim* it is the attempt that is most crucial, even if partial attainment of an ideal is all that is possible. By accepting partial achievement, he was proposing perfection (beauty) as an absolute *aim* (a perfect *telos* of sorts) rather than as an absolute *directive*. Along these lines, Alberti introduced two important notions to a possible reconceptualization of utopia: attempts to realize an ideal must include consideration of *time* and *necessity*, which outweigh any requirement for absolute achievement of the ideal in attempts to establish a *good city*. These concerns localize the ideal city of utopia by particularizing it in terms of time and place, a tolerance that introduces tension between universalizing abstraction (an ideal) and localized (mundane), present reality.

More's Utopia

Writing nearly three-quarters of a century after Alberti, Sir Thomas More proposed a pattern of perfection for the cities of his island *Utopia* (first edition 1516) that readers often misinterpret as an argument for monotonous uniformity rather than intelligible patterns that could situate citizens within the social space of their communities. More's narrator, Hythloday, describes Utopian cities with just such social relationships in mind: 'There are fifty-four cities, all spacious and magnificent, identical in language, customs and laws. So far as the location permits, all of them are built on the same plan, and have the same appearance.' He continues, 'If you know one of their cities,

you know them all, for they're exactly alike, except where geography itself makes a difference.'[25] Although Hythloday acknowledges uniformity among Utopian cities, he counterbalances this with difference as a possibility in response to situated necessity. The significant impact geography can have on city *form* and *figuration* confirms the real possibility of such generative tension.

In all likelihood, although More's description of Utopian cities makes uniformity seem a certainty, sameness among them *must* be less absolute than is commonly imagined. More implied his acknowledgment of this by countering *exactly alike* with an exception for differences that *geography itself makes*. Even if the intention is to make every part of a city the same, and even if each city is founded and distributed in the same manner, geography will defeat attempted uniformity with its own diversity. Ultimately, particularities of place present a frustrating challenge to *every* effort to install an exact replica of some original city. More confirms his awareness of this by having Hythloday describe one Utopian city as opposed to all of them. Not surprisingly, he does not present the city he describes as an interchangeable and generic abstraction of all other Utopian cities:

> [S]o I'll describe one of them [Utopian city], and no matter which. But what one rather than Amaurot the most worthy of all? – since its eminence is acknowledged by the other cities which send representatives to the annual meeting there; besides which, I know it best because I lived there for a five full years.[26]

2.1
Thomas More,
Utopia. **Louvain,**
Belgium, 1516.
Island of Utopia
Source: Rare Books
Division, The New
York Public Library,
Astor, Lenox and
Tilden Foundations

Hythloday's description of Amaurot calls attention to its specificity and to its special status among other Utopian cities. He continued with further consideration of the impact geography had on forming Amaurot's unique character. On the other hand, architectural theorist Colin Rowe's conventional interpretation of the same passage emphasized apparent, even though impossible, interchangeability among Utopian cities:

> More said of the towns of his own Utopia, 'He that knows one knows them all, they are so alike one another, except where situation makes a difference'. One may draw in horror from this calculated elimination of variety; and quite rightly so, for the ideal city, though an entertaining type to inspect, is often a somewhat monotonous environment.[27]

The intention of Rowe's selective reading was to call attention to the liabilities of Utopia, especially its apparent rejection of variety. Yet Rowe ignored the role pattern plays in making the social space of cities intelligible to their occupants. Such patterns might show themselves as a shared conception among the founders of cities and could act as a measure that situates inhabitants in all of them – or in all the parts of one. The two readings of More's description of Utopian cities – one emphasising *pattern*, the other *uniformity* – highlight how utopia's dual possibility, as either *pathological* or *constitutive*, often collapses into a single diagnosis of the concept as *always* pathological and *never* constitutive.

A place for utopias: Karl Mannheim's utopian imagination

> Thus, after a long torturous, but heroic development, just at the highest stage of awareness, when history is ceasing to be blind fate, and is becoming more and more man's own creation, with the relinquishment of utopias, man would lose his will to shape history and therewith his ability to understand it.[28]

Karl Mannheim

Sociologist Karl Mannheim's elaborate definition of utopia formed part of his more general project for a *sociology of knowledge*, which he began elaborating on in his book *Ideology and Utopia* (first English publication, 1936). Because both are kinds of mentality, Mannheim argued, ideology and utopia are important aspects of a sociology of knowledge. His characterization of utopia as a form of social imagination, as a periodic response to established order gone stale, and as locked into a developmental historical process charted from its origins to its decline (overwhelmed by matter-of-factness), makes Mannheim's argument especially relevant to the present consideration of an exemplary architecture.

According to Mannheim, utopia is the mentality of groups with no hold on power. For them, utopian mentality provides an imaginary plan they can call upon in their efforts to wrest authority from whoever controls present conditions. In this role, utopias function as shepherding visions that guide opposing outsiders into power. Conceived of in this way, utopias are an organizing image that the opposition uses to marshal its efforts toward replacing an established order. As the motivating force of social imagination, a utopian mentality is crucial for maintaining optimism, which includes evolving conceptions about *good societies* and their potential realization.

In Mannheim's view, utopia guides the social-historical process by giving it an aim: it is a characterization of utopia that harbours the possibility of returning a social dimension to architecture, offering architects a way to consciously consider the form communal appropriations of space might take and the shapes they ought to be given to receive inhabitation.

Social imagination, which is utopian in character, is never static; it is always envisioning a dynamic *not yet* in response to *what is*. Accordingly, Mannheim defined utopian mentality as 'a state of mind . . . [that] is incongruous with the state of reality within which it occurs'.[29] 'This incongruence', he argued, 'is always evident in the fact that such a state of mind in experience, in thought, and in practice, is oriented toward objects which do not exist in the actual situation.'[30] Mannheim clarified this definition with a requirement that 'only those orientations transcending reality [through incongruence with the present state of affairs] will be referred to by us as utopian which, when they pass over into conduct, tend to shatter, either partially or wholly, the order of things prevailing at the time'.[31] Desire to overcome an immediate situation is thus only utopian when it shifts from a potentially non-realizable distant goal residing in the mind alone to actual steps taken in the direction of realization in present reality.

Wish-images that remain outside the possible grasp of society help to maintain the current order and consequently are not utopian: they are neither presently attainable nor are they intended ever to be. For example, Paradise, proposed as an afterlife reward for good behaviour in this life, is not a utopia; wish-images do not serve as a means for altering the present. Wish-images are, rather, part of the apparatus for maintaining the status quo. On the other hand, if a wish-image of Paradise begins to motivate action in the present, oriented toward realization of transformed conditions during this life on this planet, it becomes utopian, or as Mannheim put it: 'Wish-images which take on a revolutionary function will become utopias'.[32]

Unique to Mannheim's conceptualization of utopia is his requirement that to be one it must act directly upon reality by initiating transformation of present social conditions. Utopia envisioned as oriented action presents a challenge to common conceptions of it as forever unrealizable. Conventional declarations of utopia as unrealistic encourage rejection of its potential out of hand, even if its project is only unrealizable under present conditions. Revealed in this is a struggle between opposing forces.

Defenders of the status quo must uphold present conditions as the only possible ones, but in doing so they also restrict their ability to envision potential. Conversely, utopian dreams are visions of social potential that arise out of the limitations of present conditions. For realists, present reality appears impossible to transcend because it *just is* – it carries with it the apparent inevitability of some objective fact. Consequently, they will label utopias impossible in an attempt to neutralize transformative potential at the outset. 'By calling everything utopian [in a pejorative sense] that goes beyond the present existing order, one sets at rest the anxiety that might arise from the relative utopias that are realizable in another order.'[33]

Utopias can guide group action because they contain 'in condensed form the unrealized and unfulfilled tendencies which represent the needs of each age'.[34] Their relationship to the present locates utopias in a dialectical relationship with it: the deficits of an existing order (its absences) become the promises of a transformed order (as realized presences). Owing to this necessary relation to a present, utopia would remain an impossibility without an existing order to challenge. Born of the present order, utopia, in turn, has the potential to 'break the bonds of the existing order'.[35]

Paradoxically, for Mannheim, realization of a utopian project ultimately results in utopia receding from the social process; that is, until a now established order is challenged by new utopian visions advanced by advocates of another order currently on the periphery with enough desire to move to the centre, and so on. This suggests utopian challenge to the prevailing state of affairs is cyclical, and thereby self-perpetuating, a permanent condition of the social process.

Ages and stages of utopia

Mannheim argued that through its life cycle, utopia has had four principal stages of development, each emerging as a response to the previous one. At the end of its life cycle, utopian mentality will collapse into decay, a course he claimed parallels the historical-social process. Proposed in this way, utopia has a beginning and an end that encompasses transformations occurring in between. At the time when he developed his sociological conception of utopia, Mannheim believed that the utopian mentality was ebbing.

The first phase of utopian mentality, 'the orgiastic Chiliasm of the Anabaptists', holds the origins of the modern utopian mentality, as well as of socialism. Anabaptism emerged soon after the Reformation in the early 1520s, especially under Thomas Münzer.[36] Sixteenth-century Anabaptist millenarianism, although partially formed by inheritances from the ancient world and early Christian eschatology, was a fundamentally new condition because it joined chiliastic vision 'with the active demands of the oppressed strata of society'.[37]

Adherents of Anabaptism wanted to locate a break in time in order to collapse the distance between *this life* and Paradise. Their revelatory project demanded rejection of prevailing conditions, which was a radical departure from ecclesiastical norms. Previously, Paradise was accepted as located far beyond *any* society's temporal reach, which made it exclusively a compensation lying outside the bounds of mortal achievement. A heavenly city might someday be attained but only after death, or as a result of Christ's return to earth to head his thousand-year kingdom. According to Mannheim, the Anabaptist's ability to redirect 'longings which up to that time had either been unattached to a specific goal or concentrated on other-worldly objectives' was epochal, especially because this gave rise to a belief that these desires could be realized 'here and now'.[38]

As described by Mannheim, the second stage of utopia is 'liberal-humanitarian'. Its adherents no longer seek a break in time to make their goal immediately present but rather believe in infinite progress. It is a project for the future that depends on an unfolding of enlightenment that evolves out of the present, extensible into an indeterminate distant future.

Mannheim's third stage of utopia is the 'conservative'. It is embedded in existing reality and seeks to justify the present as inevitable and organic by claiming that it has grown out of the past in the only way possible. With its organizing *idea* located in the past, this utopia projects its origins backward after the fact. As origin and justification, *pastness* defends a conservative present against other – opposing – claims to power, especially those of the liberal-humanitarian idea.

The fourth phase of the utopian life cycle is 'socialist-communist'. Mannheim argued that it is a synthesis of the three earlier forms. It is unique in that it would result from a process of intentioned effort and gradual concretization, which distinguishes it from the liberal-humanitarian conception of enlightenment as the result of progress stretching infinitely into the future. Socialist-communist utopias are separated from conservative utopias by locating goals in a previsioned future as opposed to embedding them in a superseded past. Socialist-communist utopia, however, shares with liberal-humanitarian utopias a rejection of conservatism's belief that present conditions are justified by being grounded in the past. Even so, the socialist-communist utopia shares with conservatism a sense of inevitability; the future is being prepared in the present and when it arrives it will be grounded in past events that made its realization possible.

Socialist-communist utopias and liberal-humanitarian utopias both reject chiliastic attempts to collapse time, although each acknowledges the usefulness of this mentality's ecstatic energy but only for so long as it can be channelled toward cultural aims. Importantly, it is the embrace of hard work and acceptance of slow evolutionary development, continuously tested in the present and rewarded in the future that decisively separates socialist-communist utopias from the chiliastic belief that some heavenly city could become immediately present through a radical break in historical time.

The end of utopias?

Mannheim argued that the fifth and final stage of the utopian life cycle is its end, a climax resulting in the eventual disappearance of the utopian mentality. Utopia's end arrives when its former incongruence comes to approximate more closely existing conditions. Utopia thus loses its necessary oppositional stance. Closer approximation of reality is inevitable because each utopian type reflects a stage in the historical-social process: 'the liberal, the socialist, and the conservative ideas are merely different stages and indeed counter-forms in the process which moves continually further away from Chiliasm and approximates more closely the events transpiring in this world'.[39] As a consequence of this more limited position, utopia finally becomes an expression of one possible hypothesis among many others about how social life ought to be.

Mannheim described the cultural conditions under which he was writing as a time of utopian decline. To him, it was an epoch of burgeoning relativism when alignment of desire with the status quo was becoming the norm. Given present conditions, his evaluation remains relevant. It is a situation in which acceptance of near infinite conflicting viewpoints makes a holistic view impossible. Although this development may be a good thing, especially because it reveals exclusionist and absolutist positions as inevitably partial, the absence of an encompassing vision for the future renders the present goalless; unbound by any purpose, progress becomes its own ultimately empty reward. The evolution of utopian mentality charted by Mannheim, from its emergence with orgiastic chiliasm through its decline and likely disappearance, left him unconvinced that the parallel movement toward rationality and inclusive relativist conceptions of reality would ultimately benefit social life:

> Whenever the utopia disappears, history ceases to be a process leading to an ultimate end. The frame of reference according to which we evaluate facts vanishes and we are left with a series of events all equal as far as their inner significance is concerned. The concept of historical time which led to qualitatively different epochs disappears, and history becomes more and more undifferentiated space. All those elements of thought which are rooted in utopias are now viewed from a sceptical relativist point of view. Instead of the conception of progress and dialectics we get the search for eternally valid generalizations and types, and reality becomes nothing but a particular combination of these general factors.[40]

The decline of utopia is, according to Mannheim, tantamount to an end of *purpose-fulness* for the social-historical process; an end that brings with it an atomization of society. Shared vision and common aims become impossible. With collective purpose lost, an approach that addresses discrete problems on a case-by-case basis replaces reality-transcending schemes. Mannheim described this as the limited vision of technique: 'I need not worry about the whole, the whole will take care of itself.'[41] His lamentation for the decay of holistic utopian visions was matched by his alarm at the decline of social imagination. Mannheim's consideration of the probable consequences of a general atrophying of utopian mentality illuminates what its lost potential might have been:

> This process of the complete destruction of all spiritual elements, the utopian as well as the ideological, has its parallel in the most recent trends of modern life, and in their corresponding tendencies in the realm of art. Must we not regard the disappearance of humanitarianism from art, the emergence of a 'matter of factness' (*Sachlichkeit*) in sexual life, art, and architecture, and the expression of the natural impulses in sports – must all these not be interpreted as symptomatic of the increasing regression of the ideological and the utopian elements from the mentality of the strata which are coming to dominate the present situation?[42]

Mannheim's attention to the relation between destruction of utopia and ideology and the emergence of a general cultural *matter-of-factness* is reflected in the emergence, during the 1920s, of the most extremely rational and reductive modern architecture, which came to be called *Neue Sachlichkeit*, normatively translated as the *new objectivity*. A characteristic of this architecture was its apparent embrace of reality *as it is* with no mediating qualities. Its results were intended to be free of any attempt either to locate transcendent meanings in, or to draw them out of, the present, the site or the building's intended use. The present *is*, and that is enough. It is architecture's job, according to this position, to present reality as objectively as possible.

Myths of objectivity

The degree to which absolute objectivity is itself thick with symbolism seems to have eluded its most ardent adherents. Even so, matter-of-factness and perseverance of ideas originating with new objectivity still shapes thinking and building throughout the world. It is an architecture disciplined by rationalized construction, a modularized building industry, and developer-given programmes for occupation. This is the case even, or especially, for architecture wrapped in a manner meant to suggest that it is driven by something other than economy, efficiency and real estate values. Because of its matter-of-factness, and emphasis on what *is*, including the facts of a building problem, the architecture of new objectivity was fundamentally anti-utopian. Mannheim characterized its tenets as including 'the conscious rejection of the past and the notion of historical time, the conscious brushing aside of every "cultural ideal", [which could] be interpreted as a disappearance of every form of utopianism'.[43]

In an epoch of apparent objectivity, Mannheim argued, relativism eclipses universality. Generalizing theories, free of reality-transcending elements (e.g., ideology and utopia), become the only way to conceptualize wholeness. Any surviving notion of universality is reduced to the elucidation of apparently 'eternal forms in the structure of human impulses'.[44] The resulting impulse theory of human action frees such action from any requirement that it be guided by spiritual elements, or a holistic vision, even one situationally located. Mannheim's concern with totality was neither determinist nor absolutist. The objective of a total vision, such as utopias suggest, is to organize effort in a holistic manner, an aspect of Mannheim's thought illuminated by Paul Ricoeur:

> [T]otality means not so much the necessity of determinism as the capacity to put all conflicts within a picture of the whole. It is this sense of general orientation that disappears in Mannheim [with the disappearance of utopia], and disappearing with it is the notion of goal.[45]

Utopia articulates the goals that make it possible for society to organize its efforts toward manifestation of the total picture it requires to orient itself and its labours. The loss of goals, and with them the possibility for organization they provide, is what ultimately concerned Mannheim:

> [T]he complete elimination of reality-transcending elements from our world would lead us to a 'matter-of-factness' which ultimately would mean the decay of the human will. . . . the complete disappearance of

the utopian element from human thought and action would mean that human nature and human development would take on a totally new character.[46]

Overwhelming matter-of-factness will so narrow vision that managing the present must become the only possibility. On the other hand, utopian thinking, of the sort Mannheim describes, allows human beings to act on history with a method that retains the dynamism of progress without surrendering to blind impulse. Utopia also balances radical initiative with a reasoned response to present reality. This contains utopia within tradition, but it is a provisional engagement harbouring the potential to supersede given conditions at any moment. Mannheim's unique definition of utopia is a promising lens through which to consider the problems confronting contemporary architecture, such as the difficulty architects have in encompassing the social. For Mannheim, utopia is necessarily bound to action and to the character of that action. More importantly, he argued that without utopia human beings relinquish their capacity to consciously act upon history.

Utopia and dystopia

Nineteenth-century debates between pragmatism (the *is* as fact) and optimism (an *ought* as potential), provide a historical backdrop for Mannheim's conviction that the utopian will to shape history must oppose the incapability of matter-of-factness to operate holistically. Nomination of *dystopia* as utopia's opposite was a result of John Stuart Mill's (1806–1873) declaration that all utopian visions are at best hopeless, thus dystopian.

As a strong, practical-minded critic of utopian impulse Mill sought not ideals but rather some moderate reforms that could arise from an existing state of affairs and be of little threat to them. His coinage of the phrase *dystopia* was intended to describe not only obviously impossible schemes, but also utopian schemes in general. Because they cannot stand up to scrutiny according to the methods of science, utopian schemes are impossible:

> [E]conomies are governed by natural laws which cannot be changed by human will, any more than the laws of physical nature can. . . . Any attempt by governments or other institutions to interfere with the operations of these laws is doomed to worse than failure.[47]

Mill's attitude, paraphrased in the preceding, led him to argue that 'it is, perhaps, too complimentary to call them Utopians, they ought rather to be called dys-topians, or caco-topians.[48] What is commonly called Utopian is something too good to be practicable; but what they favour is too bad to be practicable.'[49] John Ruskin rejected such sentiments, deeming them a direct threat to meditations on an *ought*, that he believed are necessary for good societies to take shape. In *Unto this Last* (1985), he launched a sustained attack on *Political Economy*, which Mill represented for him. In his preface, Ruskin was quite clear about his objective for the four essays that form it:

> [I]n a science dealing with so subtle elements as those of human nature, it is only possible to answer for the final truth of principles, not for the

direct success of plans: and that the best of these last, what can be immediately accomplished is always questionable, and what can be finally accomplished, inconceivable.[50]

Ruskin, though a nineteenth-century writer, demonstrates how it is possible to temper Mannheim's requirement for utopian action without relinquishing the benefits of utopian vision. Ruskin's concern was with *plans* for making society more just, though he did not call them utopian. Although he was suspicious of too easily realizable plans, he demanded that they be more than simply informing models. For him, then, plans are necessary for guiding action by way of principle, which fills them with potential. Yet, to be beneficial it is not necessary that plans be finally accomplished in full, exactly as planned.

Utopias in the present

The value of utopia, as conceptualized here, is its contribution to the formulation of exemplary architecture. Achievement of exemplary architecture requires optimism that this place as it is (including this life and reality as they are) could one day more closely approximate some *better* place. Cynics look upon imagination of, and striving for, a better place as indication of an inability to operate effectively in the real world. Intolerance for ideals is encouraged, at least in part, by Marxist critique of ideology and utopia, as much as by the thinking and operations of free-market capitalism: both are hostile to utopian thinking because it imagines an unverifiable *ought*.

Hostility toward utopia remains the norm. Even though Marx and Engels acknowledged their inheritance from Saint-Simon, Charles Fourier and Robert Owen, they always qualified the *utopian socialist* contribution as merely intuitive (rather than *scientific*), thus historically unrealistic. For Marx and Engels, these qualities confirmed the limited experiments of these predecessors as premature and ultimately ahistorical. Whatever room Marx and Engels made for their utopian socialist predecessors is mostly lost on their followers (or successors), for whom 'Utopia (or utopian)' is a term of abuse hurled at so-called ahistorical dreamers and reactionaries alike for anti-revolutionary thought and activity.

Other visions of utopia: Marx, Lefebvre and the situationists

While many Marxists remain uncomfortable with utopia, utopians and dreams, there have been several significant attempts by proponents to extend, correct and bring Marxian thinking up to date. A key objective of these efforts has been to make Marx's critical method more tolerant of dreams, imagination and utopia – whether or not they ultimately reject his ideas, critical efforts to extend or deepen Marxism definitely follow in his footsteps. Among these, the work of Henri Lefebvre (1901–1991) and the Internationale Situationniste (1957–1972+/–) are of particular interest.

Both considered the social life of cities (including architecture and urbanism) through a Marxist frame that is at once utopian and a partial negation of Marxism. Lefebvre's *Critique of Everyday Life* (1958) was a significant influence for the situationists, especially their principal theorist Guy Debord (1932–1994).

Lefebvre's work on the city in turn shows the influence of the situationists' principal urban theorist, Dutch painter and architect Constant Nieuwenhuis (1920–), especially his idea of *Play and the City*. Guy Debord and Lefebvre had both capitalism and Marxism in their sights. Most interestingly they attempted a negotiation between utopia and Marxism as reconcilable and associated concepts.

The situationists were uncompromisingly radical. Their conviction was that only revolution could recuperate reality by fully transforming society, overturning present reality in preparation for its replacement. Conversely, Lefebvre remained ever committed to positive engagement with the present. He emphasized the positive dimension of situationist potential, especially in his attempt to capture meaning and value from the seductive nothingness of spectacle. According to Lefebvre, his own vision and the situationists' are utopian. For him, this must be the case because no imaginative effort can ever be free of a utopian dimension. He was quite explicit in his view that only the most specialized activities could be liberated from utopia, but only at the cost of increasing dullness, which explains their impoverished results:

> Who is not a *utopian* today? Only narrowly specialized practitioners working to order without the slightest critical examination of stipulated norms and constraints, only those not very interesting people escape utopianism.[51]

Critique of Marxism and capitalism is implicit in Lefebvre's acknowledgment of *utopia*. The basis of capitalism is a range of separations that require specialization, including isolating art from life, theory from practice and work from play. Division of labour is, of course, the most significant separation formulated by capitalism, leading to all the others that follow. Utopia is comprehensive; it entails a picture of a whole that envisions unified social life. Capitalism is ruthlessly pragmatic. Applied Marxism, because it presupposes centralization, tends toward bureaucracy and the production of party functionaries who operate unimaginatively in the management of society. Utopia is a searching criticism of conditions at the moment of critique; reality is never complete, and reinvention of its potential as an integrated whole is constant. For Lefebvre, capitalism is the solvent of unified social life, which explains why he began his critique of capitalism with Marx:

> Marxian thought alone is not sufficient, but it is indispensable for understanding the present-day world. In our view, it is the starting point for any such understanding, though its basic concepts have to be elaborated, refined, and complemented by other concepts where necessary. It is part of the modern world, an original, fruitful, and irreplaceable element in our present-day situation, with particular relevance to one specialized science – sociology.[52]

Lefebvre's problem was not with Marx's thought but with its limitations. One such limitation is the blind eye Marxism turned toward cities, a demonstrably anti-urban attitude that neglects the city as a crucial setting of human desire. Additionally, Marxism as conventionally practiced is sober, dour and devoid of wonder, all of which encouraged Lefebvre to theorize a sociology inspired by Marx but unafraid to:

address itself to the relations between the following concepts, which are still insufficiently distinguished: ideology and knowledge, utopia and anticipation of the future, poetry and myth. Such a critical study needs to be taken up again in our changing world.[53]

He especially wished to locate within Marxist thought a place for wishes and dreams, poetry and utopia. Such desires reveal Lefebvre as essentially optimistic, underscored by his belief that it is possible to engage the present critically in order to transform it incrementally. He favoured positive engagement and reform organized according to the logic of utopia. Thus, unlike the situationists, who were absolutists, Lefebvre could envision a better future arrived at step by step. His belief was that *authentic* reality is recoverable because traces and memories of its brighter moments remain. Individuals, he was certain, continue to possess the ability to access a more authentic, directly lived everyday life. What is more, when awareness of this potential reaches consciousness, even gently, individuals will desire reform and realize it together.

Situationists and the city

Formed as a group in 1957 and disbanded in 1972, the situationists positioned themselves as the arch-enemy of contemporary consumer capitalist society, a position given its theoretical underpinning by Guy Debord in his famous book *Society of the Spectacle* (1967). For situationists the spectacle included advertising, consumption, passivity, and especially separation from direct experience.

As outlined by Debord, the society of spectacle, in order to be self-perpetuating, required generalized *separation*, a fundamental condition of alienation running throughout every aspect of individual and social life in work and leisure. Ultimately, alienation is a self-preservative measure employed by this society to defend itself against the kind of consciousness possible only when conditions of free association and communal unity prevail; conditions of disalienation such as utopias propose, which would be the direct opposite of generalized separation. According to Debord, dis-alienated individuals and collectives would lead *real* lives of direct experience, a consequence of which would be their inevitable rejection of divided labour, passive spectatorship and hypnotic consumption. Unfortunately, rejection of existing conditions will remain impossible for so long as alienation is not itself directly experienced as a solvent of individual and social life.

This society of the spectacle is not confined to the affluent West. Indeed, all societies whose economies are based on modern techniques of production, consumption and communication, left, right or centre, tend toward a world picture conditioned by spectacle. All aspects of the spectacle instigate passivity and are generally destructive of everyday life. Increasing passivity in response to the over-stimulation of perpetual entertainment, which coincides with tranquillizing regimentation, would result in banality, which the situationists saw as symptomatic of a severe mental disease sweeping the planet. Spectacle, not coincidentally, emphasizes visual (over) stimulation above all other forms of experience, encouraging an atrophy of social interaction that only the physical experience of others and the city can provide.

Cities were key to situationist critique of existing conditions because forms of alienation including work, leisure (such as tourism, visiting museums, consumption and other forms of spectatorship), as well as traffic flow all determine diminished post-World War II urban experience. The very physical reality of modern cities reinforces alienation by being physical manifestations of generalized separation as sites for its perpetuation. Isolated buildings, rationalized streets, the dazzle of abundance, and the predominance of automobiles and transport routes are fundamental determinants of contemporary cities that are inhospitable to unplanned social encounters.

Increasingly, though, the situationists' field of concern and operation – the traditional city in transition – was replaced by the capitalist city. If this city is ugly and boring, it is because it accurately images capitalist processes of specialization that lead to social alienation and the reduction of individuals to consumers and spectators. It follows, then, that any critique of ugly capitalist, bureaucratic communist or totalitarian cites must take account of the social conditions and political economy that shapes them. Negative evaluation of ugly cities exclusively based on their ugliness is empty formalism. Evaluation of an architecture presented as pure utility normally occurs according to no other criterion but utility, which requires neglect of all other evaluative dimensions. Exclusively quantitative conceptualizations of architecture and the city will always deprive both of their psychosocial dimensions.

Banality makes itself known most emphatically in cities and buildings that are inadequate for the free play of individual or social life. In modern cities, all mystery, all chance, is under threat of eradication. Rigidly programmed monosyllabic settings for work, or consumption exclusively (as an escape from work), systematically replace potential settings for spontaneous situations. In the urban environment, there is less and less tolerance for the in-between or the *other*. Rapacious consumption and commodified tourism are the only proper (accepted or even possible) activities in such new cities.

With play, there is always the possibility of wildness. A living city will provide places for play and wildness that could even encourage their spontaneous eruption. With the conquest of urban restructuring by irrational rationalism, situationists were faced with a significant challenge to their early projects for maintaining the existing city as a dynamic, unified and diverse place of mystery and spontaneity, well suited to the perpetual play of drifting. Each subsequent event of so-called urban renewal, or the structuring of new cities and peripheries, further diminished their field of operation by dulling the city, and thus spreading boredom throughout the human habitat.

Scrubbing old cities clean transforms them into entertainment zones for suburbanites and tourists to visit, while fewer and fewer residents actually live there. Accordingly, situationists saw the city as their social, cultural, artistic and urbanistic field of operation, which led them to engage in a radical critique of architecture, urbanism, society and political systems and movements throughout the world. By 1962, the group's growing frustration with the stubbornness of existing conditions led them to abandon almost all discussion of what they called 'Unitary Urbanism' or an 'Architecture of Situations'. Hotly political polemic eventually replaced the group's concern for the city and the consequences of spatial practices.

Situationist activity, whether a critique of art or politics, demonstrates a consistent characteristic throughout: an attempt to link fragments across space and time to make a dynamic, unfinished and transformable whole out of dis-unity (akin to Alberti's notion of *concinnitas*). This new whole would be non-hierarchic, non-bureaucratic, resistant to management and could engage individuals in the creation of their own social life (and its settings).

While situationists may, at first glance, seem to have ruthlessly rejected all things past and present, a deeper look reveals that their vision actually derived from some idealized pre-modern time that existed before the society of the spectacle: before state capitalism, radically free markets, or bureaucratic communism. However, the group had no tolerance for either reform, or an imitation of past conditions. If they looked in some way to a pre-modern past for clues, it was not to imitate it; rather, any use of the past would require its reinvention according to present conditions. Anything else would be formalist, serving only to validate, not negate, the present by re-forming it. Nonetheless, the past was crucial because it provides a model of what community, *real* life and experience could be. According to Guy Debord, the pre-modern past is a time before 'all that once was directly lived' became 'mere representation'.[54]

All or nothing?

Faced with a dwindling field of action and unable to hope as Lefebvre had that critical engagement of the destruction of urban social life and its setting could result in some ultimate benefit for all, situationists rejected any idea of renewal and reform. They opted instead to focus on political revolution as the only means of recovering an environment that could nurture free play and human passion. In this way, they were a bit like William Morris, who at first believed that reforming art could transform society, only to end up taking a far more radical stance precisely because art is inseparable from the individual, social, economic and political processes of life. Consequently, reform will be possible only after less brutal conditions are made to take shape.

For situationists, as for Morris, beauty was ultimately no defence against banality or brutality, or even against general ugliness, which are, after all, expressions of the conditions of the society that makes them. In view of this, utopian socialists charted a viable potential course only if practised by direct action, never as an exclusively theoretical exercise. In the end, the situationists were absolutists, which is why they failed. Their inevitable failure to vanquish and replace the society of the spectacle, however, is not a sufficient reason to completely reject them. Because their conceptualizations of a vital urban realm continue to disclose the potential of small successes, they were closer to Lefebvre than either might have recognized. Lefebvre embraced utopia to imagine an *impossible possible* as a way to construct places for recollection of general and biographical moments in the present. For the situationists, an impossible possible was not enough: utopian revolutionary efforts *must* leap into the real and become experimental revolutionary efforts that work toward a complete overhaul of existing reality. The usefulness of utopian prospects lies somewhere in between.

The situationists' all or nothing stance made it difficult for them to sustain their vision over the long run. It also deprived them of opportunities to construct their vision. That said, it is important to remember that the group accurately documented the conditions that continue to affect the social life and form of present-day cities.[55] The situationist critique of representation, especially of art trapped as spectacle in the prison house of museums, and of alienation concretized in and by the physical settings and social life of post-World War II cities, remains a challenge to the full range of spatial practices and city design fashions. Hence, situationist writings endure as reservoirs of insight into other possibilities, in particular revealing why it is that spectacular tourist and commercial cities (wherever they may be), no matter how entertaining, tend to feel emotionally empty.

Chapter 3

Real fictions

Everything of value in art has always cried aloud to be made real and to be lived.[1]

Dreams spring from reality and are realized in it.[2]

Architectural projects are a kind of fiction comparable to utopias. Drawings, including plans, sections and elevations (among other expressive representations) are the rhetorical means by which the non-reality of design is persuasively proposed as real long before, if ever, being constructed.

As a literary form, fiction presents a plausible unreality. Unexpectedly, the term *fiction* originates with *to make*, deriving from the Latin *fictio*, a making, the past participle of *fingere*, to form or to mould. Reflection on the origin of *fiction* as a verb, rather than as a noun, suggests that fictions can be constitutive – related to establishing or constructing something. Nevertheless, in common usage, a fiction is anything made up or imagined, including the making up of an imaginary happening. Hence, any invented idea or thing is a kind of fiction. Although normally thought of as unreal or as representing an unreality, by making things up, fictions reveal a potential for realization.[3]

Architectural designs, like fictions, are the making of an imaginary realm. However, architecture is profoundest when an architect's invention advances a commentary on the social activities it will house, as they are lived and as they might be lived. Its dual position between reproducing existing reality and its transformation locates architecture, Janus-faced, between *conservation* of what is and *proposition* of improved future conditions. Architectural projection presents an unreality that construction may make or form; a making that, through alteration of existing conditions, reinvents what is.

Although architectural projects are fictional inventions presented by way of various theoretical representations and justifications – visual as well as verbal, two-dimensional as well as three-dimensional – the status of a constructed project, built according to its fictitious representations, raises certain problems. Is a constructed building (or collection of buildings) an incontrovertible fact, simply because of its *presentness*? More likely, something of the fictional remains.

In its materiality, no matter how tentative, a building is certainly real; it is in existence, the process of making made it so. Nonetheless, even after construction and initial tenancy, the imagined story of a building's occupancy continues to be a fictional account of potential, which extended use either confirms or reveals as false. Following this line of thought, recently constructed buildings will only become *real* through prolonged inhabitation over time.

There thus appears to be a direct correlation between a building's long-range viability (its plausible realness through time) and how successfully it actually provides a setting for the habits and practices it was meant to house and facilitate. Any building remains *useful* only for so long as it is suitable for occupancy by its current (or future) inhabitants, and only for so long as it can engage their capacity to transform or reinvent it, without radically altering its presence (which would erase the building as it exists, making it into a different building). Buildings become real in the course of occupancy, according to the degree to which they can accommodate varied occupation during a long trajectory of use.

Consequently, an exemplary building remains alive in the imagination even after completion. Such a structure persists through time by remaining an open possibility that construction and initial occupation do not complete. This open-endedness, which opens only upon completion of construction, preserves the possibility of utopian prospectiveness even in materially present works of architecture: completed exemplary buildings encourage inhabitants to weave their own accounts of desire through the architect's fictional proposition. Occupancy, in the present and into the future, will reveal any design as originally based either on a plausible hypothesis or on unsupportable claims.

The architect's initial story of a building is a fictionalized account of some *ought* that enduring inhabitation alone can verify. Played out in a building through use, such stories can also transform that part of the world where they are situated. In buildings where the gap between the originating stories and realization is close enough, the fictions articulated by their architect can locate and transform, or at the very least, inform, the social practices occurring within. Transformation of this sort, of a particular part of the world, is conceivable as occurring through its redefinition that originates with projection, proceeds through specification, and is finally realized by construction.

What exemplary buildings appear to share is establishment of a comprehensible pattern, compelling enough to inspire in inhabitants a willingness to construe, through active engagement, how they might transform occupation of their building over a long duration. Dedication of this sort to a building is a form of attention that promotes embrace, reinvention, or rejection of what experience and reflection disclose. In *Invisible Cities* (1974), Italo Calvino's consideration of the City of Zenobia gets close to the sense of fiction in building (from invention to making and inhabitation) elaborated on here. To illustrate this as clearly as possible, in the passage that follows, quoted from Calvino, *a particular building, building* and *buildings* is substituted for *cities* and *Zenobia* where these appear in the original:

> It is pointless to decide whether [*a particular building*] is to be classified among happy [*buildings*] or among the unhappy. It makes no sense to

divide [*buildings*] into these two species, but rather into another two: those that through the years and the changes continue to give their form to desires, and those in which desires either erase the [*building*] or are erased by it.[4]

These substitutions, it seems, are permissible in light of Alberti's challenge to architects (and patrons) to view cities as large houses and houses as small cities (including something of each in the other). Alberti's argument for configuration of cities and houses was one among his many articulations of the interdependent relation of part and whole. For him, interdependency of a similar sort is as true for buildings and societies (as kinds of bodies) as it is for knowledge, made up of many parts that form a unity (made from diversity). Alberti's model endures, even though nowadays disintegration tends to provide the organizing schema for everything from individual self-experience to social life, while also pervading all forms of cultural expression.

Given the plight of cities everywhere, Alberti's appeal for the mutuality of cities and buildings is more pressing than ever. Synthesis and wholeness (made up of interrelated parts), offers a corrective for isolation and arbitrary fragmentation (without reducing complexity). Unfortunately, for so long as cities are formed according to the imperative of real estate development alone (which views highest and best use as an exclusively economic term) they will have great difficulty giving form to desires.

In the interim, rapacious acquisitiveness must continue to erase cities, transforming them from potentially beneficial settings for social life into entertainment zones of desperate consumption. Until Alberti's conceptualization of cities as houses and houses as cities takes hold, responsibility for configurative potential will increasingly fall to individual buildings, which, by their very presence, can challenge what *is* with alternative stories of what *might* be.

Imagination and invention

Utopia is an almost inescapable companion of architectural invention. Architectural projections and utopias are close relations: both argue against inadequate existing conditions while drawing upon the past to augur a transformed future envisioned as superior to the present. Unsurprisingly, their partnership is neither always *good* nor always *bad*. Constructed settings of various scales, from single rooms to individual buildings, and from urban complexes to whole cities, are attempts to actualize stories originally told through myriad descriptive representations, before any hope of realization. So important are architectural representations to the entire enterprise, that from design through construction, it is as if they somehow confer credibility on a project at its earliest stages, seemingly assuring a happy outcome if built.

Close as utopias and architecture (or urbanism) are, consideration of them together usually sets out to demonstrate how utopia must always represent impossibility, which would reveal it as an impractical practice with an exclusively negative effect on architecture. Typical of such descriptions is characterization of utopias as assuring their own defeat long before realization is ever attempted.

Conviction that utopias, literary and architectural alike, are at all times stories of self-defeat implies that existing reality is the only possible condition. The consequences of this for architecture are grave: resignation replaces hope.

Not surprisingly, surrender to conformity infuses recent discourses on architecture. For example, by focusing on utopia as excessively radical in intent, architects Robert Venturi, Denise Scott Brown and Steven Izenour dismissed utopian projections as disruptive impossibilities: 'In general, the world cannot wait for the architect to build his or her utopia, and in the main the architect's concern should not belong with what ought to be but with what is.'[5]

Using language similar to that of architectural theory, psychoanalysis also tends to diagnose utopia as a rejection of both living in reality and of complexity. French analyst Janine Chasseguet-Smirgel, for example, described utopian imagination in terms generally accepted by psychoanalysts: 'According to my hypothesis there is [in utopias] a primary wish to rediscover a universe without obstacles, a smooth maternal belly, stripped of its contents, to which free access is desired.'[6] So described, utopias are revealed as a self-deception inevitably leading utopians to invent worlds impossibly free of complication. Round city plans are, apparently, the architectural equivalent of individual desire for boundless bliss: circles (and spheres) are geometric figures believed to be analogous to the *primordial matrix* and thereby to original perfection.

3.1
The Creation of the World and the Expulsion from Paradise, Giovanni di Paolo (c. 1445)
Source:
Metropolitan Museum of Art, Robert Lehman Collection, 1975 (1975.1.31)

Notably, Colin Rowe argued that utopian city designs originate with ideal city plans projected during the Renaissance, most characterized by a circular layout. He maintained that such arrangements refer to a passage in Plato's *Timaeus* where God's creation of the world is described as demanding selection of an appropriately all-encompassing shape, 'suitable . . . for a living being [the earth] that was to contain within itself all living beings'. The obvious choice, not surprisingly, was 'a rounded spherical shape' chosen because it is

> a figure that contains all possible figures within itself. . . . with the extremes equidistant in all directions from the centre, a figure that has the greatest degree of completeness and uniformity, as he [the creator] judged uniformity to be incalculably superior to its opposite. And he gave it a perfectly smooth external finish all round.[7]

Plato's description of the sphere as a *pregnant* shape corresponds with Chasseguet-Smirgel's conviction that individual longing for an obstacle-free world (utopia) reveals a desire for return to the world-like sphere of the smooth maternal belly, which links to Rowe's contention that circles refer to perfection and totality in Renaissance ideal city plans. In the event, idealized wombs and circular cities are comparable to Plato's portrayal of the spherical world as a 'single complete whole' capable of nourishing and sustaining itself.

For his part, Rowe went further to stress that ideal cities take a circular form as 'an analogy of this divinely created sphere and as an emblem of the artificer who is declared to be immanent within it, the city receives its circular outline'.[8] Thus, according to Rowe, circular cities are analogous not only to the Earth but also to its creator. Giving the city such a shape, it seems, would guarantee its affinity with God and Earth – ascribing to the town a natural, thus perfect, character

> intended both to signify and assist a redemption of society. [Because] it is said to be a natural shape. . . . a circular city might now be considered to exemplify the laws of nature, [consequently,] how unnatural and therefore in a sense how 'fallen' the medieval city must have seemed.[9]

Rowe's explanation illuminates how classical (Platonic) and Christian ideas of perfection combined during the Renaissance to conjure up a compelling story of redemption and creation. Hence, ideal cities are circular because this form binds them to the Earth as a *perfect* shape and to God's figure, the circle, which is a symbol of original perfection and infiniteness. A city thus figured could 'serve as a representation of just the city which humanist thought envisaged. . . . a world where perfect equilibrium is the law'.[10]

Venturi and partners, Rowe and Chasseguet-Smirgel share a diagnosis of utopia as a turning away from difficult reality toward an imagined environment created in the image of unchanging or impossible original perfection. Even more explicitly, Venturi and partners argued that what they called 'orthodox Modern architecture is . . . utopian, and puristic' as well as intolerant. Moreover, utopian architects are always 'dissatisfied with *existing* conditions', wishing to change them according to their impossible schemes.[11] Apart from damning utopian dreaming, Venturi *et al.* main-

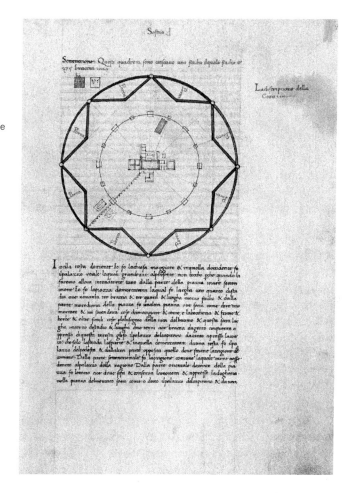

3.2
**Filarete
(c. 1400–1469):
Magliabechiano
ms: Treatise on
Architecture II–I
140–43v**
Source: Florence,
Biblioteca Nazionale
(National Library)

tained that 'orthodox Modern architecture' is synonymous with utopian impossibility. By appealing to the widely held belief that utopia is failure, Robert Venturi, Denise Scott Brown and Steven Izenour hit upon a convenient way to reveal modern architecture – utopia's doppelganger, in their view – as suspicious.

Rowe also argued that the utopian dimension of modern architecture assured its disappointing result. According to him, desire for utopia is a desire to arrest 'motion, growth, change and history',[12] attributes of *reality* that utopia must always turn away from. Psychoanalysis goes even further. Chasseguet-Smirgel elaborated on her own interpretation of utopian longing by suggesting that it reveals an unconscious desire for 'eradication of the human species to the benefit of the single self'.[13] While impossible to achieve and certain to be a letdown if it could be, such a condition is ostensibly desirable because an empty world would be always calm and forever without frustration. Chasseguet-Smirgel argued that representations of this condition include the 'perfectly straight streets, the rigorous geometry of the buildings, the sameness of the houses, [and] the passion for numbers which exists in most utopias'.[14]

3.3
View of Ideal City, Urbino, Ducal Palace
Source: Urbino, Ducal Palace

As commonly described, it is reasonable to imagine that utopias can only ever represent attempts to exit history and experience. Although there is real merit to such accounts of utopia, they do not tell the whole story. Such selective views of utopia ultimately reveal only one of its dimensions, what Paul Ricoeur terms its pathological side: the negative aspect of a roughly dual conception, which also includes the possibility of constitutive utopias as an alternative. Constitutive utopias harbour a capacity for holistic thought in tandem with longings for comprehensive alternative conditions, none of which requires absoluteness to be beneficial.

Another side of utopia

Working upon reality with the imagination, architects mediate between conditions as they are and how they believe things ought to be. Verbal, visual or textual declarations constitute first attempts to resolve the tension between envisioned ideals and existing reality. The character of such representations reveals an architect's convictions, turning on how he or she envisages his or her purpose. Architects who conceptualize themselves as members of a community are predisposed to envision their role as formulating settings upon which, and within which, social life may unfold. Because principles other than novelty, formalism, fame or technical capability alone shape their work, architects with this outlook are able to set about configuring the social realm with projects imagined for a particular place in the present.

Architecture's multiple aspects, especially its social dimension, more readily interconnect in designing minds when utopia suffuses architectural imagination. Mental tuning of this sort will reveal aspirations for buildings that surpass their identification as simple commodities. The possibility that utopia could infuse architectural projection positively should come as little surprise. After all, utopian literature persistently envisions attainment of complex, interwoven, larger communities made from semi-autonomous smaller communities. Consequently, the value of an ideal is worth considering, even if wishing for it might seem naive, particularly when present conditions offer little hope for its realization. Moreover, it appears as though settings for social life are only imaginable so long as architects entertain the achievability of some ought.

Architects and architecture

How architects see their role in society depends a great deal upon a capacity to envision the potential for establishing communities. This is important because all that architecture may reasonably do is give physical form to institutions, which in turn become a setting for their operation. Yet, with the withering away of institutions – demonstrated by the degree to which social associations such as religious, family and political life have already dwindled – the merits of the last proposition might seem dubious. Nevertheless, the alternative negative view has far-reaching consequences for architecture, chiefly that it must be meaningless and ought to represent this as exquisite autonomy. According to this view, any attempt to construct a socially meaningful setting is reactionary. Manfredo Tafuri and Francesco Dal Co, for example, revealed such a view by diagnosing Louis Kahn's attempts to give form to institutions as an expression of nostalgia for irrecoverable origins:

> [T]he new bases for architecture set up by Kahn are every bit as artificial as the myths and institutions in which he put his trust. . . . It is nostalgia that determines Kahn's language. That determinism breaks with the modern tradition no less violently than does every attempt to confine it in the display cases of a museum. Kahn's work inveighs against the reduction of architecture to a negligible object.
>
> But this signifies protecting the values from the process of history by transfiguring them into symbols, by attempting to recover their arcane properties.[15]

Tafuri and Dal Co could not locate anything more hopeful in Kahn's 'disquieting search for the "center"', as they called it, than 'a lesson without a future'.[16] They thought of Kahn's approach as nostalgic, and thus necessarily backward. According to them, because he attempted to give flesh to what Tafuri claimed are 'inoperative values', Kahn's work must be out of step with history.[17] Tafuri could not observe the reasonable hopefulness in Kahn's buildings, which are piecemeal attempts to reconstruct social life. The architect's effort, regardless of its merits, would necessarily be naively premature, at least until revolution, according to Tafuri, brings forth a reconstituted society freed from its own self-alienation. In any event, since the revolution now seems further off than ever, architecture will need to do something meanwhile.

The only hope of resisting the continuing slide of architecture into nothingness (toward becoming the 'negligible objects' of Tafuri and Dal Co's negative vision), rests with architects exerting some effort toward theorizing practices that might lead to socially richer results rather than sublimely useless objects. To begin with, such practices would need to provide architects with a place from where they could imagine some *ought* which architecture might attempt to give a form. Utopias furnish architects with just such places. However, Marxist critique and the cultural dominant of capitalism severely restrict the potential of utopia.

Utopias: theoretical and experimental

Colin Rowe diagnosed the programme of modern architecture and planning as utopian, but accepting this reading is difficult. Attempts to apply the programme of modern architecture directly and totally to cities by way of technological means – rather than through social and political change – highlights precisely how modern architecture, in practice, was mostly *not* utopian. Direct and immediate application, with little regard for those affected, deprived schemes for transforming existing cities – as well as the construction of new cities – of the distance necessary for a measured interpretation of the potential consequences of making utopias operational. To counteract this, an even larger gap ought to open between projection of ideal models and the processes that attempt to make them real; when it does not, the results will carry hints of absolutism. Henri Lefebvre argued that practices of this kind are actually positivism masquerading as utopia:

> [T]here are several utopianisms. Would not the worst be that utopianism which does not utter its name, covers itself with positivism and on this basis imposes the harshest constraints and the most derisory absence of technicity?[18]

Most importantly for architects, the absence identified by Lefebvre suggests that thoughtful research remains the practical dimension crucially lacking from redevelopment schemes affecting large swaths of existing cities and especially in the establishment of instantaneous new ones. For example, as it often occurs, the potential liveability of a city or building is characterized as a quantitative certainty, before the fact. This is an especially ill-advised conclusion, particularly considering how frequently built results disappoint because they are so poorly attuned to the qualitative dimension of liveability. Questions such as, 'what makes somewhere a place where it is good to live?' could open up this dimension to architectural projection by directing research – before construction – toward those qualities that affect the life of individuals and communities where they live. Lefebvre elucidated how this little considered practical side of utopia is relevant for inventing exemplary architecture and cities:

> Utopia is to be considered experimentally by studying its implications on the ground. These can surprise. What are and what would be the most successful places? How can they be discovered? According to which criteria? What are the times and rhythms of daily life which are inscribed and prescribed in these successful places favourable to happiness? That is interesting.[19]

The underexplored theoretical and experimental dimension of utopias separates them from the failure of modern urbanism (and architecture), which resulted in large part from practitioners proposing positivist social science solutions in the form of technological utopias. Emphasis on utopia's propensity for research calls attention to its political and social programme, qualities that do not depend upon technology for realization, regardless of how small or large a role technology might play in its establishment.[20] An understanding of utopia as a high ideal beyond the possibility of human achievement allows it nonetheless to serve as an aim – especially because its complete realization is impossible.[21] In any event, even when intended, the direct and total manifestation of utopia is in reality rarely an actual possibility.

Beyond Marxism and Capitalism

As previously alluded to, the extreme individualism of free-market capitalism is anti-utopian. It encourages depletion of social and institutional content as important features of community life and architectural projection. Conversely, the objective of Marxism (as presented by Marx and Engels) was to establish a scientific socialism. Owing to this, Marxism leaves little room for utopian thought.[22] Likewise, rejection of idealism and human psychology, in the *Manifesto* for example, reveals a significant blind spot in Marxism (identified by Lefebvre), the consequences of which are obvious enough historically.

For its part, capitalism is psychologically astute: by playing upon individual fear of inadequacy and equating acquisition with status, it sharpens primitive anxiety to the point where a free and competitive market, motivated by profit, seems to be a natural law. Although theoretically opposed, Marxism and capitalism are both anti-idealistic; the former longed to be scientific, advancing a purely causal interpretation of economic reality, while the latter is brutally positivist, exploiting human potential for avarice to its fullest.

Any effort to identify a position for architecture between Marxism and capitalism – that can resist the excesses of both – must begin with nineteenth-century utopian-socialist writings, especially those of John Ruskin and William Morris. Their consideration of contemporary life at the time initiates a reconsideration of the relationship between art and life that encourages reconceptualization of utopia's role for the imagination of architecture. This role could potentially make twenty-first-century architecture resistant to the technocratic excesses that bedeviled architects of the first half of the twentieth century and the formalistic excesses beguiling those of the second half of the century and, often enough, into the present.

Elaboration on how utopian imagination remains integral to the production of exemplary works of architecture is particularly relevant in the current period, punctuated, as it is, by the fall of the Berlin Wall and September 11, 2001. The first event heralded the official fall of Communism, suggesting that the Thatcher–Reagan mindset had 'gotten it right' – self-interest was triumphant. The second event revealed just how vulnerable the West remains, shedding light, for a moment, on globalization as interdependence rather than opportunism.

Architecture, social imagination and utopia

Karl Mannheim's proposed role for utopia in the life of social imagination remains crucial for the invention of architecture. For example, in *Space, Time and Architecture*, Sigfried Giedion considered the difficulties post-World War II architects face in their efforts to frame 'centers of social activity'. Though he did not use the term utopia, Giedion did recognize a link between social imagination and architecture:

> There is a world-wide trend toward creating centers of social activity, and this calls for far more from the architect than just technical capacity. His

task today is infinitely more complicated than that of his predecessors at the time when Versailles was built. They had but to give concrete form to an exact program placed before them by a clearly stratified society. Today the architect has to anticipate needs and to solve problems that exist only half consciously in the crowd. This involves great responsibility. The architect has to have the rare gift of a peculiar sensitivity that we would like to term *social imagination*.[23]

Giedion argued that architects require attributes that are remarkably similar to the function of utopia identified by Mannheim as necessary for social imagination. The question of *social imagination* arising in both provides the most obvious and direct link between Giedion's architect and Mannheim's utopia. For Giedion, social imagination is a special capacity that architects must possess if they are to have any hope of configuring post-absolutist centres for dynamic and diversified social life. For his part, Mannheim argued that social imagination depends upon utopia to nurture it.

Architects for Giedion and utopians for Mannheim give form to the desires, often unconscious, of the society to which they belong. Form following function in some determinist way would not be enough. Similarly, reliance on technique alone would be a serious limitation. To move beyond reductive matter-of-fact practices, Giedion argued that an architect with social imagination must possess far more than technical capacity. Likewise, Mannheim equated dependence on technique, particularly the expediency it suggests, with decline of the utopian mentality and social imagination. To sum up: social imagination is the crucial link between an architect's capacity for framing the human environment and the utopian mentality necessary for cultivation of such ability.

Paul Ricoeur: ideology and utopia

While utopia may be the life force of a social imagination as well as the engine for inventing an exemplary architecture, surely not all works of architecture can be worthy of praise for being utopian in the positive sense proposed here. Moreover, because all constructed architectural projects alter reality, to at least some degree, simply modifying an existing state of affairs cannot be the basis for evaluating utopian projects. Required are qualitative criteria that make it possible to distinguish between projects that alter reality for the better from those that do not. Giedion proposed just such criteria, arguing that projects that give form to social desires are superior to those that do not. Nevertheless, identification of social desire, which even Giedion acknowledged resides at a mostly preconscious level for individuals and groups alike, is difficult to grasp.

Maybe social imagination is actually something an architect can cultivate, a resident potential native to all, that only the particularly gifted (more likely perse-verant) acknowledge and develop? Furthermore, because even the least adept architect probably imagines that he or she has this aptitude, a more precise criterion of evaluation is required if there is to be any hope of distinguishing between projects that articulate some better end (with social imagination in abundance, which also gives form to social desires) from those that do not.

In what follows, elaboration on criteria for just such a distinction owes a great deal to Paul Ricoeur's attempt to fuse Mannheim's opposition between ideology (as conservative) and utopia (as revolutionary). By doing this, he extended Mannheim's definitions of both while enlivening them. Like Mannheim, Ricoeur believed that ideology and utopia form a fundamental part of social and cultural imagination. Contrary to Mannheim, he set out to construct what he called a single conceptual framework encompassing both, which could link utopia and ideology dialectically. As introduced earlier, Ricoeur suggested that ideology and utopia each have two traits, 'a positive and a negative side, a constructive and a destructive side, a constitutive and a pathological dimension'.[24] The positive, constructive and constitutive dimension of one can function as a corrective to the negative, destructive and pathological dimension of the other.

Ideology's two traits include a negative tendency toward *distortion* (which follows Mannheim) and a positive tendency toward *conservation* (which extends Mannheim's conception). Ricoeur argued that the negative side of utopia is a kind of social dreaming, akin to the myths Mannheim rejected because they either harboured no intention for realization or because they were so absolutist as to make realization impossible. Conversely, the positive side of utopia includes its capacity for introducing imaginative variations on existing conditions.

By interjecting dissimilarity into the present situation, utopias can subvert current conditions while fortifying social imagination, all of which, in combination, is potentially constitutive of social reality. Understood in this way, conservation, ideology's positive trait, could be a corrective to utopia's negative trait, a tendency toward escapism. On the other hand, the positive trait of utopia (a critical glance from nowhere with the potential to initiate transformation of present conditions) could serve as a corrective to the negative side of ideology (the intentional distortion of perception in order to insure the hold of a given condition on reality).

In his discussion of utopia's tendencies, Ricoeur's usage of 'pathological' and 'constitutive' are particularly helpful for elaborating on utopia's relation to architectural invention. On one side of the constructive–destructive divide of utopia's dual potential, there resides a positive tendency to *form*, on the other, a negative tendency to *deform*. Moreover, pathological (unhealthy, disordered) most closely expresses the negative dimension of utopia's capacity. Alternatively, constitutive (establish, order, frame) most closely expresses its positive potential. If utopia does indeed have this dual nature, and actually is crucial for architectural invention, then it ought to be possible to distinguish constitutive architectural projects from pathological ones.

Distinction between constitutive architectural schemes and pathological ones is useful because it introduces criteria for evaluating projects based upon the degree to which they either do or do not give form to social imagination. Not surprisingly, such a measure of architectural quality offers a challenge to the contemporary habit of basing architectural virtue on such limited criteria including novelty, surface appeal, visual effects, entertainment value, return on investment, prominence on the skyline, domination of the landscape, or its camera-friendliness. Overall, placing so much emphasis on the appeal of spectacle runs the risk of fully eclipsing architecture's social dimension.

Pathological utopia

In architectural terms, projects for buildings and large complexes envisioned as requiring total and immediate implementation reveal a pathologically utopian dimension. Motivated by a necessary obliviousness to existing conditions, such totalizing projects, especially when actually executed all at once, are deprived of the benefits that partial implementation over time offers, especially the potential for improvement that gradual rethinking permits.

The seeming necessity for immediate application limits projects of this sort to largely articulating an escape from the present. For example, specificity of location must be unimportant. What is more, speeding up the implementation process for a project leaves little opportunity to reconsider its aims. An undesirable situation that precludes corrective responses to a project's potentially negative consequences which realization always discloses. Such projects are a manifestation of what Ricoeur called the 'projection of frozen models which have to be immediately perfect'.[25]

Impossibility of achievement certainly reveals projects of this sort as pathological. A negative attribute that aptly describes the most damning characteristic of modernist city planning is its positivist excess. The multitude of attempts made during the twentieth century to install the modern city, all at once, over the traditional city, starkly reveals the consequences of such excesses. Needless to say, numerous architectural historians and critics, especially Colin Rowe, have considered the careless devastation of traditional cities as an expression of modernist hubris, proof enough that utopia has nothing positive to offer.

Absolutist utopian projects – such as those Rowe criticized – are escapist, demonstrating what Ricoeur identified as 'a logic of all or nothing which ignores the labour of time'.[26] Requirement for immediacy and absoluteness are two of the most common symptoms of pathological utopias. They are commonly so preoccupied with *time as now*, that the present is unimaginable as related to either the time *before* it or the time *after* it. Neglect of the actual effort, physical as well as mental, required to get things right reveals a conception of time obsessed with immediate presentness. In Mannheim's terms, it is a form of chiliastic longing for that break in time that would reveal an ideal city fully realized.

The demand for immediate presentness carries with it two main liabilities. On the one hand, absolute realization is forever impossible to achieve; on the other, attempts to do so require total disregard for pre-existing and ongoing patterns of life. By ignoring the pitfalls associated with concrete application, which absoluteness requires, pathological utopias fantasize frictionless conditions where everything is compatible with everything else, that only dissolution of all obstacles could bring about. For architecture, this entails total destruction of existing conditions to provide a complication-free clearing for the new.[27]

The magical thinking that conjures up (or inspires efforts to construct) obstacle-free fields for realizing the new city or society reveals how 'the pathological side of utopia'[28] tends 'to submit reality to dreams [and] to delineate self-contained schemas of perfection [that are] severed from the whole course of the human experience of value'.[29] The 'preference for spatial schematisms' of pathological utopias reveals an implicit link between them and the kind of matter-of-factness that concerned Mannheim. A schematism is a reductive figure that resists social elaboration; its diagrammatic character thwarts inhabitation at nearly every step.[30]

Unrealizability, immediateness and *matter-of-factness*, which Ricoeur argues are attributes of pathological utopia, combine what Mannheim believed the earliest utopias required to be compensatory myths (immediacy) with what absolutist utopias illustrate (their own impossibility) together with what he argued was the end of utopia (matter-of-factness). Linked in this way, Ricoeur freed Mannheim's conception of utopia, the certainty of its emergence and decline, from the limitations that his maturational schema places upon it. In contradistinction to Mannheim, Ricoeur conceptualized utopia as a permanent condition of social and cultural imagination, tending always toward either the pathological or the constitutive, a distinction that offers a valuable alternative to architectural judgment based on the degree of apparent functionality or visual attractiveness alone.

From pathological to constitutive utopia

Even though Ricoeur described the character of pathological utopias in more detail than constitutive utopias, he did make a number of suggestions about utopia's constitutive dimension. Not surprisingly, as the other side of a dual concept, simply flipping Ricoeur's characterization of pathological utopia begins to reveal his definition of constitutive utopia.

Evidently, constitutive utopias show the greatest regard for everything that pathological utopias neglect. If aggressive insensitivity characterizes pathological utopias, constitutive utopias are notable for exhibiting a deep understanding that memory, place identification and orientation are valuable qualities inextricably linked to human desire, which ought to infuse projects of any scale. In contradistinction to the speed with which pathological utopias must be realized, constitutive utopias value the benefits of slow, considered change. Moreover, utopias of this sort begin with compassion for the attachments individuals and groups establish with all aspects of the existing milieu they inhabit. How these factors situate, pattern and frame settings of human life motivates constitutive utopian thinking and doing. Obviously enough, pathological utopias are the antithesis of constitutive utopias; whereas the latter pay close attention to detail in realizing their own principles, the former, as Ricoeur put it, demonstrate 'a lack of care for the first steps to be taken in the direction of the ideal city'.[31]

Simply put, constitutive utopias are situated. They emerge out of a conviction that reasonable and intentioned progress is good, which is akin to Mannheim's description of socialist-communist utopias. The idea of progress characterizing constitutive utopias (embrace of gradual change) is in line with Mannheim's conviction that a conscientious approach to making history discloses human action as most meaningful when it is purposeful. Any utopian proposal that does not move in the direction of a good, or at least better, world will necessarily be pathological. It is for these reasons that Ricoeur placed so much emphasis on reasoned action and why he considers absolutist utopias to actually be substitutes for action: they resist verification by being unrealizable.

Constitutive utopia

In light of what has already been stated, the constitutive side of utopia offsets its pathological side, counterbalancing the negative propensity of utopia with positive potential. If rigid vision characterizes pathological utopias, constitutive utopias proffer redescriptions of reality that are flexible, remain open to the complexities and inconsistencies that always confront implementation, and do so without surrendering visions of the new society or city. This capacity derives from a conception of time that links present action, directed toward realization, with past accomplishments.

The future in turn also links present to past. This is confirmed by eventual achievement of goals, which is durational, occurring through the passage of time. Ricoeur's argument that construction of the present must be built upon the past, without losing regard for it, suggests that his conception of constitutive utopia is akin to Mannheim's conservative utopia, but only partially so. Constitutive utopias are actually much closer to Mannheim's socialist-communist utopia; both include a linkage of present and future with the past but are not limited to reproducing idealized previous conditions.

Hence, in terms of explaining existing conditions, conservative utopias and socialist-communist utopias employ history in fundamentally different ways: the former utilize the past as an after-the-fact justification for the present, whereas the latter project results worked for along the way into the future. More specifically, socialist-communist utopias link progress to the past in a critical and historical way: improvement occurs through time, partial accomplishment in the present moves goals, originating in the past, into the future, which itself will in turn become the past. As described here, the process of realization envisioned by socialist-communist utopias tallies with the emphasis constitutive utopias place on intentioned effort and planning directed toward knowable and achievable ends, ascribed to them by Ricoeur.

The determinate aims of constitutive utopias, like those of socialist-communist utopias, separate them from liberal-humanitarian utopias, which Mannheim described as based on faith in infinite progress extending forever into an indefinite future. Additionally, determinateness, or limitation anchored in exact and definite limits, relates Ricoeur's idea of constitutive utopias to Mannheim's definition of relative (or limited) utopias, which are realizable precisely because they are both piecemeal and can tolerate modification.

Unlike pathological utopias, constitutive utopias can embrace action, practice, obstacles and incompatibility. Furthermore, they exhibit tolerance for conflict between goals, embracing divergences as opportunities. By accepting tension, initial schemes for constitutive utopias tend toward elastic conceptualizations, beneficial since *all* schemes, in an attempt to justify their own logic, tend toward schematism. Elasticity opens projects up to the potential of re-evaluation during processes of implementation that are ideally comprehensive and gradual.

Multidimensional openness assures a level of awareness that keeps projects attached to the 'whole course of the human experience of value'. Moreover, constitutive utopias may 'submit reality to dreams' but unlike pathological utopias, this includes the possibility that such dreams could enter and alter reality without deforming it. The very imperfectability of constitutive utopias (a by-product of their verification through concrete action) allows them to remain reasonable possibilities. Such projects are forever partial, a limitation permitting attempted constructions of constitutive utopias to occur within the density of history. All told, utopias' most positive attributes include a propensity for experimentation and speculation, significant qualities that allow the transformations constitutive utopias suggest to enter into practice, potentially altering the real, even as their schemes are inflected by it.[32]

Précis: utopian imagination and the not yet

In accordance with Ricoeur's description, utopias are at once subversive – they call reality as it is into question – and at the same time, ordering. Destabilization created by initial subversion could lead to conditions that are ultimately more stable, the result of transformations worked out theoretically, as much as facilitated, by utopian critique of the present. Here, as elsewhere, Ricoeur's conceptualization of utopia comes very close to Mannheim:

> The utopian mode is to the existence of society what invention is to scientific knowledge. The utopian mode may be defined as the imaginary project of another kind of society, of another reality, another world. Imagination is here constitutive in an inventive rather than an integrative manner.[33]

While the value of utopian invention for architectural projection and urban design is by now hopefully unmistakable, it is worth noting that utopian subversion can be constitutive at the scale of the individual as well: 'what decenters ourselves is also what brings us back to ourselves. On the one hand, there is no movement towards full humanity which does not go beyond the given; on the other hand, elsewhere leads us back to the here and now'.[34] Movement of this sort is a kind of self-reflection possible on the personal as well as on the social level; at the scale of the social, utopias could provide the conceptual setting for such beneficial movement:

> [D]evelopment of new, alternative perspectives defines utopia's most basic function. May we not say then that imagination itself – through its utopian function – has a *constitutive* role in helping us *rethink* the nature of our social life? Is not utopia – this leap outside – the way in which we radically rethink what is family, what is consumption, what is religion, and so on? Does not the fantasy of an alternative society and its exteriorization 'nowhere' work as one of the most formidable contestations of what is?[35]

Ricoeur emphasized the role utopias can play in opening up possibilities that could alter reality for the better. It is the motivating notion of an inclusive rather than exclusive better building, city, or world, that makes this dimension of utopia constitutive, a characteristic suggesting conditions during which 'the field of the possible is . . . open beyond the actual; it is a field, therefore, for alternative ways of living'.[36] In architectural terms, this trait limits description of a project as a constitutive utopia to ones that are particularly strong in social imagination; wherein careful consideration of political, social and symbolic desire is more important than preoccupation with image, expedience or technique alone.

In light of the definition of constitutive utopias elaborated on here, it is possible to think of architecture as participating in the structuring of new institutions (in a number of senses) even before these have become operative. Buildings and cities, as settings of the social, can at the same time analogize the social and provide platforms for its elaboration. Such possibilities are latent in Ricoeur's suggestion that

> the shadow of the forces capable of shattering a given order is already the shadow of an alternative order that could be opposed to the given order. It is the function of utopia to give the force of discourse to this possibility.[37]

Projects for cities and buildings, even when constructed, are partial, remaining proposals about future occupation and action momentarily realized through the presence of sentient bodies: social life completes building. In effect, this is the discursive aspect of architecture that always engages with the possible and which utopia proposes.

Chapter 4

Varieties of architectural utopias

Yes, surely! and if others can see it as I have seen it, it may be called a vision rather than a dream.[1]

William Morris

Similarly to Ricoeur's recognition that utopia can have both a constitutive and a pathological dimension, Lewis Mumford recognized – much earlier – utopia's dual propensity: 'utopias of escape' provide compensation rather than opportunity, which makes them pathological. 'Utopias of reconstruction', on the other hand, are projective and thus constitutive. Mumford contrasted these two utopian propensities as the difference between fantasies and plans: 'In one we build impossible castles in the air; in the other we consult a surveyor and an architect and a mason and proceed to build a house which meets our essential needs; as well as houses of stone and mortar are capable of meeting them.'[2]

By employing the house as a figure for 'utopias of reconstruction', Mumford establishes a link between utopian and architectural practices. He went even further, defending utopias with architectural drawings. 'It is absurd to dispose of utopia by saying that it exists only on paper. The answer to this is: precisely the same thing may be said of the architect's plans for a house, and houses are none the worse for it.'[3] Mumford's characterization suggests that utopias of reconstruction and architects' plans are both fictions that can also be models for a possible reality.

Architectural discourse generally conceives of *utopia* as being interchangeable with *ideal*, even more so with *ideology*. Utopia, ideal and ideology intersect where an ideal refers to the highest conception of a thought or thing, brought to a perfect state by being pursued to its logical conclusion. In this sense, ideal suggests completeness, judged according to thoroughness, rather than relative goodness or badness. Because absolute thoroughness is normally beyond any possibility of total realization, ideals are implicitly achievable only in the mind, as ideas. As such, calling a notion ideal suggests that it is visionary.

Calling an idea or an individual visionary is another way of suggesting that neither is practical. Ideal is thus shorthand for declaring unexpected alternative views utopian. In turn, utopia normally signifies imagination of a place or state of things as perfect. Yet, because perfection is an ideal, it is visionary. Such a place, as imaginary, can only exist in the mind. Consequently, its realization *must* be impracticable: the thoroughness it demands is impossible to achieve, or so conventional architectural wisdom would have it.

If, according to conventional wisdom, utopia is an impossible ideal relegated to visions in the mind, popular views of ideology see it as a kind of theory used to uphold the realizablility of particular (utopian) social, political or architectural visions. In architectural discourse, theory often refers to speculative, even fanciful thought imagined as being baseless. Hence, propositions in support of a set of principles that theory puts forth are arguably interchangeable with *visionary*, *idea*, *ideal*, *ideology* and *utopia*. As such, theory has also come to signify the impracticable.

Even though theory is common enough, current discourse mostly deactivates its radical character by transforming it from a presentation of principles into an expression of wholly subjective ideas about individual practices. In this way, theoretical statements become more manifesto than treatise, leaving them with a limited general application. If theory is thought of as visionary (or fanciful) from the outset, it is drained of whatever socio-political content it might otherwise have, which anaesthetizes its ideological potential. Ultimately, theory as fancy seriously limits its own usefulness by constraining its relevance to shoring up one individual's work alone.

Portrayal of utopia, theory and ideology as fanciful tranquillizes them, which at first glance might seem a vast improvement over totalizing economic, political or architectural visions imagined as being universally applicable. De-legitimization of comprehensive world pictures ushers in relativism, which appears progressive because it diminishes the persuasive power of ideologies to explain conditions, coordinate efforts, or to create uniformity through cajoled consensus. The limitations of diffused world visions lie in a tendency towards an absolutism of their own kind, apparently rendering *all* organizing visions suspect, regardless of their scale. Architectural discourse during much of the post-World War II period exemplifies this; it attempts to liberate architects from the holistic vision that utopias, ideologies, ideas and ideals might offer them. Suspicion of organizing visions characterizes the arguments of architectural writers as apparently dissimilar as, for example, Colin Rowe and Manfredo Tafuri.

An absence of political or social frames to work within, however, leaves architects with only formalism and the empty autonomy of their work, both of which are particularly modern conditions that drain buildings and cities of their configurative potential. Anti-ideological positions portray themselves as promising a world more humane and safe, one no longer infected by the nastiness and danger of utopian visions. Without utopia, though, the result is a built environment imbued with little concern for the human beings for whom cities and buildings are a setting. In turn, because unable to touch emotion, the work of architects and urbanists will inevitably be of little concern to those same human beings.

In this chapter, an examination is made of two broadly defined lines of approach towards architecture and utopia. Writers in the first group argue that either utopia must end, or that it already has. Those in the second group propose a kind of utopia that is not really utopian. Their visions are almost exclusively technological and nearly devoid of a social dimension.

Archigram and Buckminster Fuller, for example, envisioned technological utopias in which science or technology could solve *all* human problems. On the other hand, Colin Rowe and Philip Johnson argued for an end to utopia. They imagined that draining architecture of its social and ideological content would solve all of its problems. According to them, all that ought to remain are forms freed from any desire for a better world. Writers such as Manfredo Tafuri and architects including Rem Koolhaas elaborated on an alternative position, arguing that ideology and utopia have already ended. Tafuri also claimed that architecture is at its end and that cities can now be little more than a collection of autonomous object-structures devoid of content. He also insisted that architecture, as an independent profession, is dead. According to him, architects no longer produce cities and buildings; instead, technicians employed in the building construction industry now do that work. Tafuri would also have us believe that any effort to project a social content for architecture is a pathetic delusion.

Although Rowe was a civil libertarian and Tafuri a Marxist, both considered architecture a collection of empty signs. For Rowe this was an ideal; for Tafuri it was an inevitability. Rowe argued that forms without utopia would redeem architecture by freeing it from ideology, while Tafuri argued that capitalist development, because it *must* turn everything it touches into a commodity, creates a condition where forms can *only* exist without utopia. Either way, both conceptions render architecture mute. Emptied of social purpose, architecture cannot possibly have ideological or utopian content. Rowe argued for an architecture transformed into remains to be collaged; Tafuri believed that architecture could be little more than an assemblage of remains. Rowe's ideal architecture is silent; it is freed of ideology and utopia through the distancing action of collage. Tafuri's ideal architecture is also silent; by turning away from false hopes for design, it stands in stern opposition to the conditioning perspectives of capitalism.

Colin Rowe: the end of utopia, the end of architecture?

> The hoped for condition did not ensue. For when modern architecture became proliferated throughout the world, when it became cheaply available, standardized and basic, as the architect had always wished it would be, necessarily there resulted a rapid devaluation of its ideal content. The intensity of its social vision became dissipated. The building became no longer a subversive proposition about a possible Utopian future. It became instead the decoration of a certainly non-Utopian present.[4]

In *Collage City* (1978), co-authored with Fred Koetter, Colin Rowe took it upon himself to disabuse architects of what he saw as their preoccupation with ideology and utopia. His aim was to liberate architecture from concerns lying beyond formalism. Strangely, his main theme was a lament on the ebbing awareness that urban space is constitutive of cities. He argued that the increasing thoughtlessness of architects and urban planners with regard to streets, especially the distinctions between public/ private, solid/void and figure/ground is symptomatic of the transformation of utopia from its traditional role as a conceptual ideal into its modern incarnation as an instrumental necessity for change. Utopia as a programme for direct action rather than as a prospect coincides with decaying concern for the traditional city, whose public spaces, formed by buildings related to them, gave rise to its remarkable dynamism that is now an all but forgotten resource.

More than anything, cities were vanquished in the name of science. Infinite space is the most striking characteristic of cities reformed according to the logic of scientific rationalism. According to Rowe, modern minds paradoxically pursue such cities in an attempt to return men and women to an ideal state, free of culture and closer to nature. The turn away from traditional cities reveals a conception of human creation as sinful products of the Fall. Cities brought closer to nature, even by way of irrationally rational science, would recall paradise. In Rowe's view, architects imagined modern cities as a rationalized and static utopian realm intended to be closer to nature and thereby to Adam and Eve's perfect existence in Eden before their expulsion from it. Eradication of the traditional city is thus synonymous with the purging of culture, which, in turn, brings paradise closer to hand, in the form of the new city. However, according to Rowe, this project could only be achieved by enlisting scientific rationalism and technology, which utopia represents.

The attempt to reveal paradise with utopian mechanisms was doomed to fail precisely because the two form a pair of irreconcilably contradictory ideals. By revealing this opposition, Rowe imagined he had shown how the founding premises of modern architecture were faulty: how could natural and uncorrupted conditions recollecting a time before culture ever hope to take flesh utilizing the highest achievements of culture (especially of science and technology).

Science as utopian (which includes engineering and management), combined with the collective as paradisaical (expressed by man and woman's desire to turn away from themselves and their creations), persists, according to Rowe, as the peculiar admixture informing contemporary attitudes toward the city. This is an odd condition considering that the cities of modern architecture are inadequate because impossible to construct. Moreover, the perfection they require is only possible when traditional cities disappear in their wake.

Up to this point, Rowe's equation is reasonable enough. The problems emerge with his inability to observe the other dimension of utopia, which reveals itself as also constitutive, not always pathological. Nevertheless, his anti-utopianism turns on the conviction that utopia is a greater culprit than paradise. Accordingly, utopia, more than anything else, assured the failure of the city of modern architecture from the outset. It follows, then, that real reform of architecture and planning demands the domestication of utopia, which would transform it from an instrumental necessity into a conceptual ideal, the great benefit of which would be to prevent utopia from menacing civilization any longer with its requirement for full realization, which only absolute faith in science could assure. As Rowe saw it, only removal of utopia from the equation could redeem architecture and the city.

Embarrassments of utopian politics

Unfortunately, the only strategy Rowe could come up with for pacifying utopia was to sanitize it by divesting it of passion.[5] Because the human mind has a propensity for ideology and utopian projection, a method for draining both of their threatening intensity is imperative. At last, Rowe hit upon irony as the best method for removing the threat posed to architecture by utopian excesses and ideological extremes. However, irony is unable to conquer the nagging emptiness it leaves in its wake. From the world of art, Rowe identified collage as the least dangerous way forward for architecture and urban planning:

> Which is to say, that because collage is a method deriving its virtue from its irony, because it seems to be a technique for using things and simultaneously disbelieving in them, it is also a strategy which can allow utopia to be dealt with as image, to be dealt with in *fragments* without our having to accept it *in toto*, which is further to suggest that collage could even be a strategy which, by supporting the utopian illusion of changelessness and finality, might even fuel a reality of change, motion, action and history.[6]

Because collage appropriates ready-mades for use in foreign contexts, Rowe believed the collagist attitude would be the best means for restraining utopia. As a strategy, it requires the collagist to limit his or her concern for the stories harboured by the things lifted for reuse elsewhere. Since lifting, reuse and neglect of content presuppose ironic distance, Rowe thought collaging was a convincing defence against utopian intensity.

Not surprisingly, because their emphasis on irony and disbelief is so absolute, Rowe and Koetter's desire to deaden utopia becomes itself an ideology, in this instance of acquiescence, rather than transformation:

> Habitually utopia, whether platonic or Marxian, has been conceived as *axis mundi* or as *axis istoriae*; but in this way it has operated like all totemic traditionalist, and uncriticized aggregations of idea, if its existence has been poetically necessary and politically deplorable, then this is only to assert the idea that a collage technique by accommodating a whole range of *axes mundi* (all of them vest pocket utopias – Swiss canton, New England village, Dome on the Rock, Place Vendome, Campidoglio, etc.), might be a means of permitting us the enjoyment of utopian poetics without our being obliged to suffer the embarrassment of utopian politics.[7]

Rowe's *atemporal* approach presents everything and its opposite in a manner that, like collage, suggests subdued dynamism. Collage stills motion and quietens intensity by reducing change, action, history and experience to objects of aesthetic appreciation, a strange result considering the emphasis on *dynamism* throughout *Collage City*. In the end, stillness replaces action in a way that is surprisingly like the supposed excesses of utopian projection the authors so militantly oppose.

Virtuous mediocrity

Ultimately, *Collage City* is too prescriptive in its aims. It leaves architects with little more than a disbelieving ironic framework cut off from the deep connections people might have to others or things, especially the places they inhabit. The book encourages designers to lift bits of often fine architectural and urban examples to collage them as *found objects* in new contexts, explicitly demonstrated in its 30-page concluding section, introduced as follows: 'We append an abridged list of stimulants, a-temporal and necessarily transcultural, as possible *objets trouvés* in the urbanistic collage.'[8] This flattening of antecedents and ideals has, no doubt, encouraged much ironic self-alienation while contributing to the overall flatness and cartoon quality of much post-1980 architecture and planning, betraying the wide influence of the book.[9]

What seems to have been unimaginable to Rowe is the possibility that paradise and utopia are actually two sides of the same coin. Simply put, his presentation of utopia as scientific and paradise as natural makes both share a much greater concern for the workings of nature than either could for the problems of culture.

Remaking Rowe's oppositional pair into parts of a whole might clarify his effort by showing that modern architectural theory is severely limited by its original belief that traditional cities present an obstacle to nature (paradise and utopia). If the aims of modern architectural theory were to make culture more like nature, then the traditional city, which is a symbol of culture, would have to be eradicated for the modern city to emerge. This throws into question Rowe's diagnosis of the sources of modern architecture's failure, as well as his prescription for its cure. Replacing utopia with connoisseurship and collagist facility simply gets rid of utopia but does little to address a more fundamental problem with modern architectural theory and the city of modern architecture: the dwindling concern for the social dimension of culture that continues to brutalize the human habitat (with or without paradise or utopia).

The social ignorance of Philip Johnson

> There were two directions that in the early thirties I especially and contemptuously discarded: the Modern Movement and Frank Lloyd Wright. The Modern Movement, with capital letters, is a British expression that, to me, has always had undertones of Ebeneezer Howard, William Morris, and the good, the moral, and socially aware Fabians of England. Frank Lloyd Wright I threw out as a nineteenth-century figure. . . . In the 1940s my favorite theorist was Geoffrey Scott, who in *The Architecture of Humanism* of 1914 had inveighed against Morris, Ruskin, et al.[10]

Colin Rowe was neither the first nor the only theorist of forms without utopia. From the moment he christened the international style as an architectural movement, or style phase, Philip Johnson has attempted to drain it of whatever social (utopian) content it inherited from modern art and politics. Coined in the early 1930s by Johnson, Henry Russell Hitchcock and Alfred Barr, the international style debuted in

1932 with an exhibit at the Museum of Modern Art in New York City (MOMA).[11] Hitchcock and Johnson further codified the style in their influential book *The International Style*.[12]

During the late 1950s, Johnson began turning away from the international style toward a post-modernist style, emerging with what he calls his style of *functional eclecticism* (a fanciful use of historical elements determined by pleasure alone). Johnson's shift away from an always-loose interpretation of orthodox modern architecture to a decidedly un-modern architecture reached its apex with his AT&T building in New York City (1978–1983), further confirmed by his support of Michael Graves's Portland Public Services Building (1980–1982). With the AT&T building, Johnson's apparent transformation from a follower of Mies van der Rohe to something of a follower of Robert Venturi was complete.

By 1988, it looked as though Johnson had turned again; this time he put his stamp of approval on a new style: deconstructivism, also launched with a MOMA book and exhibit (23 June–30 August 1988). In the introduction to the exhibition catalogue, he nodded toward variety, writing: 'In art as well as in architecture, however, there are many – and contradictory – trends in our quick-change generation. In architecture, strict classicism, strict modernism and all sorts of shades in between are equally valid'.[13]

A number of years before the deconstructivist exhibit, Johnson crossed paths with Colin Rowe, Michael Graves and Peter Eisenman, among others, when, in 1974, he wrote a postscript for the influential book, *Five Architects*:

> I feel especially close to them [the New York Five] in this world of functionalist calculation and sociometric fact research . . . Second, I feel close because I too have had my non-revolutionary, eclectic, copying moods, my doubts of where we are at.[14]

Quick change artist?

In 1996, in celebration of his ninetieth birthday, Johnson was applauded for playing 'a decisive role in American architecture in the twentieth century. Through his designs, writing, and teaching, he has helped to define the theoretical discourse and built form of architecture in the last sixty-five years.'[15] His own words on that occasion, in explanation of his earlier fervour for the international style, reveal Johnson's capacity for the numerous apparent quick changes that have marked his career:

> In fact, we did not have the slightest idea what the avant-garde was. Nobody told us it was an intellectual and artistic movement devoted to revolution. I did not learn that it began with Baudelaire until the other night. At the museum of Modern Art we were ignorant of the political dimension of the art; for us it was revolutionary, but only aesthetically. Our job as we saw it was to advocate, to sell these new cultural innovations to the wealthy and the powerful, . . . I never was a member of the avant-garde. . . . No, I am just addicted to the new; it helps me fight the intermediate boredom . . . I am not out to change anything. I am just fighting off

boredom. . . . What was the avant-garde has become a frantic search for novelty. . . . A desire to be famous, and a hatred of boredom. Period.[16]

Although Johnson's multiple turns might at first seem surprising, his attitude toward architecture and history actually reveals a never-changing ideological position. He has always thought of architecture in nineteenth-century art historical terms: *style* phases emerge in archaic form, develop into a classical phase, and ultimately spend themselves, falling into decline, replaced finally by something novel. Thought of in this way, movements can be neither transformative nor developmental. Conceiving of them as little more than phases of a particular *style* forever locks them into the epoch during which they arose, matured and waned.

Categorization of movements according to style development alone requires evaluation based on what is most apparent and constant: the superficial characteristics that make things appear either related or different. When appearance is the primary criterion, knowledge and evaluation of buildings depend on conformity of visible parts to make *style* designations. The possibility that meaning is actually bound to use is severely limited; so is the possibility that there are persistent themes architects can return to, time and again, beyond simply collecting forms or composing novel appearances.

The most anti-utopian aspect of Johnson's thought, revealed in his practice, is his conviction that art and architecture cannot possibly have a social dimension. His is an aesthetics of novelty alone. Past works may decorate the present but they are spent. Moreover, because the architecture of today will inevitably become the architecture of the past, there is little need to concern oneself with a social content that must soon lose all relevance.

When his fancy turned from the international style to newer developments, especially an ironic return to nineteenth-century eclecticism, Johnson viewed history with the eyes of a jaundiced curator. His idea of consulting history, which is to borrow parts from it with no concern for social context or content (beyond a schematic reduction of *pastness* to easily buildable parts in the *present*), reveals an innocence of interpretation.

Rowe and Johnson

If Rowe attacked the utopian content of historical modern architecture, Johnson and Hitchcock went after what they saw as the unrealistic social content common to the work of a group of architects that they called functionalist. They staked their battle on showing how the *new* architecture was a style development, understandable and classifiable according to formalist techniques of art history. Freed from ideology, the new architecture of the international style, could go on to develop like all great historical styles, eventually slipping out of favour.

Rowe settled on his formalist approach in response to the failure of nearly all modern architecture to deliver on its architects' extravagant social promises. He was equally discouraged by the appropriation of modernist architecture by commercial interests bent on exploiting its look and guarantee of economy and efficiency alone. His turn from an architecture of form and content to one of form alone was a sign of disillusionment, which he transformed into a virtue. On the other hand, Philip Johnson *began* disaffected. He was free from the start of what he saw as the European modernists' embarrassing naiveté, especially their programmes for social transformation they imagined they could achieve with architecture and urbanism. Johnson started out where Rowe arrived.

For Johnson, propagandizing an architecture of irony, emptiness and muteness (under the guise of purely aesthetic concerns), is neither a product of experience nor of critique. Rather, it is an intentional and perverse attempt to transform the architecture of a potentially new tradition (Giedion and Mumford's objective) into a marketable international style. The stakes are much lower for the latter. Limited expectations would obtain from the outset, making apparently adequate practice easier to achieve. Johnson's career confirms the degree to which he understands style as fashion – something ephemeral and quickly spent, requiring constant replacement as tastes quickly change. Tradition, on the other hand, suggests a manner of practice woven into the intricate webs human beings weave. By reducing modern architecture to a set of general aesthetic principles, Johnson made good use of his (and Hitchcock's) influence to establish a field where his own indifference could become the norm.

Manfredo Tafuri's forms without utopia

Consequently, in the first decades of this century [20th], there was an acceleration of the fragmentation of the functional division of intellectual work. Its position in the cycles and programming of capitalist develop-ment remains an open question, but it is certain that intellectual work which has the courage to recognize itself as capitalist science and to function accordingly is objectively separate from the background, regressive role of purely ideological work. From now on synthesis is impossible. Utopia itself marks out the successive stages of its own extinction.[17]

A third theorist of forms without utopia is Manfredo Tafuri. He differed from Rowe and Johnson in his conviction that capitalist production has permanently silenced architecture. Rowe imagined that architects could continue their form-making by freeing their work of ideology. Johnson remains a high priest of content-free formalism that, because it is empty, is fun. In contradistinction, Tafuri's writing chal-lenges complacency with negativity and inwardness. For him, history is an unfolding confirmation that the traditional (and profoundly ideological) role of architecture has ceased to exist. Consequently, architecture as anything more profound than novelty or technique must disappear, precisely because 'Ideology is useless to capitalist development'.[18]

In contrast to Rowe or Johnson, Tafuri's disillusionment, was a symptom of his Marxist critique of advanced capitalism. Everything capitalism touches becomes a commodity. It must inevitably transform all aspects of culture into objects of commerce, not value; it also must empty every ideology of its content. In the end, capitalism will convert whatever remains of ideas into commodities. According to its logic, an architecture of content is impossible.

Because it complicates the requirement of capitalism for interchange-ability and transferability, ideology – social and symbolic content – is useless to capitalist development. For Tafuri, the capitalist city, evolving since around 1750, especially in the United States, is the great exemplar of expanding architectural silence. It is a city characterized by isolated real estate development parcels, where the economic value of land surpasses any value accruable by improving it through building. Conceptualization of such cities views them as little more than assemblies of development plots. As a result, the spaces between buildings, including the infrastructure that connects them, are a collection of meaningless technical concerns devoid of configurative potential.

City of emptiness

Tafuri's negative city of capitalist development is Rowe and Koetter's *Collage City* (1978) without its empty but exemplary fragments. Its buildings would evidence a motivation similar to Johnson's philosophy of functional eclecticism.[19] Individual buildings are granted 'absolute liberty' within this city, and the whole is an accumu-lation of 'single architectural fragment[s] . . . situated in a context that [they do] not condition formally'.[20] Although this situation gives the architect a field of unprecedented inventive possibility, it results in forms emptied of content. Cities of this sort, according to Tafuri, are symptomatic of the economic development forces that make them possible: 'the crisis of the traditional concept of *form* [is] a crisis which arose precisely through the growing awareness of the city as an autonomous field of architectural invention'.[21]

Paradoxically, Tafuri argued that only silent and autonomous architecture, liberated from ideology and commerce, could resist the solvent of capitalism by opposing its own commodification:

> It should be stated immediately that the critical analysis of the basic principles of contemporary architectural ideology does not pretend to have any 'revolutionary' aim. What is of interest here is the precise identification of those tasks which capitalist development has taken away from architecture. That is to say, what it has taken away in general from ide-ological prefiguration. With this, one is led almost automatically to the discovery of what may well be the 'drama' of architecture today: that is, to see architecture obliged to return to *pure architecture*, to form without utopia; in the best cases, to sublime uselessness. To the deceptive attempts to give architecture an ideological dress, I shall always prefer the sincerity of those who have the courage to speak of that silent and outdated 'purity;' even if this, too, still habors an ideological inspiration, pathetic in its anachronism.[22]

Sublimely useless architecture evades the impossibility of meaning by being empty; it resists the marketplace by being silent. Even this, though, is not enough. Such architecture still reveals the desire for an authentic and traditional disciplinary role, which Tafuri argued is irrecoverable; architects are now little more than 'technicians charged with building activity'.[23]

For so long as architects hang on to an extinct professional self-image, they will be incapable of re-articulating the human realm in unexpected ways, though they will be able to continue practicing the kind of empty autonomy suggested by Johnson: 'Architecture, one would think, has its own validity. It needs no reference to any other discipline to make it "viable" or to "justify" its value. We might even question whether words like value or morals are applicable to an architectural style'.[24] Each conceptualization of architecture's diminished role elaborates on 'purely architectural alternatives'. However, they all lead to a dead end.[25] Only when architects have freed themselves from persistent fantasies of a disciplinary ideology, Tafuri argued, would they be able

> to take up the question of the new roles of the technician, of the organizer of building activity, and of the planner within the compass of the new forms of capitalist development . . . Today, indeed, the principal task of ideological criticism is to do away with impotent and ineffectual myths, which so often serve as illusions that permit the survival of anachronistic 'hopes in design'.[26]

The myths that Tafuri wanted to disabuse architects of are just those myths that could encourage their hopes in design; valid architecture might even be impossible without them. Johnson would view a preoccupation with utopia (a social dimension for architecture) as a profoundly pathetic expression of naiveté, Rowe would see it as a danger to vanquish at almost any cost. Tafuri would diagnose it as symptomatic of a severe case of self-delusion and false consciousness, requiring a strong dose of ideology critique.

As a Marxist critic, Tafuri could not give any credence to the possibility of reform. Only revolution could redeem corrupt culture by restoring content to empty existence. Yet, the extremity of the varieties of hopelessness elaborated on by Rowe, Johnson and Tafuri reveals them as ideologies supporting a *dystopic* vision of inevitable meaninglessness and emptiness. After all, forms without utopia are neutered and incapable of articulating desire for some *ought*. As such, worse than meaningless, they are pointless.

Bucky Fuller and technological utopianism

> Let us, too, at least give ourselves a chance to vote to commit ourselves earnestly for the Design Science Decade approach to attaining Utopia. This moment of realization that it must be Utopia or Oblivion coincides exactly with the discovery by man that for the first time in history Utopia is, at least, physically possible of human attainment.[27]

In his essay 'Utopia or Oblivion' (1969), inventor–architect Buckminster Fuller (1895–1983) proposed technological puritanism as the pathway to imminent utopia. Realization of this better world would depend upon harnessing the remarkable productive capacity of a highly developed military–industrial complex, especially its aptitude for doing more with less. Fuller argued that the immense military build-up during the quarter century between 1945–1970 had powered technological advance with unanticipated benefits to civilian life: a flood of consumer gadgets entered homes; proof enough that his utopia was achievable. Consumer convenience, as an offshoot of military research and development, promised, he imagined, a universally high standard of living that would assure world population survival.

Actually, Fuller's utopia is technological rather than social. Utopia would, according to Fuller, materialize as soon as industrial capacity shifted from arms development and manufacture to a focused preoccupation with the bio-technical conditions of planetary existence. In effect, this would be a 'design science revolution', which would make possible lives entirely free of want. The real benefit of maximizing abundance is that it would make politics irrelevant. Technological utopia could assure survival of the human species and planet Earth through what he called *ephemeralization*: doing more with less.

Design science revolution

The weakest link in Fuller's programme was the absence of some articulated method for shifting political interest away from military build-up toward maximizing abundance in the service of human survival and comfort. Nowhere did he suggest how these fundamental transformations of human character would occur. Instead, they were posited as self-evident, albeit unintended, benefits of the very military–industrial complex he hoped to replace.

However, because the design science of military build-up makes possible abundance and a standard of living unimaginable to generations preceding the twentieth century, Fuller believed we ought to model life everywhere on its accomplishments. Never mind that World War II demonstrated the dangers of technological rationalism freed of ethical restraint; Fuller naively believed that simply deciding to act in new ways would be enough.

In short, Fuller's programme for 'Utopia or Oblivion' was a proposal of economic efficiency that science and design would thread through every aspect of human existence. His utopia would be a state built upon maximization of technological capacity. With all desires satisfied by abundance, war and politics would become obsolete. However, if his utopia did not crystallize, oblivion would be the inevitable outcome.

Fuller's two possibilities, survival through abundance, or annihilation because of political conflict, do often appear as the only possible options. After all, the post-World War II period until the end of the Cold War was lived in daily fear of possible nuclear obliteration of the planet. The ensuing military competition between the superpowers during the period sank the Soviet Union. In the United States, it encouraged the emergence of a war-like mentality that privileges economy and efficiency above all other values. The results of this included development of a remarkable federal highway system, a dwindling of cities and rejection of concerns for social welfare.

Now that nuclear annihilation no longer seems imminent, maximization of abundance is the primary goal of almost all nations. Of course, in the post-September 11th epoch, the United States and Europe are confronted with a creeping fear of uncertainty equal to or even surpassing the terror of nuclear stand-off, which reveals just how spurious Fuller's confidence in technological progress was and remains.

Utopia of affluence

Faith in production undervalues the qualitative (social and emotional) by over-valuing the quantitative (scientific and industrial). Nonetheless, the threat of global terrorism aside, Fuller was to a certain extent correct: with the danger of mutually-assured oblivion abated, most humans seem happy enough to strive for a utopia of affluence and convenience. After all, the liberal dream has long been that self-interest and acquisitive desire would become a prophylactic against armed conflict and self-destruction. Passion and visions of a whole may be dangerous but the coolness of scientists and the problem-solving competency of managers or industrial designers, portrayed as universal ideals of existence, guarantee only a smallness of conception.

Ultimately, Fuller's project was a prognosis, not a utopia, which it shares with technological utopianism generally. His vision was firmly grounded in the present, making it a kind of futurology; simply offering a version of maximized existing reality extended into the future. As a glorification of a nearly verifiable potential already held within present reality, Fuller's fantasy proposed little genuine change. Extensions of this sort are a common feature of technological utopianism, which usually envisions conditions that could easily come to pass as a matter of course. Beyond maximized efficiency and abundance, technological utopias rarely envision any great overall benefit for individual or social life. On the other hand, dystopias usually elaborate on present conditions run amuck in a faintly recognizable distant future.

Kenneth Frampton identified this limitation in Fuller's project by arguing that he 'could not bring himself to acknowledge that architecture and planning must, of necessity, address themselves to the class struggle'.[28] Fuller believed that optimization alone is capable of bringing about contentment, which makes his paean to technology far less critical of what *is* than a diagram of what could easily be.

Bellamy and Morris

Technological utopianism has a long tradition, especially in the United States, where an ethos of progress is nearly interchangeable with earlier notions about perfectibility. During the nineteenth century, ideas of possibility became inextricably entangled with desires for ever-expanding material progress, a conflation encouraged in large part by the Industrial Revolution in Europe and westward expansion in the United States. Stories of this positivist dream include technological utopias. One of the most popular of these was Edward Bellamy's (1850–1898) book *Looking Backward* (1888), which is in many ways a precursor of Fuller's ideas.

A closer look at Bellamy's *Looking Backward* reveals how far technological utopias are from the notion of utopias elaborated on here. His book elaborates on a dream of optimized technology propelled by an industrial army of productive economic units. Akin to Fuller, Bellamy had blind faith in progress, understood as a developing human capacity to fully manage resources, ultimately assuring *total* control of the universe. In response to such ideas, William Morris's (1834–1896) utopia, *News*

From Nowhere (1890), elaborates on his suspicion of the mechanization of life, particularly of progress as a justification in itself.

Organized alienated labour

Morris dismissed Bellamy's belief that organized work of *any* kind could be liberation. For him, the quality (character) of the experience of labour is far more significant than the quantity of work (production). Disalienated labour, such as Morris called for, requires a social context made up of its practice, and the settings for it. Work under these conditions is not so much optimized as humane. Morris advanced *News from Nowhere* as a corrective to what he saw as the shortcomings of Bellamy's *Looking Backward*. Throughout the novel, he articulates a human realm characterized by commitment and interdependency built on social foundations more complex than work (or productivity) alone could provide. His difficulties with Bellamy's *Looking Backward* reveal yet another limitation of technological utopianism:

> The only safe way of reading a Utopia is to consider it as the expression of the temperament of its author. So looked at, Mr. Bellamy's Utopia must still be called very interesting as it is constructed with due economical knowledge, and with much adroitness, and of course his temperament is that of many thousands of people. This temperament may be called the unmixed modern one, unhistoric and unartistic.[29]

Morris draws attention to three points. First, Bellamy based his utopia on an extension of present economic techniques; second, as such, what Bellamy proposed was simply the status quo brought to an extreme; and third, because of the first two, Bellamy's utopia emphasized progress to the exclusion of tradition and imagination. A fourth, more general but equally important point, is Morris's warning against reading utopias apart from their authors. Although this limits the universality of such expressions, it hints at a crucial emotional dimension often lost when a utopia is viewed as a *game plan*.

In *News from Nowhere*, Morris depicts a newly reunified society arising out of the ashes of the old – brought down by revolution. He describes a utopia that responds to the instability of the latter half of the nineteenth century, proposing a future society rooted in an apparently more stable past represented by the medieval. When he wrote *News From Nowhere*, Morris saw terrible misery all around him, arising side by side with the factory system, mostly as a result of it. At the time, over-production required cultivation of sham needs for an excess of poor quality goods. At the same time, quality goods were becoming more difficult to come by in the wake of industrialization's final destruction of craft's traditional role.

Joy in labour

A crucial difference between Morris's vision and Bellamy's, and between Fuller's and the value of a limited utopian imaginary, turns on how each treats *centralization* and *decentralization*. Centralizing perspectives envision utopia as immanent and absolute, as a potential that could shortly be brought into being by some calculated effort. This type of thinking characterizes Bellamy's writing – as it does Marx's and Engels's –

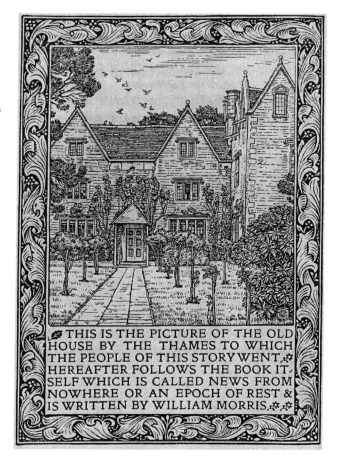

whose project, even more so than Bellamy's, was grounded in a combination of political action and optimized industrialization. All of these projects share a vision of a world where conflict is at a minimum because unmet need is non-existent. Nevertheless, the specific result envisioned by each does distinguish them.

If Marx and Engels and Bellamy believed that centralization is key for realization of utopia, Morris saw decentralization as necessary for restoration of a good (disalienated) society.[30] Fuller viewed centralization as inevitable, because the universe is finite and thus must be controllable. Mastery of nature would make world unification inevitable; a spreading energy grid was, for Fuller, both example and catalyst of this. Energy sources linked globally promised expanding industrialization, ostensibly assuring an overabundant *good life* for world citizens everywhere.

Bellamy believed his project was a viable blueprint for a better life. Realization of his plan required extreme centralization to make the (world) nation 'the sole producer of all sorts of commodities'. Similarly, Fuller argued that centralization must expand until an 'eventual unification of the world as one nation' is complete, all of which would have 'economic advantages over the present system of autonomous nations', a natural result derived from management efficiency. In Bellamy's story, the resulting world-nation would be led by 'the general-in-chief, who is the President', an exceptional manager who gained his position by passing through all the grades of 'the industrial army', the body responsible for producing all goods.[31]

Bellamy's one-world-nation would be 'a paradise of order, equity, and felicity', inhabited by docile workers trained for the jobs they could best perform.[32] Morris, not surprisingly, derived little comfort from Bellamy's conviction that '*Looking Backward* was written in the belief that the Golden Age lies before us, not behind us, and isn't far away'.[33]

> In short, a machine-life is the best which Mr. Bellamy can imagine for us on all sides; it is not to be wondered at then that his only idea of making labour tolerable is to decrease the amount of it by means of fresh and ever fresh developments of machinery. . . . I believe that the ideal of the future does not point to the lessening of men's energy by the reduction of labour to a minimum, but rather the reduction of *pain in labour* to a minimum.[34]

By making a sharp distinction between quantity of labour and the character of labour, Morris reveals *quality* of experience as the central concern of his utopia. Bellamy's (and Fuller's) unwillingness to address this issue, beyond prognostication of optimized survival as a result of world resource management and human effort in work, accentuates the exclusively technological, rather than social, dimension of their thinking.

Unifying visions

Architecture has the potential to embody numerous characteristics in common with good societies. It shelters the other arts and life while making a place for them. Art and life form architecture; it in turn informs both. Morris emphasized the degree to which, because architecture results from communal effort, it has the potential to unify art and society:

> A work of architecture is a harmonious co-operative work of art, inclusive of all the serious arts . . . Now, these works of art are man's expression of the value of life, and also the production of them makes his life of value: and since they can only be produced by the general goodwill and help of the public, their continuous production, or the existence of the true Art of Architecture, betokens a society which, whatever elements of change it may bear within it, may be called stable, since it is founded on the happy exercise of the energies of the most useful part of its population.[35]

In time, though, it became quite difficult for Morris to ignore the failure of art and craft alone to bring about positive social change. While his dream was to return art to life by making the finest products available to all, in reality, only the richest members of society could afford such high quality goods. He could not have it both ways: he would have to sacrifice accessibility to quality, or vice versa, which fed his conviction that only revolution could redeem culture. Morris's developing belief that a good society was otherwise unrealizable brought him closer to Marx while distancing him from Ruskin.

Morris's disillusionment and subsequent radicalization reveals Marx's growing influence on his thought. His earlier belief that a joy of labour in craft production was enough to disalienate society was transformed into a conviction that exemplary works of art can only arise out of a stable society, the reinstatement of which demands the violent overthrow of instability. Morris's forward-looking stance, taken from a radically conservative position in the past, presents a utopian paradox that Northrop Frye sorted out:

> It looks as though it were the distinctive social function of the creative mind to move in the opposite direction from the politico-economic one. This means that he [William Morris and his creative mind] may have to face the charge of being reactionary, but cultural developments in time, as in space, seem to go in opposition to the political and economic currents. The creative tendency is toward the prerevolutionary, back to a time when, so to speak, Socrates and Jesus are still alive, when ideas are still disturbing and unpredictable and when society is less vainglorious about the solidity of its structure and the permanence of its historical situation.[36]

Frye alludes to how *return to a time of potential in order to go forward* is a general theme of reform; Morris's project is just a particular development of this theme. Elaborating on Frye, reformers project their thought back to a time when potential wholeness could be wrought from uncertain conditions. Re-entry into a distanced, even imaginary past permits them to gain a position from which they can see a *truly* reformed future:

> Morris's 'medievalism' has precisely this quality about it of moving backward from the present to a vantage point at which the real future can be more clearly seen. I have noticed from my study of the Bible how these backward-moving pastoral myths seem to be the other side of a genuinely prophetic vision, looking beyond the captivities of Egypt and Babylon to a recovery of long lost innocence. The fact that the innocence may not have been lost but simply never possessed does not impair the validity of the vision; in fact it strengthens it.[37]

Following Frye, the recapturing of conditions in the future of a past long lost that never actually existed may be the most distinctive characteristic of utopias with a substantial social dimension. Reformers, such as Morris, express hope by situating desire for the future as the recovery of a lost past. Technocrats such as Bellamy and Fuller, on the other hand, attempt to supersede present economic and technological conditions through schematic extension of them towards what appears to be their most extreme and logical conclusion. Toward this end, Frank E. Manuel distinguished between utopian thought and other types of projects:

> The utopia should perhaps be distinguished from the religious millennium because it comes to pass not as an act of grace, but through human

will and effort. But neither specific reforms of a limited nature nor mere prognostications of the invention of new technological gadgetry need be admitted. Calendar reform as such would not qualify as utopian; but calendar reform that pretended to effect a basic transformation of the human condition might be.[38]

Manuel's definition reveals Morris's thought as embodying a utopian temperament very much of the kind exemplary architecture embodies. A paradox of Morris's utopia – and of utopias generally – is that they propose radical changes that require the overturn of existing conditions to come about; simultaneously, they envision a time of calm when individuals will no longer be alienated from one another, their labours, cities or the earth.

Archigram and high-tech

Man is on the precipice of really realizing his potential or passing out of existence completely . . . man must invent himself out of the terrifying options of his situation and invent himself into a way of life that gives him real consumer choice. We are very interested in seeing our projects as consumer objects.[39]

Overall, post-war architectural theory and practice certainly seems closer to Fuller than to Morris. With an acknowledged debt to Fuller, Archigram, a group of English architects who banded together in 1960, produced a series of unbuilt schemes celebrating the possibilities of maximization. Boundless industry and technological know-how influenced their projects as much as space exploration and consumer devices did. Principal members of the group included Warren Chalk (1927–1987), Peter Cook (1936–), Dennis Crompton (1935–), David Greene (1937–), Ron Herron (1930–1994) and Mike Webb (1937–). Even though Archigram disbanded in 1975, younger architects, including the British firm Future Systems among others, continue to show its influence.

Archigram originally formed as a response to the numbing effects of archi- tecture office work. The group wanted to shock establishment practice through a coordinated, multimedia, attack on the social structures of post-World War II architecture offices, which continuously reproduced existing settings for the routines of business culture. Serious enough in intent, their assault was largely a diversion meant to break up the monotony of professional practice.[40] Reyner Banham, an ardent Archigram supporter, confirmed this reading in his introduction to a 1973 monograph edited by two Archigram members: 'Archigram is short on theory, long on draughts- manship and craftsmanship. They're in the image business . . . It's all done for the giggle . . . You accept Archigram on its own valuation or not at all'.[41]

In 1994, nearly 20 years after Archigram's active period ended, another author proposed a more sombre evaluation of the group, emphasizing their his- torical significance and apparent radicalism. Like Banham's introduction, this essay also sits within an Archigram-approved catalogue for a retrospective exhibit of their work.

> They [Archigram] wanted the technological utopias of a 'Second Machine Age' (Reyner Banham) to enrich the architecture of the future . . . To progressive architects all over the world during the 1960s, Archigram acted like a beacon, reaffirming the purpose of their own work and giving them the strength to 'stay the course'. They sent out a signal which spoke of a revolutionary vision, a utopian atmosphere and an uncompromising pleasure-seeking approach to life.[42]

Archigram's intentions and influence rest somewhere between the poles staked out in these statements. Their challenge to status-quo architecture and practice was not so much a development of theory as a response to conditions. They argued that outmoded pre-industrial and pre-modern attitudes conditioned the work of architects more than was *healthy*. The corrective they proposed was partly an extension of Fuller's technological utopianism, but they also sought an architecture conditioned by consumer society that would reflect mass culture, advertising and disposability.

Machine age design

Inspiration for Archigram's techno-obsessiveness came from a combination of Fuller's example, the results of the space race and the apparatus of offshore oil exploration (among other technological developments). The group also derived encouragement from Reyner Banham, especially from the polemic he articulated in his *Theory and Design in the First Machine Age* (1960).

Banham argued that architecture should not simply be about the *look* of the machine but about its *facts*, a shortcoming of modernist architecture earlier identified by Fuller. Although something of a hero for Banham and Archigram, Fuller's exceptionally detailed architectural vision, with its high degree of technological and industrial reality, inspired extreme development of his ideas into a species of science-fiction-like architecture. Archigram transformed Fuller's Design Science Revolution into the sci-fi fantasies of 'Walking', 'Disposable' and 'Plug In Cities' (1960–1975), which in turn, influenced the carefully detailed exoskeletons and visible service assemblies of high-tech architecture.

The technological enthusiasm of British high-tech architecture, especially in the work of Richard Rogers and Norman Foster, reflect the influence of Archigram's vision of spectacular constructions and Fuller's preoccupation with the weight of buildings, as well as Joseph Paxton's assembly-minded Crystal Palace of 1850–1951.

Clearly, the unprecedented technological developments that took place during the years spanning from the inception of the military–industrial tool-up for World War II, until the end of the space race and Cold War era, profoundly influenced Fuller, Archigram and high-tech architects. However, where Fuller saw utopia, Archigram saw paradox, and high-tech architects saw style.

Techno politics

Archigram's vision presumes that technology can vanquish politics, which ignores a social fact: political action facilitates everyday life by mediating conflict. Rejection of politics tends toward one of two new organizational systems. One replaces political

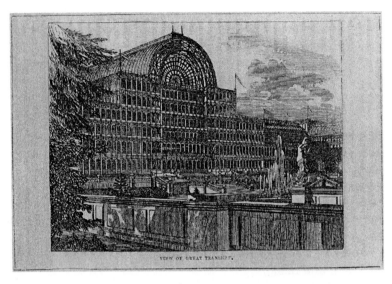

4.2
Samuel Phillips,
Guide to the
Crystal Palace,
Sydenham, R. K.
Burt, Crystal
Palace Printing
Office, 1859,
p. 149. View of
the Great
Transept.
Architect: Sir
Joseph Paxton
Source: General
Research Division.
The New York
Public Library,
Astor, Lenox and
Tilden Foundations.
Crystal Palace,
1851–1954

action with management and centralized decision making. The other replaces social obligations, normally negotiated politically, with the sovereignty of individual desire and action. The first tends toward tyranny, the second towards chaos.

In any event, replacing politics with either management or chaos would upset the delicate balance between individual desire and social obligation. Without politics to mediate action and set norms, the likely result would be either endless conflict or worsening repression. If Bellamy and Fuller envisioned an impossibly well-managed world, Archigram was unabashedly pleasure-seeking.

Archigram dreamed of buildings becoming consumer products, which would need to be flexible to remain *useful* and dynamic, essential characteristics for catching the attention of customers in the mass marketplace. Far from utopian, their fantasy was a non-critical reflection of the hedonistic character of post-war consumer capitalism, with its emphasis on pleasure-oriented consumption. The group's projects mirrored what was, and could easily be, rather than arguing for what *ought* to be. Absence of some *ought* to challenge what *is* reveals Archigram's effort, no matter how charming, challenging or even influential, to be something other than utopian. In this regard, Archigram took up the stance of being far more realist – *in line with the times* – than conventional practices could be, steeped as they were in the rehearsal of pre-war modernist pretensions.

David Greene, another member of the group, made this point emphatically: 'WE HAVE CHOSEN TO BYPASS THE DECAYING BAUHAUS IMAGE WHICH IS AN INSULT TO FUNCTIONALISM [capitals in original].'[43] Somewhat more elaborately, Peter Cook summarized the reasons for Archigram and its origins as follows:

> The first Archigram was an outburst against the crap going up in London, against the attitude of a continuing European tradition of well-mannered but gutless architecture that had absorbed the label 'Modern,' but had betrayed most of the philosophies of the earliest 'Modern'.[44]

Archigram imagined that an architecture plugged into consumer culture would bring unprecedented possibilities of choice. Up-to-date as that was, they neglected the likelihood that consumer culture does not necessarily guarantee options. As often as not, mass production and mass marketing of consumer goods tend toward limitation rather than maximization of choice. Just the same, Archigram member Warren Chalk remained committed to the supposed liberating potential of advanced technology and consumerism:

> In a technological society more people will play an active part in determining their own individual environment, in self-determining a way of life. We cannot expect to take this fundamental right out of their hands and continue treating them as creative and cultural morons. We must tackle it from the other end in a positive way. The inherent qualities of mass production for consumer oriented society are those of repetition and standardization, but parts can be changeable or interchangeable depending on individual needs and preferences, and, given a world market, could also be economically feasible . . . The order of its [Plug-in Capsule homes] design criteria are in correct order to consumer require-ments. First, a better consumer product, offering something better than, and different from, traditional housing, more closely related to the design of cars and refrigerators, than placing itself in direct competition with tradition.[45]

Archigram's notion of high-tech assembly line produced architecture is much less a vision of a transformed future than prognostication of a likely inevitability. However, even though organization of the construction industry today reflects Archigram's vision of it, the results are increasingly standardized and monotonous; liberating self-determination, especially in the housing sector, is almost nowhere to be found.

If Archigram theorized anything, it was an opening for radical experi-mentation within the confines of modern architecture. With its shock effect, their movement challenged moribund modern architecture practice during the 1960s. Archigram's most radical dimension was the group's envisioning of the spectacular architecture that would become both destination and entertainment, of the sort realized by Renzo Piano and Richard Rogers at the Centre Georges Pompidou in Paris (1972–1977), which is now the aspiration for most large-scale projects.

Rem Koolhaas's dystopian delight

> Architecture can't do anything that the culture doesn't. We all complain that we are confronted by urban environments that are completely similar. We say we want to create beauty, identity, quality, singularity. And yet, maybe in truth these cities that we have are desired. Maybe their very characterlessness provides the best context for living.[46]

An additional anti-utopian, Rem Koolhaas (1944–) demands attention because of the peculiar role he plays in current architectural discourse, in schools and in the profession. Koolhaas is an architect of Dutch origins who lived in Indonesia for four years during his youth. Before studying architecture he was a journalist in Amsterdam and later a screenwriter. He studied architecture at the Architectural Association in London; while there, in 1975, he founded the Office for Metropolitan Architecture (OMA), which he continues to head. In 1978, he published *Delirious New York*, described by its subtitle as *A Retroactive Manifesto for New York* (meaning Manhattan). Together with his Office, Koolhaas has the somewhat dubious distinction of combining many characteristics of the anti-utopians discussed in this chapter.

Koolhaas remains a global favourite of the architecture intelligentsia and students alike. Many architecture students, particularly in the US, aspire to his notoriety, primarily because they see his practice as ideal. In 2000, he won the Pritzker Architecture Prize, an award its benefactors (the Hyatt Corporation) describe as equivalent to a Nobel Prize for architects; more accurately, it is something of an architectural Oscar. The real value of the award derives from the level of respectability it confers upon the architect receiving it. Conversely, the fame of the architect selected imparts a level of credibility to the award. In a mutually beneficial way, architect and award are immediately understandable to global business interests, particularly in terms of bankable visibility. In this context, it is revealing that Philip Johnson received the inaugural award in 1979. By awarding the Pritzker to Koolhaas, the selection jury bestowed a high degree of newness value on the Hyatt Corporation for the new century; at the same time, it conferred a high level of marketplace validity on a so-called visionary architect. (Renzo Piano, who is discussed in a subsequent chapter, was also a winner.)

The multi-dimensionality of Koolhaas's anti-utopianism is remarkable. He conspicuously argues for things as they are by promoting opportunism as a radical position. With Rowe, he shares a conviction that architects should practise without harbouring too much belief in what they do. His strategy for doing this lies with mon-tage, rather than collage, probably a vestige of his screenwriting days. As a montage is a collection of episodes, each one maintaining its individual identity, it differs from collage, which is a fitting together of disparate elements to form a synthesis. Even so, in practice, Rowe's collagist technique produces results closer to montage. Similarly to Johnson, Koolhaas believes that architecture can have no possible social content, which is why he argues that its effect on the lives of occupants is negligible.

City of bits

Koolhaas's idea that modern cities are a collection of isolated elements reveals a view of architecture and urbanism close to Tafuri's. However, what Tafuri viewed as an inevitable condition of alienation, Koolhaas sees as an opportunity to optimize the success of his practice. Tafuri militated for an architecture of *sublime uselessness* as an act of resistance to the brutal alienation of capitalism; implicit in his silence was the possibility of conditions other than current ones. Conversely, for Koolhaas there is no social, economic or political dimension. He accepts the world as a *fact*. In much of his writing, he describes conditions as they are as if his point of view was no point of view at all but rather simply an objective reportage of reality, a residue of his journalist days, no doubt:

> Since we are not responsible we must become irresponsible. . . . What if we simply declare that there *is* no crisis – redefine our relationship with the city not as its makers but as its mere subjects, as its supporters? . . . Redefined, urbanism will not only, or mostly be a profession, but a way of thinking, an ideology: to accept what exists.[47]

Akin to Archigram and Fuller, Koolhaas shares a faith in optimized technology and boundless modernization. He would like to collapse architecture into engineering. In this sense, he accepts another of Tafuri's convictions: architecture is no longer a liberal profession. Architects are technicians, and their main job is to organize building activity. What is more, Koolhaas, also like Archigram and Fuller, believes that he has seen the future of architecture and civilization. It is a future reminiscent of Bellamy's vision and technological utopias generally: he presents reasonably credible, albeit emphatic, extensions of current conditions into the near future as though they were radically new. Most importantly, Koolhaas's projects originate with his vision of Manhattanizing the entire world. His schemes, many built and others under construction around the globe disclose a dimension of dark fantasy that Koolhaas himself likes to think of as *dangerous.*

Because he seems to offer a way to operate under imperfect present conditions by exploiting them, Koolhaas's acquiescence is understandably attractive. However, his exploitation of opportunity is something of a liberation theology for architects that might very well require negation of the very discipline he is ostensibly renewing. Nevertheless, his approach does amount to something of an appealing alternative, especially for architecture students. Long before graduating, many of them will already face the prospect of entering a profession unable to offer up the satisfaction they imagined it would, or were led to believe it might in school. Offices organized for production, not thought, split theory from practice, recasting the former as a liability, the latter as productivity alone.

Emphasizing the spectacle of media saturation above all else, Koolhaas models an operational mode freed from more pressing questions about the limitations and possibilities of architecture and urbanism as setting the stages upon which life is played out. Too much questioning just muddies the issue while slowing down the process; moreover, if everything is just fine as it is, even a mediocre architect can take pleasure in the things he or she makes as radical. With this consolation, intern and principal alike can more easily tolerate the seemingly unthinking productiveness of typical successful practices, which, after all, are where most architects work. Even though his indisputable media savvy distinguishes Koolhaas from such typical practices, it is his effective promotion of banality as novelty that really sets him apart.

Koolhaas's anti-utopianism received early expression in *Delirious New York*, a story about the glories of what he calls *Manhattanism*. According to him, the crowning achievement of *Manhattanism* is the Rockefeller Center, notable for its multiple programmes in numerous buildings montaged together on a single site as a series of episodes. Although portrayed as rational, Koolhaas argues that the Rockefeller Center is really a phantasmagorical conglomeration of *congested metropolitan culture*:

> Rockefeller Center is the fulfillment of the promise of Manhattan. All para-
> doxes have been resolved. From now on the Metropolis is perfect. . . .
> Rockefeller Center is the most mature demonstration of Manhattanism's
> unspoken theory of the simultaneous existence of different programs on
> a single site, connected only by the common data of elevators, service
> cores, columns and external envelope.[48]

In Koolhaas's view, Manhattanism was sidetracked by the puritanism of modernist
utopian architecture, especially Le Corbusier's *Radiant City* (1967), which is why he
is stridently anti-utopian. Decidedly realist and modernist in a technocratic sense,
Koolhaas harbours a desire to expand Manhattanism to Europe and the rest of the
world, especially China. For him, Manhattan represents 'a conscious doctrine whose
pertinence is no longer limited to the island of its invention'.[49] Yet, for as long as
thoughts linger about the city as an interrelated whole for humane inhabitation, or of
architecture as having a social dimension, the true glory of Manhattanism will be
thwarted by the traces of utopianism still nesting in modernist culture:

> My work is deliberately not utopian: it is consciously trying to operate
> within the prevalent conditions . . . it is certainly critical of . . . utopian
> modernism. But it still remains aligned with the force of modernization
> and the inevitable transformations that are engendered by this project
> which has been operating for 300 years. In other words, for me the impor-
> tant thing is to align and find an articulation for those forces, again without
> the kind of purity of a utopian project. In that sense my work is positive
> vis-à-vis modernization but critical vis-à-vis modernism as an artistic
> movement.[50]

Modernization may be inevitable, modernist ideas about reality are not, or so Koolhaas
believes. The first promises an optimization of technique and boundless progress,
the second suggests a new consciousness.

Nevertheless, certain dimensions of modernism, especially as articulated
by surrealism, sought a new unity. As a result, the art thought of as most modern
actually attempted to rethink modernity, including modernization, in a fundamental
way. Modernization is brutal and follows a strict logic of expansion. By challenging
divisions between thought and action, and rationality and irrationality, modernism,
such as revealed by surrealists, discloses a desire to reintroduce wonder into everyday life. Koolhaas longs for no such synthesis. If the modern city is ugly, he argues,
it is because people want it that way. His programme for Manhattanization emphasizes buildings as separate worlds isolated unto themselves with nondescript spaces
between them. He also believes that practice – the making of real buildings – is so
brutal, that it leaves no time to think, which suggests that ideas surpass in importance
the actual problems of making a building.

Metropolitanism

Koolhaas imagines that he has uncovered an unrecognized intent within the congestion of Manhattan. Congestion represents for him the desirability of removing the

constructed environment as far away from nature as possible. He sees in congestion a model of what he calls *metropolitanism*, which, he argues, ought to be applied the world over as a city-making strategy. Manhattanism, though, is not based on the entire city. Koolhaas, rather, emphasizes what he believes are particularly pure examples of 'A Culture of Congestion', buildings and complexes that actively exploit congestion, such as the Rockefeller Center, which through its 'hyper-density' demonstrates 'the splendors and the miseries of the metropolitan condition'.[51]

With *Manhattanism*, Koolhaas attempts to ascribe some intelligible logic to the development of New York City that it never had. It may be a vital and magnificent place and the Rockefeller Center may be a compelling example of twentieth-century urbanism, but Manhattan is far more the result of real estate speculation and development than of any carefully thought out city design. If the accumulated accidents that have become Manhattan somehow result in an often-happy condition, they do so on that particular island alone.

Drawing an inference from the congestion of Manhattan, transforming it into an *ism*, and then attempting to apply it universally, is a peculiar sequence of events. Furthermore, Manhattanization is a global phenomenon with or without Koolhaas to legitimize it. During the twentieth century, especially since World War II, cities everywhere, from Boston to Shanghai, and from Houston to Hong Kong, longed to *Manhattanize*, which seemed necessary if they were to take part in the economic dynamism that appears to go hand in hand with skyscrapers and other ultra-high-density development. Developers, planners and governments do not require Koolhaas's facile defence of their ongoing Manhattanization of the world, which they will continue with regardless. What is surprising is that Koolhaas's intellectualization of the status quo, of banality even, is able to seduce architects and critics into believing that emphasis on what *is*, is somehow radical or avant-garde.

Koolhaas's provocative embrace of conditions as they are begs the question: do people really like the modern cities they get? Moreover, if people do not complain, does that necessarily reveal the norm as an optimum condition? It seems as though Koolhaas has never considered the possibility that a mix of alienation, adaptability and long experience with unresponsive central and local authorities renders individuals passive in their acceptance of what is. Just maybe, such silence expresses frustrated muteness rather than acceptance – an inability to articulate demands for an alternative, rather than indifference to prevailing conditions. It is a possibility requiring neither return to traditional cities nor denigration of them; it simply requires sensitivity enough to fathom unspoken desires.

Rem Koolhaas's celebration of banality, whatever its charms, calls attention, in the form of a response, to the probability that neither architects nor their architecture can substantially transform social reality. Granting this, the role of utopia for architectural imagination – if there is one – *must* rest somewhere else than in a conviction that forms can determine conduct or that architects can design people. Nonetheless, architecture's limited capacity to influence society is less an argument against *any* role for utopia in architectural invention than one for why a utopian dimension is crucial.

Chapter 5

Postwar possibilities

> Prophets and artists tend to be liminal and marginal people, 'edgemen', who strive with a passionate sincerity to rid themselves of the clichés associated with status incumbency . . . Liminality, marginality, structural inferiority are conditions in which are frequently generated myths, symbols, ritual, philosophical systems, and works of art. These cultural forms provide men with a set of templates or models which are, at one level, periodical reclassifications of reality and man's relationship to society, nature, and culture. But they are more than classifications, since they incite men to action as well as thought. Each of these productions has a multivocal character, having many meanings, and each is capable of moving people at many psychobiological levels simultaneously.[1]
>
> Victor Turner

Constitutive utopias model flexible visions of possibility that could enter into reality, even if only partially. They respond through time to the actual problems of construction and the contradictions of action. Schemes of this sort, although they propose ideal futures, remain open to interpretation inflected by human experience, values and ongoing patterns of life. Comprehensibility of such projects persists through time, in large part because their inhabitation always rests between past and future. The intermediate position of the present makes occupation dynamic, a quality that cannot be accommodated by the inflexible settings of pathological utopias.

In architectural terms, constitutive works lend themselves to inflection by constant transformation, maintaining some content in reserve nonetheless. By permitting simultaneous multiple interpretations, these works establish transformational settings. They carry marks of the past even while putting forward models for potentially open future occupation. Works of this sort establish settings that articulate conditions analogous to liminality.

In the present context, liminality refers to a middle condition, or space of modification, similar to the distant location of utopias. Use of the term liminal in this way derives from anthropologist Victor Turner's description of rites of passage (which in turn owes a great debt to anthropologist Arnold van Gennep's pioneering studies).[2] It is the middle phase of a tripartite ritual process and rests between disaggregation and reaggregation. Ritual passengers move through the liminal phase as an in-between condition of transition on the way from pre-existing conditions to a new, transformed, state. As developed in this chapter, architecture is put forward as being potent for so long as it regularly revisits the *betwixt* and *between* space of change.

Liminality is not only relevant to an understanding of individual works of architecture or urban settings it also sheds light on the history and development of the discipline of architecture, especially from the late nineteenth century to the present. Removal from things as they are by way of a destabilized intermediate position makes transformation possible, but can be risky. Most importantly, safe passage is crucial for maturational development, assured only if relatively stable structural conditions exist on either side of entry into an in-between and departure from it.

The drama of modern architecture, from the end of the nineteenth century to the present, fits surprisingly well into a conceptualization of its emergence, its ebb and flow in terms of a ritual process. Liminality characterizes the condition of modern architecture when it was marginal, and could still assure its plurality and subversive potential by placing it outside the restrictiveness of style phases based in shared appearance alone. The subversive propensity of utopias for rethinking what is from an alternative position reveals them not so much as *blueprints* for some completely achievable end as *loci of liminality*, harbouring the potential for alteration that could subsequently intrude upon reality by transforming it, even marginally.

Conceptualizing utopias as a gap in between existing conditions and renewed ones suggests that their value does not lie in direct application. More precisely, utopian deviation might hint at exactly the place architects could *return* to to recollect a social dimension for their labours, making it possible to imagine an architecture that could effectively resist technocratic excess (so prevalent during the first half of the twentieth century) and formalistic excess (as prevalent now as during the second half of the twentieth century).

Establishing resistance, resisting establishment

Throughout the post-World War II period, certain problems have persistently irritated modern architectural theory and practice.[3] These problems originated with neo-classicism, when architectural rules gradually succumbed to taste, which remains the near-exclusive criterion of architectural quality. This transformation is in large part a legacy of Claude Perrault's late seventeenth-century challenge to the authority of the ancients.[4] Until then, longstanding belief held exemplary architecture to be imaginable only when conceived and constructed in the manner of ancient Greece or Rome. The point beyond which the classical tradition of architecture was no longer sustainable typically falls around 1750.[5] Yet, even today there are attempts to resurrect the past, either intact or as *found fragments*.

When the dislocating effects of the Industrial Revolution combined with the rationalism of the Enlightenment, a call arose for innovative buildings that could articulate settings for new ontological conditions. Emergent industry, machines and the character of machine production, have disrupted seemingly eternal patterns of production and human existence to such an extent that the orienting objective of architecture has become nearly impossible to satisfy. The shock of these new conditions compelled some theorists to call for a return to pre-industrial existence. In others, it inspired demands for a complete overhaul of architecture, which would come about through adoption of machine methods of thought, production and living.

If Ruskin (1819–1900) exemplifies the first group of writers, Le Corbusier typifies the second, especially during the 1920s. Françoise Choay calls theorists of the first sort *culturalist*, and those of the second *progressist*.[6] Culturalists who also include A. W. N. Pugin (1812–1852) and William Morris (1834–1896) looked backward, especially to a medieval past, for a model of reform for cities ravaged by the first decades of the Industrial Revolution. On the other hand, progressists found inspiration in the thought of utopian socialists such as Robert Owen (1771–1858), Charles Fourier (1772–1837) and Etienne Cabet (1788–1856). To a degree, each was a positivist who embraced technology; they were also concerned, though, with the problem of alienation endemic to industrialized mass society. Choay argues that the progressists are extremely important because persisting conceptions of modern space originate with them, especially ideas about zoning.

5.1
Augustus W. N. Pugin. *Contrasts: or, A parallel between the noble edifices of the middle ages and the corresponding buildings of the present day*, London, C. Dolman, 1841. Catholic Town in 1840 – The same town in 1440 Source: General Research Division. The New York Public Library, Astor, Lenox and Tilden Foundations

Progressist ideas about cities entered the mainstream of modern urbanism through Tony Garnier (1869–1848), followed by Le Corbusier, who was an even more influential conduit for such ideas. This type of planning emphasizes rationality, hygiene and industry. Culturalist ideas emphasized organic beauty, variety and the possibility of an *unalienated* person living in an environment of coherent relationships. Contemporary architecture remains caught between *return* and *revolution*, which is a legacy of conflicting visions of the city that tend to either reject modernity or embrace it uncritically. What both share, though, is a desire to do only one thing: to go either backward or forward, without entertaining the possibility of going forward through a past.

5.2
La Phalange.
Paris, Au Bureau de la Phalange.
Sept.–Dec. 1840.
3rd Ser., Tome 1,
title page
Source: General Research Division, The New York Public Library, Astor, Lenox and Tilden Foundations. Charles Fourier's Phalanstere, 1840

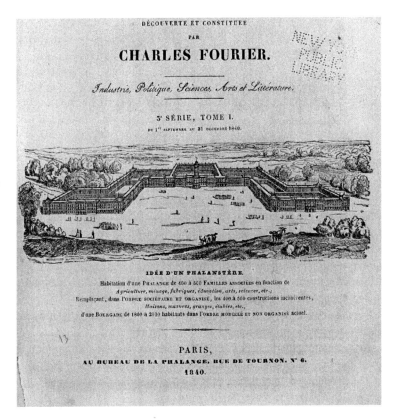

Since the 1950s, return and revolution, particularly for Western architecture, has been characterized by practices that are formalist, exclusively visual and/or radically autonomous. Such practices represent a set of mostly unproductive oppositions that only apparently resolve the persisting problems of modern architecture. Examples of this include the full range of successive stylistic movements beginning with the so-called international style, continuing with its apparent rejection by populists such as Robert Venturi, purists including Richard Meier, as well as more recent mutations, for example stylistic post-modernism, deconstructivism and hyper-modernism among others.

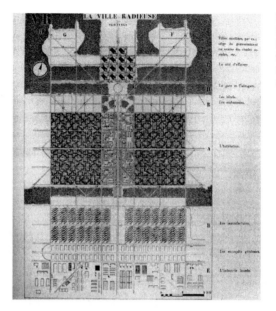

5.3
**Plan of the Ville Radieuse, 1930
from** *La Ville Radieuse,*
Le Corbusier

Tribulations of modernism

Within the very institution of modern architecture, there exists an inadequately explored path leading directly into in-betweenness and toward self-renewal. Le Corbusier (particularly in his post-World War II work) established this other possibility, characterized by social content and social structure (as opposed to formalist and exclusively visual approaches). His preoccupation with the human body as the origin of order (revealed to him especially by Phidias and Michelangelo) and the trans-historical themes at the core of his theory and practice disclosed this other possibility that extended through him to Louis I. Kahn, Aldo van Eyck and beyond.[7]

In this regard, van Eyck is of particular interest. He believed that liminal spaces are the very settings of being and potential. Going even further, he argued that humane architecture must articulate such in-between places as a counter-form to fundamental human ambivalence. Buildings, like life, are constellations, in his termi-nology, of *twinphenomena* – emotional states or building elements interdependently associated in such a way as to reveal deeper meanings.

By combining architectural theory, Corbusian as well as Albertian, with the language and methods of anthropology, van Eyck could account for problems with a psychological dimension that technical functionalism could not. The result was an extension of Le Corbusier's conceptualization of a potentially self-renewing core for modern architecture that could embrace both technology and life. By probing an unexplored potential of modern architecture through liminality, particularly the comings and goings which the concepts suggest, van Eyck avoided the conundrum presented by conventional views of return or revolution as rigidly opposed ideologies. Rather, he conceptualized them as two parts of one whole joined (linked and separated) by a third element in between them.

The ritual process of modern architecture

According to Turner, rites of passage articulate transitions of individuals from one state to another but can also account for transformations occurring to larger corporate bodies such as societies or disciplines, including architecture. Transitions of the sort Turner describes consist of three general phases: 'separation' first, followed by entry into a 'margin (or *limen*, signifying threshold in Latin)' and concluding with 'aggregation'.[8] The first phase entails departure from things as they are into a border condition where disconnection facilitates movement towards a transformed state:

> The first phase (of separation) comprises symbolic behavior signifying the detachment of the individual or group either from an earlier fixed point in the social structure, from a set of cultural conditions ('a state'), or from both.[9]

Viewed through the lens provided by ritual processes, modern architecture arguably originated with separation, bound up with a conviction that renewal required freedom from the immediate past, particularly nineteenth-century eclecticism. Some founders of modern architecture were absolute in their rejection of the past; they determined that establishment and development of a new and valid (modern) architecture required a nearly chiliastic break in time. If architecture were to develop symbols appropriate to radically transformed ontological conditions, they believed it would need to achieve a final liberation from stifling tradition. For example, in 1914, Italian Futurist architect, Sant'Elia (1888–1916) wrote:

> 'The decorative must be abolished.' The problem of Futurist architecture must be solved . . . not by foolishly adhering to the rules of Vitruvius, but by strokes of genius and armed with scientific and technical experience. Everything must be revolutionary.[10]

Sant'Elia demanded displacement of the familiar by the unfamiliar with little concern for the potential outcome, apart from newness. Crucial at this stage of development was the initial disaggregation of architecture from the past. During its second phase, rites of passage require travel through a threshold – a space in the margins resting between here and there, described by Turner as follows:

> During the intervening 'liminal' period, the characteristics of the ritual subject ('the passenger') are ambiguous; he passes through a cultural realm that has few or none of the attributes of the past or coming state.[11]

If an apparent strangeness resulting from its break with the status quo characterizes the earliest developmental stages of modern architecture, its liminal period occurred within a threshold bridging initial statuslessness with widespread adoption during the post-World War II period. As early as 1903, in a statement evocative of Turner's account of ritual processes, Henry van de Velde (1863–1957), described the ultimate renewal of architecture as needing to occur along a phased transformational process leading from initial purification to ultimate reintegration:

> Religious, arbitrary, sentimental flights of fancy are parasitic plants. As soon as the work of cleansing and sweeping out has been finished, as

soon as the true form of things comes to light again, then strive with all the patience, all the spirit and logic of the Greeks for the perfection of this form.[12]

Van de Velde's imagined reintegration, which parallels the final phase of the ritual processes described by Turner, has never materialized. As a result, modern architecture remains mostly unable to embody its own transcendent values, except by explicitly borrowing from the past in a direct manner. In this, it stands quite apart from ancient Greek and Roman architecture, which even now seems to embody and communicate something of its imperishable nature. Breaks with the past, of the sort demanded by Sant'Elia or the cleansing envisioned by van de Velde, remain elusive. Because architecture is largely socially determined it can never be completely a product of individual sovereignty. Interestingly, this condition binds present buildings to the past in the present, no matter how fully they might express attempts to elaborate on a changed future. As revealed by Sant'Elia and van de Velde, among many others, the original purpose of modern architecture was to correct corrupt practice by purifying architecture of decadent habits, such as the use of styles from earlier periods, especially evident in late nineteenth-century eclecticism.

From margin to middle

Dissatisfaction with orthodox modern architecture as expressed by Rowe, Venturi and Scott-Brown and much of the public confirms how unsuccessful its transformation from symbolic behaviour associated with separation to that of reintegration has been. Once established, the products of modern architecture tended to reveal a decisive shift in emphasis from its original potential as an agent of radical social change toward rationalization of its growing institutionalization. Irrevocably altered, modern architecture exchanged marginality to become a handmaiden to and container of emergent global capitalism. More generally, political and economic systems of nearly every stripe blatantly use modern architecture as a sign of social and economic modernization.

With its emergence from a liminal threshold into a decidedly more official, thus aggregated position, modern architecture developed symbolic behaviour appropriate to its post-war status as the new official architecture. A telling example of this transformation is the problem of monumentality, which emerged to preoccupy modern architects and theorists even before the end of World War II. Desire for a monumental modern architecture emphasizes the passage of modern architecture from lower to higher status, possible only after having moved through a limbo of statuslessness during its liminal passage.[13] In 1943, José Luis Sert, Fernand Léger and Giedion addressed this changing position of modern architecture:

> 3. Every bygone period which shaped a real cultural life had the power and the capacity to create these symbols. Monuments are, therefore, only possible in periods in which a unifying consciousness and unifying culture exists. Periods which exist for the moment have been unable to create lasting monuments.
>
> [. . .]

5. [The] decline and misuse of monumentality is the principal reason why modern architects have deliberately disregarded the monument and revolted against it. Modern architecture, like modern painting and sculpture, had to start the hard way. It began by tackling the simpler problems, the more utilitarian buildings like low rent housing, schools, office buildings, hospitals, and similar structures.[14]

By charting a passage from lower to higher realms for modern architectural production, Sert, Léger and Giedion were making an argument that a developing need for monumentality is an inevitable problem of establishment. Monumentality realized would clearly express modern architecture's changed status, definitively representing its movement from margin to centre. Ability to make monuments would also be a marker of a unified culture and consciousness: if modern architecture could produce monuments, modernity would be effectively inserted within an unfolding history of great and authentic cultures, thus establishing a new tradition supported by the appearance of pre-existing tradition (authentic monuments from the past).

Once accomplished at monument making, modern architecture would inevitably become both authentic and established, or so Sert, Léger and Giedion believed. As enchanting as their story is, it actually exemplifies how modern architecture, in the process of its own institutionalization, so often gets caught in a struggle with its radical origins – once an outsider, it now demands universality for both legitimacy and legibility.

Modern architecture's shift of status is analogous to Turner's third phase of rites of passage, characterized by reincorporation, or reintegration, into an existing structure which, although transformed by passage through a liminal threshold, remains stable enough to accommodate the ritual passenger (modern architecture) into its established setting (capitalist production):

In the third phase (reaggregation or reincorporation), the passage is consummated. The ritual subject, individual or corporate, is in a relatively stable state once more and, by virtue of this, has rights and obligations vis-à-vis others of a clearly defined and 'structural' type: he is expected to behave in accordance with certain customary norms and ethical standards binding on incumbents of social position in a system of such positions.[15]

Normalizing the new

Over-institutionalization of modern architecture during the postwar period included conventionalization of its processes and expression. By emphasizing objectivity, economy, and efficiency as (adult) virtues, while moving away from its original (youthful) social reformist position, modern architecture became tamed enough to be embraced as an appropriate means to house and represent state-bureaucracies and corporations globally. Philip Johnson, for example, held this objective from the outset. By 1952, he could confidently recount the story of modern architecture's emergent success as an international style:

The battle of modern architecture has long been won. Twenty years ago the Museum [of Modern Art] was in the thick of the fight, but now

> our exhibitions and catalogues take part in that unending campaign
> described by Alfred Barr as 'simply the continuous, conscientious,
> resolute distinction of quality from mediocrity'.[16]

Johnson's preoccupation with quality was typical, a further marker of modern architecture's changing status, highlighting its move from margin to centre. With this shift in position, modern architecture ceased attempting expression of revolutionary newness – with a clearly defined social dimension – to take up expression of established commodity value in the marketplace.

Barr, Johnson and Hitchcock spearheaded institutionalization of modern architecture in the United States with their international style exhibition at the New York Museum of Modern Art in 1932. A large part of their effort was to empty modern architecture of its original radical social dimension. Once divested of its motivating purpose, modern architecture could become simply a problem of style.[17]

For as long as its various strains were statusless cultural passengers, travelling through a liminal threshold between revolution and conformity, modern architecture's underlying principles remained unambiguous enough. Without the emotional resources of its earlier mission, it was bereft of its organizing purpose; only the inevitability of its own consumption remained certain.

Among its many far-reaching consequences, the destructive force unleashed by World War II sharpened the divide between present and past. In the war's aftermath, normalization of the new industrial age took definitive shape. An overwhelming gap had opened, revealing how extremely different modern existence was from pre-industrial life. Bridging the two was now impossible; there could be no going back. Modernity was triumphant, but at its very apex, success articulated failure. The collapse of modernity revealed its serious limitations, not the least of which was how dangerous progress could be when unbound from ethical restraint. In many ways, modernity was now spent; a tragic inevitability inscribed within the apparent accomplishment of modern civilization and architecture alike. Thus, by the 1950s, modern architecture had already been drained of much of its original optimism. This persistent loss and predicament still confronts contemporary architectural production.

While many architects and theorists had imagined that, once liberated from its own decay, a renewed architecture would emerge, reintegrated within a healthy tradition, this never took definite shape. Giedion was chief among those who hoped for such a resolution. His *Space, Time and Architecture*, for example, is subtitled *The Growth of a New Tradition*. Giedion hoped that if an original modern architecture could take root, its spread would ultimately establish a self-renewing method akin to classical architecture, which was by then apparently vanquished. Giedion's hope was rarely satisfied. As it turned out, institutionalization deprived modern architecture of its radical origins without reconnecting the bulk of it with healthy tradition.

Other possibilities

Looking backward, from a twenty-first century perspective across the full sweep of the twentieth century, one can see that only architects who practice between phases of permanence, imbued with a strong social purpose, appear to have been able to continuously and credibly re-establish modern architecture as a viable and enduring project. However, because most architecture continues to result from practices seeking either return or revolution, much of it remains disoriented in a space shaped at the end of World War II, when modernity (with its appeal to unbound progress and activity, revealing an apparently unlimited capacity for destruction as well) became suspect.

Persistent confusion regarding its purpose threatens to render architecture irrelevant. Nonetheless, when pressed, most architects will admit to desiring social (cultural) relevance (as well as status), for themselves and for their works, regardless of the obstacles. Given the social, economic and political conditions of global capitalism, such desire may, unfortunately, have to remain frustrated, as Tafuri believed, at least until after the revolution:

> Indeed, the crisis of modern architecture is not the result of 'tiredness' or 'dissipation'. It is rather a crisis of the ideological function of architecture. . . . No 'salvation' is any longer to be found within it: neither wandering restlessly in labyrinths of images so multivalent they end in muteness, nor enclosed in the stubborn silence of geometry content with its own perfection.[18]

Tafuri accurately located the crisis of modern architecture as one of content. Regrettably, Tafuri was unable to see hope even where it might lie; for instance, he rejected Louis Kahn's effort to rejuvenate architecture as a sort of self-deceiving false consciousness. Tafuri's suspicion aside, by 1944 Kahn had already begun to consider monumentality as a sphere of optimism, leading, potentially to a renewal of architecture.

At first glance, Kahn may appear to have been considering the same problem that Sert, Léger, and Giedion had attempted to sort out just one year earlier. Whereas their aim, though, was to wrestle unity of consciousness, culture and monumentality full blown from modernity in order to make this age appear grand like earlier ones, Kahn's objective was more structural, demonstrated especially by his awareness of persistent themes:

> Monumentality in architecture may be defined as a quality, a spiritual quality inherent in a structure which conveys the feeling of its eternity, that it cannot be added to or changed. We feel that quality in the Parthenon, the recognized symbol of Greek civilization. . . . Monumentality is enigmatic. It cannot be intentionally created. . . . No architect can rebuild a cathedral of another epoch embodying the desires, the aspirations, the love and hate of the people whose heritage it became. Therefore the images we have before us of monumental structures of the past cannot live again with the same intensity and meaning. Their faithful duplication is unreconcilable. But we dare not discard the lessons these buildings teach for they have the common characteristics of greatness upon which the buildings of our future must, in one sense or another, rely.[19]

Kahn's emphasis of a relation between monumentality and completeness para-phrases Alberti's definition of the beautiful: 'Beauty is that reasoned harmony of all the parts of a body, so that nothing may be added, taken away, or altered but for the worse.'[20] By drawing upon the intellectual tradition of architecture Kahn linked himself with a structured discipline, allowing him to locate an origin for future architecture in the past, while encouraging reanimation of an earlier, mostly suspended, discussion of themes rather than styles.

Section Thru Beauvais
after Auguste Choisy

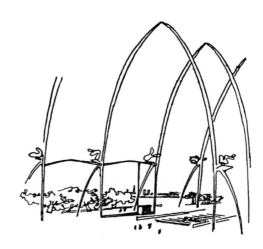

5.4 (left)
Monumentality, Beauvais Nave. Sketch accompanying Louis I. Kahn's, Monumentality in New Architecture and City Planning, A Symposium, P. Zucker (ed.), New York: Philosophical Library, 1944 Source: Louis I. Kahn Collection, The Architectural Archives of the University of Pennsylvania

Themes are permanent problems of architecture extrinsic to form and outward appearance, whereas style de-emphasizes shared concerns across space and time in favour of what is visually unique. Themes emphasize experience; style emphasizes novel images and assemblages. In truth, Kahn's argument for an architecture of thematic continuity appears to run counter to typical stories of modern architecture, which remember it as primarily requiring radical disaggregation (at least symbolically) for its development. Representative of this was Giedion's conviction that 'rejection of yesterday was understandable at the beginning of contemporary architecture, in order to regain self awareness'.[21] His point was to emphasize how invention of a new tradition, at least in its earliest stages, requires a radical break with what went before.[22]

5.5 (right)
Monumentality Nave. Sketch accompanying Louis I. Kahn's, Monumentality in New Architecture and City Planning, A Symposium, P. Zucker (ed.), New York: Philosophical Library, 1944 Source: Louis I. Kahn Collection, The Architectural Archives of the University of Pennsylvania

Nevertheless, the fact that Giedion's faith in this prospect was not absolute is confirmed throughout *Space, Time and Architecture* (1967), most emphatically in his identification of Le Corbusier as foremost among modern architects, precisely because his was an architecture of thematic continuity. Le Corbusier worked with architectural history as a repository of ideas informing current practice, which made him unique: he was embedded within history, whereas most of his contemporaries saw themselves as isolated from the past:

> Le Corbusier is the sole pioneer who never broke off contact with the past. The situation has now long since quieted and one can feel again the living forces of the past, the reservoir of human experience.[23]

Although Giedion, Kahn and Le Corbusier could each locate future renewal in the past through their encounters with tradition, modern architecture, especially as an international style, quickly demonstrated a propensity for normalization characterized by extreme abstraction. Once established, the conventions of modern architecture ossified into a structure apparently incapable of self-renewal. Had modern architecture lent itself to refreshing encounters with the past, of the sort figured by Kahn, it might have developed a renewable collection of figures able to continuously represent changes of status from strangeness to relative stability, embodying a sense that 'structure and the high-offices provided by structure are . . . instrumentalities of the commonweal, not . . . means of personal aggrandizement'.[24]

It is here that utopian potential intersects with liminality – certainty is a debilitating limitation shared by modern architecture and utopias alike. Yet, both begin in the margins with a programme for acting optimistically on the present. Utopias are typically thought of as requiring either a radical break in time for their establishment, or as a kind of perpetual stasis existing outside of time and necessity. However, utopias have another dimension filled with potential that derives from distanciation: a radical rethinking of present conditions is only ever possible from an external position (wherever it may lie). Rethinking, though, requires a past filled with clues a safe enough distance away from the present to encourage invention of a future. Thought of in this way, the past is liminal. It exists between phases of relatively stable structure: the past before it and the present after it.

Movement through a liminal phase is transitional and facilitates trans-formation of the present into a future. Every moment is in this sense liminal: each present (extended or momentary) exists between past and future. It is thus reason-able to conclude that van Eyck was correct in theorizing liminal settings, inbetweens as he called them, as the places of life. Likewise, Kahn was correct in seeing possibilities for future production in past themes, and Le Corbusier was also correct in locating the origins of his magnificent inventions in an encounter with tradition.

Evading other possibilities

Post-war practice has taken neither Kahn's nor Giedion's route nor, for that matter, Le Corbusier's or van Eyck's. Instead, contemporary architecture mostly demon-strates a kind of abandon to the whims of fashion common to all of its 'isms'. An explanation of such free-play is twofold. On the one hand, the so-called post-modern condition explains it; on the other, it appears to be a permanent condition of the cycles of avant-garde rituals that are remarkably similar to those Turner describes as charac-terizing rites of passage. The former, the post-modern condition, was identified by French philosopher Jean-François Lyotard as the dissolution of master narratives; stories previously held in common were believed to be true because of their orienting cosmological character:

> Simplifying to the extreme, I define *postmodern* as incredulity toward metanarratives. This incredulity is undoubtedly a product of progress in the sciences: but that progress in turn presupposes it. . . . [In] post-modern culture . . . [t]he grand narrative has lost its credibility.[25]

In the absence of master narratives, reasoned principles supported and explained by trans-historical themes seem impossible outside of inverted commas; only ironic detachment from experience and the taxonomies of history appear feasible. Paradoxically, this condition in itself presents a new kind of master narrative. It explains away deeper obligations to the commonweal because no such obligation could be possible if no commonweal exists. Absence of a commonweal and master narratives, even provisional ones with a very small 'm', creates a destructured condition – or an anti-structural state – akin to a condition of disorganized liminality, devoid of any chance for transformation. Comings and goings through endless thresholds are pointless; there can be no aim. Even ambivalence, such as van Eyck's inbetweens could house, is never absolute in its absence of certainty. At the end of the day, moves are made; something is done. Absolute uncertainty becomes, in its own way, just as totalizing as the worst habits of utopias. Unconditional uncertainty presents its own stifling certainty.

Tafuri viewed disaggregation much as Lyotard did, but he did so within a frame of tradition that allowed him to demystify the cyclical structure of the avant-garde. Interestingly, to do this, Tafuri employed language echoing Turner's discussion of limninality in terms of anti-structure:

> The two roads of modern art and architecture are here already delineated. It is, in fact, the inherent opposition within all modern art: those who search into the very bowels of reality in order to know and assimilate its values and wretchedness; and those who desire to go beyond reality, who want to construct *ex novo* new realities, new values, new public symbols.[26]

For Tafuri there were only two possibilities open to modern art: the expression of self-degradation consistent with a decadent culture, or an attempt to make a break in time and space to reveal, by way of limited artistic revolution, a full-blown invention without a past or a future. Explaining the first possibility, Tafuri identified artists' desires for wholeness with their conviction that they could somehow transform garbage into art (by representing once statusless objects now distinguished from a vast expanse of nothingness by the artist's touch alone).

> We have repeatedly stressed . . . how much working in degraded materials, with refuse and fragments extracted from the banality of everyday life, is an integral part of the tradition of modern art: a magical act of transforming the formless into aesthetic objects through which the artist realizes the longed-for repatriation in the world of things.[27]

Tafuri argued that degradation, even when embraced, reveals a desire for magical transformation and return – a longing to belong. If post-modern fragmentation, however, does indeed de-legitimize master narratives, then existence of even a limited or provisional organizing social structure is impossible. If this is how things actually are, then architecture – among other forms of cultural expression – has nothing to represent but itself, which leaves it to wallow only in the wretchedness of reality, attempt *ex novo* creation, or dress itself in avant-garde appearances.

Since few active architects actually build with absolutely no concern for the meaning of their constructions, a desire to practice in an intelligible manner endures. It is precisely this laudable habit that leads architects to emphasize universality, fullness and end results, which, however, makes it impossible for most to envisage their work (or its eventual inhabitation) through the threshold of liminality that utopias open. Emphasis on things already done robs architecture of something imaginary to elaborate on. Completion suggests that things are finished and can only sustain reuse as historical fragments emptied of original passion, which is how architects commonly conceptualize reform of modern architecture:

> It is no wonder, then, that the most strongly felt condition, today, belongs to those who realize that, in order to salvage specific values for architecture, the only course is to make use of the 'battle remnants', that is, to redeploy what has been discarded on the battlefield that has witnessed the defeat of the avant-garde. Thus the new 'knights of purity' advance onto the scene of the present debate brandishing as banners the fragments of a utopia they themselves cannot confront head-on. The avant-garde entrenches itself all over again in nostalgia.[28]

According to Tafuri, there was little hope of making architecture meaningful again. It is trapped by its own self-indulgence, encouraged by an economic system with no reason to value buildings as anything more than mute shelters of rationalized production. Alternatively, architecture can do little more than become commodity fetishes. Post-World War II architecture images this defeat by self-consciously articulating the entrapment Tafuri described.

Communities of communities

Multiplicity need not overwhelm common interest. More precisely, community, especially in Martin Buber's sense, takes shape when independent communities can coexist, nearly autonomously, within a much larger aggregation of population. Interdependent members joined by a modicum of shared desire and a striving for survival would make up each of these communities; their relation to specific shared concerns would be the centre that unites them. Although Buber's description of potential social cohesiveness is reminiscent of the master narratives Lyotard argued are no longer legitimate, it actually allows for nearly infinite multiplicity. Buber's conception of diverse but interrelated distinct communities might promise redemption of the kinds of stories that once provided an orienting cosmology capable of situating individuals within social space, as parts of a social body, though with a lighter touch.[29]

Such unified diversity could suggest to architects how they ought to build for life. In the paradoxical space of global villages and global capitalism, these apparently bygone conditions might seem impossible to recollect. Nonetheless, locally, social bodies remain structured, and architecture can still provide settings for them that are at once defined enough to receive social action but also open enough for inflection by it. Eurythmically related interdependent parts configure bodies. This configuration establishes complex structural interrelationships between inside and outside, between bones and skins.

Bodies suggest that harmony can occur even across and through discontinuous parts whose very diversity establishes a consonant web of relationships. Architecture could reasonably analogize just such an order by establishing settings for it, although exactly how remains an open question.[30] In turn, utopias analogize just such a conception of bodily and social order as inexorably related. Likewise, utopias model an order that architecture and institutions (social and constructed structures) could express as kinds of bodies:[31]

> [T]he organic system provides an analogy of the social system which, other things being equal, is used the same way . . . all over the world. The body is capable of furnishing a natural system of symbols . . . The Human body is the most readily available image of a system.[32]

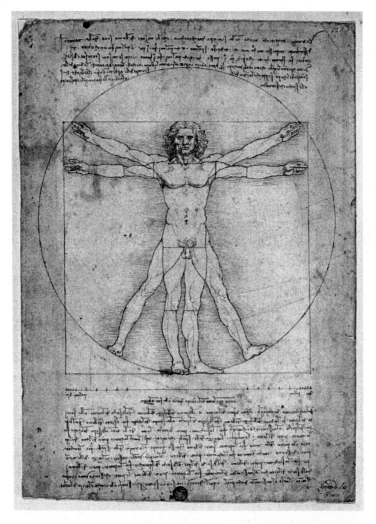

5.6
Leonardo da Vinci (1452–1519). Scheme of the proportions of the human body
Source: Venice, Accademia

The measure of architecture

Van Eyck, Kahn and Le Corbusier were each inspired by identifiable analogies between buildings and bodies, buildings and institutions, or between buildings and cities. The body/building analogy exerted the greatest influence on Le Corbusier. Kahn and van Eyck derived inspiration especially from the building/institution analogy.

Le Corbusier's continuing influence derives, in large part, from his pre-occupation with order, geometry and measure. All of these concerns manifest themselves in his Modulor system of measurement, which refers to the human body as a model of order and liveability for buildings. Most importantly, the Modulor was intended to resituate men and women in their universe, especially by mediating between industrialized production and sentient bodies:

> The Modulor is a measuring tool based on the human body and mathematics . . . The numbers of the Modulor, which are chosen from an infinite number of possible value, are measures, which is to say real, bodily facts. . . . the constructions whose dimensions will be determined by these measures are containers or extensions of man. . . . Never mind if modern mathematicians consider the formulas of the Golden Section banal! Banality may well be the very thing we should be looking for, that is, a harmonious coexistence: man-in-his-environment . . . man . . . constituted by the dimensions of the bodily numbers that determine his position in space as he goes about his everyday activities.[33]

Le Corbusier's preoccupation with devising a modern proportioning system binds him to the intellectual traditions of architecture, a conceptual framework extending backward through Alberti to Vitruvius and ancient Greek architecture that continues to suggest transformative routes in the present. The Modulor was one among the many methods Le Corbusier conceived of to help him resist the institutionalization of his modern architecture. He continuously destabilized the foundations of his own practice by challenging – even thwarting – his own desire for establishment. His cyclical transformations perpetually ran from rebellion to reflection, and back again:

> The history of Architecture unfolds itself slowly across the centuries as a modification of structure and ornament, but in the last fifty years steel and concrete have brought new conquests, which are the index of a greater capacity for construction, and of an architecture in which the old codes have been overturned. If we challenge the past, we shall learn that 'styles' no longer exist for us, that a style belonging to our own period has come about; and there has been a Revolution.[34]

In this passage from *Vers une Architecture* (1923) (*Towards a New Architecture*, 1937), Le Corbusier describes three phases of modern architecture development that mirror Turner's three phases of rites of passage.[35] Movement towards an architecture begins with departure from an existing structure, 'the history of architecture', into a period of strangeness, when 'the old codes have been overturned', that opens onto a transitional space of liminality, where 'styles no longer exist for us'. Arrival finally at reaggregation could not have occurred without movement from structure (the past), into strangeness (what was no longer is), through a threshold of inbetweenness (towards an architecture), and finally resettlement into a renewed structure: 'a style belonging to our own period has come about; and there has been a Revolution'. This process suggests that revolution is perpetual rather than final. Extended periods of flux will inevitably follow relative moments of stability.

Just as each phase of Le Corbusier's career encompassed its own rites of passage, his entire career was a process of continuous renewal dependent upon periodic passages that refreshed his practice. Indeed, Le Corbusier's recurrent transformations mirrored (or were even analogous to) the fortunes of modernity and modern architecture in general. More precisely, his earliest buildings were more or less traditionally normative, even eclectic, before he went on to reject these for his purist work of the 1920s which, in turn, began to transform itself as early as the 1930s, to evolve decisively after World War II into work far more earthbound and solid.

As characterized here, these transformations may be too neat, inasmuch as the next phase of Le Corbusier's work was always imminent in the present one, which allowed the future of his output to be forever prefigured in his previous work as much as in an enduring architectural past.[36] In short, Le Corbusier's interests were always profoundly complex and transhistorical:

> Architecture has nothing to do with the various 'styles'. . . . The emotions that architecture arouses spring from physical conditions which are inevitable, irrefutable, and to-day forgotten. . . . Architecture is the masterly, correct and magnificent play of masses brought together in light. . . . cubes, cones, spheres, cylinders or pyramids are the great primary forms which light reveals to advantage . . . these are *beautiful forms*, the most *beautiful forms*. . . . Egyptian, Greek or Roman architecture is an architecture of prisms, cubes and cylinders, pyramids or spheres . . . the new horizons before us will only recover the grand line of tradition by a complete revision of the methods in vogue and by the fixing on a new basis of construction established in logic.[37]

According to Le Corbusier, focusing on historical styles exclusively in terms of their outward appearance is a deception that hides architecture's true meaning from its practitioners. More exactly, architecture is an affair of the emotions, stirred by a continuity of themes – manifested as physical conditions – that all great buildings share. Surface effects of style, on the other hand, disconnect forms from the themes animating them, leaving the emotions unmoved. Overall, architectural renewal remains possible only for so long as tradition is comprehensible as a collection of themes perpetually refreshed through interpretation of them in the present. The newest and most vital architecture will always be grounded in the virtues of the oldest and most excellent.

> We shall not rediscover the truths of architecture until new bases have established a logical ground for every architectural manifestation. . . . Geometry is the language of man. . . . Is it not true that most archi- tects to-day have forgotten that great architecture is rooted in the very

beginnings of humanity and that it is a direct function of human instinct?
... Architecture is the first manifestation of man creating his own
universe.[38]

For Le Corbusier, tradition, the eternal values of architecture, had nothing to do
with style. Because these principles are general and abstract, they allow for infinite
investigations that presuppose no one correct outcome. Even with clear indica-
tions of what was fundamental to his own practice, Le Corbusier's approach resists
exact reproduction by others (note, for example, the work of Paul Rudolph and
I. M. Pei, or even Meier). His work also contains inestimable material for interpretation, as evidenced by the careers of Kahn and van Eyck (again in the
work of Meier and even, admittedly, in that of Rudolph and Pei, though in a far more
limited way).

5.7
Illustration of
Modular Man,
Le Corbusier

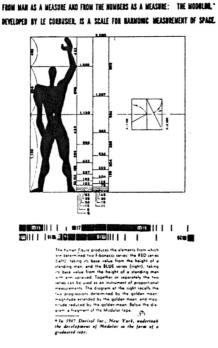

The continuing vitality of Le Corbusier's work results from his preoccupation with order as a product of geometry and measure, for which the human
body is a model of building. He elaborated on these themes in his writing as much
as in his architecture. In 1953, Rudolf Wittkower looked towards Le Corbusier's
Modulor system as he wondered how once stable immemorial proportioning systems
would be affected by modern space–time conceptions:

What bearing on proportion in the arts has and will have the replacing
of absolute measures of space and time by the new dynamic space–time
relationship? A preliminary answer has been supplied by Le Corbusier's

Modulor. In the light of history it appears as a fascinating attempt to co-ordinate tradition with our non-Euclidean world. . . . Whatever one may think of it, this is certainly the first consistent synthesis since the break-down of the older systems, reflecting our own civilization into the bargain. At the same time it testifies to the coherence of our cultural tradition.[39]

Eight years later, in 1961, Wittkower continued his discussion of the Modulor during a conference at Columbia University:

It is only Le Corbusier whose instinct guided him to the sources of our cultural heritage and transformed it imaginatively to suit modern require-ments: who attempted a new synthesis . . . It is only Le Corbusier who brings to bear on the old problem of proportion a prophetic, unceasingly searching, and above all poetic mind.[40]

A renewable modern

By 1959, Le Corbusier acknowledged the inevitability of generational shifts and the certainty of his own passing. Such recognition led him to consider prospects that might open up possibilities for the next generation, reaching far beyond the horizon of his own practice and life.

It is those who are now forty years old, born around 1916 during wars and revolutions, and those unborn, now twenty-five years old, born around 1930 during the preparation for a new war and amidst a profound economic, social, and political crisis, who thus find themselves in the heart of the present period the only ones capable of feeling actual problems, personally, profoundly, the goals to follow, the means to reach them, the pathetic urgency of the present situation. They are in the know. Their predecessors no longer are, they are out, they are no longer subject to the direct impact of the situation.[41]

The quote above was part of an open letter Le Corbusier sent to the tenth and final meeting of the International Congress of Modern Architecture (CIAM), which, in fact, he did not attend. CIAM came to its end largely because of the actions of Team X. So named because they emerged out of CIAM X (1956), Team X was a loose grouping of architects active as an assemblage from 1953 to 1984. Members included the Smithsons, Giancarlo de Carlo and Aldo van Eyck, among others, all of whom sought to replace CIAM with a body more representative of the postwar generation of up-and-coming modern architects.[42] Their success in putting CIAM to rest concluded a transformation that began with CIAM VII (1949) and took definitive shape during CIAM VIII (1951) and IX (1953). Architectural historian Spiro Kostof described this long-brewing change in terms of tribal ritual:

Team Ten (Team X) rejected the establishment guise of postwar Modernism, in which a handful of elders dominated the International Congress of Modern Architecture (CIAM), setting the official agenda for design practice and theory. . . . Team X staged a court rebellion stoked by intergenerational conflict.[43]

Soon after, Team X insider Aldo van Eyck came to challenge the group, motivated by his desire to reveal something deeper in relation to architecture's social dimension than he believed the other members were capable of doing. His aspiration was stimulated by a belief that an interlinked continuity of social, emotional and architectural themes could exist free of sentimentality for particular forms or kinds of architectural expression. Moreover, he was convinced that each architectural tradition could offer no more than a partial view of reality, that could only be augmented through interaction with parallel traditions across space and time; the main benefit of which would be a provisionally enriched and fuller conception of reality.

Van Eyck argued that engagement with tradition is referential rather than imitative, embodied themes, not the external appearances of forms, hold the refreshing potential so often sought by postwar architects frustrated as much by ossified modernisms as by enervated styles. In his response, van Eyck drew upon Le Corbusier's work as a profound resource, interpreting the older architect's modernity in an attempt to uncover transcendental ideas and transhistorical themes potentially infused throughout. Though he acknowledged his debt to Le Corbusier, van Eyck was compelled to move beyond the master in his search for an architecture capable of more adequately expressing his convictions:

> Man is always and everywhere essentially the same. He has the same mental equipment though he uses it differently according to his cultural or social background, according to the particular life pattern of which he happens to be a part. Modern architecture has been harping continually on what is different in our time to such an extent even that it has lost touch with what is not different, with what is always essentially the same.[44]

It is here, finally, that the many themes of this chapter intersect. By borrowing an anthropologist's understanding of ritual processes, especially as it concerns the transitional space of liminality, it has been possible to emphasize certain aspects of modern architecture's development from its earliest stages through the postwar period and, by extension, until today. The purpose for doing this is to suggest that that which is most vital about the modern project remains so, and that this is all too often obscured by an obsession, in equal doses, with novelty or nostalgia, both of which ultimately deplete the motive force of modern architecture. Another motivation was to propose the release of architectural culture from its obsession with history as a record of change, shifting it, rather, towards a consideration of relatively stable themes inflected according to place and occasion.[45]

A new tradition?

Architecture conceived outside of, and in response to, a more or less stable structure engages existing conditions in order to surpass them. Paradoxically, a full investigation of architecture's clearest purpose – to represent the commonweal by fixing its structures, institutions as well as the edifices housing them – will remain elusive for so long as buildings and cities merely reproduce existing conditions matter-of-factly with little concern for unexamined potential.

With impatience for the unbearably short cycles of fashion and the unrevealing short-sightedness of a journalistic approach to cultural production, in this chapter I have argued that Le Corbusier charted a course for modern architecture that could liberate it from the perpetual movement between novelty and nostalgia, which so often cripples it. There is, of course, a caveat: Le Corbusier presents a model or pattern, not a prescription. His work is thus impossible to replicate – all attempts to do so are, in fact, doomed to presentation of a superficial understanding that his method entailed an appreciation for and reworking of architectural themes:

> [Le Corbusier] always looked for the experiences of former times in his travels and he was usually interested in crystalline Greek forms and in the forms of Roman vaults or Islamic and Gothic architecture. His search for inner similarities had nothing to do with art history: it embraced the experience of the entire architectural development.[46]

Van Eyck understood Le Corbusier in much the way that Giedion did. If Le Corbusier's genius for radical invention lay in his encounter with the entire story of architecture, there would be no need to attempt a reproduction of him. To learn from him, van Eyck, for example, would need to develop his own way of seeing and thinking that nonetheless corresponded to how Le Corbusier thought and saw. In this way, it would be possible to successfully interpret and clarify Le Corbusier's method; making it possible to imagine a localized architecture as fully independent of its sources as it was equally indebted to them.

The complexity of ambivalence

Van Eyck is of particular interest because his conviction was that human existence is by its very nature liminal, which makes the job of architects primarily the articulation of in-betweens, settings ready to safely receive ambivalence, as the principal locus of life. By so identifying the in-between, van Eyck opened up an avenue along which he could distil Le Corbusier's multifaceted genius into a method capable of playing a continuing role in moving modern architecture beyond the stumbling blocks of the post-World War II era that bedevil it to this day.

The development of van Eyck's theory and practice was informed by anthropology, characterized especially by a fascination with twinphenomena, a physical condition of existence most clearly presented by thresholds, or liminality. Thresholds, however, were not the exclusive focus of van Eyck's work; he remained ever-aware that there is a *this side* and a *that side* of any threshold – the liminal space between may condition existence but it is not the only thing.[47]

For van Eyck, the multiple oppositions he considered represented an array of interdependent phenomena. He did not conceptualize two very different events, objects or conditions as necessarily antagonistic. For example, simplicity and complexity intermingle equally in van Eyck's thinking and buildings, reaching across interlinking in-betweens, rather than facing off in a conventionally opposed *either/or* condition.[48] Another younger architect, Venturi was also preoccupied with *both/and* conditions. Although at first glance he might seem to be traversing similar ground to van Eyck, he did so in a very different way. Even when Venturi invoked van Eyck, he pitched his ideas in a somewhat different, decidedly formalist, direction.

For Venturi 'both and', as he explained it in his Gentle Manifesto (*Complexity and Contradiction in Architecture*, 1966), suggests an architecture of inclusion that does not possess the conceptual complexity or social richness of van Eyck's ideas of twinphenomena.[49] Venturi's formal inclusiveness ultimately operates as a seductive hook heralding rejection of reasoned principles in favour of irony and undisciplined pleasure, mostly in the shape of self-conscious stylistic eclecticism.[50]

Whereas Venturi's approach emphasized visual perception (while his work was socially submissive), van Eyck was concerned with bodily and emotional experience as well as with the potential for an architecture of referential content.[51] Although both architects called for attentiveness to the interrelationship between parts and wholes, Venturi's architecture trades on melodramatic representation cleverly spun through a conception of architectural expression as autonomous. Van Eyck certainly included visual perception as a component of architectural delight but considered it as one among the other senses, not the primary one. To get a sense of the divergences between Venturi and van Eyck's thinking, compare the following passages, the first by Venturi, the second by van Eyck:

> But an architecture of complexity and contradiction has a special obligation toward the whole: its truth must be in its totality. It must embody the difficult unity of inclusion rather than the easy unity of exclusion. More is not less. . . . Where simplicity cannot work, simpleness results. Blatant simplification means bland architecture. Less is a bore.[52]

> I am again concerned with twinphenomena; with unity and diversity, part and whole, small and large, many and few, simplicity and complexity, change and constancy, order and chaos, individual and collective; with why they are ignobly halved and the halves hollowed out . . . Now the object of the reciprocal images contained in the statement *make a bunch of places of each house and each city; make of each house a small city and of each city a large house* . . . It seems to me that these reciprocal images furthermore upset the existing architect–urbanist hierarchy. It is what I wanted them to do – gladly [original italics].[53]

Van Eyck emphatically embraced the complexity of the concepts he was attempting to express. Venturi, on the other hand, wanted to make it look simple. While the labyrinthine quality of van Eyck's prose may frustrate, Venturi seduces with the immediate pleasures of easy comprehension. Van Eyck was not only aware of his tendency toward linguistic complexity, but believed it necessary for doing justice to the dense web of associations he was attempting to describe. To his mind, such description required a language complex enough to bring the reader into the labyrinth of experience he was weaving and presenting, which he imagined was analogous to life in a responsive built realm:

> To proceed from the idea of dwelling, in the sense of 'living' in a house, in order to arrive at the idea of living, in the sense of 'dwelling' in a city,

implies proceeding simultaneously from the idea of living, in the sense of 'dwelling' in a city, in order to arrive at the idea of dwelling, in the sense of 'living' in a house. That is as simple and as involved as it actually is![54]

What van Eyck saw as simple and involved, principally the notion of *both/and* interrelationships, Venturi attempted to codify into a system reducible to a collection of formal, or compositional, techniques.

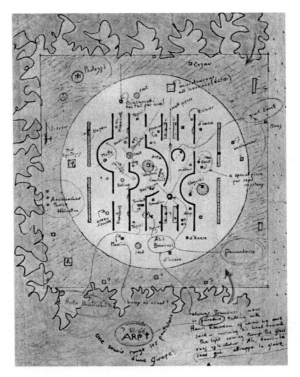

5.8
Plan of Sculpture Pavilion, Sonsbeek Exhibition, Arnheim, 1965–1966. Architect: Aldo van Eyck
Courtesy of Hannie van Eyck

5.9
Drawing, *I am a monument*. Robert Venturi
Source: Venturi, Scott Brown and Associates, Inc.

Venturi imagined that his revolutionary innovation could revitalize moribund modernist architecture. He argued that visual disjunction might be renewal enough, promising to imbue buildings with a high level of visual interest, which in itself would be a vast improvement over the aridness of orthodox modern architecture, or so it seemed at the time. In this way, Venturi advanced visual interest alone as adequate for establishing results indicative of valid reform. This novel approach, dependent as it was on visual surprise, remains a false promise. The apparently evolutionary transformations of modern architecture that it proposed occur only on a surface level – existing structure, supposedly challenged, is actually maintained.

Ironically, Venturi's project to freshen up architecture actually results in conventionalized buildings with appliqué, which are unable to do much in the way of actually proposing means for reforming the reductive tendencies of a modularized and industrialized construction industry. Through developers, the building industry dictates frames determined by real estate value that architects wrap in novel ways to make into identifiable images. It is a vision of architecture that promotes a prevailing condition under which architects can do little more than jacket positive beauty (constructed frames) with arbitrary beauty (decorative wrappers free of content). Nothing, it should be noted, could be further from van Eyck's convictions.

Into the labyrinth

Van Eyck proposed thresholds as the pathway into the in-between spaces of liminality. This was a primary focus of his thought and production; a reasonable preoccupation considering that social structure is continuously renewed and transformed via rites of passage. In his view, life is fundamentally liminal. Thus, social settings – to become settings for the social – must be places of transition that can shelter human action in a structured enough way without overburdening such action by placing too many fixed and obtrusive programmatic demands on it. Such settings allow for improvised use – a continuing existence of social life as comings and goings – without obliterating social patterns that configure a built realm or the social institutions that houses and cities shelter and present. As conceived of by van Eyck, *both/and* suggests comprehensive settings that are simultaneously unrestricted.

Early modernists wanted to institutionalize their new thinking and buildings as a way of protecting their contribution to culture. Later, when modern architecture became ossified, critics rejected the original strangeness of modernism because of its failures. In the event, some historians, architects and critics have responded with attempts to fix new norms based again on either rebellion or nostalgia. Conserving radicalism, rejecting originality (when it no longer appears novel) and the struggle to wrestle universality from inexhaustible plurality are each as limiting as they are mistaken.

Survival of the social structures that architecture shelters, defines and houses (and that make civic life possible) relies on any setting's (or institution's) liminal potential. It may be possible that modern architecture can yet become self-renewing and achieve the cultural reintegration dreamed of by its early apologists who hoped that it (as earlier architecture once could) would establish a new tradition. However, this will be a real possibility only if architects can learn to draw upon the liminal location of their discipline as the proper place of architecture's (re) invention. It is an in-between position – akin to the places of utopias – that could open up the past to architects, thus revealing as yet unknown future structures always immanent in it.[55]

Part II

Optimistic architectures

In an effort to develop the notion that imagination of exemplary architecture *always* harbours utopian content, I now turn from examining conceptions of utopia to a detailed study of works by Le Corbusier, Louis Kahn and Aldo van Eyck. The three buildings I consider were constructed during the dozen years between 1953–1965, and are important examples of a reconceptualization of modern architecture that was evolutionary in aim rather than dismissive. These architects never envisioned the abandonment of the modernist enterprise, only its enrichment. Their projects (La Tourette, the Salk Institute and the Amsterdam Orphanage) continue to demonstrate how valid architecture is imaginable and producible even in the absence of any accepted universal truths. Through its establishment, such work proposes new and situational truths that must be proven again with every new project at each new location, a theme taken up in a final chapter dedicated to more recent works that articulate reinterpretations of similar concepts. Each of these three newer works were constructed during the 1990s and include Libeskind's Jewish Museum, Piano's Tjibaou Cultural Centre and Williams and Tsien's Neurosciences Institute.

Chapter 6

Le Corbusier's monastic ideal

> Let us go back to the monastery of Ema and to our 'townhouse buildings', two forms of dwelling at human scale. If you knew how happy I am when I can say: 'My revolutionary ideas are in history, in every period and every country' (the houses in Flanders, the pilotis of Siam or of the lake-dwellers, the cell of a convent monk being sanctified).[1]

> Le Corbusier

In the previous chapter, the in-betweenness of liminality was introduced as a characteristic of an architecture at once utopian and open-ended. The value of the liminal for architecture is to make it an ongoing concern always in progress, which makes it constitutive rather than pathological. Drawing upon these ideas, this chapter and the one that follows, consider Le Corbusier's La Tourette as a limited utopia housing a partially closed (and thus also partially open) community, able to periodically re-realize (albeit provisionally) its utopian aims, by utilizing the building as a platform to do so.

La Tourette is a constructed intention, an exemplary setting continuously interpreted and reinterpreted through time by Dominicans, surrounding residents, architects, students and historians, among others. Consequently, it is constitutive of architectural culture in almost the same way as it configures and contains a Dominican conception of what a just society might be like.

In addition, La Tourette is understandable as a model for exemplary architecture that might *behave* similarly to it but certainly need not *look* like it. In terms of behaviour, the structure's multiple character, as a Dominican convent, cultural centre and architects' retreat reveals it as a locus of world-bettering desires and acts, a place of reclusion that is nonetheless cosmopolitan rather than insular.

As I have argued, exemplary architecture always seems to arise out of a play of utopian perspectives within the imagination during its conceptualization.

6.1
General view of Convent of La Tourette, Eveux-sur-l'Abresle, Lyons, France, 1953–1960. Architect: Le Corbusier

Architecture of this sort is, in Giedion's terms, a kind of social imagination. In Mannheim's sense, similarly, it would be utopian precisely because it gives tangible form to social imagination. Although utopias can tend toward either the constitutive or the pathological, it is a commonplace of architectural history and theory to consider Le Corbusier's urban dreams as utopias of a negative sort only, the aim of which is to reveal utopian dreaming as always pathological. While Le Corbusier's urban schemes may justifiably deserve condemnation as pathological, La Tourette remains a constitutive utopia. It is even, at least partially, a beneficiary of his ill-fated urban dreaming.

The trajectory of a building throughout its life will reveal it as either constitutive or pathological. Extended use of buildings and their capacity to receive changing occupation over a long duration marks them as constitutive. Moreover, transforming occupation through time discloses a building's suppleness. Given these criteria, La Tourette's long and varied occupation reveals it to be at the very least constitutive, as well as utopian. A surprising aspect of the building is a discernible relation between Le Corbusier's *monastic ideal* and John Ruskin's *medieval utopianism*, especially the correspondence of La Tourette to Ruskin's 'Nature of Gothic' (the most famous chapter of his multi-volume *The Stones of Venice* (1853), a book with which Le Corbusier was familiar).[2]

Frampton's two courses

La Tourette's very uniqueness, as a building type and as an individual structure, might lead one to think of it as too exceptional to be of any use for a discussion of how buildings ought to behave. Nonetheless, its value in this regard is undiminished. Luckily, Kenneth Frampton suggests a way forward. He argues that only two courses of action open to architecture promise a significant outcome. Although they oppose one another, their reconciliation is the only hope for architecture. He describes the first course as 'totally coherent with the prevailing modes of production and consumption' while 'the second establishes itself as a measured opposition to both'.[3]

While most architects already follow one or the other of Frampton's two courses in their work, palpable tension arises when they come into proximity with each other, a tension that only architects with the greatest capacity for synthesis can resolve. Because Frampton's principal concern is the tectonics of a suitable *built reality*, his second course (despite its opposition to the status quo) does not include escape into unrealizable, and thus *pathological*, utopian projects. While prevailing conditions are readily observable, measured opposition, because so rare, is more difficult to demonstrate. To clarify matters somewhat, Frampton advances Mies van der Rohe's work as exemplifying dominant consumer capitalist architecture:

> Mies van der Rohe's ideal of *bienahe nichts* or 'almost nothing,' seeks to reduce the building task to the status of industrial design on an enormous scale. Since its concern is with optimizing production, it has little or no interest in the city. It projects a well-served, well-packaged, non-rhetorical functionalism whose glazed 'invisibility' reduces form to silence.[4]

By doing its job well, mute product design architecture (of the sort identified with Mies van der Rohe), is well-suited to industrialized building production, comfortably conforming to the logic of real estate development while resting unobtrusively on unrelated building lots (sitting among other such lots). With little else to give a form, architects now have little else to do than invent novel packaging to make it possible to distinguish one industrial designed building from any other.

In contradistinction, Frampton argues that architectures of explicitly visible and determinate enclosure are alternatives to intentionally invisible, silent and indeterminate architecture of consumer capitalism. Such architecture is akin to *limited monastic enclaves*, or enclosures. It makes a concrete challenge to the abstract architecture identified with the prevailing modes of production and consumption.

Monastic enclaves offer a compelling alternative. They make habitations more comprehensible, and thus contribute to orienting human beings, primarily by establishing limited social settings that can accommodate, even encourage, intelligible relations of individuals to one another and to nature. It is precisely the explicitly physical presence of monastic forms that articulates their turn away from the reduction of form to silence, which modernity, by the logic of its own necessity, seems to require:

> The latter, on the other hand, is patently 'visible' and often takes the form of a masonry enclosure that establishes within its limited 'monastic' enclosure a reasonably open but nonetheless concrete set of relationships linking man to man and man to nature.[5]

By suggesting that visibility, enclosure and construction out of masonry counteracts prevailing modes of production and consumption, which are identifiable with invisibility, indefiniteness and being a product of industrial design, Frampton reveals a correlation between desirable social conditions and architectural form. Hence, monasteries (as well as convents) might well present a polemic forceful enough to subvert predominant architecture from its tendency toward non-rhetorical functionalism:

> The fact that this 'enclave' is often introverted and relatively indifferent to the physical and temporal continuum in which it is situated characterizes the general thrust of this approach as an attempt to escape, however partially, from the conditioning perspectives of the Enlightenment.[6]

Frampton's conviction that monastic enclosures, or enclaves, are configurations of escape from unsatisfactory conditions locates his critique of modernity (presumably unintentionally) remarkably close to the social form More gave his *Utopia* (1516), which was a critical negation of modernity at its inception, proposed through a model of near-medieval monastic existence.

More's critique of the modern was so powerful that it entered the Western psyche as a trope that subsequent utopian socialists including John Ruskin, would turn to when envisioning reform. More imagined his famous *Utopia* through a glance backward, identifying a good *no place* from where unforeseen possibilities might be identified. Not surprisingly, the compelling holism of More's golden age also influenced William Morris's vision for renewing life and art.

Although monastic enclaves are certainly the more humane of the two courses Frampton identifies, what interests him most is their eventual synthesis leading to an alternative: 'The sole hope for a significant [architectural] discourse in the immediate future lies, in my view, in a creative contact between these two extreme points of view'.[7] The signification Frampton hopes for requires a synthesis of opposites made up of glass and steel constructions on the one hand and masonry enclosures on the other. Resolved by an overarching vision, the result would be an architecture able to establish enclosure as a condition of social settings, advantageously brought to realization with contemporary construction processes.

Frampton's utopias and La Tourette

In effect, synthesis of Frampton's two courses would take shape as partial utopias (or *heterotopias*, as they could be many and varied). Such buildings, or social settings, would be rhetorical and polemical figures, proposing a redescription of current conditions without fully abandoning them. Opposition of this sort is optimistic, especially in its challenge to the 'vulgarization of architecture', symptomatic of its dominance by the 'modern reductionist tradition'.[8] Frampton's challenge to the status quo is at least in part utopian: it negates *what is* in hope of a renewed tomorrow. He proposes new possibilities, which would require transformed conditions for realization, conditions the new architecture he envisions could partly configure.

The partial escapes he envisions 'from the conditioning perspectives of the Enlightenment' are equally resistant and hopeful. Moreover, during the last half-century (or so), practices of the kind Frampton encourages have already resulted in works illuminating alternatives to the alienating conditions of modern industrial and post-industrial life. These alternatives, overall, embody concerns in line with those Ruskin and Morris elaborated on. Both thinkers passionately articulated powerful proposals of what *ought* to be, to far surpass what *is*. For Ruskin and Morris, trans-formation of prevailing conditions in the present would reveal superior alternatives, made more true, beautiful and equitable, in the form of a renewed and just society modelled after an idealized vision of medieval subsistence existence and collectivism. Whatever their differences, Ruskin and Morris represent a joining of social reform to art, architecture and the city.[9]

Frampton's proposal for escape from the 'conditioning perspectives of the Enlightenment' is a near Ruskinian corrective to its 'darker aspects' that have, 'in the name of an unreasonable reason . . . brought man to a situation where he begins to be as alienated from his own production as from the natural world'.[10] The newly significant architecture proposed by Frampton might seem an unlikely possibility. Nonetheless, Le Corbusier's La Tourette is just such a building. It is a partial enclosure that establishes social settings by utilizing contemporary construction processes to do so; although predominantly constructed from poured concrete, Le Corbusier treated it as a *new* masonry.

Likewise, Le Corbusier's synthesis at La Tourette harmonizes three pairs of Frampton's 'extreme points of view', the 'two courses' discussed above and two additional ones: the 'utopianism of the avant-garde' joins with the 'anti utilitarian attitude of Christian reform' (suggested by Ruskin and Morris). The paradoxical result is a 'totally planned industrialized' utopia that simultaneously embodies a 'denial of the actual historical reality of machine production'.[11]

During the 1920s, Le Corbusier could not have accomplished such a synthesis, even though earlier, when still Charles Edouard Jeanneret, he was closer to Ruskin. Only in his post-World War II work did he finally effectively synthesize all aspects of Frampton's 'extreme points of view'.[12] At La Tourette in particular, he charts a successful encounter between the avant-garde and Christian reform as well as between himself and things he earlier loved but later rejected, including Ruskin:

> My eight months in Paris cry out to me: logic, truth, away with dreams of the art of the past. Lift up your eyes and go forward! Paris says to me, loud and unmistakably, 'Burn the things you used to love, then worship what you burn'.[13]

By 1943, Le Corbusier openly claimed the past as a crucial witness to his own creation:

> Carried away by my enthusiasm for defending the laws of invention, I took the past as my witness . . . Respect for the past is an attitude that comes naturally to those who create: it is the attitude of love and respect of a son for his father.[14]

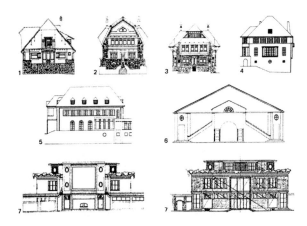

6.2
Presentation of Jeanneret's (Le Corbusier) buildings at La Chaux-de-Fonds, Switzerland, 1905–1916

6.3
Villa Savoye,
Poissy, France,
1928–1929.
Architect:
Le Corbusier

6.4
North side view
of Pavillon Suisse,
Paris, France,
1930–1931
Architect:
Le Corbusier

6.5
General view of
Chapel of Notre
Dame du Haut,
Ronchamp,
France, 1950–1954.
Architect:
Le Corbusier

A modern medieval

Ever since Claude Perrault called attention, late in the seventeenth century, to the apparent arbitrariness of the classical orders of architecture, showing them to be neither divinely ordained nor consistent, the declarative potential of architecture has steadily diminished.[15] Perrault imagined the beauties of architecture to be two: the positive and the arbitrary. The first is certain, objectively quantifiable. The second results from habit or custom and is relative.[16]

Tension between relativized taste and positive rules ultimately motivated nineteenth-century searches for an architecture of the age.[17] By the middle years of the century, such efforts turned toward invention of a new style, or styles, that could respond to new conditions by drawing upon all historical styles invented up to and including the baroque.

The ensuing cacophony of stylistic expression turned first towards eclecticism (combining elements from two or more historical styles in a single building), then later towards attempts to purify architecture through appeal to moral and structural principles, many of which found their source of strength in Gothic architecture and medieval life. The *moral* supposedly derived from medieval communal life; the *structural* deriving from the clarity of purpose persuasively demonstrated by the constructed logic of Gothic cathedrals. In this way, though not often in the same theorist's statements, attempts to reform architecture included marrying tectonics to *communitas*, which expressed a hope that if unified and principled practices could be established, architecture would again become socially relevant by resulting from common effort.

A. W. N. Pugin, John Ruskin, William Morris and E. M. Viollet-le-Duc imagined varied methods for making an architecture each believed was incorruptible, locating the wellspring of their ideas somewhere in the Gothic. Gothic architecture was crucial because it provided a link to an epoch preceding the Enlightenment, identifiable with the non-classical world. It opened up a pathway to theorizing the medieval as a way of life representing, in its idealized form, a model for restoration of a more holistic, less alienated life, such as existed long before the Industrial Revolution disrupted things. Conviction held that buildings resulting from Gothic-influenced reforms would be structurally rational (honest), or based on communal effort and meaningful labour (integrated), or some combination of the two.

While the influence of Pugin, Ruskin, Morris and Viollet-le-Duc upon development of the central principles of the modern movement in architecture is well enough recognized, most important is the degree to which these four theorists introduced a passion for reform and renewal to modern architecture that goes beyond requirements for aesthetic change alone.

Through his direct intellectual links with Ruskin, Le Corbusier would also have been familiar with aspects of Pugin's utopianism.[18] As for Morris, Nikolaus Pevsner long ago revealed the depth of his influence on the emergence of the modern movement in architecture.[19] Le Corbusier became familiar with Viollet-le-Duc's theory after moving to Paris. Ruskin and Viollet-le-Duc, in particular, played an especially important role in Le Corbusier's early artistic development. His first teacher, L'Eplattenier, introduced him to Ruskin, his second, Auguste Perret introduced him to Viollet-le-Duc.[20] Because of his far-reaching influence on elaborations of the modern project, Ruskin's utopian ideals are particularly relevant to the present discussion, especially their influence on Le Corbusier's synthesis of nineteenth-century aesthetic theory and ideas on radical reform.[21]

Lighting the way towards an architecture

Possible as it is to establish Ruskin, Morris and Le Corbusier as utopians, less apparent is the extent to which Le Corbusier was a utopian in a Ruskinian vein. There are two principal reasons for this. First, when considered as a utopian, Le Corbusier is most often associated with Fourier. Second, his uncritical embrace of the machine and his apparent blindness to alienation in relation to industrial society, particularly during the 1920s (after he transferred to Paris and renamed himself Le Corbusier) seem to confirm his complete rejection of Ruskin.

Two crucial aspects of his life militate against both accounts. First, L'Eplattenier, his profoundly influential early art teacher in Chaux de Fonds, indoctrinated him into a Ruskinian ethos. Second, his post-World War II work, the origins of which were already evident during the 1930s, reveals the incompleteness of his apparent rejection of Ruskin. Moreover, the brutality of industrialized slaughter during World War II reanimated Le Corbusier's earliest craft experience and revitalized his passion for the origin of things. These events also challenged him to reconsider his earlier non-critical embrace of the machine, leading him to temper his propensity for universalism by focusing on specificity and local tradition, concerns Louis I. Kahn and Aldo van Eyck would pick up on and develop in their own work.

In response to the futile searches, during the nineteenth century, for a style of the age, Ruskin, in the *Seven Lamps of Architecture* (1880) and Le Corbusier in *Vers une Architecture* (*Towards A New Architecture*, 1937), advanced guiding principles for what each believed would be a well-founded architecture. Both argued that the sources of valid architecture go far beyond problems of style. Le Corbusier's search brought him to valid architecture wherever he might find it. For Ruskin, Venetian Gothic provided a model of architectural virtue against which he could measure all architecture.

During his efforts to distil the principles of modern design, Le Corbusier never lost sight of the moral consequences of buildings, which remained as crucial for him as did their appearance. It is precisely this confluence of the moral and aesthetic (as much as the rational and irrational) that renders the larger part of his production exemplary:

> [Y]ou should see the intense and powerful colours which, animating the ceiling, have added a heroic touch, breath of the Middle Ages (but careful: the Middle Ages of the mind) to this industrial working place . . . the new Dominican convent school now under construction at La Tourette near Lyons; the plan embraces valid ritual, marking the spiritual and moral gestures and attitudes of the human mind – a fitting theme for the Modulor; and so forth.
>
> This is a good-humoured soliloquy because it makes a survey of our work, all organized around human values: habitation of the modern age = the

dwelling house viewed as the family's temple; the modern working place = the factory; a holy place = this convent. Yes! Why not? Yes certainly. These are resounding problems.[22]

Le Corbusier's conviction that architects must become 'engineer poets' was a radical response to the eclectic historicism of the nineteenth century; it was also a modernization of Ruskin's presentation of Gothic architecture as a purifying corrective. For Le Corbusier, such purification would derive from a fructifying cross-pollination of modern engineering products with great architecture from all historic periods; resulting not so much in a *new* architecture as in *an* architecture.

The necessary task is to give attention to places and buildings. That is the task of 'builders'. And the 'builders' are precisely the new profession that must link in a tireless and friendly dialogue the engineer and the architect, the left hand and the right hand of the art of building.[23]

Extrapolating from Le Corbusier, an architect who is both poet and engineer would be able to effectively reform corrupt practice. Poets make ordinary language extraordinary through microscopic inspection of the everyday. On the other hand, in the early twentieth century, architectural reformers, especially Adolf Loos and Le Corbusier, conceptualized engineers as a species of noble savage crossbred with ancient Greeks, which supposedly brought them closer to authentic culture, enabling them to surpass the debased efforts of alienated architects. Thus, engineers, untainted by corrupt culture and in touch with authentic tradition, could light the way for architects. On the other hand, poet architects would be able to touch emotion; made viable by engineers. By combining poetry and engineering, modern architects could offer a viable alternative to spent eclecticism.

Utopian practices, such as Le Corbusier learned from Ruskin, link history with theory, and in so doing provide a path away from obsession with style, which separates architects and their architecture from everyday life. Although Le Corbusier's modernized theory does not, at first glance, appear to sit well with the Gothic espoused by Ruskin, the crucial point of intersection lies in their shared conviction that principles are necessary for best practice.

The Gothic was convenient for Ruskin; it offered a model for a way forward through a golden age untainted by the social and artistic crises of the nineteenth century. For him, the Gothic was a utopia capable of ameliorating the alienating effects of machine production and division of labour, the greatest benefits of which would be renewed social integration of art and life. Nevertheless, Ruskin's Gothic polemic remains valuable as strategy precisely because it did not prescribe a particular style.[24] Because of this, Le Corbusier could embrace Ruskin's ethical influence without espousing an overtly Gothic approach.

However, by 1925, Le Corbusier felt the need to free himself from Ruskin, even as he placed him at the head of an extended list of early influences.

As children, we were exhorted by Ruskin. A paradoxical prophet, laboured, complex, contradictory. It was an intolerable period that could not last; a time of crushing bourgeois values, sunk in materialism, bedecked with

idiotic mechanical decoration, made by machines which, to the acclama-
tion of Homais, poured out papier-mâché and cast-iron foliage in an
unstoppable flow. Ruskin spoke of spirituality. In his *Seven Lamps of
Architecture* shone the Lamp of Sacrifice, the Lamp of Truth, the Lamp
of Humility [*sic*].[25]

Primarily, it was Le Corbusier's embrace of machine production and factory labour
that separated him from Ruskin, who saw brutality in both. He replaced Ruskin's
obsession with handicraft as *the* expression of joy in labour with a conviction that the
machine and machine labour must kill off handwork.[26] He imagined that a rational
leap would be enough to make mechanical production meaningful for alienated
labourers.

Struggling against machines was futile; any move forward would have
to account for the new realities of production. Ruskin and Morris recognized this
but could not see their way to the next step. For example, Ruskin presided over
construction of the University Museum at Oxford, which made substantial use of iron
and glass, and Morris accepted serial production by machine as a means of saving
labourers from mind-deadening drudgery.[27]

Conviction that the *good* and the *beautiful*, in social life and art, are
possible only as adjuncts to *truth* and *wholeness*, and that *honesty* and *completeness*,
even if unseen, are fundamental to any conception of truth, are among the most
important lessons Le Corbusier learned from Ruskin. His Modulor system and the
mindfulness of his works, including La Tourette, further disclose a debt to Ruskin,
revealed in his belief that every small part together becomes a whole thing, and that
individual will in construction, followed by inhabitation, is what gives buildings their
vitality.[28]

In a paraphrase of Ruskin, Le Corbusier reveals how he gained an ability
to recognize truth from him, or negatively, falsehood:

He gave a demonstration of honesty to a population gorged with the first
fruits of the nascent machine age: go to San Giovanni e Paolo in Venice
and take a very long ladder with you; lean it against the grandest tomb –
that of the Vendramin; climb up to the top of the ladder and look at the
head of the Vendramin, seen in profile as it lies on the catafalque. Lean
over and look at the other side of the head, behind the profile. *This other
side is not carved.* Disaster! Cheating! Falsehood! Treason! Everything
is false in this sumptuous, enormous tomb. This tomb is the work of the
devil. Hasten to the archives of Venice and you find that the sculptor who
was so royally paid to raise this magnificent tomb was a forger and was
expelled from Venice for forging documents!

This was how Ruskin shook our young minds profoundly with his
exhortation. . . . Ruskin had softened our hearts.[29]

Le Corbusier never fully dismissed Ruskin's ideas. His important early influence on
the architect was not some formative aesthetic theory simply to be learned,
surpassed and rejected. Le Corbusier's passion for art as the defining achievement

of life, both social and individual, made such rejection impossible. The strong idealistic thread running throughout Le Corbusier's work discloses Ruskin's persisting influence on him, particularly in his struggle to evolve consistent moral and ethical attitudes that his work could embody. Le Corbusier's post-World War II practice, interpretation of Ruskin's utopianism, and his transmission of this to the future, reveals a paradoxical relation to tradition, which for him was Janus-faced: as much a *handing down* as a *handing over*.

Excursus: towards an architecture

In his most famous collection of essays, *Vers une Architecture* (1923) (*Towards a New Architecture*, 1937), Le Corbusier boldly proclaimed the way of truth in architecture.[30] According to him, revelation of a valid architecture demanded a choice between architecture and revolution. Revolution was clearly the wrong choice but could be averted only if a new mode of building was made to rise out of the fundamentally new conditions of life evolving since the Industrial Revolution.

Le Corbusier believed that his architecture *must* become the setting for the new reality, which could take shape only if all aspects of social life were disciplined to it; otherwise, catastrophe was inevitable. In his mind, the new would need to become less strange, less threatening, so that present decay, especially the mouldering remnants of the nineteenth century, could be checked:

> The human animal stands breathless and panting before the tool that he cannot take hold of; progress appears to him as hateful as praiseworthy . . . To pass the crisis we must create a state of mind which can understand what is going on; the human animal must learn to use his tools.[31]

Though a beneficiary of the machine, modern man remains unable to take hold of it as a tool, partly because the very size of modern machines makes hand-grasping impossible. According to Le Corbusier, we remain caught between embracing and rejecting mechanization. The problem is not whether the factory system is just or not, at least not in Le Corbusier's terms; rather, the crisis resides in our reluctance to resolutely grasp machines and machine production conceptually as a now permanent condition of contemporary life:

> Let us observe to-day the mechanism of the family. Industry has brought us to the mass-produced article; machinery is at work in close collab-oration with man; the right man for the right job is coldly selected . . . Specialization ties man to the machine; an absolute precision is demanded of every worker . . . the worker makes one detail, always the same . . . The spirit of the worker's booth no longer exists, but certainly there does exist collective spirit. If the workman is intelligent he will understand the final end of his labour, and this will fill him with legitimate pride.[32]

Blinded by his overarching awe of the new technological age, Le Corbusier, during the 1920s, could not see his own absolutism. As unlikely as his programme for pride in factory labour seems, humans psychologically disciplined to the realities of machine and factory production (which entails making only 'one tiny detail' of any whole object), would no doubt be happier with their lot than individuals anguished by their diminished responsibility for the production of whole things.[33]

Unmoved by the monotony of factory labour or the disorientation it brought on by dividing tasks into ever more isolated, smaller and repetitive parts, Le Corbusier could only sing the praises of industrialization. Nevertheless, as surprising as it may seem, alienation was actually just what Le Corbusier imagined he was addressing. He believed psyches adapted to modern conditions would be enough to facilitate disalienation:

> The lodging is there, you will say, to receive and welcome the human animal, and the worker is sufficiently cultivated to know how to make a healthy use of so many hours of liberty. But this is exactly not the case; the lodging is hideous, and his mind is not sufficiently educated to use all these hours of liberty. We may well say, then: Architecture or demoralization . . . There is no real link between our daily activities at the factory, the office or the bank, which are healthy and useful and productive, and our activities in the bosom of the family which are handicapped at every turn. . . . The problem is one of adaptation, in which the realities of our life are in question.[34]

As far as Le Corbusier was concerned, offices and the factories had already become, by the 1920s, realms of rationalized production, but houses and their occupants remained inadequately adapted to these new positive conditions. For him, modernity and its requirements were inevitable, only a 'modern state of mind' was lacking, yet in time this would emerge by way of contact with the 'objects of modern life', including factories, factory production, and modern offices with their efficient, hygienic settings and operations.

Indeed, Le Corbusier believed the *normalized* world he imagined was desired, demanded even, by the modern Everyman and his family, even though they continued to reside, 'in an old and hostile environment' made up of now useless houses, streets and towns. The situation was so serious for Le Corbusier that he believed it was destroying the family.[35]

In contrast to modern conditions, 'the old rotting buildings that form our snail-shell, our habitation . . . crush us in our daily contact with them – putrid and unproductive'.[36] The shocking contrast between decrepit homes and modern settings for work and institutions would force a choice of architecture (elevated to a new standard), or revolution. To achieve architecture, to avert revolution, homes must become staging grounds of productivity and adaptation to the new, now permanent, conditions of modern existence.

Only our apparently intractable attachment to old homes and old cities obscures how much we actually *really* desire new cities and homes more akin to modern factories and offices. This circle of frustration – from wants, needs and outmoded attachments to social settings we recognize as ripe for replacement – has, argued Le Corbusier, set humanity (in the industrialized world at least) to boiling:

> Every man's mind, being moulded by his participation in contemporary events, has consciously or unconsciously formed certain desires; these

are inevitably connected with the family, an instinct which is the basis of society. Every man to-day realizes his need of sun, of warmth, of pure air and clean floors . . . Man feels to-day that he must have intellectual diversion, relaxation for his body, and the physical culture needed to recuperate him after the tension of muscle or pain which his labour . . . brings. This mass of desires constitutes in fact a mass of *demands*.

Now our social organization has nothing ready which can answer these needs . . . There reigns a great disagreement between the modern state of mind, which is an admonition to us, and the stifling accumulation of age-long detritus.[37]

Systematic operations in the antiseptic conditions of offices and factories would necessarily elicit desires for revamped homes that would inveitably intensify into demands. For Le Corbusier, these appeals coalesced around an imagined call for new homes that would be part office, factory, clinic, gym, library and theatre. If unmet, pleas for a renewed habitat would grow increasingly fervent. It is here that Le Corbusier's cry of 'Architecture or Revolution', becomes clear: until all aspects of society are brought up to date, especially the home, it will be as if 'Nothing is prepared'.[38] In retrospect, although the world that Le Corbusier demanded has more or less come to pass, the resulting environment is often alien and unfriendly, not at all a better home.

Similarly to Morris's utopia, described in *News from Nowhere*, Le Corbusier's vision of modern society required that it be made in his image of it. However, whereas Morris would have us know his utopia as primarily his dream, Le Corbusier proposed his as an inevitable fact, demanding nearly immediate realization, lest revolution ensue to bring it about. Morris presented his story as a literary utopia, Le Corbusier presented his as a programme for direct application, at least in *Vers une Architecture*.

Unlike Morris, who required revolution from the outset to redeem culture, Le Corbusier wanted to avoid it at all costs. He did not believe reformed culture (including houses and cities) would come about through a radical break with existing modern conditions. Rather, he was convinced that adaptation to new modes of labour supplemented by renewed settings would be enough to bring about general contentment. The best settings would be where neither his proposals nor his architecture would seem strange. Ultimately, he sought nothing short of the normalization of modern life in all its facets so that his necessary architecture could shift from being radical to normative.

Examination of Le Corbusier's programme for overhauling pre-existing conditions, necessary to prepare proper settings for modern ones, sheds light on a nagging paradox of his career: on the one hand, there is his architectural production, widely recognized as exemplary; on the other his urban dreams now in near total disrepute. Although none were ever fully realized, he is widely blamed for the destructive effects of urban renewal, particularly its logic of regularization through demolition.

Le Corbusier's realization of numerous remarkable buildings but no urban schemes in full suggests a surprising possibility: perhaps their intensely aggressive character provided the motive force for his ingenious individual buildings. It is conceivable that his architecture was concurrently partial realizations and models of his urban projects, which remained unrealizable dreams.[39]

It might even be possible that Le Corbusier – unbeknownst even to himself – wanted his urban designs to remain unrealized. Even so, he did once believe that his project for the *City of Tomorrow* (1929) was a necessity, not a utopia, set to replace obsolete existing cities with renewed ones supposedly able to receive and nurture inevitable conditions. Le Corbusier went so far as to imagine that cities renewed in this way would assure prevention of the revolution he so feared:

> Society is filled with a violent desire for something which it may obtain or may not. Everything lies in that: everything depends on the effort made and the attention paid to these alarming symptoms.
>
> Architecture or Revolution.
> Revolution can be avoided.[40]

Inasmuch as they present re-descriptions of social relations that would bring about a changed reality, or present re-descriptions of a reality impossible to achieve without altering social relations, Le Corbusier's writings are utopian. Although a wide gap appears to divide Ruskin's thought from Le Corbusier's early statement of belief in *Towards an Architecture*, his later work, chiefly individual buildings including La Tourette, elaborate on a set of social conditions that come close to portraying Ruskin's medievalism.[41] Moreover, monastic settings, toward which, at least in part, Ruskin guided him, made an early, significant and life-long impression on Le Corbusier.

The form of content

> The monastery of La Tourette is planned around the essentially human concept of the stark life of the preaching friars . . . what was needed was a plan catering to the needs of the heart.[42]

> I had to try to give them what men most need today: silence and peace. The Dominicans fill this silence with God. This monastery of rough concrete is a work of love. It does not talk all by itself. Its life comes from inside. It is inside that the essential takes place.[43]
>
> Le Corbusier

La Tourette embodies a synthesis of Frampton's two courses: it is a *limited monastic enclosure* built using contemporary materials and methods of construction. The complex clearly defines social relationships within its confines as well as outwards into nature. La Tourette inscribes a relation to nature that its occupants can turn to as a model of coexistence; the building carefully interprets its location, inviting the site to move onto, under and through it. The complex is also an undeniably realistic product of the age: craft is gone; serious budgetary restrictions now limit architecture by requiring a turn to standardized products, easily assembled. Stone may continue to face buildings but is rarely if ever used to *make* them.

La Tourette reveals the influence of the Certosa di val d'Ema (Ema), fourteenth to seventeenth centuries, in the outskirts of Florence, which Le Corbusier first visited in 1907 and returned to in 1911, and again, at least conceptually, throughout his career. Most importantly, Ema courses through La Tourette in the monastic virtues the Dominican brothers maintain, which suggest alternatives to lives and architecture now nearly completely conditioned by consumer capitalism. However, the fully enclosed monasticism of Ema never prevails at La Tourette; it is everywhere tempered by openness, which convincingly analogizes the Dominican's organization as a preaching, rather than an enclosed, order. Besides the obvious relationship of individual cellular unit to the overall enclosure common to both, the way in which Le Corbusier's Dominican priory sits in its sloping site recollects the mount upon which Ema rests. The two structures also benefit from carefully framed views throughout.

While the focus here is on the influence of Ema and Ruskin on Le Corbusier, it is worth noting that La Tourette also shows the influence of Le Thoronet, a twelfth-century Cistercian Abbey located in nearby Provence. In 1953, Father Pierre Marie Alain Couturier, the Dominican priest instrumental in securing the commissions of both La Tourette and Ronchamp for Le Corbusier, alerted the architect to Le Thoronet. As a result, in a number of significant ways, La Tourette reveals a debt, in terms of form and material character to Le Thoronet:

> Le Corbusier could hardly be insensitive to the harmonious arrangement of pure forms at Le Thoronet, merely placed next to each other, nor to the blind walls enclosing the inner spaces, nor to the luminous internal harmony.[44]

Nowhere in his later work did Le Corbusier simultaneously embrace and question post-World War II realities more so than at La Tourette. For example, although the building is constructed of concrete, it is conceptualized here as an analogue of stone, a *new* stone, cheaper to use and easier to manipulate, perfect for construction after craft's demise:

> In the hands of Le Corbusier the amorphous material of crude concrete – *béton brut* – assumed the features of natural rock. He did not smooth away the marks and hazards of the form work and the defects of bad craftsmanship.[45]

At La Tourette, the concrete is rough; indeed, inside and out, the entire complex is a forceful presence. Roughness, akin to *savageness* or *rudeness*, as Ruskin described it in 'The Nature of Gothic', is a virtue of poverty – presented at La Tourette in opposition to the slickness and overabundant affluence of conventional post-World War II industrialized building.

While it is customary to associate Ruskin primarily with Gothic architecture and its revival, this is an oversimplification. Apart from rejecting much Gothic revival architecture, especially when architects attempted a direct imitation of sources, for him, it was an exemplar, a means of getting at those principles he believed great architecture shares across space and time. By making the object of his argument great architecture of all ages, rather than the great architecture of

6.6
**Apse, Le Thoronet,
Provence, France,
c. twelfth century**

6.7
**Entry portal, east
side. La Tourette,
1953–1960.
Architect:
Le Corbusier**

one age alone, Ruskin could use the Gothic and the virtues it embodied for him to elaborate on a collection of general principles valuable for evaluating *any* architecture. He did exactly this in 'The Nature of Gothic', where he lists the virtues of Gothic builders and their products as interchangeable.[46]

According to Ruskin, not all of the virtues he describes need be present for a building to be Gothic, though he argued each is present, to a degree, in all great architecture.[47] He asserted one virtue – emotional strength – as being as fundamental to Gothic architecture as to humanness, in its material form it conveys *savageness*; its mental expression, or key moral element, includes *rudeness*, referring to robustness and vigorousness. According to Ruskin, both are identifiable in all noble art.[48]

For Ruskin, a Gothic building would be virtuous inasmuch as it expressed the savageness and rudeness of its builder in material form. The attachment of material form to mental expression makes the presence of a building in the world akin to the comportment of its maker. In short, buildings are in the world as their makers are, or at least they can share the same aspirations. If the maker is virtuous because he is savage and rude, then his creations, including buildings, must express these moral elements. The virtues of a man are the same for any building he makes. A building does not picture or image these virtues; it makes them present.

Savageness in building is virtuous precisely because it expresses the fundamental fallibility of human beings. No actual person or building may ever achieve perfection. Humane virtue turns on a capacity to accept one's own fallibility and requires tolerance of the same in others. Considered in this way, perfection is only possible if one's aims are so limited, or one's work so debased, that achievement of perfection is actually possible. Ruskin and Le Corbusier did not reject perfectibility, only achieved perfection, with the shallowness of thought it demonstrates, especially the precision, smoothness and finish that expresses it.

Anything wild in thought or imagination, that is, anything genuinely inventive, eludes perfection, showing itself in admirable forms that are rugged, rough, powerful, savage. Forms and finishes that are varied, which is to say vigorous, disclose a vitality analogous to that of living creatures who are the more beautiful the less they are perfect; beautiful because they are alive, decaying and growing all at once. Perfection of the sort unachievable by humans is reserved for God, or Nature as an expression of God's genius. In sum, no person or work of architecture is noble, argued Ruskin, unless imperfect: 'Of human work none but what is bad can be perfect, in its own bad way.'[49]

At the end of the day, present conditions must necessarily restrict the aspirations of most architects. The limited expressive capacity of an industrialized construction industry, whose labourers are semi-skilled assemblers rather than craftsmen, determines the scope of possibilities. When perfect construction is demanded and an absolute smoothness of finish is readily achievable, it is best not to challenge the relatively unskilled labour of modern construction with too wild an imagination or thoughtful an architect.

Le Corbusier twisted just such limitations to serve his thoughtfully emotional architecture, which he accomplished by pushing twentieth-century building practices toward enduringly humane ends. Echoing Ruskin, he accepted the limits of budget and labour without allowing either to restrict his imagination. Consequently, La Tourette confronts the twentieth century with its own materials. It makes of concrete, so central to the century, a rough and wild medieval masonry that is never melodramatic.[50] Le Corbusier made, as did Ruskin, the highest virtue of roughness and imperfection, which analogize tolerance and a willingness to accept humans as they are, valuable qualities that could redeem Le Corbusier's utopian vision from whatever tendency it had toward preternatural perfection.

6.8
North wall of church with chapel, La Tourette, 1953–1960. Architect: Le Corbusier

Ruskin's virtues, if they are virtues, do not go out of style, even if their disclosure differs according to specific times and places. Through his revelatory process, Ruskin brought to light the prospect that artistic virtues are independent of any fixed form or style, likely to outlive particular time-bound examples of both. The wild confrontation between nature and culture that La Tourette mediates is but one emblem of Le Corbusier's success in embodying Ruskin's highest virtue for architecture in a post-World War II building.

Chapter 7

The life within

Town planning is profoundly traditional if we accept the truth that tradition is a continuous sequence of all innovation, therefore the most reliable guide to the future. Tradition is like an arrow pointing to the future, never to the past. Transmission – tradition's real meaning, its reality. Thus town planning emerges once again from the depths of time; its mission to give our civilization a home of its own.[1]

Le Corbusier

Like utopias, Le Corbusier's buildings are arguments for particular ways of living. Each one made his developing commentary on existence increasingly perceptible. His works are so much more than pretty pictures or isolated objects that disinterested aesthetic appreciation is insufficient for understanding them. By providing dynamic settings for possible action only partially limited by their very presence, Le Corbusier's architecture demands active engagement on the part of its occupants, and certainly never quietly recedes into the background. In fact, Le Corbusier saw this as the criterion of good architecture:

An architecture must be *walked through* and *traversed*. It is by no means that entirely graphic illusion certain schools of thought would like us to believe in, organized around some abstract point that pretends to be a man . . . Good architecture is 'walked through' and 'traversed' inside as well as outside: that is living architecture. Bad architecture is frozen around a fixed, unreal, artificial point that is utterly alien to any human law [original italics].[2]

However, buildings that invite full-bodied experience emphasize the tension between arguments for a way of life set to architecture and the dynamism invited by it. Experience will inevitably open gaps between architects' intentions for a building and its occupants' actual experience of it. Above all else, no matter how decisively architects may form buildings, their inability to determine behaviour will always prevail.

The richness of Le Corbusier's social imagination comes through in his architecture to reveal its utopian dimension. Even when partially built, his vision of communal harmony remained mostly a concatenation of social dreams. To become operable in exactly the way Le Corbusier imagined, the settings he proposed would require individuals content to renounce a fair degree of individualistic desire in favour of the collective's greater good. Life in utopias requires agreement; actually, limitation – determining who is or is not welcome – is their defining feature. More's *Utopia*, for example, argued for a sort of enclosed monastic life as the most beneficial, a conclusion Le Corbusier also arrived at by 1911. Most people, however, do not really want to lead lives restricted in any way. Not even the relative permissiveness of More's ideal society, which endorsed the pleasures of sex and family, would be likely to be enough to change negative opinions of utopias. Regardless of its potential benefits, the prospect of any utopia becoming a reality remains an understandably horrifying prospect for most modern people.

Perhaps the values of socialist utopias must be rejected, at least for so long as identity and desire are largely defined by the consumption of goods and pursuit of freedom from all interpersonal and institutional constraints. Radical subjectivity seems still to promise at least a modicum of self-liberation, regardless of the isolation it entails. In short, utopian worldviews touting interdependency would present for most a terrifying prospect. Thus, the intense social interdependence of living in a community that fascinated Le Corbusier is hardly ever entertained as a serious possibility for modern secular societies. Nonetheless, the substantial confrontation between self, world and others that retreat makes possible might be one of the few ways for contemporary individuals and families to intermittently withdraw from the solvent of mass society without rejecting it completely.

Ruskin, Ema and Le Corbusier

In 1907, Le Corbusier set off on a study trip that brought him to Florence, among other destinations. His guide there was Ruskin's *The Mornings in Florence* (1876), which includes five daily itineraries. At the end of the first he encourages the reader to make a side visit, beyond the city's walls, to a Carthusian monastery for a momentary experience of monastic life.[3] Known as both the Certosa (Chartreuse) del Galluzzo and the Certosa di Val d'Ema, the monastery is located approximately two and a half miles west of Florence's Porta Romana.

In addition to *Mornings in Florence*, Le Corbusier would have also had with him Ruskin's *The Stones of Venice*, which includes the famous chapter 'The Nature of Gothic'.[4] In it, Ruskin presented his beliefs about labour and the virtues of art. He encouraged empathy for art originating in a humane social and economic life akin to that found in monasteries and related to medieval cathedral building. With a frame of mind prepared by his earlier reading to discover what Ruskin had taught him to see in nature and culture, Le Corbusier made his first visit to the Carthusian monks' house at Ema.[5]

Even though no longer occupied by Carthusians, the monastery still contains what Ruskin found there and continues to give clues to the discoveries Le Corbusier made during his visit, particularly how he could go on to synthesize this information into an approach that would guide him throughout his career. On 15 September 1907, after visiting Ema, Le Corbusier wrote: 'I would like to live my whole life in what they call their cells. It is the [perfect] solution to the working man's house type, unique or rather an earthly paradise'.[6]

Ema is a monastic masonry enclave that establishes clear relationships among the monks and between them and nature. Most impressive for Le Corbusier must have been the striking location of the monastery on Monte Sacro and the variety of framed views opening out toward the landscape throughout the complex. He would also have been impressed with how social life was enclosed at various scales throughout, from the monks' individual apartments to the whole complex on its hill – organized around a number of enclosed open spaces of different sizes.

7.1
General view. Chartreuse d'Ema (Certosa del Galluzo, or Certosa di Val d'Ema), Florence, Italy, c. fourteenth to seventeenth centuries

7.2
Framed view. Chartreuse d'Ema (Certosa del Galluzo or Certosa di Val d'Ema), Florence, Italy, c. fourteenth to seventeenth centuries

135

His greatest discovery, attested to by sketches, was the graceful repetition of each individual monk's home. Every cell is a domestic enclave formed by rooms for work, study, meditation, eating and sleep, as well as a small garden. All of the cells are discernible from within the monks' cloister as well as from beyond the walls of the complex. In the relationship of the individual cells to the cloister – unified by an arcaded passage – and of these combined units to the whole complex, Le Corbusier detected implications for the social life of institutions at all scales, from house to city. The cellular structure of much of his subsequent work shows this. At Ema, each cell is a small house, and the monastery as a whole is a small city:

> [T]o solve a large proportion of human problems you need locations and accommodation. And that means architecture and town planning. The Ema charterhouse was a location, and the accommodation was there, arranged in the finest architectural biology. The Ema charterhouse is an organism. The term *organism* had been born in my mind.[7]

Le Corbusier's capacity for intensely close observation – indebted as it was to Ruskin's eye – allowed him to get far deeper than surface appearances to reach the internal organizing structure. At Ema, his concentrated vision revealed a fundamental synthesis of opposites: the reconciliation of individual and collective. His perception of surfaces remained paramount but he viewed them primarily as a pathway to form. In turn, he saw form as the expression of an object's essential content, which made it possible for him to draw *persistent* themes from the structure and internal logic of nature and culture across time.

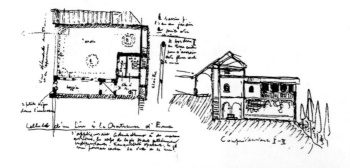

7.3
Plan and cross-section of Ema. Le Corbusier

7.4
Interior, monk's cell Chartreuse d'Ema (Certosa del Galluzo, or Certosa di Val d'Ema), Florence, Italy, c. fourteenth to seventeenth centuries

Le Corbusier identified Ema as a social and spatial model for how individuals and families might participate in collective activity without losing their privacy. With his first visit to the monastery, Le Corbusier inaugurated his strategy for making houses and cities responsive to the problem of individual longing for *a place* in mass society. When he visited Ema again in 1911, he codified earlier lessons into the beginnings of his mature theories of architecture and urbanism:

> So here I was again at the Ema Charterhouse . . . I did some sketches this time, and I understood things better too . . . My first impression of the charterhouse was one of harmony.[8]

In his subsequent schemes for individual houses and apartment blocks, each cell of a Corbusian collective is an enclave: a retreat, a place to withdraw from the stresses of modern mass society. The individual's room is a sanctuary for meditation, rest and preparation for return to the collective for a greater degree of socially beneficial productivity. As such, it is akin to the role Le Corbusier envisioned for houses in 'Architecture or Revolution'. If, in his various housing schemes, Le Corbusier was unable to fully replicate an intentioned community as rigorously configured as that of the monks at Galluzzo, it is because modern man is decidedly anti-monastic. However, at La Tourette all the threads did come together.

Location and accommodation

It is possible to make much of Ema's influence on La Tourette. Peter Serenyi did so persuasively in his 1967 essay, 'Le Corbusier, Fourier and the Monastery of Ema'. In it, he convincingly inventoried the varieties of influence Le Corbusier synthesized to formulate the social framework of his urban and architectural vision. For example, he showed how Fourier's vision of integrated social life in Phalanstère had a lasting influence on Le Corbusier, who was probably introduced to Fourier's writings by Tony Garnier in 1908, sometime after his first visit to Ema. Serenyi also identified the significant influence of steamship organization on Le Corbusier, first discussed as a model in his *Vers une Architecture* and a short time later in *Précisions* (1930). Serenyi then turned to the Monastery at Ema, revealing it as a concrete example of a complex Le Corbusier could refer to, organized like a steamship, which might also be an appropriate setting for a *Phalanstère*.

All of these influences coalesced in distinct proportional admixtures in Le Corbusier's various solutions to the problem of how modern individuals could interact with a collective to the benefit of both. Serenyi exemplifies this with projects Le Corbusier designed for collectives, including the Immeubles Villas (1922 – unbuilt), the Cité de Refuge (begun 1932), the Unité d' Habitation in Marseilles (begun 1947), and La Tourette (1953–1960).[9] For obvious reasons, La Tourette stands out among these as the Corbusian setting most influenced by the Monastery of Ema. Le Corbusier's own words confirm his admiration for the Carthusian monastery as a golden model from the past that he could draw upon in his efforts to reform architecture in the present:

> The beginning of these studies [for dwellings of a human scale], for me, goes back to my visit to the Carthusian monastery of Ema near Florence,

in 1907. In the musical landscape of Tuscany I saw a *modern city* crowning a hill. The noblest silhouette in the landscape, an uninterrupted crown of monk's cells; each cell has a view of the plain, and opens on a lower level on an entirely enclosed garden. I thought I had never seen such a happy interpretation of dwelling. The back of each cell opens by a door and a wicket on a circular street. This street is covered by an arcade: the cloister. Through this way the monastery services operate – prayer, visits, food, funerals.

This 'modern city' dates from the fifteenth century.

Its radiant vision has always stayed with me.

In 1910, returning from Athens I again stopped at Ema.[10]

Le Corbusier's later interpretation of Ema at La Tourette confirmed his uncanny capacity for recognizing future architectures in past ones. In these models, he identified possible solutions for a wide variety of difficult problems confronting contemporary architecture:

[B]ut not until later did the essential, profound lesson of the place sink in on me – that here the equation which it is the task of human wit to solve, the 'reconciliation of individual' on the one hand and 'collectivity' on the other, lay resolved.[11]

For Le Corbusier, problems of a social dimension always demanded an appropriate setting. This attitude, although it depends on form to present its results, is not formalist. Le Corbusier imagined that the forms he invented, as solutions to social problems, were the content of these solutions made manifest. As such, form is content and requires no meta-discourse to explain intent; sentient bodies will experience the meaning of charged forms through their five bodily faculties. They will, in turn, comprehend settings made up of such forms by way of reference to their experience of them.

Such an architecture, comprehensible through reference rather than representation, assumes that a no longer, or never, alienated individual is moving through it. Alternatively, especially by the time Le Corbusier designed La Tourette, he might have imagined that a force of will alone would be sufficient to establish a setting powerful enough to challenge contemporary alienation. If successful in its aims, such a building could model potential social wholeness while collapsing the divide separating form from content. Le Corbusier implied as much in his understanding that a reconciliation of individual and collective requires a setting that models the possibility of this condition:

But in the resolution of this problem ['reconciliation of individual' on the one hand and 'collectivity' on the other] another equally decisive lesson was to be learned [from Ema]: that to solve a large proportion of human problems you need locations and accommodation. And that means architecture and town planning. The Ema charterhouse was a location, and the accommodation was arranged in the finest architectural biology.[12]

An *architectural biology* would be an architecture of life. It *must* be a holistic setting allowing for the fullness of human existence. Consequently, Le Corbusier's project for a full architecture is reminiscent of Alberti's contention that because they are bodies, buildings are organic – made from interdependent parts forming a comprehensible whole. Le Corbusier's conception also echoes Alberti's conviction that cities and houses are inextricably linked in the formation of a *complete* human environment, which becomes the setting for individual bodies who make up extended social bodies, requiring *location* and *accommodation*.

Just as Alberti encouraged a striving for ideal cities, even though time and necessity must always frustrate their total realization (and be allowed to), Le Corbusier saw Ema as a golden model for a valid modern setting, open to wide-ranging interpretation. It was certainly not, as far as he was concerned, a fixed idea requiring exact reapplication. His imaginative work with the past, and upon it, was inspired. The models from the past that Le Corbusier referred to never boxed him in. In much the same way as Alberti imagined that ideal cities could learn from Plato without strictly conforming to the philosopher's laws for them, Le Corbusier did not permit his own abstractions to eclipse his sensitivity to the concreteness of lived reality.

Responding to the sway Ema held over his imagination, La Tourette shares many of the remarkable features Le Corbusier found there. For example, La Tourette, like Ema, crowns its hilltop location, but here the structure juts out from the hilltop. At both complexes, views from each of the dormitory cells are extremely important, although at La Tourette only one side of the three blocks of cells faces the valley. Shared as well is an emphasis on communal spaces, including the church, chapterhouse, refectory, atrium and passageways. Each cell of Le Corbusier's convent opens onto a passage, but unlike at Ema, it is enclosed and communal activity rather than nearly absolute seclusion is the norm.

Although La Tourette also includes a cloister, it is non-traditional. Instead of being an arcaded walk around an open court, like Ema, here, fully enclosed hallways

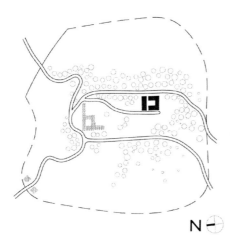

7.5
**Site plan.
La Tourette,
1953–1960.
Architect:
Le Corbusier.
Drawing by
A. B. Dixon after
Le Corbusier**

N

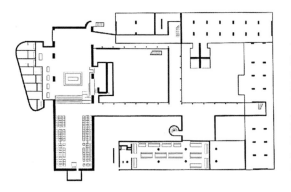

7.6
**Plan of lower
ground floor.
La Tourette,
1953–1960.
Architect:
Le Corbusier.
Drawing by
A. B. Dixon after
Le Corbusier**

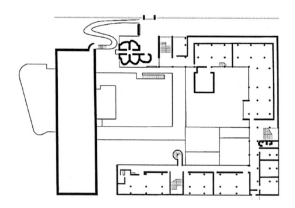

7.7
**Plan of entry level.
La Tourette,
1953–1960.
Architect:
Le Corbusier.
Drawing by
A. B. Dixon after
Le Corbusier**

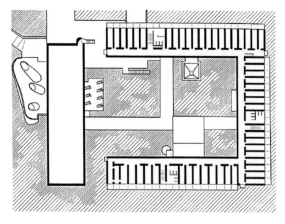

7.8
**Plan of level five.
La Tourette,
1953–1960.
Architect:
Le Corbusier.
Drawing by
A. B. Dixon after
Le Corbusier**

7.9
**East–west section.
La Tourette,
1953–1960.
Architect:
Le Corbusier.
Drawing by
A. B. Dixon after
Le Corbusier**

separate the interior from the cloister. At Ema, the cells form a **U**, closed at the end by the block including the church. At La Tourette, the church is both linked to the rest of the convent, by passages cutting through the cloister, and physically separated from it, by being pulled away from it. The **U** housing the cells and other uses faces off against the massive block of the church. Everything La Tourette shares with Ema and with Le Thoronet and all of its departures from both are responsive to the peculiarities of Dominicans as a religious order.

7.10
**General view.
La Tourette,
1953–1960.
Architect:
Le Corbusier**

Le Corbusier's free interpretation of monastic models at La Tourette demonstrates his capacity for recognizing golden models as fertile territory for invention. Even so, at least one writer viewed these modern inconsistencies with historical monasteries as an indication of irony rather than engagement. Reyner Banham, for example, discounted interpretations of La Tourette that draw upon Serenyi's observations, introduced above.[13] According to Banham, by denying absolute claustral closure to the Dominicans at La Tourette, Le Corbusier was intentionally mocking the monastery at Ema. Banham went so far as to interpret La Tourette's partially closed court, filled with Corbusian objects, as an attempt by the architect to thwart what Banham must have believed were the inflexible monastic aspirations of Dominicans:

> And one does not have to be much of a cynic to observe that just as the monastery may be seen as a caricature of Corbu's intentions in the reform of urban housing, so La Tourette can be interpreted as a satire on the monastery [Ema] . . . Here is a building aggressively claustral in form that contains no useful cloister, for its central square is too clogged with miscellaneous structures to be used.[14]

If La Tourette were a monastery, in the strictest sense, and if drawing upon models meant doing so without reflection, Banham's commentary would have merit. Unfortunately, he neglects to distinguish between Carthusians and Dominicans, who are, after all, not interchangeable; they organize their communal lives in quite different ways.[15] True enough, both sleep in individual cells rather than in dormitories, but whereas Carthusians sleep, eat and work in their cells, Dominicans primarily sleep

7.11
View into court.
La Tourette,
1953–1960.
Architect:
Le Corbusier

7.12
Cell interior.
La Tourette,
1953–1960.
Architect:
Le Corbusier

and study in theirs. Thus, a Dominican cell is a simple room with a bed, desk, wardrobe and washbasin. Carthusians live in small independent houses.

At Ema, the Carthusian houses consist of five rooms on two levels. The entry level, entered from the monk's cloister, includes an antechamber, a library and bedroom cell. Lay brothers would have delivered the monk's meals to them through a small hatch in the wall next to each apartment's door. Located one level below on the ground floor there are two rooms fronting a garden. Timber and fuel were stored in one; the other was used as a workshop.

Dominicans eat in community and are preachers. Carthusians eat in isolation and hardly ever speak. They are hermits who require the solitude that radically claustral settings provide. Dominicans engage the world through preaching and teaching and were, until church and state divided in France, most often housed in convents located in university towns.

With the actual daily practices of Carthusians and Dominicans in mind, it is no wonder that La Tourette, while an interpretation of Ema, differs from it in fundamental ways. Reflecting on Banham's commentary, it appears that his concern was not with the actual life of monasteries, such as that of Ema, or with the special requirements of a Dominican convent but rather with some kind of claustral *idée fixe*; a mental representation confirmed by the following:

> And if those structures were to be cleared from the central square [of La Tourette], then the claustral form would be revealed as a cruel joke in itself, for the fall of the land and the elevation of much of the building on *pilotis* and buttresses together mean that a large segment of its perimeter, far from being closed, is dangerously open to the distractions of the world outside.[16]

7.13
Refectory.
La Tourette,
1953–1960.
Architect:
Le Corbusier

The partial openness of La Tourette and even the *miscellaneous structures* in its cloister emphasizes it as a city on a hill while referring to many unique characteristics of the Dominican order, not the least of which is the prior location of their convents in cities. Dominicans are not monks, although they desire to live in community. They are worldly and urban but not secular, and because they are not monks, La Tourette is not a monastery, certainly not in the sense that Banham imagined it should have been.

Utopia and La Tourette

> [S]taunchly virile . . . [La Tourette] constitutes a magnificently positive reaction to the slick glass and shiny surfaces now emasculating architecture. Concrete is the means, raw potent concrete, the concrete of the twentieth century, but employed here with almost medieval strength of expression.[17]

Given the evidence of bodily experience, much of what is written about La Tourette is exaggerated (the quote above, though, is mostly accurate). For example, the North

Wall of the Church holds back much less than it receives, defining a boundary rather than holding back energy (as Rowe observed). The parapet walls of the roof-walk are not so high as to preclude views toward the mountains, town or ground (as Giedion claimed). The church, modern as it may appear, has a remarkably medieval tuning both aurally and visually, made physically present by experiences of light and sound during mass.

La Tourette is also far more humble than it appears in most photos. Walking along the approach to the convent reveals how remarkably present it is in the landscape – a presence that is interdependent, relying upon a compromise between building and nature that resulted in the happy outcome still evident. The structure is also regional. It shares a number of characteristics with buildings in nearby Lyon, especially the bold presentation of clear geometry expressed as large unrelieved areas of wall. La Tourette also shares these qualities with Le Thoronet, the twelfth-century Cistercian abbey Le Corbusier visited before designing La Tourette. Notably, openings at La Tourette are punched through the concrete as if it were a thick masonry wall, much as at Le Thoronet.

Le Corbusier's Dominican convent is homely and defers to the forces of nature. It exists in time and shows its vulnerability, having begun to crumble. It is outward looking, directing attention away from itself and toward nature, the horizon, the village in the valley, the mountains beyond and the world beyond them for which the way of life contained, more so than the container, might be a model of possibility. Nature acts forcefully upon La Tourette and begins to occupy it in places, including the overgrown court and roof-walk, the roofs of the various passages cutting through the court, and the roofs of the atrium, sacristy and chapel. Eventually the earth will subsume La Tourette – a building already deeply rooted to its ground.

7.14 (left)
**Church Interior.
La Tourette,
1953–1960.
Architect:
Le Corbusier**

7.15 (right)
**Framed view
into valley.
La Tourette,
1953–1960.
Architect:
Le Corbusier**

The court is much gentler and more hospitable than imagined. It establishes a series of squares or spaces, providing views of and access into nature, which runs beneath and over the building and through the court. The 'ideal' Corbusian forms located in the court (cubic, pyramidal and cylindrical) are neither strictly Platonic nor precious; these objects appear inevitable because the imperfection of the court makes appropriate places to receive them.

Only a visit to La Tourette can fully reveal how it engages and accommodates the body everywhere. At almost every step, the structure reminds occupants of their own presence and of the building's. This occurs at every sensory level and through a myriad of inventive details that inform occupants of how they might use the convent, all the while allowing individuals to alter certain parts of it in order to make the body more comfortable.

Two examples of such accommodation include the parapet wall of a balcony extending off the lower of the two floors of cells and two operable panels found in each of the cells. The balcony has a concave cavity at the top of its surrounding waist height wall that suggests taking a forward looking stance with arms spread apart and forearms resting comfortably in the cavity, directing one's attention toward the church. This arrangement also promotes conversation: when two people are on the balcony, one forearm of each would fit very comfortably into the concave space, encouraging them to face each other.

The same position also facilitates contemplation of the many structures arrayed in the court below, as well as the walls surrounding it that clearly explain the occupation of the building to the left and right. Rising up directly across from the balcony looms the massive wall of the church, which defines the court's far edge, echoing the thoughtful bodily position assumed while occupying the balcony. When

7.16 (left)
Stair tower in court. La Tourette, 1953–1960. Architect: Le Corbusier

7.17 (right)
Court, view toward church. La Tourette, 1953–1960. Architect: Le Corbusier

reflectively resting there, it is possible to smell and see nature within and beyond the complex. One can see plants in the court along with the occasional bird, and hear birdsong and the wind through the rustle of trees beyond it.

Of the many bodily accommodations throughout the complex, the one occurring at the interior and exterior facing walls of the brothers' individual cells is of particular interest. Each of these walls has an operable panel, one in the wall separating the small room from the common interior passageway facing the court, and the other in the wall separating it from the individual balcony to its exterior. Both panels form an operable, semi-permeable, membrane positioned between the inner sanctum of the cell and the world beyond; linking the world of community within to the world of Nature and ordinary life beyond.

When the panel facing the passageway is open, it communicates the occupant's desire for some contact with the community, even if the entry door to the room is secured. However, the panel and door can be shut for solitude. The operable panel facing the balcony allows the cell's occupant to further fine-tune the quality of contact with the outside world. For example, it is possible to leave this panel slightly ajar to let in a little natural light and fresh air, even though the balcony door and window are shut and curtained.

The facades of Xenakis

A seemingly infinite variety of formal and visual effects makes up La Tourette, each of which is in part a deception. Visitors, often architecture students, focus on sketching its myriad compositions and novel details, including its forms, surfaces and details, as if the whole was meant to be sorted out as a collection of discrete compositional devices, rather than experienced as a configured whole made up of interdependent parts, all working together to shelter and present the community within. A propensity to forget the life within persists, it seems, even when its assemblage of unique characteristics, including the lighting and architectural promenade that weaves everything together, are apparently apprehended.

One particularly engaging collection of effects at La Tourette is the glazing scheme of the floors below the brothers' cells, especially the south and west facades facing outwards as well as the facades of the corridors that cross through the court, all of which Le Corbusier's principal collaborator at La Tourette, Iannis Xenakis (1922–2001), designed. (Xenakis was a musician and engineer who went on to become a well-known composer of modern – especially electronic – music.)[18]

Each of these facades is composed in part with a series of *ondulataires* – non-structural concrete fins spaced according to harmonic divisions based on progressions of the golden section. A fixed sheet of glass rests between each of the fins, except where operable panels called *aérateurs* replace them; so named because of their ventilating function (similar to those found in the cells). It is a novel arrangement, modulating light entering the building while altering views out from it. Le Corbusier called the invention 'musical glass panes'.[19] Nevertheless, these fins on the facades can appear more as clever effects than as interdependent parts of the whole. The description of them as *musical glass panes* begins to reveal the problem.

7.18 (left)
**Architecture
students.
La Tourette,
1953–1960.
Architect:
Le Corbusier**

7.19 (right)
**Atrium exterior.
La Tourette,
1953–1960.
Architect:
Le Corbusier**

Xenakis began designing his facade scheme by inverting the notion that *architecture is frozen music* to make it become something like 'music is architecture in movement', even though he stated that, 'on a theoretical level the two statements may be beautiful and true, but they do not truly enter into the intimate structure of the two arts'.[20] Despite his suspicion, he nevertheless appears to have attempted to make the facades represent movement, even though, apart from the *aérateurs*, the building, its intense vitality aside, does not move – at least not perceptibly.

Nonetheless, in a description of his efforts in designing the three facades facing into the court, Xenakis asserted his musical intentions: 'I had chosen four elements, *a*, *b*, *c*, *d*, of the golden section and their twenty-four permutations, which I arranged on the unfolding of the facades like a variation of a single theme in time'. Le Corbusier altered Xenakis's designs for these.[21] On the other hand, his designs for the aforementioned exterior and corridor facades (based on his compositional experiments for music) were realized:

> The criterion [for arranging the concrete fins] was that of the densities of the points (blips [on magnetic tape]) on a straight line (time). . . . So

> the solution is to juxtapose on the facades patches containing dense, upright casings of reinforced concrete with patches containing rarefied ones.[22]

While the music/architecture analogy may be fruitful for attempts to describe the deep structures shared by the two arts, they operate differently as lived experience. Music moves through time by marking it. On the other hand, architecture persists through time by showing time's marks upon it. Another crucial difference between music and architecture is that whereas music acts upon individuals who listen to it, individuals act upon architecture by making use of it. In any event, Xenakis's propensity for representing theoretical abstraction makes his facades *feel* less a part of an interdependent whole than many of La Tourette's other elements.

To know La Tourette only through its effects, surfaces, forms and details, though, is to remain alienated from what renders it remarkable: its capacity to support the community by providing a clarified setting for the life within. How Le Corbusier accomplished this architecturally is of special interest. Identifying and drawing principles out from the building could potentially inform the making of other exemplary platforms for life. Whatever lessons La Tourette might hold for the invention of social settings, these do not reside in its effects as isolated tableaux. Imagining that they do is a failure sadly demonstrated by the results of buildings such as Boston City Hall (1962–1968), supposedly modelled after La Tourette.[23] Actually, Boston City Hall is a collection of unexpected and arbitrary visual effects that appear alien to its setting and social objective, effects which make it incomprehensible. In contrast, Le Corbusier's ability to synthesize aesthetics and ethics in establishing social settings sets La Tourette apart.

Not a monastery

Dominicans are members of an Order of Preachers, founded by Saint Dominic (1171–1221); it was formally sanctioned in 1216. Dominicans are Friars Preachers (Black Friars in England), a non-enclosed order, and thus La Tourette, which is a Dominican House, or a convent (a word that in American English conjures up the place where nuns live) is not a monastery. The monastic analogy holds nonetheless because monasteries were the source of Le Corbusier's effort to give form to a manner of living capable of balancing individual desire with collective requirements. In addition, monastic rule does, after all, influence Dominican life. That Dominicans are not monks and La Tourette is not a monastery serves to emphasize the degree to which Le Corbusier was able to explain his monastic ideal via a convenient programme for sympathetic clients.

When Saint Dominic set up the first Dominican Houses, they were centres of study established in urban centres, often major university cities. Organized in this way, Dominicans played an important role in the development of intellectual and spiritual life wherever their houses were located. Unlike enclosed monastic orders, the Dominican order is not organized as a collection of autonomous houses (or convents); rather, each is a part of an extended community of communities. Individual members belong to the order, not a particular house. As a preaching order

that chooses to live in community, Dominicans have struggled since their establishment to synthesize the conflicting requirements of a contemplative life with the
demands of an active ministry.

With this struggle in mind, the Dominican project is shaped by a perpetual
attempt to invent a middle way between the clarity and certainty of monastic life
and the confusion and uncertainty of worldly experience. This search, which requires
continuous reinvention of the balance between conflicting forces, is a permanent
condition of the order. It is also an expression of the order's particularly dialectic
organization. Because of the certainty it promises, monastic clarity has often tempted
Dominicans. Monasticism, although a dimension of the order's dual character,
threatens to dominate when members lose sight of their searching and apostolic
purpose (expressed by their historic role as preachers and teachers).

Colin Rowe was one of the few architectural writers to have observed
that La Tourette is a building uniquely bound to the dialectical exercise Dominicans
play out in their daily life as members of an order that attempts to synthesize apostolic
and monastic desires. Rowe, however, could only see this demonstrated by the forms
Le Corbusier invented and in the relationship of the structure to nature. This makes
Rowe's reading less an interpretation of the relation of the setting to its occupants
than an attempt to draw meaning out of the forms by seeing them as representations
of veiled content, which need not have all that much to do with the actual life of the
community within the walls of the convent.[24]

Dominicans are not monks[25]

When Le Corbusier conceived of La Tourette in the late 1950s, French Dominicans
had adopted, since the nineteenth century, a non-traditional tendency toward monastic organizational and physical structures. Strict separation of Church and State
was initiated in France during the post-Revolutionary period. During the nineteenth
and twentieth centuries Dominicans came to be housed in box-like structures outside
of towns that neophytes enter to be indoctrinated into the order by other Dominicans.
Le Corbusier no more envisioned this kind of arrangement than did Père Couturier,
who, as was noted in the previous chapter, guided Le Corbusier in his development
of La Tourette, even providing him with sketches of the convent he envisioned, and
also encouraging him to visit the Cistercian monastery of Le Thoronet.

Couturier was drawn to Le Corbusier because of his conviction that
Christian art could only be renewed if the most gifted contemporary artists were
engaged to make it.[26] Accordingly, Le Corbusier allowed both Le Thoronet and Ema
to course through La Tourette but neither dominates; interpretations of monastic
virtues do. By suggesting Le Thoronet to Le Corbusier, Couturier was being at once
radical and conventional. As an ideal of community life transferable to Dominican
practice at La Tourette, Le Thoronet provided a radical model – Dominicans are, after
all, neither Cistercians nor an enclosed order. Nonetheless, the medieval roughness
of Le Thoronet inspired Le Corbusier to interpret Ema on his own terms. What is
more, Le Corbusier understood enough about the Dominican order to introduce a
degree of openness appropriate to their particular traditions that Le Thoronet does
not have. It is, in fact, such openness that continues to sustain La Tourette.

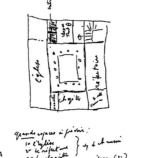

7.20
**Sketches, an idea
of a monastery
based on Le
Thoronet, by
R. P. Couturier**
Source: Reprinted
from J. Petit,
*Un Couvent de Le
Corbusier*, Paris:
Les Editions de
Minuit, 1961

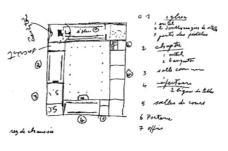

7.21
**Sketches, an idea
of a monastery
based on
Le Thoronet, by
R. P. Couturier**
Source: Reprinted
from J. Petit,
*Un Couvent de Le
Corbusier*, Paris:
Les Editions de
Minuit, 1961

Paris, le 4 août 1953

Cher Ami,

Je suis heureux que vous soyez allé au Thoronet. C'est
là un monastère à l'état pur. Maintenant, il n'y aura plus d'in-
convénients à ce que je vous montre des monastères modernes, où,
dans une habitation embourgeoisée, nous vivons cependant la mê-
me vie qu'au 13ième siècle. Ce qui est t absurde !

7.22
**Cloister.
Le Thoronet,
Provence, France**
c. **twelfth century**

Paradoxically, almost from the moment of its completion, La Tourette suffered because of the remarkable changes that took place in Catholic religious life after Vatican II (1962–1965). La Tourette's fortunes were further influenced by later transformations in Western culture generally, especially as a result of the 1968 student rebellion in France, which empowered French Dominicans to call into question the monastic organization they had taken on during the nineteenth and twentieth centuries. This questioning included an expressed desire to leave *boxes* of Dominican learning for a return to their tradition of being educated in universities, followed by working and living in cities.

Dominicans did not abandon their traditional settings in cities voluntarily, but were forced to do so because of social and economic conditions. The most important event leading to this was the decisive split between Church and State that occurred in France at the end of the nineteenth century, when the new Republic eclipsed the Restoration. In the aftermath of this split, church status changed. For example, religious study was removed from state universities. Because the state would no longer serve Dominicans' educational requirements, the order had to construct its own colleges. Lacking adequate financial resources, their new colleges, including La Tourette, had to be located outside cities in more isolated countryside areas where real estate was cheaper.

Reforms during the 1960s returned religious studies departments to state-run universities, where postulants of the Dominican order could again train. Subsequent to this, Dominicans sold off many of their rural convents to reclaim their search for a way between asceticism and activism in French cities. As it turned out, La Tourette's countryside location made it a less than desirable place for such pursuits.

Nevertheless, although French Dominicans sold off many of their box-like properties, they determined to keep, maintain and, in part, reinvent La Tourette. From the moment of its construction, La Tourette has been a focus of intense international interest, which has long assured its survival beyond the loss of its original use. Reinvention has allowed La Tourette to become a hub of contemplation beyond the exclusively, or obviously, religious sphere. It is now a centre of study where spirituality in contemporary life remains the guiding theme. As such, the building operates as a retreat for thoughtful individuals generally but also as a pilgrimage site for practitioners, students, researchers and friends of architecture who seek access to the mysteries of one of the finest architectural minds of the post-baroque period. It also offers clues to how exemplary buildings might continue to be (re) invented.

Flexible concrete

In light of its persistence, it is possible to observe how the setting provided by La Tourette presents the community occupying it with opportunities to continuously experiment with perfected means of inhabiting the complex. Reinterpretation of the building mostly reflects ongoing and transforming conditions of conventual life, but also occurs in response to the needs and desires of the individual brothers who occupy the structure. Originally constructed to house more than 100 Dominicans, as of July 1999, 16 Dominicans were living at La Tourette, but it did not seem empty of either people or purpose. (At the time of this writing, the convent is undergoing a major restoration and reworking of its purpose that promises to assure its continued long-term survival.)

In response to transformations in religious, political and social life occurring since its construction, a number of spatially defined practices at La Tourette have been altered from their original state, yet none of these modifications required radical alteration of the building. For example, separation between priests and worshippers is much less pronounced than it was originally. Women are now welcome to enter the convent even though they were previously barred. The community and its famous setting are also now open to interested visitors, religious and non-religious, architects and non-architects alike. In fact, very few sections of the convent remain off-limits to visitors.

Occupation of the church during services is much altered from when the convent was first constructed and occupied. These modifications clearly demonstrate how occupation of the complex has been transformed without altering the structure. For example, the public originally entered the church through a back entrance with direct access from outside the convent (brothers entered the church from within the convent, as most still do), whereas outsiders, whether from the surrounding community or visitors from further afield, now enter the church from wherever they may be in or around the complex.

The original area for the public is at the back of the church near the confessional, separated from the main body of the room by the altar. Previously, this was the only place where outsiders could sit for mass; they can now sit wherever there is an appropriate place for them in the church. Originally, only brothers could occupy the pews on the other side of the altar, in the main body of the church. These pews have since been extended and are now open to the public. Women and lay people are now also invited to take part in performance of the mass.

Another notable transformation is that of the former visitors' room, which is actually a series of five free-form pods located beside the entrance to the complex. The first of these pods was the porter's lodge. It is now the main reception for

7.23 (left)
Hall from atrium to
church.
La Tourette,
1953–1960.
Architect:
Le Corbusier

7.24 (above)
Church interior.
La Tourette,
1953–1960.
Architect:
Le Corbusier

all who wish to enter the convent. While it is not clear who originally greeted visitors, the desk is now manned by young local women who confirm reservations and take payment for stays, partial or full-board, and yes, credit cards are welcome. The four other pods are located to the church side of this first one, arranged so that two pairs of pods face each other across a narrow passageway. When the convent was closed to outsiders, this was where Dominican brothers from within met visitors. These four pods now house displays of Dominican publications, books by Le Corbusier, others about La Tourette, postcards and Modulor measuring tapes, among other souvenirs.

Since the institution of these changes, the community has become a retreat and a centre for probing questions of contemporary life in the areas of architecture, the social sciences, psychoanalysis and, of course, religion. And in the process the convent has been urbanized, despite its rural location. It is metropolitan, scholarly, thoughtful and intense. A relevant example of this is the Centre Thomas More housed at La Tourette. It studies questions related to, or within, the human sciences. A brother with an interest in Le Corbusier and utopia who organized the Centre, argued that the concrete out of which the convent is predominantly constructed is actually, paradoxically, quite flexible, which accounts for the remarkable responsiveness of the complex. Because of this, as the building becomes known through occupation, the perfection and reinvention of its use can occur without requiring abandonment of its original and traditional purpose, a purpose analogous to the order's perpetual search for self-perfection through experimentation rather than violent change.

That Le Corbusier's building allows for, and maybe even encourages, such investment is a testament to the architect's utopian vision for modern life in the contemporary city. La Tourette is a model for Dominican occupation of it that is elastic enough to allow for imaginative reinvention of the purpose and programme contained within. In this respect, the building becomes a model of Dominican life in particular, while also being a laboratory in which the brothers can experiment with how best to utilize the resource of their building. Thus, La Tourette, by the example of the ongoing life within, becomes also a model for civil life in general that goes on beyond its walls.

Had La Tourette been an indifferent building that did not demand engagement, the Dominican order would have sold it off. Had they abandoned the building, it might very well have come to house another appropriate occupation. Its dynamic story and unfolding patterns of use make La Tourette a particularly persuasive argument for the possibilities that utopian imagination holds for the invention of an exemplary architecture. Most significantly, the building persists as a viable pattern for occupation, flexible enough to encourage reinvention and reuse of it by the same order without either becoming indeterminate generic space or necessitating its radical physical alteration.

Giving form to desire

To conjure up La Tourette, Le Corbusier appealed to a golden age he discovered in the social and spatial elaboration of the Carthusian monastic life that he first experienced at Ema. This model remained with him for the rest of his career and, not surprisingly, came to particularly influence his efforts after World War II, when modernity could no longer conceal its central fiction: that unending progress as the self-justifying objective of progress is an unquestionable *good*. At La Tourette, Le Corbusier elaborated on monastic ideals as a social and spatial critique of affluent industrialized consumer society. Though now nearly half a century old, the building might still have something hopeful to offer an insecure twenty-first century.

The lessons of La Tourette reside in its specificity at every level, a specificity subsumed within a general conception of community attuned to the particular group of people occupying it. What stories of La Tourette usually do not reveal is the trajectory of its occupation through time. Interpretations tend to consider it as if today were still the day of its completion. In this way, it becomes ossified. Such temporal hardening encourages rigid interpretations that focus on either its intended programmatic occupation, or on it as an object relevant exclusively in terms of the exact period of its creation. The usually untold story concerns the changes which a particular building can either sustain or not and the degree to which, over the course of decades, it survives and supports reconceptualizations of it. Italo Calvino identified this capacity with great precision. (In the quote, I have inserted 'La Tourette' where Calvino identified one of his invisible cities, 'Zenobia'. I have also substituted 'buildings' where Calvino had 'cities'.)

> [I]t is pointless to decide whether [*La Tourette*] is to be classified among happy [*buildings*] or among the unhappy. It makes no sense to divide [*buildings*] into these two species, but rather into another two: those that through the years and the changes continue to give their form to desires, and those in which desires either erase the [*building*] or are erased by it.[27]

Following Calvino's line of reasoning, Le Corbusier's La Tourette is identifiable as an example of the first *species* of building described above: even after many changes it continues to give form to the desires of the Dominicans who occupy it and the visitors who seek it out. In this way, La Tourette remains a model of the possible that exists, it is responsive to the contradictions of time and necessity, and thus may be considered a constitutive utopia. What may be surprising, considering how frequently utopia is conceptualized as static, is that La Tourette establishes a setting that exists between past and future and *through time* by being both liminal and establishing a liminal setting. In a sense, this liminality is comprehensible in the degree to which La Tourette circumscribes a container ever ready to be filled anew by life.

Chapter 8

Fairy tales and golden dust

> Only from wonder can come out new institutions . . .
> they certainly cannot come from analysis.
>
> . . . If I could think what I would do, other than architecture,
> it would be to write the new fairy tale,
> because from the fairy tale came the airplane, and the locomotive,
> and the wonderful instruments of our minds . . .
> it all came from wonder.[1]

Louis I. Kahn

In the previous two chapters, Le Corbusier's La Tourette was argued for as an exemplary building and a constitutive utopia. Both conclusions draw heavily upon Le Corbusier's interpretation of monastic living as a golden age and model of possibility for reconciling individual and collective identity within a liminal setting. La Tourette, though unique in itself, actually shares qualities with settings that came before it, such as Michelangelo's Campidoglio, and after it, such as Louis I. Kahn's Salk Institute. While the golden age drawn upon is not always the same, these exemplary settings nonetheless interpret shared and persistent social and architectural themes. With this in mind, the discussion turns to Louis I. Kahn (1901–1974) and his efforts at the Salk Institute (1959–1965).

Needs and desires

Recognition as one of the great architects of the twentieth century came rather late to Louis I. Kahn. During the 1950s, when he had already been working for several decades, Kahn's thought appears to have taken a remarkable turn. It was only after this that he became celebrated worldwide as a notable architect. His transformation is of particular interest: it was utopic in character and came after years of experience as an activist architect, producing social housing to fulfil essential needs. After his conversion, Kahn came to see housing more as a *need* than as a *desire*. (Yet, in his language, a house could speak of desire if it made present an approximation of the original desire that led humans to want houses where it is good to live.) Nevertheless, the earlier stages of his career continued to serve as the foundation for his later work.

In Kahn's mind, needs and desires were two different things. Needs are basic requirements, including food, shelter and clothing, which make biological survival possible. Any civil society, according to Kahn, ought to provide for needs as a matter of course. Desire, on the other hand, is a realm of dreams required for psychological survival. By 1950, he came to believe that the basic need for shelter was achievable. As a result, he felt himself free to focus on aspirations, which lend themselves to symbolic expression, and are actually bound up more with desire. Exploration of this sort evoked architectural responses that are referential in character, communicated most effectively to the body through experience.

For Kahn, the architect's special obligation to society is to interpret institutions in such a way that they become settings for human aspiration once more. Houses are, of course, institutions as much as schools are, and Kahn would continue to build them, but these later houses were different from the social and emergency housing that preoccupied him during the early part of his career. Kahn struggled throughout the 1950s to express the psychological role of institutions in the life of a society. During the last quarter century of his life, his primary architectural concern was with individual and social dreams, particularly with how institutions, as places of both *availabilities* and wonder, come about.

Because they maintain much in reserve, Kahn's buildings are mysterious, which distinguishes them from the post-World War II banalities of reductive modernism. Kahn's achievement is especially remarkable considering that he came of age – architecturally – during an era of unprecedented affluence in the United States. From the late 1940s when Kahn began thinking about monuments until the 1970s and the oil crisis, the United States achieved worldwide prominence by providing the increasingly dominant model for all things from art to business. American pragmatism combined matter-of-factness with extreme rationality to promise economy and efficiency, and thus, apparently, limitless affluence. In buildings, the fabling of these traits found expression in retail and corporate architecture, as well as in the art that decorates the public areas of such structures. These developments, but especially the professionalization of architecture with its division of the discipline into discrete specializations, confirmed for Kahn how much what he called the *marketplace* was overpowering cultural life.

Kahn's metamorphosis from an admirable to a noteworthy practitioner would not have taken place if he had not shifted from satisfying *essential needs* (shelter) to interpreting *institutional essences*: social settings that he rendered as concrete fairy tales. The architectural results of Kahn's transformation stood as a challenge to the organizing perspectives of the marketplace, especially notable because they occurred against a backdrop of sustained cultural levelling and acquiescence, particularly in the mainstream.

Though built in their moment, Kahn's fairy tale settings were profoundly future-oriented. His constructions concretized a vision of institutions as settings of and for human desire at a time when it appeared certain that pursuit of streamlined management alone would drive cultural decisions, particularly in the realm of architecture. Kahn made his stalwart and unique opposition to *what is* manifest through the erection of fragments – located in the United States and elsewhere – of a utopic land of *ought*, configured with institutions made of dreams and desire. The legacy of this achievement stands as a reminder to architects and their clients that buildings are where human beings live, not simply where people are stored or produce. Among Kahn's exemplary settings, the Salk Institute in La Jolla, California is especially poignant.

If realism conveys something in line with an economic organization meant to sustain status quo conditions which are thought to be rational because they are apparently quantifiable (measurable and certain), then Kahn's work is anything but realistic. His overriding concern was with the *unmeasurable*, the qualitative and the emotional. He demonstrated this conviction in his belief that architects must take the briefs their clients hand them and set about transforming them from prescriptions to be filled into mechanisms for getting at, and ultimately presenting, a deeper, emotional, symbolic and radical meaning that institutions harbour. Recovery of this content, however, is only possible when wonder effectively tips the balance in its favour by exceeding the inescapably narrow vision of realism, extreme rationalism and obsession with quantity and measure.

How Kahn turned

Explanations of Kahn's transformation from a capable architect into a great one are hardly ever satisfactory. They include describing his turn as dependent on an artistic debt owed to Paul Cret (his teacher at the University of Pennsylvania and an early employer), who instructed Kahn in the rigorous methods of the Beaux-Arts. Others suggest it was his introduction to archetypal geometry by Anne Tyng (who worked with him from 1945 onwards), or even his three-month stay at the American Academy in Rome in 1950–1951 (during which time he also visited Greece and Egypt).[2]

It is true that Kahn's post-1950 buildings share with Cret's best work a concern for dynamic symmetry and procession, but it is much more modern than Beaux-Art (Kahn had even planned to go to Germany to learn more about Walter Gropius before the Depression hit). Pure geometrical forms, such as circles, squares and pyramids – rendered in plan and three-dimensionally are certainly a trademark of his work after 1950 but these share little with Anne Tyng's independent work. His post-1950 buildings, beginning with the Yale University Art Gallery (1951–1953), developing with the Trenton Bath House (1954–1959) and Richards Medical Research Laboratory Building (1957–1965), but coalescing with the Salk Institute – all designed after his stay at the American Academy – do show the powerful influence of ingenuously interpreted Roman ruins.

As important as any stay in Rome might prove for an architect, it is worth noting that Kahn had already travelled to Europe in 1928, but that earlier trip did not result in the work that evolved after 1950. It is thus unwise to look for an epiphanic

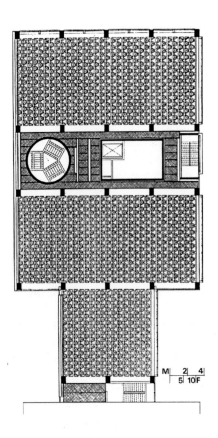

8.1
**Plan. Yale Art
Gallery, New
Haven, CT,
1951–1953.
Architect:
Louis I. Kahn**
Source: Louis I.
Kahn Collection,
The Architectural
Archives of the
University of
Pennsylvania

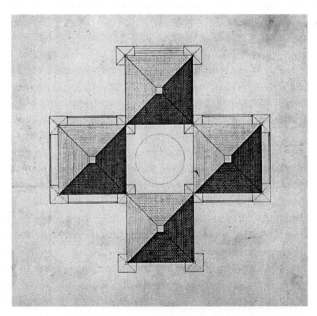

8.2
**Plan. Trenton Bath
House, 1954–1959.
Architect:
Louis I. Kahn**
Source: Louis I.
Kahn Collection,
The Architectural
Archives of the
University of
Pennsylvania

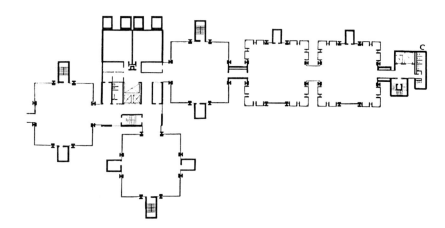

moment in Kahn's development. There was no break in time after which a previous Kahn died off to be replaced by a crystallized Kahn.[3] His striking work for institutions is rather the result of a long maturational process, a gradual development, influenced by all that came before.

Intimations of Kahn's later development showed up as early as 1931. For example, in his essay 'The Value and Aim of Sketching', he already demonstrated a concern for the 'intrinsic character' of objects that drawing could reveal. As a method of inquiry, drawing was presented as a search that is necessarily interpretive because 'the presence of our own individuality causes it [any object or thing] to appear differently than it would to others'.[4] This comment reveals an attitude toward drawing that would mature into Kahn's ability to encounter the ancient and the modern without the threat of either eclipsing his singularity. His concerns of 1931 suggest that by 1950 he must have long been preoccupied with interpretation as generative:

> We should not imitate when our intention is to create – to improvize.
> . . . We can never think clearly in terms of another's reactions; we must
> learn to see things ourselves, in order to develop a language of self-
> expression. The capacity to see comes from persistently analyzing
> our reactions to what we look at . . . I try in all of my sketching not to
> be entirely subservient to my subject, but I have respect for it, and regard
> it as something tangible – alive – from which to extract my feeling. I have
> learned to regard it as no physical impossibility to move mountains and
> trees, or change cupolas and towers to suit my taste.[5]

Much of Kahn's matured approach comes through in this quote, albeit in seed form. His later preoccupation with *forms* as continuously existing patterns of things, especially institutions, relates to the transformation described above. Forms are necessary for new institutions (or individual instances of anything) to come into being. For instance, *House* is a general idea about where it is good to live; *a house* is a specific example of it as an idea made particular by individual subjectivity, or circumstance, as Kahn called it. Forms inform all making but are out of reach. Because each circumstance of a form's appearance is an interpretation of something that has no presence, only approximate manifestations of any form are ever possible. Individual subjectivity always makes the representation of a form unique, each instance is an interpretation often initially made by way of drawing.

By the 1960s, Kahn argued that forms are the ideas of things (such as institutions) that design makes incompletely manifest because forms, as the origin and idea of a thing, have no dimension. Design is thus always an interpretation of a pre-existing idea of human desire (a *form*) that exists outside time, and because circumstance always comes into play, it is reconfigured differently (and refreshed) with each instance of its appearance:[6]

> Form has no shape or dimension. Form has a nature and a characteristic. It has inseparable parts. If you take one part form is gone. That's form. Design is a translation of this into being. Form has existence, but it doesn't have presence, and design is toward presence. But existence does have mental existence, so you design to make things tangible. If you make what could be called a form drawing, a drawing which somehow shows the nature of something, you can show this.[7]

> Form is *what*. Design is *how*. Form is impersonal, but design belongs to the designer. Design is prescribed by circumstances.[8]

Collating the source material of Kahn's later buildings, such as the Salk Institute is arguably less valuable to an understanding of his method than is insight into his interpretive process. In a summary way, Kahn's interpretive method was a hermeneutics of hope as opposed to one of suspicion.[9] The latter seeks to unmask and reveal the false consciousness or bad faith of an individual, artefact or group (Freud and Marx, for example, were suspicious rather than hopeful). The former seeks to recover some content currently lost to consciousness. It is a recovery imagined to carry with it possibilities for enriching life as a deeply experienced optimistic event.

A large part of the motivation for Kahn's interpretive project came from a desire to restore social life by recovering the aspirations that originally inspired institutions. He came to invent settings for institutions that dignified them as places of social wonder and desire. Not only did they extend the possibilities of moribund post-World War II architecture, especially in the United States, but also effectively inserted a hopeful challenge into the grey flannel cultural landscape of 1950s management culture:

> You say *the institutions of man*. I don't mean institutions like the establishment. I mean, really, institutions being this: that it is an undeniable desire to have the recognition, that man cannot proceed in a society of other men without having certain inspirations that they have – this [must] be given a place for their exercise.[10]

Even if Kahn's method of inquiry was a hermeneutics of hope, this does not yet give access to the metaphors or content he referred to in his quest. He constructed the framework of his search out of origins more psychological than historical. More than anything, his desire was to recover a future from the past he believed existed outside of time. Consideration of Kahn's key words, such as *form*, *design*, *order*, *nature*, *Volume Zero* and *institution* indicate what motivated him. Although he had a reputation for being obscurantist, if one listens carefully, his descriptions of his driving beliefs were really quite precise:

> What was has always been. What will be has always been. And what is has always been. It's the sense that reflects the beginning, and the beginning is the confirmation of all things that follow'.[11]

Resisting the marketplace

In Kahn's architectural drama, the corrosive propensity of the *marketplace* and *professionalization* was an almost insurmountable obstacle. For him, 'marketplace' had nothing to do with markets in traditional towns and cities but instead referred to a particular kind of commercial organization that emphasizes quantitative, rather than qualitative, evaluations of worth. Motives of profit alone condition the marketplace, making it subservient to economy and efficiency. Because of this, it traffics in decidedly unemotional ideas and products, which is why Kahn found the marketplace uninspiring, if not repulsive.

Professionalization of architecture, according to Kahn, required a levelling of aspiration in the service of marketplace demands. Credibility of professional architecture organizations depended on their capacity to present the public with a vision of professionalism based on quantifiable criteria as an indicator of individual and group competency. Kahn saw in this a tendency toward diminished results that was inevitable precisely because professionalization required standardized practitioners whose individual accomplishments were quantifiable.[12]

Kahn's post-World War II buildings for American institutions dramatically clarified the problem of how to house them without resorting to oversimplification. He elaborated on a kind of fairy tale of institutional possibility. In his stories, willpower would be enough to gain access to the essences of institutions, which would empower him to redeem them. Kahn's conviction was that if architects provided a setting for an institution as an *availability*, its operations could adjust to meet the challenge of the setting. Thus, the form of an institution becomes its content. Consideration of self-selection shows that this belief is less naive than it might first appear. Any institution that had a desire to be housed within a Kahn building would have already begun to envision itself in a particular manner. His best buildings, for example the Yale Center for British Art in New Haven Connecticut (1969–1974), demonstrate the happy outcome of auspicious pairings of client, architect and brief.[13] His dramatic relationship with Jonas Salk, his favourite client, confirms it.

Ultimately, Kahn's buildings achieve their drama as settings for social wonder with clearly drawn figures, especially by suppressing all details except those necessary for comprehensibility, such as construction joints. Though his buildings are demonstrations of intense consideration, they are almost never melodramatic or overly fussy. In a wondrous way, Kahn was able to render the typicality of an institution without homogenizing it. He did this by grasping institutional essences and rendering what he caught as a presentation of this. Such acts of will made

Manfredo Tafuri uncomfortable with Kahn's effort, in much the same way the never-to-be-repeated efforts of nineteenth-century *utopian socialists* troubled Marx and Engels. A Fourier phalanstère might be out of time with its historical condition but it was a result of that condition, as well as a commentary on the present within which it might exist. Even if they fail, which they often do, such attempts remain models of possibility for future reformers who come upon them.

The inevitability of failure for reformist efforts seems to be in direct correlation with just how out of step they are with the conditions of present reality, which tends to so overwhelm them that they cannot endure. Even though Tafuri viewed Kahn's effort as doomed because it was anachronistic, those institutions that he did succeed in housing, because they wanted to be housed in buildings by him, remain among the most clearly rendered examples of social wonder produced anywhere after World War II. Although Kahn's vision did not convincingly survive him in any architects beyond himself, his institutional structures – from houses to research institutes – demonstrate that other ways of thinking and doing are still possible.

The 1950s and beyond

It was during the 1950s that Kahn's language transformed along with his architecture. His emerging linguistic and architectural strangeness was a reward for coming into his own after many long years of practice. The hardship he endured during the Great Depression, and in other areas of his life, probably confirmed his conviction that he was a worthy hero of his own fairy tales. However, Kahn's refreshing encounter with ancient architecture during his time at the American Academy in Rome and during travels further afield, provided him with direct and emotional access to many of the primary sources of architecture.[14] Beyond these encounters, Kahn's trips to India introduced him to people and places he considered transcendent. Even amongst all these influences and experiences, Kahn trusted Jonas Salk enough to take his guidance to heart. For this reason, he considered Salk a true leader and his favourite client, even collaborator:

> When you ask me who has been my favorite client, one name comes sharply to mind, and that's Dr. Jonas Salk. Dr. Salk listened closely to my speculations and was serious about how I would approach the building. He listened more carefully to me than I did to myself, and then he recorded these things in his mind. During the time of our study, he constantly reminded me of premises which were not being carried out. These premises, which he thought were important, were also the basis of his questioning in his own way of thinking. In that way he was just as much the designer of the project as myself.[15]

Kahn's cryptic language, as he called it, took definitive shape between his address at the first international meeting on architecture organized by Team X in Otterlo, Holland in September 1959 and December 1959, a short time after his first meeting with Salk. Entering into a dialogue with Salk was fortuitous; it brought Kahn into a direct and sustained encounter with a fellow traveller. Even as Kahn's language became ever more enigmatic, his association with Salk materialized into one of those rare working relationships that frees both partners to express their own singularity.

Not a neoclassicist

From the 1960s until his death (and even posthumously), bits of Kahn's fairy tale land were constructed in New Haven, Trenton, Philadelphia, La Jolla, Rochester, Fort Worth, New Hampshire, Ahmedbad, Dacca and elsewhere. Each of these settings is heroic, not as a setting for an individual personality but rather as a platform for the heroic adventure of living an ordinary life. Although monumental in their way, Kahn's institutional buildings are not aloof or cold like the cultic stages of personality erected in Fascist Italy or Nazi Germany, where the focus was always on a single dominant figure. Some of Kahn's buildings may indeed have a dominant focus, but for reasons very different from the individual dwarfing objectives of French neoclassical architect Étienne-Louis Boullée (1728–1799), or the grotesque pomposity of Nazi and much Italian Fascist architecture.

Any central focus in Kahn's work was devised as a means of orienting individuals in their procession through institutions as settings of civic life. Comparisons of his work with totalitarian architecture and neoclassical architectural fantasies are not particularly helpful.[16] In contradistinction, Kahn's utopian fragments are places of inhabitation for real people. This was for him a crucial difference between his own work and Boullée's (or Claude-Nicolas Ledoux's, 1736–1806) fantastical drawings:

> I was asked to write a comment on the work of two eighteenth century architects, Ledoux and Boullée. When their drawings were shown to me for the first time (I mean the original drawings) I was struck by two impressions: of the enormous desire of their drawings to express the inspirational motivations of architecture, and how outrageously out of scale they were with human use. But still they were highly inspiring. They were not projected to satisfy function or living in, but belonged to the challenge against narrow limits.[17]

In so-called visionary architectural drawings, Kahn observed a youthfulness close to original inspiration that was capable of challenging the status quo by pushing the limits. The value of such audacity lay in its revelation of possibility rather than in establishing blueprints for direct and immediate application. Thinking about Ledoux and Boullée provided Kahn with an opportunity to conceptualize fairy tales as analogous to the opportunities utopian practice presents:

> If you eliminate the fairy tale from reality I'm against you. It's the most sparkling reality there is. Utopia somehow is a reality, it's in reality. That's the point: Utopia is real. . . . I would say that Utopia inspires. But Utopia itself? – no, there's no Utopia.[18]

It is worth emphasizing that in the above quote, Kahn discloses a crucial paradox: despite their unreality, fairy tales and utopias may actually be the most radical contents of reality. How, though, can utopias be real and concurrently not real? For Kahn, utopias and fairy tales are the most real contents of reality precisely because of the power they have to inspire. This reality, however, need never become wholly manifest (measurable); in fact, it ought to remain always a *not yet* condition (unmeasurable) so that it can maintain its inspirational role as a source of wonder, and as a challenge to present limits.

In explaining these ideas, Kahn used the prefix *un* instead of *im* to indicate that his intent was not negative. *Im* expresses no, not, without, non, not able to do, or not a possibility. Had Kahn employed the more standard *immeasurable* (instead of his non-standard *unmeasurable*), he would have conveyed a sense of impossibility, which was not at all his intent. *Un* expresses the reverse, removal or release of the thing mentioned from the condition indicated. Thus, *immeasurable* conveys that which cannot be measured, whereas *unmeasurable*, in Kahn's usage, conveys a return of the immeasurable – boundlessness, vastness – to qualities already limited by attempts to measure them. If successful, measurement would restrict, reduce or nullify immeasurable qualities by measuring them. In short, *unmeasure* promises a return of wonder (possibility) to things no longer questioned.

An architecture of life and death

The materials of Kahn's buildings were locked into an ethical dilemma revolving around determining what they wanted to be, which required resolution before construction could begin. According to him, each material could do certain things, or do certain things better than others could. However, only the materials themselves, if attended to, would be able to communicate this aptitude to an architect. After construction, the marks left by its process persisted as a complete record of this drama by telling the story of a building's emergence, most emphatically at the joint. Furthermore, Kahn believed that construction of the joint was the origin of ancient and contemporary ornament and would continue to be the source of future ornament as well.

The question is not one of one material being good for one thing and bad for another; it is more an ethical question based on an ethos of materials. A material wants to be like that which it can most identify with. Thus, if a brick is believed to identify most with an arch, it wants to be an arch – or at the very least, arch-like. An analogous identification obtains equally for buildings and individuals – what will the building be like? Whom will I be like? This is significant because it suggests that everyone and everything is like someone or something else. No new thing comes from nothing, everything has a past: a future is only desirable when constructed out of this. For Kahn, two brothers – silence and light – exemplified the drama of architecture but they are not so much autonomous as interdependent parts of a whole:

> Now when I was speaking about silence and light or the desire to express and the means, I tried to say that all material is spent light. It is light that has become exhausted. Creation makes me think of two brothers who were really not two brothers. One had the desire to be, to express; the other had the desire to be something that becomes tangible which makes the instruments upon which the spirit of man can express itself. If the will

to be is to become something of the predominance or prevalence of the luminous, then the luminous turned into a wild dance of flame, spending itself to become material, this little lump, this crumpled lump made the mountains, the streams, the atmosphere and we ourselves come from spent light.[19]

8.4
Joint. The Salk Institute for Biological Studies, La Jolla, CA, 1959–1965. Architect: Louis I. Kahn

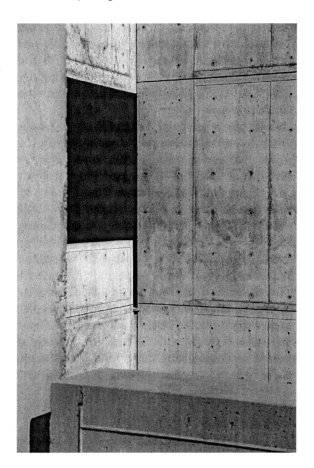

Kahn believed that light makes all things present. Surprisingly, according to him, material presence is spent light – something apparently dead. Yet, because everything comes from spent light – even living human beings – deadness cannot really be the whole story. Light is energy, a force from which we and our world come, to which we and our world will one day return. For Kahn, the drama of architecture was implicitly one of life and death, of material not yet existent because it is light and of material that has become present through a death dance to become spent light.

Concern with a good death indicates a preoccupation with death as that event which configures life. Hence, a good death is not possible without a good life, and a good life cannot be constructed out of perpetual escape from the big questions about existence, self-worth, love and death. Neither dazzling entertainment architecture nor mutely efficient buildings, can provide adequate settings for pondering such questions, no matter how much more apparently pleasant it might be to be dazzled to distraction or numbed out of self-awareness. It is not that a setting for situating mortal anxiety will somehow make thoughtfulness about life's drama a certainty, but it is certain that settings more carefully attuned to receiving life's drama do provide a more adequate stage upon which to confront mortal anxiety.

Can architecture ever really concern itself with mortal anxiety; if the intent is to alter the character of human disquiet, then the answer must be no. However, if conceived of as a setting for life, architecture could provide a reassuring container for angst. Inevitably, there is no more persistent pattern of life than preoccupation with its processes and outcome; it was Kahn's desire for his architecture to be places where it is good to live in a meaningful way.

Certainly, architecture cannot guarantee thoughtfulness or a happy outcome to a life. But if architecture is a world within a world, as Kahn argued, or is a living thing, as he also argued, then a fundamental question arises: what kind of world nourishes, and what kind of being facilitates a good life? The answer seems to be that a world receptive to life's drama nourishes it most, and beings most full of care for human dilemma facilitate a good life and a good death. Kahn's fairy tale settings of availabilities in the form of institutions attempt to 'take the sting out of the narrow limits of our time' by collapsing time without going backwards.[20]

Occupation of a setting outside time offers individuals the possibility of something like a permanent present. This challenges progress and the myth that epochs are distinct, with no shared themes across them. Kahn's institutions inscribe an eternal appeal to history as circumstance by somehow existing outside time without ever leaving it. Ancient history is present, but so is the promise of a future related to aspirations that were vital at the moment of an individual building's design and construction, and may remain so. Consequently, Kahn's buildings convincingly respond to yearnings for permanence in a way that little other post-World War II architecture has.

The yet not said. The yet not made

Of all the phrases that show up in Kahn's writing, two, *Fairy Tales* and *Golden Dust*, more so than any others, promise access to the nature of his quest. It is the story of a search for good beginnings to an optimistic future of social wholeness that he intended his buildings to establish at least partially. For Kahn, the fairy tale is fundamentally future-oriented toward fulfilling desire rather than for solving problems:

> The wish of a fairy tale is our inheritance of first desires. When you have a desire but you have no means, all you can do is wish, and it is still a fairy tale.
>
> It is the wish which drives us forward, not know-how, not technology. What drives us is the yet unmade thing. The whole basis of this century is only to satisfy the not-yet expressed. Not that which is available. That is not exciting at all.[21]

Kahn did not instrumentalize his fairy tales. Nor did he intend them to be a means to some economic or technological end. Even if a building was the result, the fairy tale remains an imaginative practice for envisioning the *not yet*, which Kahn thought of as forthcoming: 'The yet not said, the yet not made is what puts sparks of life into you'.[22] 'What has been made already is just an indication of the wonder of the mind'.[23] If a fairy tale was to organize action in a meaningful way, it required a sense of purpose. For Kahn, fairy tale origins long ago and far away were worth recollecting because they could continue to inform establishment of even the newest institutions:

> We must admire deeply the original examples. Those which came out of sheer inspiration and what may have been the source of inspiration, those which lead you to choose one or the other to express a mystery.[24]

Access to these origins is through *form*, which relates to desire, *existence-will*, which is what a thing really wants to be, and through *order*, which encompasses all the laws of nature, and is the nature of a thing. Order is first (earliest, or deepest), existence-will is next (something of a middle ground between order and form), form is last (form is what design attempts to make present).[25]

Design interprets order, existence-will and form. It is a process informed by circumstance and the singularity of an individual. As a process, design works on what an architect can get at of order, existence-will and form. Only golden dust can make the most striking presence of each of these available to practitioners. Golden dust is a residue of the past blown forward into the future. It is a configuration of tradition lending itself to interpretation because it is not complete. Interpretation of it in the present, motivated by the wish of a fairy tale, is how golden dust becomes something new.

> The value of tradition is that it gives you the powers of anticipation, that you are able, with tradition, to find the courage to express that which lasts for a longer period of time than what circumstantially you can judge. It is beyond the circumstances you express in it. So the golden dust is only an expression of nature-man which distills out of all of this, from which you get the essence of the meaning of tradition.[26]

> You cannot recapture what has happened. What is valuable is the golden dust that fell from this, which was man's nature. If you can, from what happened, derive man's nature, and if you could put your finger through the golden dust, you would have the powers of anticipation.[27]

Kahn's idea of tradition is anticipatory. Golden dust falling off the past is what gives an architect (anyone) the power to anticipate, dream and desire. The wish of a fairy tale is possibility made up of a recollection of archaic (originary) residue. Genuine human existence and experience were, for Kahn, a realm of dreaming, where what *isn't* is dreamed into reality:

> The true reality is the fairy tale, not the every day course of things, which is only circumstantially living the fairy tale, full of disappointments, full of less than what you'd expect. That's not man at all. Experience is purely

incidental. The unattainable, the yet not made, yet not said, is what motivates man.[28]

With this, Kahn made a bold challenge to the matter-of-fact condition that is all too often seen as the only reality. What if what is usually thought of as reality is actually a sort of unreality? What if existence as commonly lived is a defective simulacrum of *real* life?

The fairy tale logic of Volume Zero

For Kahn, then, real life is not a place where institutions crush desire by deadening it; nor is it a place where architects fill clients' programmes like prescriptions, or where marketplace values are the only truth. Fairy tale reality is a location of wonder, anticipation, desire and fulfilment. It is a milieu where architects interpret clients' programmes to get at the nature of institutions so that these may become places of availabilities for human desire, where quality of thought is far more valuable than quantity of production. It is the realm of architecture and institutional life that Kahn attempted to embody in the social settings he invented, which he hoped would guide their occupants toward a more holistic community. Kahn is an exemplary architect precisely because the content of his buildings remains intelligible, at least tacitly, to those who occupy them.

Kahn's fairy tale was a story of human mutuality made possible by strong institutions. Recollection of the imaginative spirit of *first* institutions ought to inform invention of new institutions. As the residue of first occurrences, golden dust is crucial for interpretive recollections. Fairy tales are invaluable because they envision a future *like* the past (but not exactly).[29] The particulate nature of golden dust (it is dust after all) allows for an inventive reconfiguration of its contents in the present. It includes those good and fundamental things that the past carries forward. Golden dust is gold because it is incorruptible, which makes it of supreme value; it is dust because it is past and faded – dead even, returned by way of scattering to nature and the cosmos to be recollected and reconfigured in the present by imaginatively sifting through it. This sifting is necessarily a situational (circumstantial, in Kahn's words) interpretation of what *always* remains of origins – even if all that remains are precious particles blown forward from the past toward the future.

> Tradition is just mounds of these circumstances, you see, the record of which is also a golden dust from which you can extract the nature of man, which is tremendously important if you can anticipate in your work that which will last, that which has a sense of commonness about it.[30]

Fairy tales permit access to the unconscious by giving it access to consciousness. They provide room for fantasy by challenging the dominance of *reality* over possibility. By opening up pathways to the dark side of human being and the unconscious; fairy tales confront death, aging, the limits of our existence and the wish for eternal life – in short, *all* the basic human predicaments. To do this, fairy tales must 'state an existential dilemma briefly and pointedly', presenting problems in their most essential form.[31] In this way, they come very close to Kahn's desire to get at the essential forms of institutions. Kahn's buildings are about possibility that strong institutions (firmly ordered and presented) could be settings for enduring social bonds and desire.

As forward-looking stories, fairy tales give clues, suggestions really, to how golden dust could, or ought to, be reconfigured to resolve the impact of current social crises on institutions. In this way, fairy tales are future-oriented wishes that for Kahn promised a time once again when things would be how they were before the first books brought literacy. Kahn's concentration on fairy tales, institutional essences and wonder represents dimensions of his fascination with the possibility of a *Volume Zero*: the book that comes before *Volume One*, or, more precisely, a non-volume of collected wisdom that continues to exist before writing and literature.

Pre-literate communication appears to have held for Kahn a promise of redemption for alienated modern man. He thought, it seems, that oral communication is closer in time, probably space as well, to the first instances of things, especially institutions that originally emerged out of a human desire to be with other people joined by common interest to become members of a community. The written word tends toward academicism, which potentially closes off knowledge from further experiment by relegating it to books. Thought, so contained, becomes a history of ideas analogous to the taxonomies of art historical styles. The limitation of such an approach to knowledge is that it tends to make of each epoch, no matter how cogent its virtues, continuing interest or even relevance, a thing of the past, relegated to histories with little capacity for informing present action.

Oral tradition transmits living knowledge; each retelling of it is generative, capable of transforming, thus refreshing what it communicates. It is a form of interpretation able to keep knowledge vital. On the other hand, committing knowledge to writing risks making it ossified and easily forgettable. Such is the case even when literate knowledge attracts written commentaries, which tend to interpret it as given. Such commentary encourages a sense of the already written as concluded: it can now only be revitalized if operated upon from the outside. Kahn's *Volume Zero* redressed precisely this academic tendency.

Volume Zero, *forms* and the *unmeasurable* resist being turned into ossified book knowledge because they elude *capture*. Like the stories of fairy tales or the societies of utopias, *Volume Zero* is a book that does not exist, which made it the most important book for Kahn. Forms, although key for giving institutions a presence, can never be made concrete, only interpreted and approximated. The unmeasurable is infinite, qualitative not quantitative, and is among the most important qualities with which architecture transacts. However, it eternally resists apprehension. With these key ideas, Kahn theorized a way for architecture to resist its capture by style, fashion, and conventional art historical periodization. His chief desire was to thematize architecture by exploring those things – psychological and social – that are always the concern of exemplary buildings.

According to Kahn, each building for an institution is a retelling, extension and interpretation of the original story of human desire for that institution. Fairy tales carry condensed cultural knowledge configured so that its transmission can occur by way of reference, apprehended through a direct experience of content on a preconscious level. If made explicit, a fairy tale would have no resonance for listeners or readers because too direct a presentation of the content would rob the story of its emotional impact. Kahn's understanding of what he saw as the essential content of institutions operates similarly. He attempted to configure institutions in such a way that their emotional resonance, existent because it is a response to human desire, is neither suppressed through reduction nor lampooned by explicitness. His objective was not to fix an institution once and for all at a particular point in its social development but rather to present it in a manner that would make it emotionally understandable.

Kahn's architecture as fairy tale analogy was useful for him in at least three ways: first, fairy tales are future-oriented even if they tell stories about something far away and long ago. Their future orientation derives from fairy tales being carriers of cultural knowledge intended to introduce possibilities to successive generations. What is more, the future orientation of fairy tales reveals their utopian dimension – both fairy tales and utopias are stories of potential told in the present about future possibility. Second, fairy tales and architecture have a social dimension – both establish the context of a given society. Fairy tales do this by transmitting deep insights about life in a particular culture. Architecture does this by establishing, as a physical presence, the settings for institutions that make social life possible and intelligible. Third, experience and comprehension of both fairy tales and architecture occur in distraction. Fairy tales rely on distraction to get something across through a story that communicates on a manifest level while transmitting a latent content to the listener or reader that operates on an emotional level; comprehension of architecture occurs in a similar manner but the story it tells is told directly to the body.

Architecture is never a picture; experience of it is always by sentient bodies moving through it during some event that the setting provided ought to communicate and facilitate. The primary concern of a participant observer for a building is that it be a place where it is good to do whatever it is he or she is attempting to do there. In this way, meaning is drawn from use; whatever meaning an architect wishes to communicate must be transmissible and comprehensible through use. Thus, if an architect wants to transmit a story of use that is richer than a tale of limited functionality, the content of this story must be comprehensible even to distracted occupants moving about his or her building. Hence, the logic of fairy tales is directly applicable to architectural meaning. Both tell their stories through manifest content that must not completely obstruct the latent content, which is of greater resonance because it communicates more directly to the emotions.

Fairy tales also facilitate imaginative displacement of intolerable emotions onto the characters of the tale, which helps to render difficult emotions manageable. They provide a safe space to play through actual problems in the imagination, which is why fairy tales tend not to threaten individual security, even though their concern is with the sources of profound psychic anxiety. Modern stories, like modern buildings and institutions, are often too direct. Consequently, because many buildings do not offer any kind of imaginative relief, they are often just frightening. For example, consideration of the despair associated with so much post-World War II public housing in the United States, United Kingdom, France and elsewhere, demonstrates how directness can play itself out architecturally and psychologically to disastrous effect.

By telling their stories in a casual way, fairy tales resist being either moralistic or too demanding. In much the same way, Kahn invented buildings for institutions that resonate psychologically, despite the tendency of clients to cast architectural problems as requiring simply a nicely packaged technical response. He saw this as his responsibility and the responsibility of architects in general. According to him, getting at the unique psychological core of an institution is an architect's first obligation to humanity (no matter how unrealistic this might appear according to the logic of reductive realism or the functionalist elevation of minimum standards to maximum possibility):

> I know of no greater service an architect can make as a professional man [or woman] than to sense that every building must serve an institution of man, whether the institution of government, of home, of learning, or of health, or recreation.
>
> One of the great lacks of architecture today is that these institutions are not being defined, that they are being taken as given by the programmer, and made into a building.[32]

Also, fairy tales are for children; they are stories of eternal wonder, which is why they were a potent force for Kahn's invention of vital settings for institutions. Children are closer to their affect and instincts than adults are partly because a child, owing to his or her more recent arrival, is closer in time and space to primal desires that persist – although submerged – within adults. Adults, more often than children, are conditioned by a limiting conception of *rationality* and *reality* that can too easily cripple imagination. Kahn's preoccupation with the residue of the archaic (golden dust) does not suggest that he believed traditional cultures to be societies of undeveloped children. Rather, for him, tradition held things closer to the heart than is possible for dissociated moderns confused by false promises of progress and rationality. Fairy tales recreate a realm of the child's mind and thus can bring adults closer to radical desire. Thus, it is no wonder that, at the age of 72, Kahn would write:

> I have so damned much fairy tale in me. I never lose sight of the thing. I believe the wish, the fairy tale is the beginning of science. I think if I were to trade my work for something equally strong in me – as impelling in me [it would be] to write, to be the writer of the new fairy tales. And maybe to use whatever talent I have in drawing to illustrate them.[33]

The explicit and the enigmatic

Fairy tales facilitate a purging of mortal anxiety without overtly confronting individuals with this very condition. On the other hand, horror stories hit one over the head with mortal anxiety. Similarly for architecture, there is a fundamental difference between displaying emptied signs of past ages as if they were hollow cultural trophies (or attempts to sharpen the modern condition of dislocation by being as disorientating as possible) and engagement of persistent themes through interpretation.

The first sorts of architectures are representational (and can be terribly unsettling); the second are referential, requiring no overt picturing of recognizable content to be comprehensible. Individuals can experience this comprehensibility during their encounter with a structure in which forms present content directly to the body. Such direct presentation of meaning requires a deep fluency in persistent architectural themes (not to mention the symbolic language of architecture) and a powerful interpretive capacity, in much the same way that uniquely effective film directors can translate emotion (even action) into images in an associative way with no discernable loss of power. In fact, such effective translation often amplifies meaning.

The experience and knowledge of architectural themes can only occur through forms, even though these themes can be extrinsic to particular forms. Because of this, an architect's ability resides in a capacity to interpret and to represent architectural themes in new forms. Direct comprehensibility, occurring on a pre-conscious level, is precisely what allows the Salk Institute (and exemplary architecture in general) to communicate at a deep emotional level. What, though, is the nature of this direct apprehension of meaning? How does it occur? How does it present itself to sentient bodies? Why is it comprehensible? The following four hypotheses attempt to account for these effects.

1. Direct apprehension of meaning is made possible by fitting together architectural elements (which embody and present architectural themes) in such a way that the result neither forces poetic intent to a point of caricature nor suppresses it so that it becomes incomprehensible. Thus, a door, window, column, passage-way, and so on, as well as kinds of occupation, are elements of a whole and at the same time part of the presentation of symbolic and psychological content.[34]

2. Direct apprehension of meaning is possible because common elements of architecture, including patterns of use and occupation (as well as forms and institutions), have a long duration in any culture (sometimes across cultures as well). Meaning accrues over time and is not easily disposed of. Thus, while an elevator may not communicate upward movement in as direct a manner as a stair, an elevator articulated as a tower might begin to communicate this as both a functional and symbolic meaning.[35]

3. Architectural elements and occupation, fitted together thoughtfully, present architectural meaning directly to individuals. Individuals can apprehend this meaning because most of us are aware of our place within the moment and of the relationship of this moment to preceding moments (including the degree to which both may prefigure future ones). This continuum is comprehensible inasmuch as this moment emerges out of the past, not so much as a teleological extension of some plan but rather because time passes. Individuals are historical beings whose link with the past is through their bodies and the settings they inhabit.[36]

4. Directly apprehended meaning is comprehensible because the human body has changed little over the course of millennia. In short, *the best form is always thus*

already given, which does not mean that there is nothing that can be altered, but rather refers to the reality that *sitting makes chairs, chairs do not make sitting*.[37] An architecture that is careful in this regard will be comprehensible, no matter how *modern* it is. Kahn's fairy tale buildings engaged in telling such directly comprehensible stories. Because they communicate them directly to the subconscious, they can purge emotion.[38]

Experience of Kahn's buildings occurs primarily by way of a body in movement through, around and over them. They are not pictures; nor do they display signs. To clarify what was unique about Kahn's approach, it is worth considering a couple of architects who attempted to follow his example. They did so in one of two primary ways. Romaldo Guirgola (of Mitchell/Guirgola), for example, appropriated Kahn's formal and constructional rigour but drained both of their fairy tale conception. For Guirgola the problem is a formal one, solved by using forms mostly emptied of comprehensible referential content. Mitchell/Guirgola's various Philadelphia projects demonstrate this, including their University Parking Garage (1963), United Fund Headquarters (1969), Penn Mutual Life Insurance Company Addition (1969–1970), and their addition to the University Museum, at the University of Pennsylvania (1969–1971). Since, it appears, they were unable to come to terms with Kahn's challenging language and the way this found its way into his buildings, Mitchell/Guirgola opted for an extremely reasonable though far more technocratic approach.[39]

By apparently intentionally misreading his words and architecture, Venturi, Scott Brown and Associates defused Kahn's challenge to the status quo by transforming it into a collection of flat architectural effects. The result reduces Kahn's concern for the past to a caricature of it. Venturi, Scott Brown and Associates translated Kahn's preoccupation with historical continuity and his play with past, present and future into a representation of historical motifs collected and displayed with irony informed by advertising and pop-art vacuousness. The firm's Philadelphia buildings that demonstrate this include the Guild House (1960–1963), Franklin Court (1973–1976), ISI Building (1978–1979), the Clinical Research Building, at the University of Pennsylvania (1991), as well as the firm's addition to the National Gallery (Sainsbury Wing) in London (1986–1991) (among others).[40]

Kahn's endeavour was exemplary, a morality play, in which the virtues of building as a setting for human behaviour struggled against a decadent architecture of professionalization and the marketplace. For him, fairy tales were presentations of *typical character*, and *golden dust* was the stuff from which a golden age could be recollected; his buildings project both into the future.

As testaments to their own possibility, the wish fulfilment offered by Kahn's buildings was not unrealistic. His architecture transacted in an interpretation of permanent themes represented according to circumstances. The legibility of Kahn's buildings comes, in part, from his bidirectional conversation with the past, and the future. Kahn believed it would be possible to reform institutions by recovering their origins, but he had no desire to resurrect them in their archaic form; rather, he wished to nourish new institutions with the golden dust blown *forward* from a distant past.

Chapter 9

Kahn and Salk's challenge to dualistic thinking

I'm doing a building for Dr. Jonas Salk in San Diego. Though it was presented to me as a biological research center, of which there are many examples, I sensed from the start from a little remark that Dr. Salk made that this was not the same. He said, 'I am more interested really in the nature of man. It's what really activates my sense of wonder more than does all this business of being able to make contraptions which can make microbes talk and what not.[1]

Origins of the Salk Institute

The Salk Institute was meant to be a setting for challenges to technocratic dualistic thinking where a forum of thinkers in the humanities, art and science could reconcile the irrational and rational.[2] Jonas Salk's (1914–1995) conviction was that science belongs to society, is part of culture and therefore ought not be imposed upon a population from above. As part of his conception of science, Salk understood research as a creative act akin to the production of any other cultural artefact. To his mind, a research centre ought to be as much monastery as artists' colony; what was crucial was that the setting would provide a retreat where researchers could find the necessary comfort to set about exploring. Considering this, Salk and Kahn's architectural objective was to devise a setting to house and present an attitude toward knowledge that brought art within the sciences and the sciences within art, and both within a humanistic domain. Thus, Salk's aim in founding his institute was to reunify multiple branches of human knowledge in response to 300 years or more of movement in the opposite direction.

Salk consulted with Kahn, but did not originally intend to retain him as architect for the institute. Nevertheless, once they had met, a remarkable meeting of minds occurred, resulting in a lasting monument to Salk's aspirations but also to Kahn's idea that institutions make the city and the city ought to be a forum of availabilities. Salk summed up his wish for the Institute as wanting it to be a setting for biological research where Picasso would feel welcome. What he meant by this was that his research centre should be a meeting ground, a place of assembly, for thoughtful individuals from all disciplines who could bring insight to the role of science, especially biological research, for human beings at large.

For Salk, this coming together would begin a rapprochement between science and art, which then, as now, were habitually pitted against one another as though they represented irreconcilably opposing camps made up of irrationality on one side and extreme rationality on the other. Even though the Institute has never quite developed in the way Salk had envisioned, his intuition has shown itself to be prescient. As genetic research evolves alongside the biotech industry, ethical questions regarding appropriate application of research reveal themselves as unanswerable according to the logic of science, progress and rationality alone. Equally important are the discoveries of neuroscience that promise to mount a challenge to oppositional thinking.

Salk and Kahn came to professional maturity when the limits of modern techno-science had become too obvious to ignore. The most enlightened scientists began to realize that for inquiry into the ethical function of scientific research (and its consequences) to have a benefit, it would need to come from beyond the orbit of scientific research. The consequences of progress has at times proven to be so profound that certain developments eclipse the capacity of secularized rationalism alone to make sense of them. A profound example of this entered world consciousness the moment atomic bombs fell upon Hiroshima and Nagasaki. Combined with the Nazi holocaust in Europe, these events glaringly revealed the extreme dangers nesting within technological progress. Scientific rationality alone could not envision the long-term consequences of either. What is more, the work of philosophers of science, including Michael Polanyi and Thomas Kuhn, have made it impossible to maintain a belief that science is always disinterested and objective research.[3] If scientific research is a product of human desire, rationality alone cannot be enough to guide it.

Modern architecture and beyond

By the late 1940s, architects had begun to acknowledge the symbolic and psychological limitations of a modern architecture.[4] During the 1950s, it became even more apparent that most of what was being built was severely restricted by positivist reductionism. Unfortunately, what had begun in the late nineteenth century as a movement for radical architectural reform was, by the 1950s, resulting in an increasingly alien environment. Wonder and hope were overwhelmed by management agendas characterized by a near sacralization of economy, efficiency and the quantification of human need and desire.

In contrast to typically limited perspectives on contemporary life, Kahn was one of the very few American architects to envision an emotionally expanded modern project. As with a number of his European contemporaries, but especially

Aldo van Eyck, Kahn was inspired by Le Corbusier's ability to render modern construction poetic, especially by deepening its possibilities without rejecting the more humanistic aims of modernity. Simply put, Kahn worked anthropologically. He searched for themes of cultural continuity that, by way of interpretation, could refresh existing institutions while giving clues to the formulation of new ones, including the Salk Institute. Conventional modernists worked with a near-blind commitment to progress, explicitly demonstrated by their faith in an idea of modernism tied to reductive models of social science, especially behaviourism.

After CIAM

Kahn had his first encounter with Salk less than four months after giving the concluding talk at the Otterlo, Holland gathering of CIAM in September 1959. CIAM had originally been formed in 1928 after Le Corbusier's winning League of Nations competition entry was disqualified for being too *modern*, but by 1959, the organization was at its end. Just a year later, Team X, including Aldo van Eyck as a member, went on to position itself as a replacement to CIAM, which had already split into *old* and *new* factions during its tenth congress in 1956 (the first Le Corbusier did not attend).[5] The Otterlo gathering was, in effect, a requiem for the organization, which made the Salk Institute a post-CIAM building both chronologically and ideologically.

Kahn's invitation to the Otterlo congress came primarily on the merit of his Richards Medical Research Laboratories Building (1957–1965), then under construction at the University of Pennsylvania. Participation in the congress promised both international exposure and an opportunity to organize his thoughts for presentation to a sympathetic audience attuned to his ideas, especially about how to achieve refreshed institutions through an encounter with origins:

> Preform is archaic form. In the preform actually exists more life, more of the story that can come after, than anyone who walks from it and nibbles at it can ever attain. In the perform – in the beginning, in the first form – lies more power than anything that follows. And I believe that there is much to be gained by this thought if it comes through your minds, not only through mine, in what it can mean to you.[6]

According to Kahn, architects are responsible for reviving the existence-will of institutions, which they can do by returning to origins whenever called upon to establish settings for existing or new institutions. Because each instance of an institution is *circumstantial*, bound to a particular historical moment, establishment of any particular institution is never definitive. Rather, each expression of an institution is an interpretation of its original appearance. Hence, it is crucial for architects to conserve access to the seeds of a particular institution's *first* emergence. Carried within these seeds are the organizing principles of an institution, not its actual operation or appearance, which are circumstantial. Without access to these seeds (or radical origins), it would be impossible to configure an effective circumstantial instance of an institution in the present.

An important dimension of Kahn's approach was his conviction that the central concern of architects is to provide settings for events. The particular event itself, though, remains the concern of those who occupy the setting provided for it. Therefore, for example, an architect may provide a house both as shelter and as a symbolic expression of 'house' but only the occupants of a specific house (an instance of a particular institution) can make it a 'home', a place suited to their own singularity. When occupants vacate their 'home', it again becomes a house for occupation by others, who, as part of their own uniqueness, can again make it a 'home', although one that is different from the home that the earlier residents occupied, even though it might be the same building:

> A 'home' has to do with the people in it, and it is not his business [the architect's], except that he must prepare this realm to make it suitable for 'home'.[7]

In this sense, Kahn distinguished between 'house' and 'home', even though the two are often thought of as interchangeable. A house is a place established where it is good to be home. In his language, house is the setting; home is the unique occupation of that setting. The symbolic house has something to do with what all houses share, which leads to the problem of how a particular house might be arranged. Each instance of a house is circumstantial: a unique instance of a historical house. To make a house somewhere where it is good to live, so that it can become a home, does not necessarily require the formal ingredients of conventional houses.

According to Kahn, the circumstantial aspects of a problem are not the essence of it. For example, contours, design, material, location and imagery (the tangible things) are circumstantial. On the other hand, the essence of the problem of an auditorium is that people come to it to hear and see others who perform. It is an event of hearing and seeing, as well as performing. Accordingly, the first concern of an architect ought to be whether or not the auditorium he or she has offered up is a place where it is good to hear, see and perform – all else is circumstantial, thereby secondary to the primary problem of housing the potential of an event well. Such preoccupations, whether for a home, an auditorium, or a biological research institute, far outweighed formalist concerns for Kahn, van Eyck and others in attendance at Otterlo. Settings for events must always take a form; just the same, this was no call for reductive functionalism. It was, in actuality, just the opposite. Otterlo was a forum for formulating a clarion call for modern architecture to become more anthropologically oriented, and thus again capable of touching emotion.[8]

A compelling antecedent

Salk consulted Kahn for the same reason Kahn was invited to Otterlo: the Richards Medical Research Laboratories.[9] Compared with the cool glass and steel buildings which were then the norm in the United States, the Richards Medical Research Building was a vision of some other, richer way of housing institutional research. The structure begins to establish a magical landscape on the University of Pennsylvania campus. When viewed from the vantage point provided on the upper floors of high-rise graduate student housing some distance away, the multiple brick and concrete laboratory towers dominate the skyline, not because of their bulk, but because of their thoughtfulness and wonder.

The Richards Building gestures in several directions. By being an agglomeration of vertical structures, it partakes of the emotional power nearly always ascribable to towers. For example, towers are sky-bound places of domination associated with the organization of spaces below and around them. Towers of churches, city halls or the defensible towers of castles can become a focal point of the social landscape. Even commercial skyscrapers, such as the now-destroyed Twin Towers of the World Trade Center, can serve an important orientating function simultaneously at the local and regional scale. A collection of towers is appropriate for medical research, at least in part, because the fundamental preoccupation of medicine is, after all, defence of the first temple – the human body. Medicine holds the promise of making human bodies free from disease. If medicine serves, cares for and protects life by conserving or returning health, medical research is the sentinel of medicine.

The Richards towers also gesture toward the campus. In a remarkable way, they are a marker that stands sympathetically between the Gothic revival buildings of the old campus, including the residential Quad standing before them, and the promise of an emergent modern campus. The brick and concrete of the Richards towers are analogous to the brick and stone of the Quad and share a balance of material and colour with them and other buildings of the pre-existing campus. Not surprisingly, the Richards towers also share a pronounced verticality with the earlier neo-Gothic campus buildings; both announce an upward striving for enlightenment.

There are other references as well; the Richards towers refer to Frank Lloyd Wright's Larkin Building in Buffalo, New York, 1903 (demolished in 1950 to make way for a parking lot.) The Larkin Building was an administration building notable for the separation of services into independent towers that freed up internal space. As such, Wright's building explored, much earlier and in a somewhat tentative way,

9.1
**Richards Medical
Research Building,
Philadelphia,
1958–1960.
Architect:
Louis I. Kahn**
Source: Louis I.
Kahn Collection,
The Architectural
Archives of the
University of
Pennsylvania

what after the Richards towers became Kahn's defining approach: careful articulation of what he called *servant* and *served* spaces such that each thing has its own clearly defined place in a building. At the Richards Building he was particularly interested in moving contaminated air away from the researchers; at the Salk he elaborated on *servant* and *served* spaces through the distinct characterization of rooms for work, reflection or rest, as distinct from each other but even more so as distinct from spaces set aside for circulation and services.

A crucial difference, however, between the Larkin Building and the Richards Laboratories is that whereas the former was a highly defended collection of masonry blocks and towers that appeared impenetrable, the latter is as elegant *as* it is defended. An additional difference shows up in the organization of interior spaces: at the Larkin clerical workers occupied an enclosed central space at the bottom, easily observed by upper management above and surrounding them; spaces within the Richards towers highlight the individual efforts of scientists at work. In any event, Wright's building was paternalistic whereas Kahn attempted to maximize research as an endeavour of wonder and creativity.[10] Kahn's description of his main concerns for the Richards Laboratories discloses how his preoccupations for the building were divided equally between the technical requirements of scientific research and how to appropriately express its character as cultural work:

> I simply said, in a university building which was a laboratory for medical people, that the air you breathe should never come in contact with the air you throw away. That's all. Then I said that a scientist is like an artist – he is like an architect: he does not like to work as they do at M.I.T., in corridors with names on them. He likes to work in a kind of studio. A place which he can call all his own, or with his confrères, working on a problem.[11]

Kahn, Salk's visionary

Salk first learned of Kahn after a talk the architect gave in Pittsburgh. He approached him in December 1959 to seek his advice for selecting an architect to design the Institute of Biological Studies (later called the Salk Institute) that he intended to build in La Jolla, California (just north of San Diego). In the event, Salk selected Kahn as the architect for his Institute in light of personal first impressions rather than in response to their subsequent tour of the Richards Medical Research Laboratories. Money to set up the Institute came from the March of Dimes; the San Diego city council donated the land for it. Salk's fame and fortune, which enabled him to embark on such a project, came as a reward for his development of the first safe and effective polio vaccine, released on 12 April 1955 in the United States.

Kahn recollected his first encounter with Salk and their visit to the Richards Laboratories many times. Retrospectively, it is not surprising that Salk, considering his broad interests, would retain Kahn to develop a project intended to go far beyond mere functionality. Of course, he was also concerned with determining an appropriate size for his needs so that he could commission a convenient and functional building, but he was, it seems, most impressed with Kahn's ability to make something special out of a laboratory building:

> I am designing a unique research laboratory in San Diego, California. This is how the program started. The director, a famous man, heard me speak in Pittsburgh. He came to Philadelphia to see the building I had designed for the University of Pennsylvania. We went out together on a rainy day. He said, 'How nice, a beautiful building, I didn't know that a building that went up in the air could be so nice. How many square feet do you have in this building?' I said, 'One hundred and nine thousand square feet.' He said, 'That's about what we need.'[12]

Salk's desire for an architecture that could accommodate the primary requirement of a laboratory, that it be a place where it is good to do experimental research, was enlarged further by his conviction that an expanded notion of what a research environment ought to comprise would concurrently enhance its cultural role while augmenting the potential of scientists working there. Kahn highlighted this in another description of his first encounter with Salk.

> It has to be a laboratory, we are interested in one thing – we believe that cancer does not belong to medicine. We believe it belongs to population, not to medicine. We believe we can have people come in who can use their minds, who have powers of realization. What do you think the building should be like?[13]

Salk's initial impression of Kahn's capabilities, that he could provide a setting of the right size and do it beautifully, encouraged him to further elaborate on his desire that the Institute should become a place of encounter for scientists, artists and humanists. His embrace of a link between science and art as realms of shared creative inquiry was a powerful conception, which Kahn put into play in the invention of the Institute. Salk encouraged this line of enquiry by placing few restrictions upon his architect, which set Kahn free to develop the possibilities of the project. Salk's primary concern for the Institute remains abundantly clear in Kahn's recollection of what his client most desired:

> He said 'There is one thing I would like to be able to accomplish. I would like to invite Picasso to the laboratory.'[14]

Kahn took this to mean that Salk was seeking a setting where the *measurable*, quantifiable, could coexist with the *unmeasurable*, that which resists measure.

In the problem he set for himself, Kahn saw potential for a fundamental corrective to the limitation he believed continued to bedevil science; that it is overwhelmingly concerned with what *is*, whereas it ought to be more like art, which concerns itself with what *isn't yet*. While Salk observed this limitation in technoscience, he did not see it as a problem confronting the higher, more independent realms of research, of the sort members of his Institute would engage in. Nonetheless, no matter how hard he tried to reconcile the two, Kahn continued to see the measurable and unmeasurable as opposed, even though he believed that the 'wish in the fairy tale is the beginning of science'.[15]

Salk was much more at home with the idea that the unmeasurable and measurable form parts of an interdependent whole. Though Kahn may not have been able to resolve the antagonism he saw between art and science as fully as Salk could, the two nonetheless remained in fundamental agreement. Near the end of his life, Kahn recalled his collaboration with Salk in a manner that suggests he did finally come to see it as possible to reconcile the measurable with the unmeasurable:

> At the Salk Institute of Biological Studies, two of the buildings are not yet built but one is. Salk told me that he wanted to have a laboratory to which he could invite Picasso. He stayed overnight in Philadelphia to talk. I came up with the idea that what he wanted was a place of the *measurable*, which is a laboratory, and a place of the *unmeasurable*, which would be the meeting place. Biology is not just scientific or a simple task of finding that which is measurable. There is an *unmeasurable* quality, even in matters scientific [original italics].[16]

It is worth noting that in the quote, Kahn alludes to the three institutions he envisioned for the Salk Institute: a meeting place, housing, and laboratories, of which only the laboratories were constructed. (It is also worth noting that the reference to Picasso was particularly close to Salk's heart. In 1970, Salk married the artist Francoise Gilot, who had previously been involved with Picasso.) Interestingly, although Salk shared Kahn's belief that scientists are like artists, he was unconvinced by the studio-like laboratories at the Richards Laboratories. Instead, his preference was for open-plan lab-spaces, which have proved to be infinitely more adaptable than would be possible in studio-sized labs.

Their initial disagreement, and its resolution in Salk's favour, has had a profound impact on the endurability of the Salk Institute as a viable and self-renewing research centre. Because open-plan labs facilitate change, they are able to accommodate the requirement of unanticipated changes in research habits. Equally

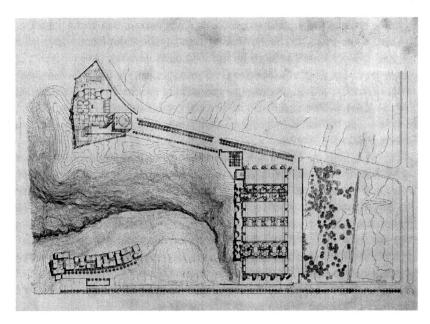

9.2
**Master plan. Salk
Institute for
Biological Studies,
La Jolla, CA,
c. 1961.
Architect:
Louis I. Kahn**
Source: Louis I.
Kahn Collection,
The Architectural
Archives of the
University of
Pennsylvania

9.3
**North–south
section through
laboratories and
service floors. Salk
Institute for
Biological Studies,
La Jolla, CA,
1959–1965.
Architect: Louis I.
Kahn.
Drawing by A. B.
Dixon**

important for the adaptability of the Salk is its novel section. Laboratory floors alternate with mostly clear-span service floors, the openness of which have permitted the introduction of new technologies and services without affecting the character of the building.

Kahn's world

As noted above, Salk brought few if any architectural preconceptions to the founding of his biological research institute. Most importantly, this included not burdening his architect at the outset with programmatic prescriptions to fill. His desire to find the feeling of an institution before committing either himself or his architect to any fixed spatial or functional requirements for it, beyond a specific amount of lab space, confirmed that he and Kahn shared an unconventional approach. Recalling his selection by Salk for the Institute project, Kahn remarked 'I had no program whatsoever', later elaborating on this by adding:[17]

> Without the restriction of a dictatorial program it became a rewarding experience to participate in the projection of an evolving program of spaces without precedence. This is only possible because the director is a man of unique sense of environment as an inspiring thing, and he could sense the existence will and its realization in form which the spaces I provided had.[18]

By giving him only the vaguest suggestion of a programme, Salk encouraged Kahn to invent a new institution freely. Allowed such latitude, Kahn found inspiration in the fairy tales of human settings he had long been devising, which included an inquiry into the qualities of buildings he had yet to project. His was a fundamentally future-oriented approach, permitting exploration of various institutions according to a conviction that the circumstances of a building are secondary to the necessity of determining the kind of setting in which it would be good to enact the events a building is intended to house.

In a house, for example, 'In a certain space it is good to sleep'.[19] Such a statement applies to all houses everywhere, yet it has nothing to do with a specific instance of house; all that is necessary is that a house, wherever and whenever it is brought into existence will have spaces where it is good to sleep, others where 'it is good to dine or be with others', and so on.[20] What these spaces will be is never fixed once and for all, but it is certain that if a house is going to become a place where it is good to live, it will have to respond to basic requirements that are the responsibility of the architect to re-establish. In addition to house, Kahn had fairy tales for institutions generally, and more specifically the room, street, city, school and library. For example, according to Kahn, school begins with a man under a tree:

> [T]alking to a few people about a realization he had – a teacher. He did not know he was a teacher, and those who listened to him did not consider themselves pupils or students. They were just there, and they liked the experience of being in the presence of one who had a realization – a sense of order. This is the way it began.[21]

Thus, a school where it would be good to learn must draw upon the origins of school as the satisfaction of a desire to know and to be around one who knows, but this in no way indicates that a school ought to be a tree or should in any way look like a tree. What is crucial is that the architect struggle to gain access to the original inspiration of school. According to Kahn, the street, as a place of agreement, is the first institution. The virtue of cities consists of their many streets:

> The city is the assembly of the institutions of man. In other words, the city is the place where the institution occurs to man. The gathering of man and legislation establishes the institution. I believe *availability* is a more meaningful word than institution. The measure of a city is the character of its availabilities, how sensitive it is to man's pursuit of well being. The traffic system and other needs are only the servants of availability.[22]

Armed with this approach, Kahn set out to invent the Salk Institute as a collection of institutions; a place of availabilities, where it would be good to do those things which each setting would be established to support. However, before Kahn could begin proposing shapes, he needed to develop a deeper understanding of the events he was charged with housing. He resisted any attempt to house the programme or to give visible forms to functions until he had a clear grasp of the availabilities implied by Salk's desires:

> The institution is not the building. The institution is the agreement to have that which is supported. It is an agreement that this kind of activity is natural to man. It is an undeniable part of the way of life.[23]

Kahn envisioned the Salk Institute as a small city whose primary spaces were laboratory, meeting place and living space. As a city, the Institute required specific settings for communal gathering, solitary contemplation, chance encounter, retreat and different kinds of work. Conceptualization of the Institute as something like a monastery was Salk's idea as much as it was Kahn's. The result reconciled the two courses Frampton argued remain open to architecture (discussed in Chapter 6). For example, the Salk 'is patently "visible"' and 'takes the form of a masonry enclosure that establishes within it's limited "monastic" enclosure a reasonably open but none-theless concrete set of relationships linking man to man and man to nature'.[24] It is also 'well-serviced' and in harmony with modern technology.

      Overall, the Institute is an example of what Frampton considered the 'sole hope for creative [architectural] discourse in the immediate future': 'creative contact between modern technology and a limited monasticism'.[25] The monastic analogy is not a stretch, as both Salk and Kahn had monasteries in mind, which, among other characteristics, associates the building with La Tourette.[26]

As a form of life, monasticism remains a powerful model of how individual and collective can come together for mutual benefit. Monasteries model a social order based on dedication to a shared purpose. As such, they present a challenge to a social life that is diffuse, highly specialized, competitive and extremely individualistic. Psychological and social confrontation of this sort can present itself in spatial practices by establishing forms that oppose the physical sprawl of modern development with a comprehensible compactness.

Nevertheless, the experience of modernity, which includes a weakening of enclosed social and spatial practices, such as those presented by monastic life, has brought with it an openness of possibility that makes any return to a closed society difficult to imagine. Therefore there exists a tension between holism, which Kahn and Salk desired, and the inevitable dissipation of social life and its settings, which corresponds with secularization: it is just this tension that Kahn and Salk sought to address at the Salk Institute. Paradoxically, the diffuse sprawling environment of modernity is in alliance with the *measurable* (science in Kahn's mind) while the enclosed and more readily comprehensible environment of monasteries is in alliance with the *unmeasurable* (art in Kahn's mind). Salk, though a scientist, was sympathetic to this view. His retreat to the Monastery of San Francesco in Assisi, in the early 1950s, during a difficult stretch of research work confirms this:

> The spirituality of the architecture there was so inspiring that I was able to do intuitive thinking far beyond any I had done in the past. Under the influence of that historic place I intuitively designed the research that I felt would result in a vaccine for polio. I returned to my laboratory in Pittsburgh to validate my concepts and found that they were correct.[27]

Salk's sensitivity to the potential benefits of a setting led him to desire an environment where scientists could engage in intuitive research that was also equipped with laboratory facilities where they could attempt to test the soudness of their findings. In a sense, the Salk, like La Tourette, is an attempt to invent a setting for an institution adapted to the epoch *after* modernity. Even so, much as Salk and Kahn drew inspiration from monasteries as models for their new institution, they were both shrewd enough to recognize the impossibility of negating transformations (social, spatial and technological) that have occurred. As early as the 1940s, Kahn had begun developing his understanding of the difficult encounter between ancient and modern:

> Some argue that we are living in an unbalanced state of relativity, which cannot be expressed with a single intensity of purpose. It is for this reason, I feel, that many of our confrères do not believe we are psychologically constituted to convey a quality of monumentality to our buildings.[28]

Even though relativity seems inevitably to preclude monumentality, Kahn acknowledged that a desire to mark one's own time or place is a permanent condition of being human. Individuals and communities have a psychological need to make their lived world recognizable. Kahn's conviction was that psychological need, as the basis for emotional desire, is an architectural topic that is far from exhausted:

> But have we yet given full architectural expression to such social monuments as the school, the community, or cultural center? What stimulus, what movement, what social or political phenomenon shall we yet experience? What event or philosophy shall give rise to a will to commemorate its imprint on our civilization? What effect would such forces have on our architecture?[29]

As one of the persistent themes of architecture, monumentality endures because it is at the root of how human occupation of some place can distinguish it from all other places. It is impossible, though, to intentionally create monumentality. Any attempt to do so, believed Kahn, would be as hopeless as endeavouring to achieve monumentality by resurrecting superseded circumstances. Monumentality, as a quality, such as the Salk has, could only enter a work through a deep feeling for the original and contemporary inspiration of a particular institution.

Land and building

In Jonas Salk, Kahn found a like-minded spirit and a favourite client who gave him an opportunity to project what at least one contemporary publication described as 'Salk's ambitious castle'.[30] Kahn worked out his scheme for the Salk in great detail, particularly by distinguishing the character and location of the three main parts that would constitute the research village – laboratories, meeting place and residences. He did this so that each of the three key programmatic areas would lend itself to specific expression of the individual events that so intrigued him. He further delineated these so that servant and served spaces could be both provided for and recognizable as distinct:

> The original concept of the three parts which expresses the form of the Salk Institute – the laboratory, the meeting place, the living place – has remained. The acceptance of the separation has made Dr. Salk my most trusted critic.[31]

Division of the complex into three primary use groups remained a possibility throughout design and construction of the project. Salk's willingness to accept Kahn's elaborate scheme for the institution (even if only as a future possibility) inspired him throughout the process and long after. Ultimately, only the two laboratory buildings and the court between them were constructed (during the 1990s, Anshen + Allen architects added two additional buildings to the Institute).

Interpretation of the site is the beginning of any project. For example, Kahn sited the three separate parts he envisioned for the Salk in such a way as to uncover and accentuate the unique qualities of the land. This approach depended on his ability to see potential for a setting that could orient occupation and use in the absence of the buildings not yet constructed. Kahn interpreted the Salk Institute site, located at the head of and around a dramatic canyon facing the Pacific Ocean, in just this way. His positioning of each of the three main uses clarified the institution's occupation of the land while accentuating the site's unique topography and its role in the invention of the institution.

9.7
**Plan, current state,
including
additions. Salk
Institute for
Biological Studies,
La Jolla, CA.
Architect:
Louis I. Kahn.
East Building
addition, architect:
Anshen + Allen,
Los Angeles, 1995.
Drawing by
A. B. Dixon**

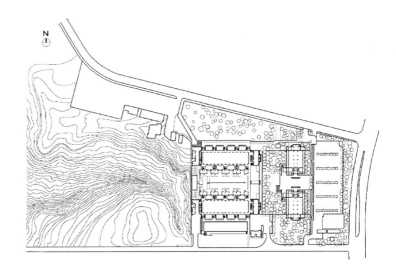

The laboratories were sited furthest inland to the east end of the development area at the head of the canyon, which opens before them, spreading outwards toward the Pacific Ocean. The residential component, located some distance in front of the laboratories, would have defined the south edge of the canyon (and the site). The meeting place, which Kahn described as a castle or chateau, would have defined the north edge of the canyon. As envisioned by Kahn, the meeting place would have occupied the broad plateau directly across the canyon from the living place, some distance in front of the laboratories and slightly to the north-west of them in the direction of the ocean. Such an arrangement would have maximized the natural virtues of the site, but it would also have clarified use by rendering each element comprehensible in terms of its location.

For example, as built, the court between the laboratories is the focal point of the Institute, its location at the head of the canyon calls attention to this. However, had the meeting place and living place also been built, the court and laboratories would have been even more clearly identifiable as the core of the complex. The living place would have extended a perpendicular line moving westward from the laboratories, and the thinness of the residences would have clarified this edge of the site; their position facing into the canyon would have emphasized the private nature of the living space. The shape of the meeting place, located on a broad plateau, would have been roughly square. Its omni-directional shape would have underscored its role as a forum of exchange, making it a link between the laboratories (measurable) and sea and sky (unmeasurable). This location would have also pinned down the north-west corner of the site by emphasizing the character of the land at this spot.

Kahn's thoughtfulness in siting the complex, including the small part actually constructed, depended on his elaborating on a vision of it as a potential whole, informed by careful interpretation of site and institution. Because of this, his world-making objectives, in the play between site and building, remain comprehensible even though only a fragment of the whole was constructed. Kahn began his interpretive process by resonating with the site, drawing inspiration from it for the institution he was inventing:

> The choice of the site of Torrey Pines, La Jolla, San Diego, overlooking the sea and protected surrounding park and university property is the first inspiring act towards creation of the environment for the Institute for Biology. From the presence of the uninterrupted sky, the sea and the horizon, the clear and dramatic configuration of weather beaten land spare of foliage, the buildings and their foliage must find their position in deference to Nature.[32]

As constructed, the Salk Institute effectively accentuates those things about its site that inspired it. First, because all buildings ultimately decay and fall into ruin (assuming they are not demolished prematurely), they are, in effect, always positioned 'in deference to nature'. The sparse plaza that links and separates the two identical laboratory buildings further emphasizes this, as it is something of a sundial or suncatcher. The weather-beaten teak infill panels are an expression of how human conquest of nature by building is never more than tentative. These panels form the walls of all rooms (studies, offices, administration and cafeteria) that are neither service nor laboratory. The four perimeter walls of the six laboratories (three in each building) are glass-filled steel frames. Windowless and nearly windowless concrete conveys service areas throughout. The central plaza (or court) is paved with travertine, and includes travertine benches, while a watercourse defines its central axis. In addition to these materials, light and shadow play a significant space-defining role at the Salk.

The Salk court is the building's signature feature, yet it was a long journey from Kahn's initial desire to fill the space between the laboratories with trees to its present austerity. Interestingly, it was not exclusively Kahn's invention. He consulted with Mexican architect Louis Barragan (1902–1988), who suggested that the plaza should be free of obstructions.[33] Barragan argued that it 'should be a plaza of stone not a garden. If you make this a plaza, you will gain a facade – facade to the sky'.[34] In his own architectural work, Barragan mastered the use of water as a material. In his hands, water became a kind of moving solid, usually flowing through well-defined channels that empty out into a pool (as it does at the Salk).

Barragan's use of water, particularly at the Salk, refers to earlier models, especially the Lions' Court at the Alhambra in Granada, Spain (thirteenth–fourteenth centuries). Besides a similar organization of directional water channels in a court, Barragan's symbolic intent for the Salk appears to have been consistent with Islamic garden courts, again at the Alhambra.[35] Enclosed Islamic gardens, such as the Lions' Court, refer to and are representations of two principal sources: Solomon's temple and paradise.[36] Accordingly, the Salk is as much an enigmatic monument as it is both a garden and a marker that mediates between built platform and natural expanse. This is reasonable enough considering that, after all, biological research concerns the very essence of life and creation.

9.8
**Looking east
across canyon.
Salk Institute for
Biological Studies,
La Jolla, CA,
1959–1965.
Architect:
Louis I. Kahn**

9.9
**Plaza looking
west. Salk
Institute for
Biological Studies,
La Jolla, CA,
1959–1965.
Architect:
Louis I. Kahn**

The stark combination of colours and materials of the Salk Institute work together with the disposition of its forms to establish a site platform that defines a presence amidst, as Kahn described it, the 'uninterrupted sky, the sea and the horizon, the clear and dramatic configuration of weather beaten land spare of foliage'. Orchestration of these features allows the building to become an event of the landscape without either dominating it or suppressing itself. The Salk is a human-made realm that orients occupants to their tentative location within the vast natural expanse, by carefully interpreting all the natural forces at play in its immediate environment. A day in the court is very much like a day at the beach under the movements of the sun, sea, sky and moon.

9.10
Sunning at the Salk. Salk Institute for Biological Studies, La Jolla, CA, 1959–1965. Architect: Louis I. Kahn

Partially closed, partially open

Even though it is possible to slip into the central court of the Salk at several points, especially from the main entry to the east, the organization of the complex presents a closed aspect toward the outside world. From the north, south and east the Institute seems surrounded by impenetrable solid walls. What is remarkable is that even though the Salk is actually permeable, its overall aspect is both defended and monastic, which reveals it as a setting concurrently open to public visits that provides private retreat for its researcher occupants. Towers housing servant uses requiring little or no light wrap the laboratories on the north, south and east outward facing

9.11
**North elevation.
Salk Institute for
Biological Studies,
La Jolla, CA,
1959–1965.
Architect:
Louis I. Kahn**

sides of the building, establishing the closed–open condition of the complex. There are ten service towers in all, five on the north side and five on the south side. Together they present an apparently solid concrete face outward on the north and south sides of the building. Stairs, elevators or lavatories fill each of the ten towers.

A massive windowless concrete structure defines the east-facing side of both the north and south laboratory buildings; each is filled with services including air-handling units, transformer units, mechanical room, electrical room, incinerator, storage, photo lab and an inward-facing special laboratory in both wings. These structures flank the main point of entry and extend beyond the edge of the court to form a transition zone that marks movement from the outside of the complex into its main symbolic space (the central court). A subtle change in level further emphasizes this transition. As one moves from the east to the west, from the outside inward, it is necessary to climb several steps to reach a slab that effectively forms a bridge between two areas planted with lime trees. These planted areas flanking the bridge rise slightly above it to further enclose and define it as a link and separator. The trees elaborate the closed–open nature of the Salk, legible even though fences surround all openings into the complex, and are locked in the evening.

9.12
**East front. Salk
Institute for
Biological Studies,
La Jolla, CA,
1959–1965.
Architect:
Louis I. Kahn**

From the vantage point on top of the entry bridge, the Salk still appears defended and impenetrable. All one sees when facing west from this point are angled sheer concrete walls facing into the court and the horizon beyond. From this point, the court opens up toward the vastness of sky and sea beyond. Depending on the light, these two apparently infinite bodies can appear as one. Only the sun, which presents itself through its play on the architecture and in the sky, is able to separate sky from sea as it defines both. The drama of this entry point, where the vastness of the unknown (the *unmeasurable*) eclipses the individual, silently demands a pause. Here, the sense that inquiry is never complete is brought home with majestic power – an emotion appropriate for encounters with both art and science – before one has entered the laboratories, or even the court.

From the entry bridge, it is a few steps down into the court. A water channel inscribes the centre-line between the mirrored buildings, emphasizing the westward processional flow of the complex. The watercourse, whose colour alters with the changing light of the sky, begins at the eastern end of the court in a raised blocky square of travertine. It then flows westward to a pool invisible from the vantage point of the entry point, definitively ending – at the plaza level – with a waterfall beyond that drops in stages to pools in the lower court.

Even though this channel clearly inscribes westward movement through the court, reinforced by the angled walls gesturing toward the canyon, sea, sky and sun beyond, a long travertine bench, perpendicular to the entry bridge and parallel with steps down from it, blocks the way, demanding a shift of position to either the left or right. With this necessary move off the westward axis, the building begins to reveal itself as simultaneously closed *and* open. Exploration of the north and south sides of the building reveals a similar quality. With this movement, what at first appeared to be impenetrable towers reveal open slots in the corners, but only when seen from the west. Movement along, around and through the complex toward the west also reveals the glass walls of the laboratories, which are in shadow behind deep protective walkways.

9.13
Fountain fall. Salk Institute for Biological Studies, La Jolla, CA, 1959–1965. Architect: Louis I. Kahn

Although the laboratories have glass walls, the floors above and below them nevertheless extend far enough to project a highly defensive aspect. Service floors between the second and third laboratory levels and on top of the third laboratory level (including an invisible service floor between the first and second laboratory levels) have narrow slits in the wall that further emphasize the closed–open defensive nature of the complex. Approach toward the service towers reveals that deep black voids visible in them are penetrable. The first and fifth of these provide access directly into the inner court. Actually, the disposition of these outer towers is defensive. Aside from allowing the building to communicate its own security, everything has been calculated to protect the laboratories from the extremes of direct sunlight and glare of southern California. In the central court, defence against glare and the self-defensive nature of the building is especially apparent.

9.14
Sun control. Salk Institute for Biological Studies, La Jolla, CA, 1959–1965. Architect: Louis I. Kahn

Westward movement through the court reveals that the gesturing angled walls are actually towers pulled away from the laboratories. Together, with walkways spanning between them, these towers establish an ambulatory opposite the laboratories on the ground level and balconies on the second level. Study cells for the principal scientists at the Salk, on the same level as the service floors and directly across from them, occupy the first and third levels of these towers. The towers' defensive purpose is to insulate the laboratories and the walkways fronting them from disturbance and glare but also to isolate the principal scientists in an optimal introspective environment. A dry 'moat' drops two levels down between the defensive layer of the towers and the laboratories on the court level. Its purpose is also protective, further insulating the laboratories from disturbance. It is also functional – it brings a surprising amount of natural light two levels down into the lowest laboratory.

Beyond the fifth service tower and a retaining wall, which are furthest to the west, the land drops down a level to reveal an additional floor. At this point, the building pulls in from the service tower to reveal a five-storey office wing capping the west end of both laboratory wings. These buildings have openings framed in the

9.15
Study cells. Salk Institute for Biological Studies, La Jolla, CA, 1959–1965. Architect: Louis I. Kahn

9.16
Office wing. Salk Institute for Biological Studies, La Jolla, CA, 1959–1965. Architect: Louis I. Kahn

same weathered teak infill panels used on the walls facing north, south and west. There is also a loggia on the ground floor and a partial one on the first floor of the office wings attached to both the north and south buildings, which partially frame the main court above and lower court.

A pair of massive concrete **L**s, shields the rest of the complex behind them while forming the backdrop of the lower court, which is where institute fellows and staff can meet to share an outdoor meal, close to the cafeteria nearby. The concrete **L**s pull away from the main laboratory building while separating the office wing from the westward side of the angled sheer concrete walls mentioned above. From this prospect, the sheer walls that appeared solid from the east now disclose both their occupation and openness. From the west, it is possible to observe that these occupied walls also have windows framed within weathered teak panels. The sheer walls are actually projections extending out from towers made up of alternating open and closed levels, pulled away from the laboratories. It is only when facing east and inward into the court from the west that the complex reveals itself as quite open.

Movement westward from the north or south while facing east, especially in the central court, reveals the Salk Institute in all its openness. Even though the Institute's objective is to serve human beings generally, it projects a defensive prospect from the north, south and east to protect researchers from external distraction as they ponder the stubbornness of certain diseases. In a most eloquent gesture, the Institute opens toward the west, toward the infinite sea and sky beyond. It opens as well toward a declining sun falling into the western horizon, which, rather than symbolizing defeat, implies a humbling of metaphysical hubris, indicating, perhaps, acceptance that there will always be more questions, most unanswerable. Thus, in this honorific limited monastic setting – with inner court, defensive outer walls, study-cells and ambulatories – dedicated as it is to scientific research and the cure of intransigent disease, charity reveals itself as an embodiment of the most desirable qualities of Western religion surviving into a secular age.

Chapter 10

Aldo van Eyck's utopian discipline

I am again concerned with twinphenomena; with unity and diversity, part and whole, small and large, many and few, simplicity and complexity, change and constancy, order and chaos, individual and collective; with why they are ignobly halved and the halves hollowed out; why too they are withheld from opening the windows of the mind![1]

Aldo van Eyck

An enriched reality

By now it will, hopefully, seem quite reasonable to suggest that utopias are stories very much like architectural projections. Both forms of expression argue with existent conditions, draw upon the past and augur a transformed future envisioned as superior to the present. Aldo van Eyck (1918–1999), the focus of this and the following chapter, told his utopian architectural stories in three principal ways: written presentation of his vision, emblematic expression of it and various attempts to realize it with buildings. Van Eyck's essay 'Steps Toward a Configurative Discipline' (1962) was a compelling textual expression of his *story*; the Amsterdam Orphanage (1957–1960), discussed in the following chapter, was among his most convincing constructed expressions of it, and the Otterlo Circles (1959) was an exemplary emblem of it. In each, van Eyck transcribed an increasingly enriched expression of his utopian vision for a new dynamic reality.

'Steps Toward a Configurative Discipline' stands as van Eyck's most comprehensive statement of his architectural principles.[2] It was an attempt to elaborate on a systematic working method, *a configurative discipline*, which, according to van Eyck, would entail exploration of dynamic complexity that could be organized fugally to maintain a comprehensive whole. He argued that his new theory and practice of architecture would deliver more compassionate human habitats than orthodox modern architecture could ever hope to deliver.

The essay is primarily a theoretical statement motivated by van Eyck's effort to draw principles out of his then recently completed and occupied Amsterdam Orphanage building. While the structure could aptly illustrate the intent of the essay, no illustrations of it, or of any building, were included with its original publication. Nor did van Eyck refer directly to his building in the essay text.

Without illustrations to direct or limit their understanding of his intentions, sympathetic readers have had to interpret his words according to their own imagination. Van Eyck's statement was a plea for enrichment of contemporary practice, rather than justification of one style over another: he wanted to let his words stand on their own without colouring a reader's sense of them. The message of 'Towards a Configurative Discipline' is generative rather than prescriptive; van Eyck was arguing for a shift in mentality, not a particular outcome.

Van Eyck wanted to evolve a way of thinking about architecture and urbanism that would be as widely applicable as it was free of any suggestion that constructed results should look a particular way. The record of his practice bears this out. Although he never abandoned the vision presented in his essay, the buildings he produced during the next four decades were never simplistic stylistic restatements of the discipline he proposed. What he demanded, though, is that buildings act in certain ways, which stands out as the utopian message of 'Steps Toward a Configurative Discipline'.

10.1
Hubertus House, Amsterdam, 1973–1981. Architect: Aldo van Eyck. Interior with Hannie van Eyck

10.2
**View of Tripolis
Office Complex,
Amsterdam,
1990–1994.
Architect: Aldo
van Eyck with
Hannie van Eyck**

What van Eyck proposed was no less than a way out of the limiting perspectives of abstract and academic twentieth-century architecture and urbanism. More precisely, he sought to reveal a richer whole than CIAM's reductive myth of four distinct functions (*housing, work, recreation (during leisure) and traffic*), parcelled out as isolated sectors in buildings and towns, could tolerate.[3] He argued that CIAM's four functions were far too *coarse* to provide places for the full complexity of life. For contemporary cities to be distinguishable from traditional ones, architects and urbanists would need to evolve a discipline capable of constituting enriched environments analogous to historical cities (without either mimicking them or neglecting what is uniquely modern), while learning from the combined cultural inheritance of developed, traditional and developing world cities and villages alike.

Whole parts

Unification of elements into a complex and legible larger whole, at all scales ranging from an individual building to an entire city, was the main objective of van Eyck's configurative discipline. Arrangements of this sort are capable of carrying multiple meanings (or multi-meaning, in van Eyck's terms), which would contribute to an object's enduring interest. In a more literal sense, configuration of a building entails enclosing space with structures that clearly express what they do; for example inside is usually separated from outside by walls, an arrangement of architraves held up by columns might support the roof, and so on. Together, these structural elements join to do a job but also remain legible as parts whole in themselves, simultaneously forming a larger whole.

Combining building elements into comprehensible patterns to form an evocative whole would result from more than a simple synthesis of constituent parts into an integrated structure. Accordingly, rather than getting lost, individual elements constitute a whole in which they remain intelligible as articulated forms in themselves. Harmonious arrangements of elements comprehensible as complete, of the sort van Eyck envisioned, surpass the individual meaning of each part by creating an intelligible overall form. If effectively configured, even buildings constructed from pieces more or less clipped together could be much more than the sum of the basic elements out of which they are assembled.

Practicing a configurative discipline would, van Eyck believed, make buildings and cities into comprehensible patterns, offering welcoming places for the human occasions they shelter. Configured places could be emotionally, sensually and intellectually perceptible as amiable settings for human relations precisely because they are rich enough to house desire and psychic anxiety. When not carefully articulated throughout (spatially, structurally and materially), as a set of determined relations between part and whole, buildings elude comprehensibility. The absence of readily legible patterns (configured out of parts) complex enough to sustain intelligibility and interest throughout an entire building or city, results in the undesirable condition of incomprehensibility. On the other hand, richly textured patterns and reciprocity among parts would make buildings and urban environments into what van Eyck called *counterforms*, forms that are complementary to human complexity and interrelatedness because they can receive and contain existence in all its contradictory depth.

Appearance is important, but it is not the whole story, even if the first perception of any place is by sight. Rather, physical and psychological tangibility of an enclosure as a place arguably offers a fuller experience. Places become present through a fitting together of a certain number of things in particular ways. Configured places, though, are perceptible as such only when it is possible to make physical and psychological associations with them. Hence, a configured place will invite movement through it. Configured architecture is figurative; it is not a literal representation of social forms, but rather analogizes relationships and interdependencies by establishing places for them.

When configured into a whole, elements combine to establish a significance far surpassing their individual connotative and denotative potential. For example, a single column is *readable* as a support, a standing human figure, or both structural support and figure. When combined in one setting, many columns together begin to form a community of bodily figures working in unison without losing their individuality. Conceived of in this way (as columns have long been), they connote human uprightness in addition to being necessary structural supports.

In van Eyck's Amsterdam Orphanage, for example, two columns surmounted by an architrave form the basic structural and communicative unit of the building. Four such units joined at right angles to one another define a square in two dimensions and a cube in three; these form the basic spatial cells out of which the building is assembled. A dome caps each individual unit, except in a few instances where a much larger dome surmounts nine such units grouped together, to form a larger square or cube. Arranged in this manner, all of the elements combine to define a configuration of cellular units forming a complex body much richer, connotatively and denotatively, than a standing column alone could.

Configuration of elements into a form is not simply a literal expression of structure; the result is as figurative as it is analogical. It operates metaphorically – a body is a building and a building is a body. Both are indivisible wholes made from parts. Moreover, a body is also like a building and a building is like a body: both are complex wholes that gesture and relate. Building gesture and relation emerge as perceptible through reference to human occasions that buildings make places for. Thus, individual bodies and communities of interacting bodies figure significantly in van Eyck's configurative discipline, not only because a body is a figure or a shape but because a configured place is a setting for forms of human conduct and the human forms that enact it.

Configured places gain in familiarity (meaning) when assembled from individual units intelligible as analogues of individual bodies. Bodies and buildings are unities harmonized from diversity (not simply a synthesis of it). In both, individuality is identifiable through a relation to a collective. Modern buildings are unique wholes made from extensible parts; analogously, an embodied person can elaborate his or her uniqueness only as a member of a collective.

Relativity

Van Eyck's architectural ideas as elaborated on in 'Steps Toward a Configurative Discipline' were an outgrowth of his understanding of relativity. This understanding is a theory based on the hypothesis that all motion is relative, suggesting that understanding is always relational rather than absolute. In relativity, he saw a world view that could make a configured architecture imaginable. Since any particular cultural perspective is partial at best, other views, distant in space and time, promise to make valuable contributions to elaboration of a comparatively more complete conception of reality, which could reasonably inform much richer architectural practices.

Relativity theory states that although light has a constant velocity, there is no observable absolute motion, only relative motion. Accordingly, time is relative. Space and time are interdependent, while form is a four-dimensional continuum. The consequence of such a conviction is that while all motion (action, behaviour) may be situational, in that it occurs in the way it does according to the circumstances of its setting, it is nevertheless relational because it occurs under the same light and is made up of the same particulate matter. Modern thinking of this kind informed van Eyck's visits with traditional cultures; he saw in the ancient and the distant simultaneously situational and relational outcomes.

Drawing upon ideas of relativity, van Eyck believed that universal and local, ancient and modern, as well as classical and vernacular could all coexist alongside each other to the benefit of all, which his Otterlo Circles emblematized. In terms of architectural practices, he imagined he would find in the unique expressions of each epoch and place, but especially in the responses of pre-industrial societies to particular circumstances, clues to how advanced Western societies could humanize their own

10.3
**The Otterlo
Circles, second
version of the
original design for
the CIAM
congress, Otterlo,
1959. Aldo van
Eyck**
Courtesy of Hannie
van Eyck

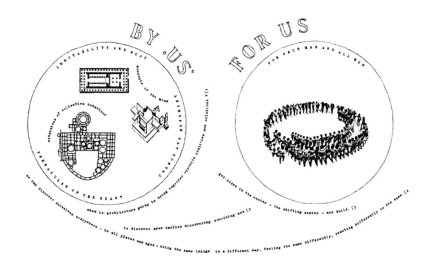

habitats. In light of the importance of relativity for van Eyck, is crucial to emphasize that relativity is not relativism. Because relativity proposes a reality made up of interdependent relations, it is ultimately a theory of unity. Relativism, on the other hand, is a vision of atomized reality.

Reciprocity

According to van Eyck, the interdependent relations of relativity form a web of reciprocal associations. In certain respects, reciprocity describes relativity and by extension, the kind of interdependent relations a configured architecture facilitates. Reciprocity is primarily a condition of mutuality understandable as a back and forth relation. For example, although conventional wisdom tends to understand inside and outside as opposites, reciprocity shows them to be complementary. One is a counterpart of the other. Accordingly, inside and outside have an equivalent rather than an opposed value. Even so, they are not the same.

Reciprocity is a mutual action characterized by a balanced give and take. For a building 'to breathe both in and out (as we do)', as van Eyck demanded, its organization would need to be in accord with the balanced give and take of reciprocity. Most importantly, for reciprocity to occur as *twinphenomena* (see below), articulation of both/and relations must not result in *this* versus *that* conditions, or be rendered as an abstraction of some condition of reality. Van Eyck argued that as a coequality of parts, reciprocity can make the lived realm comprehensible and full, legible because articulation of each part, including rooms and houses (but not only these), would establish a web of determined relations.

Twinphenomena

Van Eyck's notion of reciprocity, although it suggests reconciliation of split phenomena, has little to do with Robert Venturi's notion of *complexity and contradiction* (discussed in Chapter 5), which presents twinphenomena binarily as a display of irreconcilable oppositions. Reconciliation of *twinphenomena*, though, does not subsume individual parts into a new, fully unified entity. Rather, *twinphenomena* suggests the coexistence of individual parts conventionally characterized as split phenomena, associated as elements of a richer whole. The coming together of these parts, however, requires an additional condition, but this harmonizes rather than reduces them; van Eyck named this the *inbetween realm*, which forms a third place, or threshold, that links as it separates two previously opposed conditions.[4]

Van Eyck's idea of part/whole interrelatedness is analogous to his conviction that human beings are everywhere *both* the same *and* different, which clarifies his sense that all traditions can inform any tradition – a conviction derived from reciprocity as an organizing principle learned from his understanding of relativity. The principles of relativity may be universal but not absolute (relations occur everywhere, though differently in response to specific local conditions, natural as well as human-made). This application of the principles of relativity to a method, such as a configurative discipline, depends on the particular situation of their individual elaboration. Principles may be widely applicable in the abstract but actual conditions inflect these when practiced locally.

Twinphenomena are counterparts coexisting in reciprocal relation to one another, which is why van Eyck believed they could rejoin abstractly split phenomena such as inside and outside. The possibility of giving such both/and conditions expression suggests how buildings might begin to embody the richest possible social and emotional experiences by becoming counterforms to them. Demonstration of this occurs at the Orphanage where, in places, inside is like outside (such as the interior street) and outside places next to it are like inside places (enclosed, or covered, outdoor spaces), where inside slips into outside (and vice versa). At the threshold to the entry court of the Orphanage, for example, a sequence of associated places unfolds in such a way that outside becomes increasingly like an inside, mostly through changing levels of enclosure that shift from open to closed.

> [I]t is still a question of twinphenomenon, a question of making the inbetween places where they can be encountered, readily mitigating psychic strain. What is direly needed is a dimensional change in both our way of thinking and working which will allow the quantitative nature of each separate polarity to be encompassed and mitigated by the qualitative nature of twinphenomenon combined: the medicine of reciprocity.[5]

An architecture that *breathes* in and out is a unity made of coexistent diversity in which part and whole amplify the meaning of the each other, and that confounds inside and outside as absolute opposites. This was van Eyck's challenge to the Western tendency for binary thinking. His aim was nothing short of wanting to collapse false and non-productive oppositions, particularly the propensity for presenting *twinphenomena* as polar opposites. Examples of such thinking include the persistence in conceptualizing the mind and body as split and of individuals and collectives as divided into nearly irreconcilable opposites. Split reality is inimical to human beings because, according to van Eyck, we are psychically most at home in *inbetween realms*.

Inbetween

A human habitat, van Eyck argued, ought to provide for fundamental human ambivalence by reconciling *twinphenomena* in an *inbetween* realm. By doing so, buildings and cities could become *counterforms* to ambivalence among other individual and social conditions. Psychic anxiety is unavoidable, precisely because it is an emotional expression of the liminality of human existence, caught as it is in between the twinphenomena of the perpetual comings and goings that characterize individual experience:

> As soon as the equilibrating impact of the inbetween realm – extended so that it coincides with the bunch of places both house and city should be – manifests itself in a comprehensibly articulated configuration, the chances that the terrifying polarities that hitherto harass man's right composure may still be reconciled will certainly be greater.[6]

A paradox of the in-between realm – even though it is a counterform to ambivalence – is its 'equilibrating' potential. Ambivalence, when embraced by a both/and sensibility, rather than rejected by a narrow either/or mentality, could balance private and public experience because it suggests that, for example, 'both house and city' could become 'a bunch of places'. It permits this by inscribing the in-between realm of human beings in architecture, especially through articulation of windows and doors as direct presentations of this realm, which also includes streets, spaces between buildings, corridors, hallways, stairways, entry halls and so on.

Examination of van Eyck's work reveals just how much in-between places preoccupied him. For example, delayed entry into the Orphanage extends as a leisurely procession through carefully articulated light and dark – in-between – spaces, all of different sizes with different formal and social qualities. Each inbetween at the Orphanage is a carefully articulated linking/separating space of much greater significance than simply being residual, or a functional necessity for circulation:

> [M]ake a welcome of each door and a countenance of each window: make of each a place, because man's realm is the inbetween realm – the realm architecture sets out to articulate.[7]

Van Eyck's plea, it is worth noting, was no call for buildings to *look* like people. Rather, he wanted his buildings (buildings and cities generally) to be *biomorphic*, not *anthropomorphic*: the latter suggests that a building is humanlike, that it looks human. On the other hand, the former suggests that a building be lifelike, a place where it is good to live.

Right-size

By reconciling rather than resolving twinphenomena, the in-between realm encourages an approach in which each part is clearly articulated as equal but different. In turn, articulation of each part of a whole and the whole itself requires that each part be given what van Eyck named *right-size*, a condition arrived at by considering parts in terms of themselves and reciprocally with all other parts of any given whole.

When achieved, *right-size* renders a building (or city) comprehensible across each part of it and throughout the whole of it. Such places will be of the 'right-size', because they facilitate 'man's right composure', right because he would have his equilibrium in a realm attuned to the basic human condition of inhabiting inbetweens during the journey through life to death. In sum, right-size is a kind of twinphenomena made up of *both/and* reciprocal relationships:

> What has right-size is at the same time both large *and* small, few *and* many, near *and* far, simple *and complex*, open *and* closed; will further-more always be both part *and* whole and embrace both unity *and* diversity [original italics].[8]

As with other aspects of his configurative discipline, right-size is a desirable end, the aim of which is to assure specificity in an overall form. Van Eyck's interpretation of relativity as a universal principle was crucial for his conceptualization of right-size, which is not so much a question of absolute scale as it is a concern for the '*right or correct effect of size*'. In a sense, right-size is a question of size-propriety. As an objective, appropriateness is a general (universal) desire even though specific ideas about it may be situated both spatially and temporally. Likewise, positive manifestation of size-propriety depends on an enriched comprehension of the specific place and occasion of its occurrence. Interestingly, right-size analogizes the eurythmic relations among parts that occurs across human bodies.

> If a thing is too much and too little the same, it will also be too much and too little different. Right-size will flower as soon as the mild gears of reciprocity start working – in the climate of relativity; in the landscape of all twinphenomena.[9]

Unfortunately, the absence of right-size is all too common to architecture and urbanism designed and constructed since World War II. Very often, the result is indistinct environments with 'no room for emotion', which make settings of this sort 'a wasteland', characterized by rigid compartmentalization devoid of reconciling inbetweens.

The problem of vast number

Ever since the example of Joseph Paxton's Crystal Palace housing the Great Exhibition in London (1851) was built, contemporary architecture has become increasingly determined by the apparent advantages of modularized and industrialized construction techniques. Unfortunately, these advantages operate in a climate almost exclusively conditioned by economy and efficiency as ultimate virtues. Under such conditions, emotional need and desire for a built environment as a counterform to psychic distress must remain frustrated. Therein lies the failure of industrialized building technique (generally an assembly on site of parts prefabricated off site): first instances of repetitive units used in most building construction are typically so meagre that their qualitative vitality (associative potential) cannot survive beyond even the first instance of a particular unit.

In turn, repetition only highlights the emptiness of such elements; it is a problem that stubbornly resists the redress offered by ever more *interesting* visual forms or appliqué alone. The main problem is that each prefabricated element of a building is usually so large that when deployed individually, even more so when combined, it tends to defy comprehension. According to van Eyck, smaller scale prefabricated elements would be a partial solution to this.

If nothing else, a richer array of prefabricated elements could inscribe a greater degree of necessary complexity to any building assembly. As a problem of meaning, first instances of repetitive elements must be much more than *beautiful* to sustain figurative potential through each repetitive phase. The figurative potential of initial units, or elements, is sustainable across vast repetitions only when each begins with abundant connotative and denotative investment. In the first instance, such a requirement rebuffs ironic reuse of historical building elements, which tends to recast them as empty commodities. Unsettling and incomprehensible architecture is also rejected: both frustrate memory and anticipation, which are, after all, the primary sources of denotative and connotative potential in buildings.

According to van Eyck, vast number could be solved if 'significant content' were 'transposed through structural and configurative invention into architecture' at every stage of multiplication.[10] Yet, because the modularized construction industry so often determines building character, vast number continues to elude the capacity of most contemporary architects to master its configurative potential:

> Failure to govern multiplicity creatively, to humanize number by means of articulation and configuration has already led to the curse of the new towns!

> They demonstrate how the identity of the initial element – the dwelling – has hardly proved able to survive even the first multiplicative stage – those in Holland are terrifying examples of organized wasteland. The fact is that in most cases the initial elements had no identity to lose anyway![11]

Instead of establishing a configured whole, overly rationalized (unimaginative) approaches to vast number, utilizing excessively large multiple units of structural elements and cladding, generally results in buildings (or districts) that are emotionally flat and painfully monotonous. If vast repetitions of meagre initial modules have a propensity for banalizing the human habitat, it must fall upon architect/urbanists, not the building industry or clients, to bring to the problem the level of thoughtfulness it deserves.

Reciprocity, according to van Eyck, is a positive way to mitigate the problem of vast number. If repetitive units come under what he called the '*laws of dynamic equilibrium*', general conditions will never overwhelm individual elements. This is so because strong individual units (the particular), by virtue of their strength, could survive their first presentation and subsequent combination with other elements in a way that meagre units cannot.

Individual and particular elements would achieve enrichment by continuously reasserting their identity throughout any collection of assembled parts generalized as a whole. Van Eyck named this give and take between part and whole 'harmony in motion', which operates according to the 'laws of dynamic equilibrium': a balanced tuning of elements that impart 'rhythm to repetitive similar and dissimilar form'. Thus, individual, singular and particular units and elements not only show in their opposites but are also a part of them; in turn, all of the various parts together constitute the collective, plural and general (the whole); the column/architrave arrangement at the Orphanage for example.

> What is essentially similar becomes essentially different through repetition instead of what is but arbitrarily 'different' becoming arbitrarily 'similar' through addition.[12]

This story of richness, attained through repetition, has as much to do with configuring buildings, districts and cities as it does with how individuals find their place within collectives. Reciprocal, rather than dualistic (oppositional), relations might assure a happier outcome in both instances. The only way for legibility of part and whole to hold throughout a building (house or district) is when greater comprehensibility is sustainable at each stage of multiplication. This is achievable only when clearly defined places and elements are intelligible at all levels. Such wide-ranging environmental comprehensibility is a real possibility if careful articulation of determined relations occurs not only at the scale of individual buildings but also across districts and throughout entire cities:

> It is a question of multiplying dwellings in such a way that each multiplicative stage acquires identity through the significance of the configuration at that stage.
>
> I say, through the 'significance' of the configuration in order to make it clear that it is not merely a matter of visual form, since this alone would be purely academic, but of significant content transposed through structural and configurative invention into architecture.[13]

By providing amenable settings for social encounters, it is conceivable that reciprocal relations between houses and cities could support similar relations between individuals and society, and vice versa. Nonetheless, the built environment can only become a counterform to a society if that society *already* has a form. However, because contemporary society generally lacks a tangible social form, van Eyck believed counterforms to social relations would only come about once society adopted reciprocal relations between individual and collective. Once instituted, such reformed conditions might well encourage establishment of an analogous built environment as its counterform, which persists as the utopian desire provisionally presented by van Eyck's architecture. Actually, his buildings were settings for the very possibility of realizing his utopia.

House and city

Van Eyck's ideas on design, elaborated on in 'Steps Toward a Configurative Discipline' and at the Orphanage, are equally applicable to cities. Actually, his configurative approach is urbanistic in its very nature. The Amsterdam Orphanage is as much house as village; it carries implications for both. He argued that each house is a small city and each city a large house and that streets can be thresholds for both. His desire was for each citizen to be able to live and dwell concretely in his or her individual house as well as in his or her city at large. Van Eyck envisioned a habitat where individuals would feel at home in both city and house, precisely because they could recognize the two as interrelated:

> Now the object of the reciprocal images contained in the statement *make a bunch of places of each house and every city; make of each house a small city and of each city a large house* is to unmask the falsity which adheres to many abstract antonyms: adheres not merely to small versus large, many versus few, near versus far, but also to part versus whole, unity versus diversity, simplicity versus complexity, outside versus inside, individual versus collective, etc., etc. [original italics].[14]

In his association of city and house, van Eyck reveals his debt to Alberti, with whom he shared the conviction that houses are cities writ small and that cities are houses writ large. Thought of in this way, house and city pair up as part of an interdependent web in which every individual part is significant in itself and as a vital part of the whole it forms.

By linking house and city, van Eyck challenged what he considered the non-productive, even destructive, disciplinary separation of architects from urbanists. His conviction was that division of once-unified disciplines into opposed professional entities creates a mental climate for practice conditioned by abstract antonyms. Dualistic thinking is, in his view, antithetical to comprehensibility; it splits phenomena in two, opposing them across near-absolute divisions. The risk of this is a lived environment which is no longer comprehensible. Van Eyck was convinced that rejoining architecture to urbanism was fundamental for reforming both disciplines. The resulting single discipline would then be able to think of cities as house-like and houses as city-like.

It is worth noting, though, that he did not recommend his configurative discipline for application to already richly evocative and configured traditional cities. When an architect/urbanist makes projects for a persisting urban habitat, his or her responsibility, according to van Eyck, is to embrace existing conditions as a challenge. By entering into a fruitful interaction between past and present, designers can determine what the latter might inherit from the former as much as what the present could contribute to an understanding of the past. Dialogue and configuration of this sort helps to render newly developed areas both welcoming and comprehensible, despite their newness and production according to the logic of an industrialized and modularized building industry.

The cure van Eyck recommended to ameliorate the disciplinary separation of architects from urbanists is what he called 'the medicine of reciprocity'. If left untreated the result would be 'heterogeneous monotony', an apparent difference that is actually monotonous because 'the open space between them [individual buildings] is so casually articulated and emptied of every civic meaning that they loom up like oversized objects, pitilessly hard and angular, in a void'.[15] Considering that most buildings in city, suburb and rural settings are construed as autonomous objects set into isolated sites, even a cursory glance at new development throughout the world confirms the validity of van Eyck's lament.

By basing his configurative method on a repetition of 'essentially similar' parts, van Eyck could make diversity out of apparent sameness while resisting monotony. Moreover, this approach takes account of the realities of contemporary industrialized construction. In consciously confronting these realities, he was able to make a virtue of apparent limitations. He engaged modularized construction methods, yet resisted defeat by the tendency toward mindless standardization that they generally assure. Careful repetition of familiar parts permits a degree of legibility not possible with either arbitrary difference or thoughtless sameness, both of which are quickly transformed into stultifying monotony:

> Each individual dwelling possesses the potential to develop, by means of configurative multiplication, into a group (subcluster) in which the identity of each dwelling is not only maintained but extended in a qualitative dimension that is specifically relevant to the particular multiplicative stage to which it belongs. Whilst the resulting group is, in turn, fortified in the next multiplicative stage by a new identity which will again enrich that which precedes it.[16]

Enlightened architecture, of the sort suggested by van Eyck's utopian vision, could prefigure new or reformed social relations by becoming counterforms to these, even before they gained widespread acceptance. The Amsterdam Orphanage is an instance of such a building with potentially wider social implications for both cities and citizens. Because cities are good (desirable) rather than simply being accidents of history, practical necessities or even economic resources alone, van Eyck was vehement in his conviction that they will continue to play a crucial social and psychic role in the life of individuals:

> We must do all that can be done in our field to make each citizen know why it is good to live citizenlike in a city built for citizens, for a city is not a city if it is just an agglomeration for a very large 'population' – a meaningless accretion of quantities with no real room for anything beyond mere survival.[17]

No matter how emotionally and poetically reasonable van Eyck's vision was, it must remain a dream – a utopian vision – for so long as social, political and economic perspectives inimical to comprehensive thought continue to condition the education, practice and, maybe especially, procurement of architecture and cities. Indifference towards enriched visions of the human environment, as a place of multi-meaning configured from twinphenomena and reciprocal relations, remains the norm. In contradistinction to conventional architectural and urban practices, van Eyck called for the transformation of present conditions by challenging them. Key to realizing this would be a reversal of the common conception that cities are collections of unrelated parts governed by no qualitative organizing principle.

Application of a configurative discipline could render a city comprehensible by encouraging citizens to move through its many parts, as they inhabit them through use. The objective of this transformation is a proposal of form only inasmuch as constructed environments first present themselves to inhabitants as forms. Much more significantly, configured houses, districts, or whole cities, would provide a social benefit by modelling for inhabitants a vision of individual elements reconciled to a collective with which they could comfortably coexist. In a configured city, each part would link up reciprocally with all other parts, and to the whole. Configuration would not result in a decentralized city, nor in a city without a centre, rather it results in a patterned city of *multiple* centres – a city occupied by each citizen throughout:

> *Each citizen would thus 'inhabit' the entire city in time and space* . . . It may sound paradoxical but decentralization of important city-scale elements will lead to a greater appreciated overall homogeneity. Each subarea will acquire urban relevance for citizens that do not reside there. The urban image – awareness of the total urban cluster – is then no longer represented by personal place-reference, different for each citizen, and a center common to all, but, apart from such personal place-reference, by a gamut of truly civic elements more or less equally distributed and relevant to all citizens [original italics].[18]

The 'new reality' van Eyck envisioned would be made up of social places that analogize individual and collective relations. He did not intend these settings to form or dictate the outcome of the civic life they would house; they should not be deterministic in any way, no matter how carefully articulated. He believed that a configured setting – comprehensible at the local and general level – could encourage social interactions to occur in such places that would eventually evolve into a configured social whole.

He believed his project could be achieved because the structures he argued for would take account of human emotion and human being as in-between conditions, provided for by places where spontaneous occupation and elaboration of relations into expanding webs of association is possible. Configured rooms, houses, complexes and cities can articulate just such a realm of human being by situating inbetweens as a focus of human habitats, rather than attempting to eradicate them – as the rationalizing tendencies of urban renewal does.

Wholes and parts

> A city, however, is a very complex artifact and, like all artifacts, fits no pseudobiological analogy. It is a man-made aggregate subject to continual metamorphosis to which it either manages or fails to respond. Accordingly, it is either transfigured or disfigured. Our experience is founded on the latter, our hopes on the former – that is the plight we are in now.[19]

In a configured city, every citizen would be aware of the many parts that form it. Cities would have a centre legible at the macro level of the metropolis, as well as multiple centres legible at the micro level of the neighbourhood. According to van Eyck, the more or less even distribution of identifiable civic elements throughout a city's many centres would weave its individual areas together as viable parts of a potential whole. A city so configured would be intelligible as a whole, not because it is a juridical or economic agglomeration of population and infrastructure with a single geometric centre, but because citizens would have occasion to go where identifiable civic elements are located. Growing familiarity with a city's multiple parts and the memory of them would make it more comprehensible, which in turn would facilitate development of an effective cognitive map (or mental image) of it. Experience of a whole city as a *whole* would reveal it as a bunch of places, and the possession of all its inhabitants:

> At a city level many closely related identifying devices will be necessary to establish a rich scale of comprehensibility. Identifying devices can be artifacts – new or historical – or given by nature and more or less exploited. In the past it was often a church, a palace, a great wall, a harbor, a canal, an important street or square – often, too, a river, valley, hill, or seafront. Many of these are still valid beyond their visual impact.[20]

So-called urban regeneration continues to make cities less *city-like*. It usually employs a strategy to make cities more attractive as entertainment destinations. Transforming cities in this way requires suppression of those city-like qualities, especially the complexity of pattern that might make it less attractive to developers, revellers, shoppers and tourists. These particular consumers of cities seek out economy and efficiency above all else. Spontaneity is a threat to the repackaging of cities, even to a city seeking to recast itself as a party-town.

To accomplish regeneration of this sort, places accommodating an articulated in-between realm must be eradicated or, at the very least, be sterilized. Inevitably, a sanitized city is a city of extremes. It is a city of insides opposed to outsides, of good places opposed to bad, of rigidified oppositions. What it cannot be, therefore, is a city of reciprocal relations across in-between places. Rationalization of the urban realm and its transformation into zones of easy surveillance and control deprives cities of their ambivalent spaces, which leaves them less able to accommodate psychic tension.

Most people know, albeit unconsciously, what cities offer and why they are drawn to them. Unknown or unspeakable desire, though, makes it difficult for individuals to take responsibility for their own habitat as a setting for spontaneous human encounters. Even though many people have great difficulty communicating their desires for cities, van Eyck felt that he had understood just how much people long to find homecoming in them.[21] He argued that configured cities are magnetic because they carry an intense web of emotional and social association across an extended range of settings and experiences.

When the web of association is effectively extended into expanding areas, a city will become even more magnetic, and thus larger and larger, presenting citizens and visitors with even more possibilities to satisfy their basic desire to communicate.

10.4
**Site plan.
Amsterdam
Orphanage,
1955–1960 and
Tripolis Office
Complex,
1990–1994.
Architect: Aldo
van Eyck with
Hannie van Eyck
(Tripolis Complex).
Drawing by
A. B. Dixon**

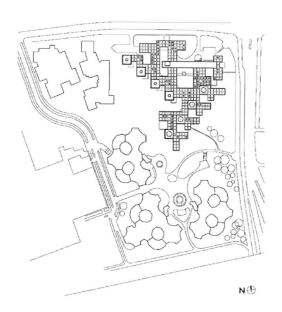

N⊕

The Orphanage is an example of this in two ways. It sits at the edge of Amsterdam and continues to draw people toward it. In addition, it demonstrates how an individual building can introduce city-like qualities within itself as much as to an urban edge, which, in turn, has transformed a non-place into some-place. Proof of this is the newer development that has grown up around the Amsterdam Orphanage in recent years.

Because he believed that cities fulfil a basic human longing, need even, van Eyck was keen to present them as the result of desire, not simply of economic necessity. Cities, he argued, are a response to positive human needs, inventions conjured up to actually satisfy these needs, rather than some outmoded anomaly just as easily replaced by entertainment centres, malls, telecommuting, gated communities or the promise of an Internet-based virtual community.

Envisioning cities as places of desire stands in clear opposition to typical real estate development and governmental conceptions of cities as 'a *statistical, economical and technological inevitability*'. The rift between these two conceptions is significant: the quantifiable (development) approach is *impersonal* and *negative*. The qualitative approach views cities as well tuned emotionally and thus as psychically positive.

If van Eyck was correct in his estimation of cities and human desire for them – a conviction that turns on whether or not human beings really are social animals – then architects and urbanists have too pressing a task ahead of them to permit themselves the luxury of embracing a despairingly cynical, self-justifying abdication of their responsibility to the social. Cities and culture may well be part of an ongoing process of evolution, but no matter how much past elaboration informs present visions, according to van Eyck, contemporary conditions demand new solutions to age-old questions.[22]

An authentic modernity?

In van Eyck's architecture, reciprocity and twinphenomena were two consequences of relativity that made it comprehensible when articulated. What is more, inbetweens (thresholds) were places where individuals (perceiving subjects) could enter into an awareness of relativity as a four-dimensional conception of reality that links the generalized concepts of space and time, which become place and occasion when particularized. Four concepts: relativity, reciprocity, twinphenomena and inbetween were the fundamental building blocks of van Eyck's project for a configurative discipline. His interpretation of relativity provided the theoretical basis of the method. Reciprocity suggested how one might practice with his theory. Twinphenomena implied the desired outcomes of this practice – not its specific results. Inbetweens described inhabitable conditions that slide in, out and through twinphenomena.

By highlighting temporality (movement, occupation and occasion), inbetweenness discloses architecture as four-dimensional: perceiving subjects in movement complete architecture and cities by reinventing them through inhabitation and use. Architecture and cities may be works of art but to be humane, they must be more than simply visually appealing. According to van Eyck's theoretical statements, temporality, accommodation of the relation between occupant, social action and building, can only come to full awareness if relativity (interdependence) replaces absolute frames of reference.

'Steps Toward a Configurative Discipline' expressed how van Eyck's concept of 'built homecoming' could be thinkable; the Orphanage demonstrated how in a specific instance. His essay, Orphanage, and Otterlo Circles drawing were partial presentations of what van Eyck saw as a 'new reality', which he believed originated with the discoveries made by early twentieth-century avant-garde artists. Most notable of these was the emergent awareness that a basic unity constituted from the local and the universal permits artists to gather the ancient into modern art. Concurrent with this embrace of difference, artists explored how to rejoin related phenomena as parts of a whole that extreme rationalism continues to veil or split in two. Reconciliation of this sort revealed itself as a possibility when modern artists discovered that dream life may actually disclose a profounder consciousness, capable of enriching waking reality.

An authentic avant-garde, as van Eyck called it, promised a new and enriched reality, characterized by awareness that 'all dual phenomena' are 'inseparably linked' and, despite conventional understanding, impossible to 'split into conflicting polarities'.[23] According to him, artists (Picasso, Klee, Mondrian and Brancusi), writers (Joyce), architects (Le Corbusier), composers (Schönberg), philosophers (Bergson) and scientists (Einstein), all possessed this sensibility, making them all members of what he called 'the whole wonderful gang'. He argued that they 'set the great top to spinning again and expanded the universe – the outside and the inside universe. It was a wonderful riot – the cage was opened again'.[24]

Van Eyck's utopian objective was to return the efforts of architects and urbanists to that which their work 'sets out to articulate . . . the inbetween realm'. It is the business of both to continually articulate this territory precisely because 'man's realm is the inbetween realm', a setting impossible to locate when abstract antonyms

– *either/or* divisions – form lived conditions compartmentalized into collections of dissociated 'terrifying polarities'. According to van Eyck, rigid divisions terrify by alienating us from our own *both/and* domain. Life entails endless mental and physical transitions; it is through the inbetween that humans constantly pass as they go from here to there. Van Eyck believed that amelioration of terrifying polarities would only be possible if inbetween conditions were introduced to buildings and cities.[25]

If the human habit is to provide for basic emotional needs, something of the self must be recognizable in it. Not, though, in a direct, melodramatic or literal manner, but as a web of determined relations to which individuals can make bodily associations through reference. A human habitat is human because it is constructed. However, for any human realm to be truly humane, it must not offend the complex and contradictory inbetween place of human being. If it does, it will be terrifying. Any setting devoid of inbetweens and twinphenomena, as van Eyck saw it, will be incomprehensible because it makes no place for the human predicament of ambivalence.

Chapter 11

Story of another idea

It seems to me that past, present, and future must be active in the mind's interior as a continuum. If they are not, the artifacts we make will be without temporal depth and associative perspective. My concern with the ultimate human validity of divergent, often seemingly incompatible concepts of space and incidental or circumstantial solutions found during past ages in different corners of the world is to be understood in the light of the above. Time has come to reconcile them; to gather the essential meaning divided among them.[1]

Aldo van Eyck

Aldo van Eyck's ability to conceptualize better places through reversal or inversion of hidebound ideas about social optimism is largely what made his achievement remarkable. The Municipal Orphanage of Amsterdam (designed 1955–1957, built 1957–1960) was the first fully worked-out application of his configurative discipline. Notwithstanding its present condition (it is no longer an orphanage) the building continues to tell the story of another idea that architects and clients can return to as a built poem of potential. As such, even now the Orphanage presents a physical challenge to conventional practice, especially the view of architecture as irrevocably diminished. Until his death, van Eyck railed against the fatalism betrayed by declarations that the domain of architecture must shrink, especially the assertion that salvaging it requires freeing it from the burden of usefulness:[2]

What is gradually making good architecture impossible – and is worryingly widespread and accepted – is the ardent ambition of Post-Moderns etc. . . . to disburden architecture of every social, humane or even practical motivation so that, now autonomous, it can take its place among the fine arts. . . . One might expect that the architect-become-artist, now the creator of autonomous works, would wish to be in complete charge. But

214

that is not what has happened for on the threshold of liberation things took exactly the opposite turn. Architecture-become-art (and at the same time inconsequential) together with all the new obstacles preventing architects from doing their job well, produce a paralysing and chaotic situation.[3]

By articulating a significant social setting for the possibility of an enriched reality, the building stands in concrete opposition to the willing acceptance by many practitioners and theorists of the apparent unfeasibility of a persisting social dimension for architecture. As an exceptionally tactile building attuned to the needs of its intended occupants through emotional understanding, the Orphanage was an expression of van Eyck's idea of an *emotional functionalism*, not so much the opposite of technical functionalism as an augmentation of it. Whereas technical functionalism tended to reduce use to instrumental convenience, emotional functionalism would take at least as much account of the qualitative dimension of building and experience.

Van Eyck's preoccupation with patterns (of the sort that organize everyday life as well as the kind that configure the built environment as counterforms to the first) aligns his work with the kind of patterns utopias devise as a way to give society a form. His vision of patterns made from a multiplicity of parts is presented most concretely at the Orphanage through doorways, which are direct expressions of inbetweens that reconcile twinphenomena. For example, doors, according to the logic of abstract antonyms (dualistic oppositions), separate inside from outside, one room from another, here from there, and so on. As applied at the Orphanage, doorways are thresholds – direct presentations of liminality (an in-between condition). They are not so much boundaries as links, a third condition articulated by delaying entry (not confusing it) and through a careful definition of entry that goes beyond functional necessity alone.

At the Orphanage, streets, rooms and structural elements are all parts of an intelligible pattern continuously formed and presented throughout by an assemblage of clearly articulated elements that make the whole. Consequently, each part gains in meaning (associative richness) as it comes to form an intelligible structural whole.

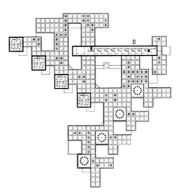

11.1
Ground and first- floor floor plans. Amsterdam Orphanage, 1955–1960. Architect: Aldo van Eyck. Drawing by A. B. Dixon after Aldo van Eyck

N

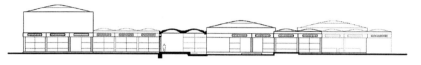

11.2
Section.
Amsterdam
Orphanage,
1955–1960.
Architect: Aldo
van Eyck. Drawing
by A. B. Dixon

Enriching modernism

The Orphanage was van Eyck's first major independent commission; it brought him international attention, which confirmed the building as the capstone achievement of his early career.[4] The complex communicated his conviction that a desirable enrichment of post-World War II architecture required a different kind of functionalism. Rather than rejecting CIAM outright, he recognized a beginning in its limited tenets, especially because it provided a direct link to the ideas of early modernist architects. However, much as he sought a way to open up and deepen modern architecture without rejecting it, he had little patience for the growing prominence of Walter Gropius's conviction that architecture must always result from teamwork.

> Teamwork has rapidly come to mean no more than beating about the bush, because the original aspiration long ago changed into something else: pass on, hand over, delegate or contract out whatever you can, and at the same time hire in unlimited resources to carry out what remains to be done.[5]

Van Eyck was certain that this conception of teamwork would lead to architects completely losing their responsibility for the building process. He feared that commercial indifference would fill the gap. Through the years, his suspicions were confirmed by architectural practices that have come to increasingly resemble Gropius's management model, with the careless results van Eyck expected.

The distant and the near

During the late 1950s, van Eyck developed an interest in how anthropology could inform modern architecture, inspired at least partially by avant-garde artists who had sought inspiration in non-Western traditions.[6] Although he had begun travelling to Africa in the late 1940s, it was during the 1950s and 1960s that these activities became formalized as a search for sources to renew hidebound modern architecture. During these journeys, he collected artefacts in much the way he had been collecting modern art. Just as modern art expressed the cosmology of a new reality for van Eyck, he likewise observed a unified cosmology in the ethnographic materials he collected from the African villages he visited, expressed by an interrelationship between each thing that made life possible and comprehensible, from the smallness of a basket to the largeness of the world.

Especially impressive for van Eyck were the Dogon people of sub-Saharan Africa, who wove a rich web of orienting relations from the elements of their daily life, including baskets, homes and the arrangement of their villages, and so on at all scales. Contact with the rich cosmological patterns of village life, which continued

11.3
**Dogon village
plans. Aldo van
Eyck**
Courtesy of Hannie
van Eyck

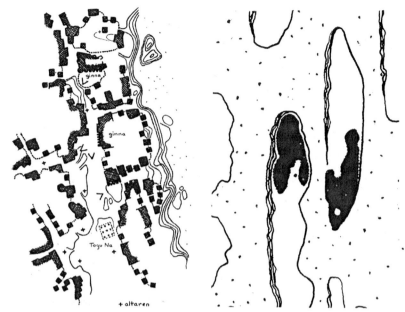

Plan of Upper Ogol.

Upper Ogol left, Lower Ogol right.

217

to exist parallel to the more diagrammatic settings of affluent industrial societies, convinced van Eyck that narrow *functionalism* would never be able to provide an adequate home for Western men and women.[7]

Van Eyck's visits with the Dogon people inspired his growing frustration with the limitations of orthodox modern practices, but also convinced him that architecture's poetic potential could be relearned from people who, by necessity, lived much closer to a particular place, within an articulate circle of individual and communal relations. Out of these experiences, he developed his interest in the inbetweenness of space and architecture (discussed in the previous chapter). Although his ideas of the inbetween were somewhat akin to Kahn's servant/served conception, their considerable difference was that they were reciprocal rather than dualistic: for Kahn's idea to be intelligible, servant must be clearly distinguished from served.

Overall, though, van Eyck's objective was to develop a new kind of emotional functionality extending beyond the poetic impoverishment of technical functionality that characterized the majority of buildings. His project to deepen modern architecture seemed even more possible in light of his contact with the Dogon people. From then on, van Eyck cultivated an intense concern for those who would occupy his, or any, buildings. He hoped to infuse his structures with an enriched functionality deepened by the poetry of emotion.[8]

Present in the past

Throughout earlier chapters, exemplary architecture is posited as both liminal and utopian. It is utopian inasmuch as its architects envision it as a superior setting for improved, though as yet unforeseen future conditions, and liminal because it always keeps enough in reserve to encourage open rather than fixed habits of occupation. Architects of such buildings do not so much foresee transformation of use and conduct as give it a platform upon (and within) which it can unfold. In this way, an exemplary architecture can remain vital no matter its age; revitalized by occupants constantly reinventing its purpose through occupation, who, in so doing, more fully approximate its completion.

Potential for continuous renewal through transforming occupation is a function of the paradoxical relationship between utopia and liminality that exemplary architecture embodies. Le Corbusier and Kahn certainly understood their architecture as important cultural work with a social dimension. However, even though they understood what they were doing and why, van Eyck was unique for his development of a method that actually elaborated on improved settings for social and civic life as fundamentally liminal, which he could do without neglecting common psychological (and physical) desires for enclosure and shelter.

Van Eyck's distinctive anthropological conception of architecture permitted him to sustain a radically modern outlook even as he gathered past into present. His facility for pulling together disparate spatial and temporal influences immeasurably enriched his architecture. Indeed, this capacity facilitated his extended exploration of return *and* revolution as coequal parts of a new reality, each as separate from the past as it is inextricably linked to it:

Architects nowadays are pathologically addicted to change, regarding it as something one hinders, runs after, or at best keeps up with. This, I suggest, is why they sever the past from the future, with the result that the present is rendered emotionally inaccessible – without temporal dimension. I dislike a sentimental antiquarian attitude towards the past as much as I dislike a sentimental technocratic one towards the future.[9]

Utopias are distant non-places resting between present and future. When articulated, the place and occasion of utopias is liminality, not fixity, as is commonly imagined. Separation of this sort allows for a surprising possibility: optimistic redescription of everyday reality, including the social relationships momentarily departed from.

By embodying his own rethinking of conventional institutional structures, van Eyck's Orphanage building expressed the possibility of transformation. Conventional views of utopia as placelessness might make a utopian perspective seem a peculiar resource for the establishment of a building like the Orphanage, which powerfully communicates its meaning through structure and material. However, utopia's placelessness, expressed by permanent *communitas*, *liminality* or *betwixt and between*, introduces to architecture, which is necessarily static, the potential of an enriching responsiveness to changing conditions of occupation. Surprisingly, inbetweens are the architectural counterform to utopia, places of threshold, where transformation and reconciliation of twinphenomena can occur.

By giving form to ambivalence through building, van Eyck disclosed his acceptance of the coexistence of opposing ideas, attitudes or emotions within the same head as a fundamental condition of being human. The architectural correlate of ambivalence is the inbetween, which van Eyck articulated as a place for occasions of human homecoming at the Orphanage. His development of the inbetween as the basis for significant settings reveals thresholds as a fundamental location of transformative comings and goings. Moreover, van Eyck's efforts to reconcile indigenous cultures (anthropological in approach) with the heritage of pre-modern Western thought (exemplified by classical antiquity) were combined with his conviction that modernity has its own traditions. The temporal inclusiveness of his approach decisively separated his work from the technocratic practices of so-called utopian high-modern architects.

Van Eyck's approach to past, present and future (communicated in the form of an emblem by his Otterlo Circles) is an example of how even radical newness (utopia) is possible only when elaborated out of existing structure. The traditions van Eyck interpreted, though, are anything but inert. He believed that only ongoing patterns of life that are constantly reinvented (unchanging and constantly changing) could accommodate life.

Twinphenomena, articulated as thresholds or passages linking apparent opposites by way of a third condition, are expressed most deliberately by the liminal moment presented by doorways, which figuratively resolves the apparent opposition of structure to anti-structure by reconciling them as coequal parts of a comprehensive whole. By focusing on thresholds as the psychological place of human drama, van Eyck could envision an architecture practiced through the transformative inbetweenness of utopia even though it makes no claims to be one.

11.5
Former staff residence wing. Amsterdam Orphanage, 1955–1960. Architect: Aldo van Eyck

The paradoxical relationship between built structures as fixed entities, with specific materiality, and their existence, at least in part, as structureless settings (counterforms), to changing occupation, is a striking example of how van Eyck's idea of twinphenomena is a model for utopian settings that are not absolute. His buildings were utopian inasmuch as his objective was an architecture of open-ended possibility specific in its social aims with a carefully articulated agenda.

Van Eyck's utopian state, then, would be a place where individuals are at home because they can find their equilibrium. This equilibrium is won by embracing ambivalence, the inside and outside of desire. The dynamism of van Eyck's ideal place may be surprising, especially considering how rejection of utopia is usually based on claims that it is an inimical and unchanging non-place outside of time and experience (which supposedly confirms that the hopefulness utopias disclose is pathological). In just this way, so-called realists smugly attempt to marginalize thought about a more humane realm. Shameless declarations of utopia's unreality, or unrealizability, are the means by which matter-of-factness – the immediate and limited – is fabled as the only acceptable demonstration of reality.

A configurative discipline provisionally illustrated

At the Orphanage, van Eyck's vision of a *new reality* of more open social relations was given a place. His psychological and spatial aims were so fully articulated at the Orphanage that even though it is now emptied of its original use, it persists as a model of possibility for enriched architectural and urban practices. Neither van Eyck, nor his client, nor chroniclers of his work at the Orphanage refer to the complex as utopian or as a utopia; nevertheless, the explicit objective for it was to become an ideal city of sorts. Client and architect alike desired to construct an ideal city form, writ small, to house an institution with an enlightened social programme.[10]

11.6
**Interior street,
current state.
Amsterdam
Orphanage,
1955–1960.
Architect: Aldo
van Eyck**

As a setting, the building is still comprehensible as a considerate urbanizing form, even though its original occupants left long ago. Contrary to conventional conceptions of utopias, there is no attempt to arrest time at the Orphanage, nor is it organized with perfectly straight streets. Streets do figure prominently, but it is a major interior one that was originally full of surprises. It was a place of experience that in no way evidenced any attempt to exit time. Embedded in time and open to experience, the Orphanage was dynamic rather than static, making it a constitutive rather than pathological utopia.

Van Eyck configured the Orphanage out of a limited palette of standard elements that together form a series of multiple units repeated throughout. Even though limited, his considerate assemblage of repetitive elements results in a surprising presentation of near-infinite combinative and reciprocal possibility. Consequently, the building is simultaneously simple and complex. Individual parts have both a primal and distinctly modern quality, communicated by their concurrent status as referential and structural elements, which makes each initial part, through its subsequent combination, into a very clear assemblage, readily comprehensible at the moment of perception.

Maintaining the identity of each individual structural element through inventive repetition enriches rather than impoverishes the overall effect, which the fugal arrangement of the Orphanage assures. The elaborate resulting pattern of repeated and varied architectural themes establishes a dynamic tension that is structurally engaging and invites exploration. In this concrete example of van Eyck's configurative discipline, the combination of identifiable elements into larger repetitive units augments individual element identity to present his theoretical and social aims directly to the body, while clarifying the structural, social, functional and artistic intent.

To begin with, the basic structural unit of the Orphanage is a concrete column augmented by the addition of a second column placed a uniform distance from the first. Next, an architrave with a rectangular slot cut into it caps these standing columns by traversing them. This assembly forms a threshold by establishing a portal with a 'this-side' and a 'that-side' of it. It is worth noting that this assemblage, however modern it may be, also refers to the Doric order of ancient Greek architecture. Initial orthogonal extension of this first combination of elements encompasses four columns, each a uniform distance from the others. Architraves span each pair of columns. These structures form the basic constructive structural unit of the Orphanage.

Conceptually, and concretely, four columns traversed by four architraves form a primary structural element of shelter, comprehensible as a house-room, which refers to Laugier's 'Primitive Hut' but also to Le Corbusier's Dom-ino structural system. Even though it is a distinctly modern assembly, the structure also refers to aboriginal architecture and classical architecture simultaneously. As a richly textured combinative element, this structural unit embodies multiple references that could continue to enrich the particular methods of construction required by modern architecture.

11.7
Basic structural unit. Amsterdam Orphanage, 1955–1960. Architect: Aldo van Eyck

In actuality, there are places in the Orphanage where two or three house-room units are combined, forming larger squares, or rectangles. Nevertheless, the basic unit remains comprehensible throughout. It is a legibility attained by clearly articulating it in the interior and exterior alike. Restatement of the basic spatial unit occurs most emphatically at the roof level. Here, individual domes reassert and define each house-room by capping it with its own roof, which gives the Orphanage its distinctive roofscape.

11.8
**Larger unit.
Amsterdam
Orphanage,
1955–1960.
Architect: Aldo
van Eyck**

A total of 336 precast concrete domes cover all of the basic house-room units, except for eight much larger units, each equal in size to nine initial house-room units combined but rendered as a single entity capped by a far bigger dome. These distinctly larger elements originally housed the children's residences, and were organized according to age for infants to ten year olds, and by gender for ten- to twenty-year olds. Housing units originally intended for the older children were distinguished further by being two storeys in height. Living areas of these duplex units were on the lower levels with bedrooms above; both were on a single level for the younger children.

11.9
**Aerial view.
Amsterdam
Orphanage,
1955–1960.
Architect: Aldo
van Eyck**
Courtesy of Hannie
van Eyck

Apart from the four exceptions for older children, and one other, an administrative bridge establishing the main point of entry, the Orphanage building is on a single storey relieved within by subtle shifts of level, and throughout by changes of materials, colour and infill. The complex comprises two main wings, each of which included four of the eight children's residential units. The four large duplex units are all on the west side of the Orphanage, while the four large single-storey units for younger children are on the east side. Articulation of age-distinct areas went even further; the two wings slip past each other, separated by the large entry court. Additionally, the wing for older children is further north while the one for younger children slides further south.

The administrative bridge noted above defines the outer edge of the entry court, sheltering the main threshold into the complex below it, while effectively linking the two wings of the complex. Precast concrete panels, with openings as required, enclose second-level sections of the building here as elsewhere. The administrative bridge and the spaces next to it originally housed support functions with staff apartments and a staff meeting room in the second storey.

11.10
Entry porch. Amsterdam Orphanage, 1955–1960. Architect: Aldo van Eyck

11.11
Main court. Amsterdam Orphanage, 1955–1960. Architect: Aldo van Eyck

Inside the complex, a meandering interior street – actually articulated as a street – threaded together the children's housing, support areas, including the infirmary, dining hall and administrative wing, according to what van Eyck called *labyrinthine clarity*, which suggests paths enriched by derivations analogous to unfolding experience. It was a conceptualization of architectural paths related to twinphenomena, envisioning an arrangement of buildings where the possibility of wandering, as analogous to intuition and wonder, persisted as an alternative to the pervasiveness of rigidly diagrammatic planning practices.

The assemblage of the more than 400 house-room units extends outward from the entry court, which once established the social rather than geometric centre of the Orphanage. The main court and many other smaller courts created by a careful assemblage of multiples continue to give the Orphanage its unique village-like character. Even though these basic units extend orthogonally toward the cardinal points to form a grid, the result is anything but foursquare; rather, it is remarkably diverse and dynamic, resulting in part from the opposing stepped diagonal arrangement of each wing in plan.

Stepping the two triangles, effectively established by the two main wings provided van Eyck with the opportunity to include a wide variety of open-air places (or courts), which are either fully enclosed by the exterior walls of the building, or only partially protected by them. There are also loggias in a number of places that form thresholds between inside and out. Overall, the effect of such thoughtful articulation – materially, spatially and psychologically – is a building of great social legibility.

Van Eyck added his extensible units together with great ingenuity to make smaller and larger places, places that are directional, places that are not, and so on. A remarkable feature of his configurative method was the nearly infinite figurative

11.12
**West side court.
Amsterdam
Orphanage,
1955–1960.
Architect: Aldo
van Eyck**

potential it could draw from a surprisingly limited number of elements. So, although the basic unit and the whole are all of the same *stuff*, openings established by a repetition of two columns and an architrave allow for almost limitless possibilities of infill: from open to closed, door to window, wall to aperture and from transparent to translucent. Clearly defined places, less determined ones, as well as enclosed open places and open enclosed places were also established.

What results is a myriad of places made from twinphenomena and clearly determined relations, dependent on a sophisticated architectural order that established an internally consistent logic throughout. The outcome is a building that invites understanding by way of exploration and open interpretation. It was a setting for individual and collective that permitted each to elaborate a clear spatial identity. Such determined relations accommodate a process of social configuration out of which social wholes could form. The process was played out through thresholds (in-betweens) where individuals came together, or at least once did, and in part still do, even after an architecture school replaced the Orphanage.

At the Orphanage, although the parts are all quantitatively similar, their application reveals them as having been 'extended in a qualitative dimension' through 'configurative multiplication'.[11] A large part of what makes the building comprehensible as a whole turns on the reciprocal relations among its parts, intelligible at every scale. Application of a persuasive basic unit, assembled from two columns and an architrave, established dynamism rather than monotony throughout the complex.

The various materials used to infill walls at the Orphanage were not deployed fancifully or arbitrarily. They related to and explained what surrounded the building and how the building began to configure the abstract environs of its site (at the outer edge of the Amsterdam's historic core) through its presence. The openness, closedness, opacity, transparency, translucency, solidity and permeability of walls throughout the complex derived from a variety of materials including glass and glass block, steel, as well as brick and concrete. Each originally defined a particular social, functional and emotional relation throughout the building. Sun, light, interior occupation and social objectives all conditioned the choice of infill materials for the walls relative to the desired character of places within. For example, the north and east sides of the building are the most solid, precisely because they define the outer boundaries of the site and front major roads.

The youngest children found protective enclosure behind the walls on the east side of the complex, while the solid north side marks an open yet secure main entry point to the building. On the other hand, the south and west walls are far more open than those on the north and east. This side of the complex fronts the former playing fields of the Orphanage, it also originally housed the older children. However, even though differences between the north and east, as well as between the south and west sides of the complex are legible, they are by no means absolute.

Open never contradicts closed in a rigid way, and there is also no attempt to confound comprehension or to establish dualistic relations through such an opposition. Rather than becoming a pair of abstract antonyms, open and closed weave together, according to van Eyck's method, in a qualitatively appropriate manner. For example, although the south and west sides of the building are more open than the north and east sides, the former living quarters of the older children carefully establish protective enclosures. Another example of multi-meaning includes the extreme south wall of the whole Orphanage: it is solid, a condition that clearly defines the extreme southern edge of the building, but also would have made the infirmary, originally located behind it, among the quietest places of all.

What is left? Significance

The Amsterdam Orphanage was the most important building of the first half of van Eyck's career, decisively demonstrating the results of his artistic development from the 1940s onwards. Built as a counterform to the kind of life meant to be contained within, the Orphanage remains a welcoming setting for particular individual and social occasions, open to inflection, rather than simply representing functions, or being an expedient container for them. Hence, his building encourages emotional occupation even though it might not make immediate sense according to the requisites of physical functionalism, with its overly rationalized and narrow conception of building fitness to use.

> Immersing himself thoroughly in the mental world of the building's youthful inhabitants, the architect [van Eyck] succeeded to quite an extraordinary degree in transposing this world into spatial qualities. It is through such profound identification with its users that the building has become a manifesto against the habitual lack of interest among architects in those who are to occupy their buildings. It is a manifesto advocating a sorely needed change of attitude in the profession, namely to use every architectural means to be generous in one's concern for what people expect of their surroundings, both physically and mentally.[12]

In contrast to physical functionalism, van Eyck's building elaborates on his notion of emotional functionalism as a corrective. He believed that buildings conditioned by the myth of reductive functionalism must remain nearly incomprehensible, since they are impoverished assemblies of minimally sized and economically efficient adjacencies of use. According to van Eyck, modern architecture expresses its severest limitation by way of its adherence to physical functionalism, the logic of which elevates minimum existence to the status of maximum possibility.

Rather than succumbing to the limitations of physical, or technical, functionalism, the Orphanage encourages comprehensibility and emotional function in a wide variety of ways. For example, through multiplication of the principal constitutive assemblage of the building, the repetitive trabeated pavilion structure capped by a dome discussed earlier, the building as a whole gains a village-like character akin to the sub-Saharan Dogon villages admired by van Eyck. Furthermore, the numerous domes capping the complex's many modules lends it a biomorphic quality, like a desert or dune landscape.

Repetitive geometries, invention of a strong initial module, and embrace of contemporary means of construction adapted to an emotional functionalism are attributes that van Eyck's building shares with Kahn's work. Also resonant is how protective the Orphanage appears from the outside while being cave-like cosy on the inside, articulated materially and by means of lighting and colour. Reflecting on such relationships, van Eyck compared the inside/outside character he hoped to achieve at the building as akin to a winter coat, benefiting from a rough protective exterior counterbalanced by a comforting soft interior. Overall, the Orphanage explored a method for establishing considerate spatial articulation, the basis of which is a system of moderately scaled screens with a variety of infill. These screens offered a wide spectrum of physical and emotional possibilities, expressed by material fluctuations.

Articulation of the sort that characterizes the Orphanage makes the whole complex comprehensible via sentient experience of it, emphasized by way of reference to the body. By beginning with a body-related module (at its most basic, a column), van Eyck was able to elaborate a small-scale approach to a large structure, providing a home-like setting where children could feel secure. His conviction was that the particular atmosphere of the building would allow an occupant to find him or herself at home within an otherwise institutional structure in a *concrete* rather than *abstract* way. It is precisely because he so carefully articulated his physical and emotional aims that the building remains anything but conventionally institutional long after its original construction.

Although it is no longer occupied as originally intended, the building continues to demonstrate van Eyck's vision of a new reality. The Orphanage's transformed present condition distinguishes it from Le Corbusier's La Tourette, which persists in housing new occupations still based on the original intent for the building. It also differs from Kahn's Salk Institute, which houses an ongoing occupation close to the original intent of its architect and client. But even if the Orphanage may have lost its original purpose, it is arguably the *most* utopian of the three buildings examined so far in this study. To elaborate, it is the most utopian precisely because its continuous occupation by whatever use (orphanage, school, office), is sustained by re-readings of it as an impressive expression of social imagination, which opens up utopian perspectives:

> And yet potentially the space this building has persistently managed to generate as an open structure is present still, ready and waiting for a more propitious age.[13]

Its specificity, intimacy and openness to spontaneous occupation, made the Orphanage in its past incarnation as an architecture school, a building free from depersonalization, the deadening quality commonly associated with most modern institutionalized structures. For the same reasons, as a current collection of offices, it provides settings that give workers a humane place to work, as opposed to the anonymity of typical office environments, which fosters a sense of individual expendability. By elaborating on principles of a humane architecture, the Orphanage building remains a viable model; it perseveres in its capacity to support alternative conceptions of institutional space.

The Orphanage confirmed van Eyck's ability to configure a large-scale, complex, institutional structure in such a way that it clearly communicates its purpose while avoiding the abstract banality of typical bureaucratic settings. Such laudable qualities can endure, even if they are only mildly acknowledged and embraced, regardless of the limitations of the present occupation. For example, an advertising agency can be as much the beneficiary of the Orphanage's humane architecture as children once were.

This ability to introduce intimacy to institutional structures for a changeable mass society, that frequently empties buildings of their original purpose, stands as van Eyck's greatest achievement. The Orphanage was the earliest fully worked out expression of this special capacity, which all van Eyck's subsequent buildings embody, albeit in ever-evolving ways. Even though the Orphanage is remarkably specific in its materiality and arrangement, this very specificity holds enough in reserve to permit each new occupation of it at least the potential to effectively renew and recomplete the building.

A concern for concreteness that was structural rather than social can also be seen at the building. Actually, van Eyck was obsessed with the exact material out of which buildings are made, a preoccupation that remained constant throughout his career, even though the way he presented this concern transformed over time. Materiality in this instance not only confirmed the physicality of the building, but also rendered phenomenal van Eyck's very concern for material as the first point of contact, or encounter, between occupants and a building. The Orphanage is thus not

11.13
Lunch room, current state. Amsterdam Orphanage, 1955–1960. Architect: Aldo van Eyck

11.14
Inside-outside. Amsterdam Orphanage, 1955–1960. Architect: Aldo van Eyck

so much an expression of materialism as it is a demonstration of the architect's awareness of touch. By acknowledging the haptic, van Eyck gave due recognition to the persistence of how the world makes itself known primarily through bodily experience.

Occupation of the Orphanage never had a chance to evolve exactly in the way envisioned by either van Eyck or its patron, Frans van Meurs, who was its original director. By the time the building was operational, he had already retired and the Orphanage came under less sympathetic supervision. Subsequent to this, from its opening in 1960 until 1986, when it was threatened with partial demolition, those charged with its maintenance subjected the Orphanage to abuse.

Over the years, as new ideas about homes for children gained favour, the building was much altered and allowed to decay. These difficulties culminated in 1986 with plans to demolish half of it. In response, Dutch architect Herman Hertzberger, who is very close in sentiment to van Eyck, organized architects and others in an international campaign to save the building. The resulting scheme included selling the Orphanage and surrounding land to a developer who was required to restore and renovate it, after which it was partially occupied by the Berlage Institute (then a new architecture school).[14]

> The history of this 'house for children', in actual fact a tiny city, has been a story of changes from the outset. Even before the building was appropriated a discussion raged over how the programme was to be housed in its various units. And when in 1987 the insensitive regime of its then occupants, who were all set to demolish large parts of the Orphanage, came to an end, the building became a place of learning with the arrival there of the Berlage Institute.[15]

The developer who purchased the Orphanage building was permitted to build three new office buildings on open ground at the site, designed by Aldo and Hannie van Eyck (1990–1994). These buildings now cradle the Orphanage.[16] Rising rents ultimately forced out the architecture school. This event is an indication of the building's newfound success, or at least its viability as prime commercial real estate. Various business interests now fully occupy the building, including the administrative offices of a clothing retailer and an advertising agency that holds the largest portion of the structure.

Reflecting its new use, the entire complex has now been rebranded the *Garden Court*. The Orphanage is now a business location particularly desirable for its many courtyards, non-institutional character, convenience to the Amsterdam ring road, ample on-site parking, and because of the cultural cachet that its modern architectural monument status lends to the commercial tenants who now occupy it.

> Then came evidence of the building's great power, or rather its capacity to take these changes of occupancy in its stride. Although now wholly used as an office building and with little of the former ambience left, a complete disaster it is not. However unfortunately its interior has been treated, as a structure it is still very much in control.[17]

11.15
**Tripolis office
buildings 'cradle'
the Orphanage.
Amsterdam
Orphanage,
1955–1960.
Architect: Aldo
van Eyck**

In its present state of occupation, the Orphanage building nonetheless continues to give form to van Eyck's lifelong challenge to architects and urbanists that their responsibility is to make places '*For Us, By Us*'. Such places articulate determined relations that are at once constant and variable, a counterform to the reciprocity that exists between individual and society. Furthermore, the Orphanage building embodies a reconciliation of three great traditions he identified according to his understanding of relativity: the classical, embodying *immutability and rest*; the modern, embodying *change and movement*; and the tradition of spontaneous building, embodying the *vernacular of the heart*, effectively depicted in his Otterlo Circles.

Together, this multiplicity and simultaneity demonstrates a reconciliation of world heritage, individual dreams, and the universal desire for a home (localized according to specific demands at any particular location). Van Eyck's conviction was that each tradition, although unique in character, has something to share with every one of us, augmenting what we can know about ourselves, even if distant in time and space from the present.

Utopian patterns

In their endeavour to create a just society, utopians eagerly attempt to discern unchanging patterns. A utopian society would, no doubt, be embodied in the buildings that shore it up, give it form and present it to the human beings who inhabit it. Unchanging patterns are intriguing because they represent a kind of golden age. They permit proximity to an unrepeatable epoch in an unreachable place, returned to as a reservoir for ideas about how human beings might find their home on Earth.

For van Eyck, this golden age was multiple; it comprised not only traditional and classical architecture, but modern architecture as well, especially modern architecture of the early years of the twentieth century. According to him, early modern avant-garde architecture remains of vital importance because its invention occurred at a moment when optimism prevailed about times that were in many ways fundamentally different from those of its immediate past.

Van Eyck, though, was not content with a golden age lacking a verifiable past or the real possibility of a present. Ancient traditions, especially ongoing traditional societies such as the Kayapo Indians of Brazil, depicted in the left Otterlo Circle (later version), were as crucial to his vision of a humane ideal as was the new. Pre-existing traditions and patterns of life provide a familiar ground upon which humans stand and from which Westerners (and others) can learn about themselves. This is especially the case for parallel traditions such as those he encountered in Africa. His concern was as much with what is *unchanging* as with what *constantly changes*.

Mutual traditions of architecture and the mutuality of traditional societies, with their emphasis on interdependency, were for van Eyck an enduring model of possibility for cities and buildings, which can suggest how a more humane habitat might come about in any age. Not surprisingly, considering his preoccupation with part and whole, van Eyck's theory found its origins with Alberti, who defined *beauty as wholeness*.[18] Actually, his writings and buildings often appear to paraphrase Alberti:

> Make a bunch of places of each house and each city, for a city is a huge house and a house a tiny city. Both must serve the same person in different ways and different persons in the same way.[19]

Alberti was quite specific about intelligible patterns made from harmoniously interrelated parts at all scales. Although van Eyck considered these same inter-relationships, he did so from his mid-twentieth-century position.[20] In his discussion of configured wholes made out of interrelated parts, van Eyck elaborated on Alberti's tolerance for time and necessity, or experience, and the particular in terms of place and occasion. By so doing, he made an ideal of what Alberti considered inevitable, which could make utopian prospects into real possibilities on a limited scale.

With this unique vision of better situations (occasions) and places, van Eyck added a surprisingly complex dimension to utopian thinking and projecting that rescues both from the limitations of a speculative ideal fixed to an idealized and unchanging moment in time. His conceptualization of an ideal city is in direct opposition to idealized geometric figures that typically represent utopian cities.

As a dynamic ideal city, limited in scale, and geometrically complex, the Orphanage demonstrates that partial utopias need be neither totalizing nor static. Van Eyck's method for achieving this dynamism includes conceptualization of how to transform abstract notions, such as *space and time*, into concrete and humane forms, by representing them as *place and occasion*:

> I came to the conclusion that *whatever space and time mean, place and occasion mean more, for space in the image of man is place, and time in the image of man is occasion*. . . . Place and occasion constitute each other's realization in human terms. . . . Make a configuration of places at

each stage of multiplication, i.e. provide the right kind of places at each configurative stage, and urban environment will again become liveable. Cities should become the counterform to man's reciprocally individual and collective reality [original italics].[21]

By conceiving of architecture as a counterform to human realities, van Eyck offered a solution to the problem of social imagination that Giedion argued faces post-World War II architects in their efforts to frame 'centers of social activity'.[22] Van Eyck's exploration of polycentric cities and multivalent buildings was an ingenious way to address the lack of centre, or form, confronting most societies. It is significant, then, to observe that his enterprise was so challenging precisely because it was an exercise of social imagination, which is the crucial link between his capacity for framing a humane habitat and the utopian mentality necessary for this ability.

Van Eyck's utopia was a place where humans could be at home. Its dynamic character would probably be its greatest surprise, especially in light of conventional wisdom which has it that utopias must ultimately always stubbornly stand as static non-places outside of time and experience. Moreover, configuration of human habitats discloses an impulse to render them comprehensible; it does not disallow diversity (or difference) but rather emphasizes situatedness through careful repetition of familiar parts, strengthened by being legible throughout.

Van Eyck's remarkable achievement is that he was able to imagine wholeness in terms of the inbetween, equilibrium in terms of dynamism, and permanence in terms of relativity. More remarkable still, is that he constructed a limited utopian realm voluntarily occupied for a while in just such ways, one that in its present transformed condition continues to tell a *story of another idea* that architects and clients could return to as a *model* of real possibility for configuring the human realm. All of these characteristics effectively distinguish his vision from the narrow concerns of economizing reductionism, excesses of visual novelty and fantasies of autonomy that characterize so much contemporary practice.

Chapter 12

The unthinkability
of utopia

> Meanwhile, though he is a man of unquestioned learning, and highly experienced in the ways of the world, I cannot agree with everything he said. Yet I confess there are many things in the Commonwealth of Utopia that I wish our own country would imitate – though I don't really expect it will.[1]

> Sir Thomas More

When human needs periodically appear met and biological survival seems assured, utopias' rebelliousness persists, especially by putting up generative resistance to the limitations matter-of-factness places on social life. At the very moment when a utopia seems realized, restless spirits emerge yet again to push for something that goes beyond simply meeting the barest requirements for human habitation. Such individuals challenge minimal expectations with visions of an enriched reality. Thomas More's *Utopia*, for example, contested a reduced social realm with the possibility of augmented and clarified relations among citizens, at the very moment when commons lands were being fenced in (enclosed) and social relations divided.

Throughout the modern (post-medieval) period, from More's time until today, there have been restless spirits who remain unsatisfied with the *apparent* realization of utopia in the form of affluence, technological sophistication and assured survival. Such individuals differ from deterministic technological utopians, who see in progress, as its own reward, not so much a promise of meaningful abundance but rather an impoverished reality based on scarcity.

Utopians of the sort discussed here however, tend to view utopia – as a description of their longing – as derogatory. Accordingly, especially during the twentieth century, the title 'utopia' came to imply a guarantee of failure, becoming a marker of impossibility. Consequently, no *true* utopian is comfortable with the title of *Utopian*, precisely because such designation is tantamount to marginalization and

12.1
Thomas More,
Utopia, **Apud**
inclytam
Basileam, 1518.
Frontispiece
Source: The New
York Public Library,
Astor, Lenox and
Tilden Foundations.

rejection. What crypto-utopians such as Le Corbusier, Louis I. Kahn and Aldo van Eyck envisioned, was a new reality more real than present reality could ever be without some transformation. Still, to call a utopian a utopian is typically an assertion that his or her vision is doomed from the outset.

Utopia, in its current use, is primarily an invective that proponents of limited vision hurl against possibility. In architecture, hostility to all things utopian derives from four primary sources. First, Marx and Engels's critique of what they called utopian socialism highlighted the unscientific and thus unverifiable character of utopias. Second, the failure of supposedly scientific socialist visions (China and the USSR for example) to bring about a more humane existence confirmed that socialist ideology is no more scientific than utopias are. Third, the failure of totalizing visions of modern architecture to produce a more humane human habitat, whether aligned with Western democracies, communism, utopian socialism or technological utopianism confirmed that architecture alone is not enough to assure utopia. The fourth source of anti-utopian feeling was the collapse of Soviet communism, which appeared to confirm that ideology of any sort is hazardous, a reasonable enough conclusion considering the devastation of World War II, Nazism, Fascism and Stalinism. (Somehow, the technocracy of the atom bomb seems to have washed whiter because of the apparent pragmatics of its use, though it too casts a very long shadow.)

Since World War II, worldwide capitalism has come to prominence as the only system apparently capable of guaranteeing survival of the human race. With ideology under a dark cloud and in disarray, self-interested liberalism and capitalism can finally, and conclusively, replace religion and other social visions with a worship of technology, progress and profit. Specialization and matter-of-factness are adjuncts of self-interest, so pervasive that they lend a gloss of reasonableness to retreat from social dreaming. Under present conditions such reasonableness is commonly represented as a virtuous opponent to the kind of social dreaming utopia makes possible.

In short, given the worldwide success of capitalism as the dominant cosmology (the only possible vision), only a fool would willingly embrace a position remotely definable as utopian. Smart players embrace dominant social visions and join in. One way to demonstrate membership is to claim matter-of-fact reasonableness (representation of reality *as it is*) as a bulwark against dangerous unifying social visions of harmony in motion.

It seems, then, that if utopia has a positive dimension, rather than being exclusively a term of abuse, it is crucial to explain how this can be. In the context of this study, this has entailed showing how utopias also include a potentially constitutive force capable of empowering architects to form architectures out of social, humane and practical motivations. The proposed formulation of architecture and utopias is in direct opposition to conceptions of architecture and urbanism that view them as either solutions to technical problems, commodities or as autonomous art objects, emptied of powerful social motivations. Even so, architectural projection does seem always to harbour a utopian dimension – sometimes constitutive, at other times pathological.

In previous chapters, architectural imagination was examined as an implicitly utopian practice. What remains is to argue how architecture conceptualized (theorized and/or practiced) as the production of autonomous aesthetic objects, as a business practice, service industry or as a representation of matter-of-fact *realism*, reflects and maintains a disciplinary crisis of purpose. The crisis of architecture arises, at least in part, out of its necessary condition as a so-called 'weak discipline'. The uncertainty – actually, non-existence – of absolute architectural truth – in a positivist science manner – tends to enervate its confidence while agitating its quest for novelty.

Proposals of architectural truth usually end up revealing just how indefinable the disciplinary parameters of architecture actually are. The uncertainty about what architecture is or does encourages architectural education, theory and practice to become ever more amorphous. Alternatively, there is an opposite, though no more helpful, tendency toward peculiarly restrictive conceptions of what the limits or ends of architecture are. Such premature certainty reveals a desire to achieve cultural and economic parity with stronger disciplines such as law or medicine.

Discomfort with architecture as a weak discipline prompts displacement of its possible configurative principles in favour of conceptualizing it as something either unbound or, alternatively, as extremely restricted. In some instances, the activities of design are thought to so liberate the spirit that process is fetishized and results are viewed as unimportant. Design as liberation turns education into a kind of play therapy and is oblivious to the burden of use. Seeing architecture as a process so tightly controlled that it might actually lead to predetermined results also diminishes its configurative potential; as would the celebration of architectural 'newness' as an end in itself. These various preoccupations, in differing degrees, characterize so-called 'avant-garde' practices as much as they do conventional commercial ones.

If architecture's condition as a weak discipline could be reconceptualized in ways that freed it from its apparent disciplinary inferiority, architects (theorists, practitioners and educators) might then begin reformulating this very weakness in terms more appropriate to the particular problems of architecture. For example, cognitive science provides space for what it calls 'ill-defined problems', which include writing and other creative endeavours. What characterizes such problems is that they have no one definitive solution or single correct response. If architecture is a weak discipline, or the objects of its investigations constitute ill-defined problems, and this is a permanent feature of its practice, then disciplinary crisis is probably less a result of architecture's *weakness* than efforts to make it *strong*. Attempts to make architecture strong run the gamut from struggles for its complete autonomy to efforts to circumscribe it as one service among others within a global service economy.

However, as a weak discipline, architectural comprehensibility (for theorists, practitioners, educators and the human subjects for whom architects propose settings) depends, at least in part, upon the embrace of architectural invention as a utopian practice. Even if not so named, utopian projection reveals a preoccupation with stories about places and occasions, especially with how the second finds its settings in the first. Disciplinary comprehensibility, and the comprehensibility of results, requires a way to play at total pictures of buildings and cities that concurrently resist the finality of absolute application, as well as resisting the prevailing tendency toward technique and specialization that make such limited completeness attainable. In consideration of this, German philosopher Hans-Georg Gadamer has suggested how utopia might be reconceptualized in just this way:

> Utopia is a dialectical notion. Utopia is not the projection of aims for action. Rather the characteristic element of utopia is that it does not lead precisely to the moment of action, the 'setting one's hand to a job here and now'. A utopia is defined by the fact that . . . it is a form of suggestiveness from afar. It is not primarily a project of action but a critique of the present.[2]

The 'suggestiveness' of utopia that Gadamer points out as central to practice (which would include architecture), meets action, or its potential, in Ricoeur's conceptualization: 'Because the concept of utopia is a polemical tool [in its critique of the present and redescription of it], it belongs to the field of rhetoric. Rhetoric has a continuing role because not everything can be scientific.'[3]

Conceived of in the manner suggested by Ricoeur, utopias are rhetorical figures intended to persuade, not by cajoling (in the manner of advertising images) but through presentation of a potential articulate enough to be a real possibility for future action and its settings. What is crucial in my new re-reading of utopia and architecture presented here is the reconceptualization of utopias as offering a comprehensible or configuring picture able to assist individual and group organization of thought and action without requiring total application of any picture all at once, or ever.

Such reworking of the concept offers a corrective to the common view of utopia as fantasy or escape – a picture of impossibility at best left unrealized, and at worst dangerous. Gadamer is also helpful in this regard; he argues that utopian thinking is a means to something more practical than merely impossible wishes or retreat into fantasy:

> It is the creative capacity of human beings to come up with wishes and try to find ways to satisfy them, but that does not change the fact that wishing is not willing; it is not practice. Practice consists in choosing, of deciding for something against something else, and in doing this a practical reflection is effective, which is itself dialectical in the highest measure. When I will something, then a reflection intervenes by which I bring before my eyes by means of an analytical procedure what is attainable: If I will this, then I must have that; if I want to have this, then I have to have this . . .; until at last I come back to my own situation, where I myself can take things in hand.[4]

Architectural imagination as utopian practice suggests a method for configuring comprehensible projects via conception of them as something more complete. Totalizing play of this sort can locate individual projects within the realm of the possible while inscribing them within a relationship to the whole they invent.

In short, an initial wish can be effectively negotiated into reality – albeit in a limited form – as partial realization. Simultaneous combination of this with remembrances of original total pictures sets up the possibility of a dialectic. The relation between an originating ideal and the substantial effort required for even imperfect realization promises to guide utopian projects into configured existence as the fragments of a desirable whole. It follows, then, that total conception and partial realization act as checks and balances to one another. Moreover, if the envisioned whole of a utopia is conceived of as an immanence concealed by present conditions, as it surely must be, then utopian wholeness, as a desirable objective, is revealed as an unspoken method for inventing exemplary buildings, with positive implications for cities as well.

The unthinkability of utopia?

The idea of practice introduced above is novel inasmuch as it recalls forgotten attitudes. For example, in *Space, Time and Architecture*, Sigfried Giedion argued for a kind of architecture that becomes a setting for an *ought* before the fact. The setting is real, that is, it exists as a construction, but the life (social and individual) it is intended to house may not yet exist; not when the project is first constructed, nor even after its occupation, or possibly ever, at least not exactly as envisioned. His idea, that a structure (or collection of structures) can be projected and constructed as a setting for a kind of life to be realized in the future suggests a number of possible avenues for reconfiguring contemporary architectural theory and practice, especially in terms of what might, or ought to, organize the efforts of both.

Giedion's interpretation renders projects (in their conceptualization and realization) utopian – they are an interpretation of a social life and a setting for it that responds to the present by critiquing it. It is a utopia, however, that is neither a 'vest pocket utopia' in Rowe's sense nor 'distinctly "out of it"' in Franco Borsi's sense.[5] The implicit utopias of Giedion's description maintain their ideological dimension while being real possibilities.

Rowe sought to neutralize utopia and ideology such that the 'Campidoglio, etc., might be a means of permitting us the enjoyment of utopian poetics without our being obliged to suffer the embarrassment of utopian politics'.[6] His desire to neuter utopia by separating its forms from the social content it carries was meant to tame utopia so that it could become one among many urban adornments that may be attractive but are ultimately inconsequential.

Borsi's understanding of utopia as pathetic in its ineffectuality is even more common: 'Utopia is infeasible: a utopian project is an unfeasible project. It may be so by default or by choice . . . In a more positive vein, it is generally acknowledged – at best – that utopia is a question of "imagination" or "fantasy"'.[7] Both Rowe and Borsi appear to have relied on Engels's essay 'Socialism: Utopian and Scientific' for the substance of their estimation of utopia and utopian projects as escapism. Consequently, both miss the potentially configurative social dimension that even piecemeal projects for change hold.

In comparison to Rowe, Tafuri's negative criticism of modern architecture (since 1750) was explicitly embedded in Marxist critique of ideology, utopia and capitalism.[8] Tafuri wanted to evolve a critique of ideology and utopia that could reveal the mechanisms of architectural practice as now bound to capitalist production, which would also explain how, as he saw it, the retreat of architecture into irrelevance was inevitable. Any other conclusion, according to him, is self-deception. Hence, division of labour can be honest, whereas utopia, which always proposes a synthesis, is regressive and anti-revolutionary.

For Tafuri, a robust critique of ideology and utopia was necessary because both are kinds of dangerous distorting magic that promote impossible dreams of escape from capitalism, which obscure the destructive effect it has on cultural work. Most negatively, persistent attempts at escape must prolong capitalism's survival by indefinitely putting off genuine, revolutionary renewal of social and cultural life. The significant benefit of Tafuri's approach is that it allowed him to recognize what Rowe and Borsi could not: utopia as ideology is significantly more vital than utopia as escape.

Rowe opposed the 'activist utopia' he believed emerged during the nineteenth century (which he argued was the blueprint for postwar urban renewal) to the 'speculative' or 'classical utopia' of Renaissance ideal cities that he thought of as 'image rather than prescription'.[9] In the opposition he established, one kind of utopia is *good* because of its apparent contentment to remain a hypothesis while the other is *bad* because it is anxious for realization. Binary thinking of this sort cannot locate any possibility that nineteenth-century ideas had anything of value to offer.

Rowe shared his rejection of piecemeal utopian efforts with Tafuri. Both also needed to describe architecture as empty: Rowe to make it safe, Tafuri to demonstrate the ideological bankruptcy of capitalist production. Rowe, though, was far less comfortable with politics than Tafuri. His discomfort with transformation, which he acknowledged borrowing from Isaiah Berlin, ultimately rendered his project an apathetic one, the aim of which was to turn cities into museums of utopian collectibles domesticated and purified of context and content, but especially of *dangerous* ideology.

Tafuri's critique of ideology reveals a significant weakness in Rowe's debunking of post-nineteenth-century utopias and the city of modern architecture that followed. For example, although Tafuri was no friendlier than Rowe to modern architecture as it developed out of nineteenth-century utopian thinking, he could see the crisis of modern architecture as one of meaning or content or, as he put it, of ideology:

> The crisis of modern architecture is not the result of 'tiredness' or 'dissipation'. It is rather a crisis of the ideological function of architecture . . . it is useless to propose purely architectural alternatives. The search for an alternative within the structures that condition the very character of architectural design is indeed an obvious contradiction in terms.[10]

By revealing the predicament of architecture as an ideological crisis, Tafuri implied that its resolution would also be fundamentally a question of ideology. On the other hand, Rowe proposed 'purely architectural alternatives' that, while potentially entertaining, would do little to alleviate the problem of content confronting modern architecture and the modern city. He left meaning behind. Moreover, whereas Rowe would turn architecture into commodity, Tafuri saw this as the very crisis (and inevitability) of architecture as one branch among many of capitalist production.

If the limits of Rowe's project arose out of his binary thinking and absolute suspicion of ideology, the limits of Tafuri's developed out of his belief that architecture must be dead because under present conditions it can have nothing to communicate. In Tafuri's view, this was an inevitable outcome of architecture's subjugation to the logic of capitalist production (which must eventually empty everything it touches of all ideological content). Yet, Tafuri's decidedly pessimistic reading neglected the real possibility that human will can persist even under the worst conditions. Furthermore, he was, it seems, unable to believe that focused desires still have the capacity to inspire meaningful action. For Tafuri it was all or nothing; either revolution would redeem culture or it would wither.

Thinking with utopia

In contrast to Rowe's de facto acquiescence, or Tafuri's negative revolutionary perspective, the real possibility of bit-by-bit reform is the focus here. Such possibility revolves around conception of an *ought*. Distinguishing between *ought* and *can* (or is) is required if reform is to become a conceptual possibility generative of humane architecture on a project-by-project basis. Ruskin, for example, distinguished between *ought* and *is* in *Unto this Last* (1985), an example of nineteenth-century speculation about the good life that seems to have eluded Rowe.

Conception of an *ought* links architecture with utopia and ties invention to Giedion's interpretation of architectural potential as holistic and prospective. An *ought* of this sort concerns not only the ethical obligations of a project but also of the setting and social institutions that a realized project proposes and might shelter. This *ought* may even have little to do with the technical–functional requirements of the client, rather it will more likely be the content an artist desires to transmit to present and future alike as a commentary or interpretation of contemporary conditions and aspirations, especially as these might be revealed through a specific project in a particular place. What is more, settings given a new form have the potential to contain new forms of conduct by proposing a place for them to occur.

Rowe and Tafuri's attempts to neutralize architecture and tranquilize utopia notwithstanding, there have been a few recent attempts to renovate utopia as relevant to architectural invention. Even so, the character of this requires further development. For example, at the close of *The Ethical Function of Architecture* (1997), Karsten Harries muses: 'let us dream of utopia'.[11] What, though, would be the character of this dream if realized? According to him, it will consist of 'introducing into the city theatrical and festal spaces, punctuated by works of architecture that, lacking authority and responsible to no one, are greatly revolutionary'.[12]

Unfortunately, Harries does not really offer concrete suggestions for just how this 'revolutionary' city would come about. In fact, he hazards not even a guess about the conditions required for establishing such a realm. Open though his proposed city might be to possibilities of spontaneous inhabitation, his conception appears too weak to enter into reality by transforming it. His praiseworthy advocacy of *weak thought* – provisional and open rather than absolute and fixed – is not at issue. Rather, his lack of clarity about what he believes would be configured by such dreaming, not to mention how it might come to pass, does seem a serious limitation.

Nevertheless, what appears certain is that revitalization of utopia requires emphasizing its social and political aspects while simultaneously stimulating its capacity to resist its pathological propensity. To do both, utopias must continue to have something substantial to say about reform, holistic settings and desirable outcomes.

In *The Roots of Architectural Invention* (1993), David Leatherbarrow, similarly to Harries, addresses the configuration of a more open, provisional, realm. While his proposal is implicitly utopian compared to Harries's, his elaboration on hopes for reform is far more concrete. In brief, Leatherbarrow argues that architectural potential is most achievable when comprehensive schemes are conceptualized with the ethical function of architecture in mind, which, obviously enough, associates his ideas with Harries but also with Ruskin's ideas on *ought*:

> The work of site definition involves the invention of a more perfect order, one that closely approximates what ought to be. This task is never fully accomplished because the conditions in which one finds oneself are always changing . . . The definition or fixity of a design intends the 'right' order of human affairs, but such a definition always emerges from contemporary conditions. Architectural definition can be envisaged only in view of what is right in a given situation. . . . Design solution intends constructions that will endure and approximate ideals, but do so in view of, or in response to, demands, requirements and interests that are bound

> to a time that will be superseded by another. . . . As it makes up the spatial and material correlates of typical forms of human conduct, architecture aspires to persist in time but can do so only because it is situated in a time that remembers inadequate solutions so that better ones can be projected.[13]

Like Giedion, Leatherbarrow recognizes the centrality of memory to utopian-like projection, athough he presents it in the negative. Whereas Giedion, for example, interpreted Michelangelo's Campidoglio as a figuration of the artist's remembrance of a free (republican) Florence and his dream of returned freedom in a future republican Rome, Leatherbarrow argues that memory informs present-day commentary on earlier inadequate solutions by encouraging current projects to convincingly surpass the limitations of previous ones. Memory is thus proposed as configuring the future by either superseding past (or present) conditions, or by reclaiming and reconfiguring some ideal past in the present towards a better future.

Both configurations are utopian in their redescription of reality based on a critique of the present. They are also examples of constitutive, rather than pathological, utopia: the concrete results envisaged (or even realized) are partial, not as applied, but under present conditions. A project may be constructed, but either its situation will change at some point or the social situation for which it is intended as a setting may forever remain unrealized as a permanent condition of openness. The crucial difference between both Giedion and Leatherbarrow's positions and the argument developed here is that neither openly mentions utopia as an organizing feature in the imagination of an exemplary architecture. For example, while Giedion implies the role of a golden age, the presence of utopia is even subtler in Leatherbarrow's argument.

Rowe's identification of 'vest pocket utopias' as a way to benefit from utopian form alone freed from social content differs from the inventions Leatherbarrow was considering. Rowe proposed purely architectural alternatives of the sort Tafuri warned against, which, it is worth recalling, he argued disregard architecture's crisis as a loss of its 'ideological function'. This is a serious debilitation precisely because, without an ideological function, architecture inevitably becomes an object of fetishized consumption.

Leatherbarrow appears to have located a way out of this conundrum by arguing that buildings 'are the result of something other than architecture'.[14] This 'something other' includes 'likely forms of conduct . . . patterns of conduct . . . [and conception of a] "right" order of human affairs . . . demands, requirements and interests that are bound to a time that will be superseded by another'. Architecture, then, proposes the 'spatial and material correlates of typical forms of human conduct'. Most importantly, perhaps, it is an approximation of 'what ought to be [for the moment, situated] in a time that remembers inadequate solutions so that better ones can be projected'.[15]

What Leatherbarrow proposes is very close in intention to Aldo van Eyck's conception of a 'configurative discipline'. The biggest difference between the two is one of scale. Leatherbarrow is mostly concerned with individual sites and the buildings that occupy them as the primary location of potential wholes deriving from thoughtful practices. Van Eyck, however, took a leap in scale by applying Alberti's calculus that 'the house is a small city and the city a large house' to the contemporary city.

Van Eyck did not so much want to make cities into houses or houses into cities. He believed, rather, that house-like cities would be more welcoming, while city-like houses would be more cosmopolitan. By proposing configuration of the whole city so that it becomes comprehensible as situating human habitation and human society, van Eyck attempted to reform architecture as a discipline into a forward-looking utopian practice of memory, potential, repair and reconciliation.

Towards a configurative discipline

Giedion, Harries and Leatherbarrow may be implicit utopians in the sense developed here, but for the most part the contemporary city remains conceptualized as a diseased entity requiring radical surgery to cure it. Or, in more enlightened approaches, it is promoted as a vast entertainment zone at its rebranded best when approximating the programmed qualities of shopping malls and theme parks. Van Eyck would have rejected both attitudes. The first is morbid in its efforts to rid civilization of its setting, and the second is perverse in its surrender of the human realm to extreme free market capitalism, which necessitates abnegation of the civic.

Van Eyck believed that human beings choose to live in cities because they allow for a kind of human interaction impossible in any other setting. He warned that the way we approach the city, for example by introducing suburban spatial practices into the centre, remains antithetical to its relevance as a setting for human life characterized by civic interaction. It is no wonder, considering his passion for city life, that van Eyck was one of the few recent architects willing to criticize his profession by challenging critics, educators and practitioners to resist the seeming inevitability of deurbanized cities filled with inhospitable architecture.[16]

Although van Eyck may not have called his vision utopian, this does not preclude the possibility that it was nevertheless utopian. Like a true utopian, he grounded anticipation of 'a person-friendly-humane-architecture'[17] in memory; recollecting possibility untainted by current cynicism, informed as much by traditional culture as by classical antiquity and modernity. No matter what present conditions might suggest as realistic or inevitable, van Eyck continued to see people as better than they might actually be. Accordingly, he endeavoured continuously to provide what he called 'built homecoming', a human environment able to contain individuals and groups emotionally as well as socially.

If van Eyck's desires were not utopian, it is difficult to say what else they might have been. Moreover, the prospective nature of architecture is its permanent utopian condition, especially when the aim is to surpass the limitations of inadequate previous solutions. Nevertheless, architects must deny, even denounce, utopianism if their projects are to have any hope of being accepted as viable, more valid, possibilities. It is thus not surprising that van Eyck would not describe himself or his work as utopian, but neither did he think it necessary to incessantly reject utopianism as unreal or hopeless. Embrace of social reality was, in fact, of paramount importance to him, he reserved his fiercest criticism for any architecture that did not assist individual and social well-being:

> The present generation of architects dismisses as errant hypocrisy the theory that we build with the intention of providing a pleasant environment for society. They spurn such 'humanism' and accordingly . . . reject [my approach].[18]

It anguished van Eyck to imagine that an architect would intentionally construct an unsettling building, yet he recognized such an attitude in the air. He identified its source in a *desire* (self-abnegating as it might be) by some contemporary architects to represent a diminished role for themselves and their architecture in consumer society. Nevertheless, he remained surprised that any architect would want to elaborate on the demise of his or her own discipline.

According to van Eyck, even if society seems more and more to have no form and citizens have little idea of how to ask the right questions of those who shape the built realm, or lack the confidence to formulate demands for a more humane habitat, architects, nonetheless, remain responsible for making the human environment a home for people:

> To the extent that the user of our buildings is indeed, literally, the well-fed consumerist society, this rejection – this cynicism – becomes understandable. I as much as anyone am aware of the malodorous side to the architectural pond. [It might seem as though] [e]verything functions but man himself . . . If this is so, rejection, criticism and cynicism are all to be expected. But that doesn't exclude a humane standpoint. On the contrary, it IMPLIES it. You don't have to be a philanthropist to argue for a person-friendly – humane – architecture. Such a thing as a person-unfriendly architecture is a priori unthinkable. It's not architecture at all but something else altogether. Even though the human collective does little enough to inspire a love of one's own species, the task remains the same and it is this: to work in a way that achieves something that's positively useful to people. JUST AS THE DOCTOR OR THE BAKER ON THE CORNER DOES [original capitals].[19]

Van Eyck argued against the impersonal and abstracting tendency of binary thinking, which was a characteristic of the striving for objectivity and idealized absolute truth the natural sciences once mythologized and laid claim to. The opposite of the impersonal includes the subjective or emotional, which are equally the opposite of objective ideals. A configured, comprehensive city would be partial in the sense of both biased and unfinished, a city made up of relationships between part and whole and whole and part that can render it understandable as a configured pattern that is never fully complete. Specificity (in its partialness), emotionality and subjectivity, when understood as rhetorical, guard a configurative conception of utopia from becoming impersonal, impartial and objective.

By the same token, rejection of scientific method out of hand would be premature; scientific method is especially useful when it models a kind of testing of wishes to see their fitness for reality, such as Gadamer described. At any rate, van Eyck's approach was utopian in its optimism born of critique and its conception of the city as total, which is necessary for civic comprehensibility to become a real possibility. The memorial aspect of van Eyck's utopia resides in his conviction that cities are a permanent – past, present and future – condition of civilization, crucial settings for the elaboration of human beings in community.

Concinnitas, *configuration and utopia*

Van Eyck's considerable concentration on wholeness discloses his intellectual debt to Alberti. For example, his complaint against the limited nature of *mere survival* indicates awareness of a continuing devolution that already concerned Alberti nearly 500 years earlier.

For Alberti, the *beauty* of the whole commonwealth was of the utmost importance – configuration of all of its aspects was necessary for it to be persuasive. Strangely enough, progress has disfigured this ideal into its opposite: increasing bureaucratization and a muting of the civic realm now renders institutions more and more abstract (not to say ugly). Alberti long ago warned against such reductive tendencies:

> Most notable is beauty, therefore, and it must be sought most eagerly by anyone who does not wish what he owns to be distasteful. What remarkable importance our ancestors, men of great prudence, attached to it is shown by the care they took that their legal, military, and religious institutions – indeed, the whole commonwealth – should be much embellished; and by their letting it be known that if these institutions, without which man can scarce exist, were to be stripped of their pomp and finery, their business would appear insipid and shabby. When we gaze at the wondrous works of the heavenly gods, we admire the beauty we see, rather than the utility that we recognize.[20]

Alberti's separation of beauty and utility could lead to a misreading of his intent. He might seem to be justifying the practice of thinking of buildings as construction with architecture added on as an aesthetic wrapping, a separation of structure from cladding that confuses architects in their attempts to determine over what part of the process their expertise obtains. While conceptions of art and architecture, or understandings of them, frequently separate form from content, Alberti's apparent opposition of beauty to utility intended no such thing; his definition of beauty bears this out.[21] What is more, it prefigured van Eyck's conviction that part and whole and whole and part are interdependent.

According to Alberti, beauty is a hope rarely granted in full. Nonetheless, striving for it is vital. Aiming for an ideal by utilizing language to persuasively argue for its virtues reveals Alberti's and van Eyck's efforts as rhetorical: both sought to convince the reader of the correctness of their proposal of a specific *ought* that, at least conceptually, encompasses a prospective view of the whole city. Their mutual objective across time endures as the presentation of a convincing beneficial outcome that other architects, in van Eyck's case, and patrons, in Alberti's, might be tempted to shepherd toward reality. Alberti was certain that it is rare for anything to be 'complete and perfect in every respect', but this demonstrates his hopefulness rather than expressing resignation.[22]

Whereas his partiality has subsequently been deformed into the kind of bureaucratic 'realism' which many architects select as a default position, neither Alberti nor van Eyck were dissuaded from pursuing wholeness (no matter its complexity) as an aim. In fact, convinced that achievement of a configured city is the greatest difficulty, both redoubled their efforts to persuade the reader that their proposals disclosed a necessary good. Accordingly, Alberti argued:

> Anyone who builds so as to be praised for it – as anyone with good sense would – must adhere to a consistent theory; for to follow a consistent theory is the mark of true art. Who would deny that only through art can correct and worthy building be achieved.[23]

Writing nearly 500 years later, it was much more difficult for van Eyck to imagine that anyone who builds 'builds so as to be praised for it'. Paradoxically, just such resignation borne of frustration was the motive force of his optimism. As he saw it, if most architects and urbanists care little for the hard work necessary to realize a configured city, to say nothing of the governments and individuals who hire them, van Eyck saw it as his responsibility to project a voice of resistance, reason and emotion, even though it was mostly unheeded.

In a wilderness of resignation, his partiality was that much more necessary. Van Eyck asserted that the configurative possibility of cities and the elements that form them, which could become identifying devices for citizens, 'is sorrowfully forgotten the moment architects and urbanists grab a pencil'.[24]

It is worth noting that his conception of identifying devices has little to do with Rossi's 'Architecture of the City' (1982). Whereas Rossi proposed apparently fixed and recognizable figures employed for their familiarity and organizing potential, van Eyck proposed a constancy of desire, which figuration transforms:

> The time has come to invent new significant identifying devices that perpetuate in a new way the essential human experience the old ones provided for so well. At the same time these new ones must provide for equally essential experiences the older ones no longer provide for or never did.[25]

Just as Alberti recommended, van Eyck's theory is consistent but does not propose an outcome adhering to a fixed formal or aesthetic image. Moreover, design, construed as technocratic problem solving, style development or adherence, formal play, or ironic manipulation of elements, is refreshingly absent from van Eyck's thought and practice. In this way, his project was close in spirit to Aberti's, whose objective was to propose the '*Art of Building*' as an approach, as an optimum state of mind, and as a discipline of practice, not as a technique for arriving at a particular look or result. Theoretical elaborations for both were a way to evolve a best possible approach, not a means to arrive at some predetermined end.

If van Eyck's proposals are convincing and can inform the discipline, that is, if architectural practice responds by reforming itself as a configurative discipline, cities and buildings would be approached positively rather than negatively:

> We cannot solve the problem of the expanding metropolis if we continue to approach it negatively. That the metropolis 'explodes' instead of expanding naturally – I am thinking among other things about suburban disease – based on the negative status quo.

> Even if the vicious circle qualities are evident, we must start from the simple positive truth that cities expand because man today is drawn toward them for intrinsically human reasons – because the desire to communicate and participate is a primordial attribute of consciousness.[26]

If architects, theorists, or educators began with the 'simple positive truth', posited by van Eyck, that cities get bigger because people require them more for emotional than economic satisfaction, their practices, at a variety of scales, from individual buildings to the whole city, might become more configurative. The partiality such a method entails discloses human desire for a home, as well as individual longing for places, as potentially the fundamental content of building.

Attending to this play between individual desire and human condition raises the possibility that the city could indeed become comprehensible through eurhythmic relationships (in both directions) between part and whole and whole and part. Van Eyck's wish could then slowly enter reality to re-render the human realm in such a way that individuals might find more than adequate shelter in both house and city.

Correspondence between van Eyck's elaborations on a configurative discipline and Alberti's discussion of compartition, ideal cities and the city–house house–city relationship, form a dialogue of themes across several centuries of architectural theory. In the event, van Eyck's effort relied heavily on Alberti's ideas; moreover, the thought of both is crucial for conceptualizing architecture as a constitutive utopian practice.

In Book One of his Ten Books, Alberti discussed *Lineaments* as those parts of architecture that derive from the mind, which suggests that the beginning of architecture resides there. In Chapter Nine of Book One, he considers *compartition*, which is touched upon at several points throughout *The Art of Building* (1988); as an idea, it is both prologue and explanation of his much-quoted city/house house/city analogy. In Book One, Chapter two, Alberti defines *compartition* as 'the process of dividing up the site into yet smaller units, so that the building may be considered as being made up of close-fitting smaller buildings joined together like members of the whole body'.[27]

In this instance, the site is construable equally as that of an individual building or of an entire city (maybe even region). Thus, the town is comprehensible as a body, made up of interrelated parts, in much the same way that a single building is. Here, body refers as much to the physicality of a human being or animal as to the organization of individuals into a civic structure, equally made out of single people as single buildings and institutions. Conceptualized in this way, buildings and cities analogize bodily structures, even as bodies provide a model for such structures.

For Alberti (and van Eyck as well), bodies were an acceptable as well as valuable model for both building and city, primarily because bodies are experienced as a unitary whole made up of interdependency among its variety of parts (akin to Vitruvius's discussion of eurhythmy in Book I, Chapter II, especially in paragraphs three and four, of his *Ten Books*). Alberti reflected upon order of this sort, experienced bodily and achieved in buildings and cities, considering it (following Plato) of the same stripe as beauty: both depend upon harmony (or at the very least coherence) among interdependent parts to reveal them. Order, argued Alberti, is 'the chief ornament in every object', assured only when it is 'free of all that is unseemly'. *Compartition*, adequately realized, goes far toward disclosing an object that is seemly:

> Neither jumpy, nor confused, nor disorganized, nor disconnected, nor composed of incongruous elements; it should be made up of members neither too numerous, nor too small, nor too large, nor too dissonant or ungraceful, nor too disjointed or distant from the rest of the body, as it were. But in terms of its nature, utility, and methods of operation, everything should be so defined, so exact in its order, number, size, arrangement, and form, that every single part of the work will be considered necessary, of great comfort, and in pleasing harmony with the rest.[28]

Alberti's ideal condition for buildings reflects his definition of beauty. A building becomes beautiful only with the achievement of an extremely high degree of internal coherence, at which point *nothing may be added nor taken away but for the worse*. However, although less explicitly stated than when he defined beauty, Alberti clearly believed that partial realization of complete internal coherence is generally the best that can be hoped for. His acceptance of such partial success discloses how important the aims modelled by ideal mental images are as a guide to actual work.

What is more, Alberti's identification of *the requirements of necessity and convenience* as a serious concern locates the ideal he proposed within real possibility, while still making it more than 'the utility we recognize', though weaker, more partial, when compared with attempts to fully realize and apply a utopian scheme, geometrical or political, all at once.[29]

Architecture as utopian practice is less the realization of a rigidified ideal image than recognition of design as commentary and critique, as a means by which the existing may be redescribed with some improved new condition in mind. The usefulness of mental pictures of *wholes* is that they serve to guide action as they bring projects into material existence; further, such a picture implies obligation, which could recall architects from the widespread contemporary belief that buildings are autonomous objects, and cities are simply fields of commerce and development.

Holistic envisioning also suggests that building and city are inextricably bound in any formulation of comprehensible settings for human being and action, such as van Eyck pleaded for. It is unlikely, however, that he would have devised his imperative that architect/urbanists ought to 'make a bunch of places of each house and each city' without Alberti's earlier introduction of a similar, albeit somewhat more elaborate equation.[30] He argued that compartition, order and interdependency are as necessary for projecting and constructing comprehensible houses as they are for projecting and constructing configured cities:

> [A]ll the power of invention, all the skill and experience in the art of building, are called upon in compartition; compartition alone divides up the whole building into parts by which it is articulated, and integrates its every part by composing all the lines and angles into a single, harmonious work that respects utility, dignity, and delight.[31]

According to Alberti, it is vital to consider every element of houses and cities with the greatest care and attention to ensure harmonious works that satisfy need and desire. The result would be a setting appropriate for human being at all scales from detail to city (even entire regions). Van Eyck mirrored such convictions, even going so far as to extend them. Whereas Alberti was preoccupied with the appropriateness of the setting (believing that propriety could be enough to facilitate satisfaction of need and desire), van Eyck reordered this relationship at all scales, in terms of human subjects – something explicitly named by Alberti.

Van Eyck further *modernized* Alberti's proposal by considering the individual parts out of which contemporary buildings are assembled, at a variety of scales – from detail to house to city and beyond – in terms of repetition and modular construction. In conjunction with his concern for the human subject, this consideration of the realities of industrialized construction could potentially humanize repetition. His focus upon the connotative and denotative capacity of first units as crucial to their success across subsequent multiples of them reveals a method for rendering even the extreme size of modern buildings intelligible.

The ideal proposed by van Eyck turns on expansion of multiples that extend the identity of prior and future conditions through further multiplications of them. Crucial to this approach are the qualities of the initial unit that, if adequate, will allow it an identity that, in a twist on Alberti, not only depends on interdependent conditions for success but requires that it could exist on its own as an independent whole.

In short, according to van Eyck's model, each element is a whole that when joined to other wholes, or multiples of it, extends the identity of the resulting, expanded whole rather than diminishing it. It is worth noting that this approach reveals the weakness of most modern multiples, which are incapable of supporting so much conceptual weight. It thus remains an ideal as yet mostly unachieved: modularized and industrialized building practices tend to doom repetition because most first units only reveal their own initial conceptual emptiness when multiplied.

For his part, van Eyck proposed a way of working that, like Alberti's convictions about house and city and city and house, moved in two directions at once. Both considered the part and the whole at the scale of the city as made up, ultimately, of details. However, for van Eyck, unlike for Alberti, it is the identity of the first unit as a whole in itself that assures legibility of an assemblage of parts – this is a radical departure from Alberti's conviction that the parts form a whole that can be neither added to nor taken away from, except for the worse. It was nevertheless necessary, made in consideration of contemporary construction methods motivated by an effort to humanize them. Van Eyck recognized the necessity (if need and desire are to be accommodated by buildings and cities) for a revision of Alberti's notion of beauty, which could accommodate a crafted building but would have great difficulty moving multidirectionally, from part to whole and back again, in the manner that an assembled building demands.

As with Alberti, van Eyck's ideal can accommodate necessity. In fact, it is a product of it; it is both the cause and result of comprehensibility bound to an industrialized building process. For Alberti the state was a corporate entity made up of the humans forming it, a concept closely related to his conception of the building as a body. The condition of beauty in a building, a body and a state is produced when as many of the potential meanings of propriety as possible contained in Alberti's term *concinnitas* are present.

Concinnitas conveniently gathers up the many senses of comprehensibility examined here.[32] It suggests a kind of architectural practice that could be capable of envisioning a holistic human realm by way of utopia without requiring immediate or total application. Utopian imagination provides architectural thought with a means by which to conceptualize the coincidence of all the parts of buildings, cities, states, bodies and governments as interrelated and interdependent. Ideas of the city as a complex association of all the elements that form it present a challenge to conventional attitudes of the city as a collection of whimsical objects determined by market forces alone.

The body/city analogy developed here, as drawn from Alberti and van Eyck's conceptions of city and house, is also present in Plato's *Republic* (1984), employed by him as a means to emphasize the relationship of part to whole. After an extended discussion of how the best city is the one most like a single man, Plato has Socrates say: 'We compared a well-managed city to the body as to how the parts and the whole were connected in pain and pleasure'.[33] Such a notion of the city, as a body of interrelated and interdependent parts, has little to do with the modern idea of the city as an organism that lives or dies dependent upon *efficient* circulation of goods, traffic and people. The interdependency of parts making up a whole proposed in the *Republic* is an expression of *common purpose* as crucial to the inauguration and survival of a just city. Alberti, and to a lesser extent van Eyck, assumed common purpose among citizens. Even so, he did recognize the possibility that such common cause could be locally based, rather than universal.

Plato's idea that just cities are like bodies infuses Alberti's organizing principle of *concinnitas*, which he considered the means and process for organizing thought and action at *all* scales and *across* all disciplines, while describing the interrelationship and interdependency of both.[34] In Alberti's universe, *concinnitas* would necessarily be most abundant in Nature, precisely because it is the model of order for all things that human thought and action, at its best, might imagine.

Concinnitas, however, cannot be quantified: its relative presence as a proportional content of any thought or thing is recognized but eludes observation, touching awareness only through that which it operates. In short, there is no scientific proof for its existence. It can only be understood, or recognized, as either a presence or an absence. When present, *concinnitas* is immediately observable, argued Alberti, to 'the workings of a reasoning faculty that is inborn in the mind'.[35]

As a faculty, condition or process, *concinnitas* is no easier to observe (except through its representations) than is morality, the absence of which is ordinarily viewed as a deficit. Although both may be culturally bound and locally organized, notions of each, as well as of propriety, appear in their own unique ways at almost all times and in all places. Further, the body and its care may be a model for all three: *concinnitas*, morality and propriety.

The prospect of wholeness

Although van Eyck's approach is identifiably utopian, especially in the degree to which he pictured wholes (made out of parts) at the outset meant to result in comprehensibility at all scales, he discussed his proposals for a *configurative discipline* in terms of intelligible cities rather than ideal ones. Alberti was more forthcoming in his estimation of the usefulness of contemplating such cities in the establishment of comprehensible places (rooms, houses, cities and institutions).

In Book Four of his *Art of Building*, after describing the purpose of buildings and the nature of institutions and locations for pleasure, Alberti surveyed the divisions of society in terms of classes of people and classes of buildings, each with a role to play in composing the city and the social body. He proposed that the descriptions of states (cities, governments and people) he had surveyed are actually parts of a whole comprehensible through consideration of each as a part forming it. Moreover, each of these parts is conceptualized as a different institution requiring a particular presentation as a building appropriate to its status and purpose; it is a distinctiveness which is as applicable to populations as to buildings.

In this arrangement, Alberti establishes a productive tension between the universal and the local. The former can establish general principles enabling organizing conceptions of humanity (the universal) that inevitably change when encountering the specific (the local). Accommodation of such apparently opposed conceptions facilitates contemplation of a *best city* as a means to organize thought about cities in general, without obligating any of them to mirror in reality the ideal *in toto*.

It is in this way that utopia can set in motion redescriptions of reality in terms of ideals on a local level, potentially doing so also by allowing for alteration during establishment of a project. Alberti's consideration of the viability of an ideal state elaborated on in Plato's *Republic* suggests he would have accepted the reading of his intent advanced here. For him, institution of the *ideal* is difficult at best, but difficulty is not the point. Recognizing the vulnerability of plans for ideals is not in itself productive; at stake is developing awareness of the necessity of an ideal for envisioning the real as it ought to be.

In his description of ideal cities, Alberti introduced items crucial for an understanding of utopia as generative.[36] First, his suggestion that 'we too should project a city by way of example' helps to clarify Giedion's claim that Michelangelo's Campidoglio refers to prior examples of good government, while establishing a setting for a future good government specifically by giving it an anticipatory form.

Second, Alberti's caution that an ideal city must 'conform to the requirements of time and necessity' offers a significant corrective to the pathological propensity of utopian schemes (especially the violence inherent in attempts at total application all at once, which must ultimately make ideal projects impossible to realize). Accommodation to time and necessity could bind projects to a particular location in space and time, which shields the ideal from universalizing notions of it.

Utopian visions so imagined, especially when applied slowly and partially over a long duration, allow changing conceptions of time and necessity to operate on them, thus making any city 'projected by way of example' potentially responsive to the actuality of human practices in continuous transformation. Consequently, by minimizing the utopian propensity for fixed ideas without relinquishing their crucial ideological dimension, utopias could recuperate their generative potential, especially by offering up models *for*, rather than blueprints *of*, ideal cities.

Fluidity of conception permits utopian (mental or projected) images to organize architectural imagination over time. Gianni Vattimo touches upon this in his argument for a 'weak' (or *soft*) utopia that could organize the efforts of architecture and urbanism as soon as both finally accept that form cannot impose conduct as if from above. Vattimo characterizes this potential as a benefit arising out of the eclipse of architects' strong metaphysical conception of their tasks:

> Once the architect is no longer the functionary of humanity, nor the deductive rationalist, nor the gifted interpreter of a worldview, but the functionary of a society of communities, then projects must become something both more complex and more indefinite.[37]

Vattimo's multivalent view echoes Martin Buber's conviction (elaborated on in *Paths in Utopia*, 1996) that world survival depends on a decentralized conception, promoting reconfiguration of continents and states as a collection of communities of communities.[38] Conditions realizing such a vision could assist individuals to become situated as members of local communities that are part of a larger national or even global community, all of which might be interrelated in a mutually interdependent relationship without any loss of local identity. In fact, smaller communities, with augmented identities, could form around shared goals, fuller and more complex than present notions of constituencies based on shared self-interest can allow for.

Architecture and urbanism responsive to, and as settings for, such a condition, could result from a sense of shared obligation to smaller limited communities as well as to the larger, more diffuse, community of which they are also a part. Vattimo considered just such a possibility:

> In this sense the plan is a contract, not something that the city can simply apply straight away. It has the form of a utopia, so to speak, that guides the real future project, but which will itself never actually be realized as a project 'put into action' and 'applied' on the landscape. Gathered together in this statutory form of the project are all the conditions of rhetoric, persuasion and augmentation regarding the cultural tradition of the place in question, those different cultural traditions within the community that

significantly modify and redefine the activity of the contemporary architect and planner.[39]

Vattimo proposes a utopianism that is neither grandiose nor totalizing, but makes good use of the configurative possibilities holistic schemes offer, even while honouring the crucial restriction that application occurs over time, which allows for reflective modification of plans. In addition, it is key that such schemes are responsive to the practices of the community for which they are projected. Vattimo's 'weak' utopia can do this because it resists the potential excesses so common to attempts to apply projects all at once. The pathology of utopian schemes intended for complete application, within a short time span, is most acute precisely because accelerated establishment permits little or no possibility to consider the probable consequences of such projects during their realization.

Utopianism is so often associated with impossible dreams that its real concern, the quality of present conditions with an eye toward how existing social reality might be positively transformed to emphasize its best aspects, is generally neglected if not forgotten outright. Nevertheless, individual and social well-being are primary concerns of utopias. Thus, considering conventional expectations, van Eyck's *poetic utopian* vision is paradoxically utopian precisely because it concerns social potential as a very real topic of architecture:

> What is it then that must be done to ensure that buildings do assist well-being? Well . . . lots of things, like for instance that they belong to where they are put and that one can truly say of them: they haven't got what they needn't have (but do have what they need). In both cases this is a lot – all sorts of things.[40]

In the realm of architecture and urbanism, denial of social dreaming – a general *unthinkability* of utopia, or of the terrifying possibility that one might be a utopian – is a product, at least in part, of the awful social failure of so much modern architecture and urbanism, especially because much of it had an apparently self-professed utopian objective. CIAM's vision may have originated with a conviction to defend Le Corbusier's poetic modernity, but it quickly became an organ for promoting an international style that Giedion denied existed. In this role, CIAM's radical origins were abandoned as it changed into a kind of technological-utopian think-tank, preoccupied with four functions and minimum existence.

In response to CIAM's significant limitations, van Eyck and Team X attempted to elaborate a programme for an enriched modernity with a tacitly utopian dimension. For example, in one of the few statements where he mentions utopianism overtly and positively, van Eyck counters projects by *unpoetic utopists* with the alternative of an altogether more satisfying *poetic utopianism*.

> We're not going to let unpoetic utopists (what a paradox) browbeat our realism which has as much utopianism in it as society can absorb. We cannot do more than we can without doing less. Others may one day do more, but the pseudo-utopian browbeaters do less, usually very much less.[41]

In light of his statements from the 1940s onward, one can only imagine that an unpoetic utopist practises a species of technological utopianism, akin to the work of orthodox CIAM and commercial practitioners, which cannot really be utopian because utopia is always poetic. Poetic utopianism, on the other hand, it appears, *must* derive from an authentic modernity, which argues that split phenomena are really coequal parts of twin phenomena ignominiously split into dualities by a binary habit of mind common to positivism, which, according to van Eyck, include, among others:

> [T]he conscious and unconscious world (reality and dream, reality and myth, romanticism and classicism, imagination and common sense, order and confusion, movement and rest, mind and body, organic and inorganic, simplicity and complexity, change and constancy, past and future.) You can carry on endlessly until you meet good and evil, life and death, man and god.[42]

Reconciliation of phenomena long ago artificially separated from one another, to be represented as diametrically opposed, presents architects and urbanists with an enriched reality they could potentially analogize to the great benefit of their projects. Moreover, utopias, expressive of holistic habits of mind, model just the kind of mental tuning suited to envisioning a reality optimistically transformed through enrichment of it.

Utopia: the tacit coefficient of exemplary architecture

To conclude, although architects do not like to think of themselves as utopians, exemplary architecture continues to be imagined with a utopian mindset nonetheless, whether embraced or otherwise. Furthermore, architects' unquestioning acceptance of economic, social and political conditions makes it exceedingly difficult to invent exemplary buildings. Similarly, negating the present offers no panacea. It will not automatically result in exemplary architecture, particularly when present conditions are rejected in a superficial manner, either by emphasizing visual or formal novelty as difference or by ignoring architecture's social dimension.

When change is merely cosmetic, it serves only to re-establish what *is* by repackaging it and marketing it as new. Over the decades since World War II, modern architecture has consistently found itself in just this situation. Ultimately, there is always the potential for another (superior) possibility for social life that architecture can give form to, which is precisely what this investigation has endeavoured to reveal.

Because social life always occurs in, around and upon the artificial environment that humans make for themselves, utopic possibility as generative is very much an architectural concern. Be that as it may, the results of this investigation should in no way be construed as suggesting that utopia is or could be a technique for establishing *quality*; nor do these results imply that all architects should become utopians. Most importantly, these findings do not show how to instrumentalize utopia as a domesticated practice. Rather, these findings hopefully demonstrate that – individual protestations to the contrary aside – *all* exemplary works of architecture from the past, present and into the future *will* continue to harbour a utopian dimension at the moment of their invention, through to the long process of concrete realization.

A tacitly utopian dimension reveals itself as an apparent necessity for works of architecture and urbanism to be construed as exemplary or to have the possibility to become so. Yet, when a utopian propensity of art or architecture is made conscious to the maker, or is the self-conscious, but unnamed, objective of the maker, the first impulse is to either deny a utopian dimension or conversely to caricature it. Disdain for utopian projection is further encouraged by the arid projects for social housing and so much of the remaking of city centres in the United States, United Kingdom and elsewhere, associated with it.

When utopia becomes classified, or understood in a typological way, rather than apprehended as a dimension of this or that unique example of architecture harbouring utopian desire, it quickly becomes an ideal ossified into the rigidity of an *idée fixe*. In its disfiguration as a fixed idea, utopia is transformed into a type that can only be most imperfectly shadowed in the concrete world of reality, which will always confound rigid schemes with the messiness of time and necessity. Ossification of utopian longing, as a kind of established practice (or technique) that results in particular kinds of buildings that look a certain way quickly washes any utopian dimension out of the result. However, Le Corbusier, Louis I. Kahn and Aldo van Eyck were each able to conserve the utopian dimension of their work by leaving it mostly unspoken, often calling it something else in the name of a reality each wished to transform through clarification.

In the final analysis, this investigation reveals a paradox: the necessity of some utopian dimension for construing exemplary architectural inventions counter-balanced by the necessity that it be simultaneously suppressed, which has something to do with the reason why utopian experiments tend toward failure just when they seem to have nearly achieved total application. Once it enters consciousness and nears realization, utopian vision is likely to become myopic and brittle, a consequence, at least in part, of its utopianness entering awareness, transforming into a schema as it does. As a strategy for achievable perfection, the resistance of former utopian inventiveness – the generative achievement of utopianism – becomes instrumentalized, and when it does, it fails. Bureaucratization of utopia concludes its generative potential, especially as it moves from a liminal to an apparently fixed condition.

In a sense, the unthinkability of utopia is what calls it to the mind's attention. Le Corbusier, Kahn and van Eyck were professed anti-utopians; in fact, it is highly unlikely that any of them would have appreciated their thought and work being the focus of a narrative extolling the positive – even essential – role of utopia in the imagination of their, or any, exemplary architecture. Paradoxically, the very unthinkability of utopia, revealed in characterizations of their own practices, protects the utopian dimension of their work from becoming an *idée fixe*, or a typology of utopia, such as Colin Rowe's round cities revealed. This is so even for Kahn, whose desires to give form to *first things* once and for all discloses a tendency in his work to slip toward typification.

What, then, is the point of revealing the utopian dimension of an exemplary architecture if the very unthinkability of utopias is what permits such works to harbour a utopian dimension in the first place? It may be that the very unthinkability of utopia conceals its *other* from ridicule: an unspoken, often seemingly unspeakable, hope that the world could again be full. Such hopefulness elucidates potential, maybe even confirming that human beings and their relationship to nature and society is not bound by any necessity, any more than it is predestined to become ever-more abstract, as a painful expression of alienation. After all, is not the real possibility of recuperation exactly what humane settings, from Michelangelo's Campidoglio to van Eyck's Orphanage, propose and provide for?

The very concreteness of the settings examined here (their partiality and specificity) reveals a range of attempts to force, by their very presence, the possible realization of altered conditions, conditions within which fuller experience could take shape, embodied by individuals elaborating on operative social conditions, in settings remarkably suited to them. It might even be possible that these settings could sustain the inside and outside of self-experience in a realm tuned to interactions between public and private, self and other, and between subject and object.

The concreteness of such constructed settings resides as much in the material of their making as in their direct presentation of meaning, experienced by embodied minds including emotion and intellect, through the full five senses. This meaning requires no explanation; it is not abstract meaning that requires some meta-discourse to reveal it; rather it is *felt* meaning, experienced through reference to lived experience, both profoundly immediate and emotional. Such settings give form to desire, retrospective and prospective alike, because they can contain it, and in so doing, a fullness of experience, whose corollary is a kind of utopian wholeness, is made into a real possibility – at least for a moment.

In this sense, each of the settings considered in this study is a negation of the conditioning perspectives of the present, which is characterized by abstractness, ironic distance, commodification and the isolation of spectacle. Each of these qualities finds its mirror in an architecture represented as visual stimulation alone, to the near exclusion of other sorts of experience. In comparison, it is the very concreteness of La Tourette, the Salk Institute and Amsterdam Orphanage, then, that offers a challenge to arbitrary and positive beauty alike, especially as the two have become isolated from one another (mirroring an ever-increasing marginalization of architects) during the past 250 or so years. What the settings of Le Corbusier, Louis I. Kahn and Aldo van Eyck propose, by way of example, is a partial reconciliation of subject and object. In so doing, each challenges the logic of isolated beauties in the first instance. What is more, this challenge is the utopian dimension that each of these projects harbours.

Chapter 13

Into the present

I do not want to design anything, nor construct anything that does not carry with it a strong and clear message of responsibility, not only aesthetic but also of an ethical and moral sort. In short, I would like to carry into the new millennium a sort of rapproachement between scientific and ethical progress. I believe that this is likely the most important thing to carry into the year 2000 [translation by author].[1]

Renzo Piano

The enduring value of inhabited architecture turns ultimately not on its aesthetic appeal as an art object or even upon its technical functionality but rather on its persisting adequacy as a platform upon which social life can occur and transform itself. Even the most intentionally autonomous architecture will ultimately, over the long haul, be valued or discarded based on its capacity for receiving intended events while simultaneously remaining open to unexpected or unimagined ones without becoming obsolete: buildings freed from the burden of use are unsustainable.

Each of the projects examined in this chapter can be paired in some way with the three earlier projects at the centre of this study. Daniel Libeskind's Jewish Museum, Berlin (1989–1999) pairs with Le Corbusier's La Tourette in at least two ways. Both structures are dedicated to inward contemplation ideally leading toward potentially transformative reflection. Moreover, the construction of both hints at fallibility as a crucial humanizing characteristic, reserving perfection for the unknown or unknowable, or for the much too easy. Tod Williams and Billie Tsien's Neurosciences Institute, La Jolla, California (1992–1995), pairs with Kahn's Salk Institute, most obviously by being a research centre located just up the road from the earlier one, which established La Jolla as a prime location for such institutions. Both buildings make extensive use of concrete and engage in a significant dialogue with the land, at varying distances from the Pacific coast.

Renzo Piano's Jean-Marie Tjibaou Cultural Centre, Nouméa, New Caledonia, (1991–1998) pairs with van Eyck's Orphanage in more surprising ways. Whereas van Eyck incorporated traditional and foreign sources into his building in an effort to expand the scope of the institution while humanizing it, Piano's building introduces the height of sophisticated European building methods, materials and services to a local institution infused throughout by interpretations of indigenous building methods and forms. Van Eyck enriched his modern architecture by introducing ancient and alien traditions that he saw as parallel and equally valid. Piano goes in the opposite direction: advanced Western architecture is inflected by a local and pre-modern tradition as a means of interpreting both, rendering each relevant for a unique condition. In addition to the correspondences that Libeskind's, Williams and Tsien's and Piano's buildings examined here have with my earlier examples, each is courageously optimistic about the positive role architecture can play in the civic life of individuals, institutions and cities.

Piano, interestingly enough, has some direct connections with Le Corbusier, Kahn and van Eyck. He was obsessed with Le Corbusier's work when he was young and worked with Louis I. Kahn for a short while in Philadelphia.[2] Moreover, van Eyck was a member of the jury that selected Piano's winning competition scheme for the Jean-Marie Tjibaou Cultural Centre.

Berlin utopia: Libeskind's Jewish Museum

Three basic ideas formed the foundation for the Jewish Museum design: first, the impossibility of understanding the history of Berlin without understanding the enormous intellectual, economic and cultural contribution made by its Jewish citizens; second the necessity to integrate the meaning of the Holocaust, both physically and spiritually, into the consciousness and memory of the city of Berlin; third, that only through acknowledging and incorporating this erasure and void of Berlin's Jewish life can the history of Berlin and Europe have a human future.[3]

What could be more audacious, more optimistic, more utopian, than to imagine that a single building, overflowing with artefacts and evidence, might harbour the possibility, or even be the evidence, of an ongoing Jewish culture in Berlin, or Germany in general. There is something remarkably prospective, though never nostalgic, about the agenda elaborated on by the Jewish Museum Berlin. Libeskind's first commissioned work attracted hundreds of thousands of visitors to it when still empty, some even lamented that it would be filled with evidence of tens of centuries of Jewish participation in German culture. Yet, the building on its own, without the artefacts, would seem only a memorial, a remembrance of people now gone, testifying to loss alone with no hopeful dimension.

Although it is filled with documentary evidence of a community nearly destroyed, the Museum is not simply a storehouse of relics recalling an extinct civilization; rather, it heralds a continuing, though fragile presence. The building itself articulates this hopeful drama, slicing across its site and rising up into the baroque building that serves as its entry hall. These qualities, including the various concrete voids, announce that something is going on here; this building is a marker of joy as much as of sorrow.

13.1
**Site plan. Jewish
Museum Berlin,
1989–1999.
Architect:
Daniel Libeskind.
Drawing by
A. B. Dixon**

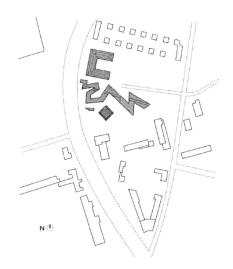

N

Even if the Museum were to lose its purpose, somehow be emptied of its contents, physical, historical and emotional, it would arguably remain an indicator of loss and hope on the Berlin landscape. The building promises to resist unforeseen occupations unsympathetic to its original purpose. 'Nazism and the Holocaust' may well, as psychoanalyst Chasseguet-Smirgel argued, 'remain the great mystery of the twentieth-century and have opened up vertiginous glimpses into the depths of the human mind', equally mysterious, though, is why any Jew would return to, or remain in, Germany.[4]

Libeskind's determinism

The Jewish Museum confronts the human propensity for forgetting with its own dark past. It demands engagement, but does so in a hopeful manner, permitting individual appropriation through bodily experience. Libeskind's work is audacious, but this is a sign neither of extravagant novelty nor of blind self-indulgence. While he would like visitors to consider his buildings in a particular way with a particular frame of mind, these suggestions are but one possibility among others. Choice, individual action and the inscription of self into shared reality are the most overt possibilities.

Libeskind's obsession with how the building is received (confirmed by several plaques posted throughout the basement level that indicate how the architect would like visitors to perceive and experience its main symbolic spaces) dislocates him for a moment to the position of critic, rather than artist. All the same, it is very likely that even without his directive statements to guide them, most visitors would feel something very close to what he wanted them to feel, particularly because the building actually does analogize what he wants you to feel. Paradoxically, though, by telling visitors how to feel, he risks igniting the reasonable human inclination to feel otherwise.

If Libeskind is directive, it must be because he wants Berlin, Germany and Europe to remember what, reasonably enough, it would be easier to forget. Even if his attempt to stage-manage experience is discomfiting, at the very least, it calls to mind the uncomfortable outcomes of the actions that most Germans and Europeans did little to prevent. In this museum, in this city, there is often a strong feeling of dislocation that Libeskind's building effectively analogizes.

> The task of building a Jewish Museum in Berlin demands more than a mere functional response to the program. Such a task in all its ethical depth requires the incorporation of the void of Berlin back into itself, in order to disclose how the past continues to affect the present and to reveal how a hopeful horizon can be opened through the aporias of time.[5]

Europeans in most parts of Europe lived alongside Jews with differing degrees of mutuality and tolerance for over 1,000 years. That coexistence is mostly all gone now, after Germans and others following their orders completely destroyed most Jewish communities. The consequences of such destruction for Europe are unfathomable and continue to unfold. Libeskind's determinism, as it turns out, is the expression of a not-so-quiet outrage at the forgetfulness that is widely on view in Berlin (grand expressions to the contrary notwithstanding), which is obsessed with the present and future of the post-wall city arising out of its ruins. Remembrance, at least in this context, might actually reveal the potential for real transcendence.

Why they come

The Jewish Museum is a declaration of the absent presence that continues to haunt Berlin and much of Europe. Libeskind's building might encourage reflection but it could just as easily be ignored, which is the potential fate of any statement. Architecture, though, is a peculiar kind of communication. If its aim is high art alone, making it akin to sculpture or even painting, it might be freed from the burden of use, but it will also be useless. Although architectural expression is symbolic in character, it is most powerful when comprehension of it unfolds through experience directly perceived by the body.

The building itself may be the reason why people visit it, many on some sort of architectural pilgrimage. In that case, the questions foremost in such a visitor's mind would be: does it deliver? Does actual experience of it stand up to the hype? However, in order to find out, the architectural visitor would need to experience as much of the building as possible before making a decision about its aesthetic effectiveness. Obviously enough, exploring the building as though it were pure form alone, or simply an objective of architectural interest, would quickly run into the *problem* of the Museum's curatorial mission.

At that moment, the social dimension of the building's purpose will intrude upon any possible experience of it as pure form. The curation speaks through the building, which in turn emphasizes the objectives of both. The building and its contents engage in an ongoing often-uneasy exchange: which will dominate the other? Ultimately, neither is dominant, as conditions of supremacy shift throughout, never quite resolved and always somewhat tense. This condition is similar to the survival of Jewish identity in Europe, no matter the good faith or forgiveness of each party.

Nevertheless, the willingness to present the drama of this tension, more or less in the open, reveals a utopian perspective that could be considered constitutive rather than pathological. It is utopian because the project of both the Jewish Museum building and its permanent collection is prospective and optimistic; faith in continuity is always future oriented. In the case of a continued, even thriving, Jewish presence in Berlin, it is doubly so. Likewise, the utopia projected is constitutive precisely because it is taking shape in the present, fully aware of the audacity of its project and the tensions that make up its territory.

If the building might bring architectural pilgrims to it who go on to learn about the stories it houses, a similar exchange could occur for those who come to the building primarily for the content. It seems reasonable to suppose that it would be all but impossible to remain indifferent to Libeskind's building, no matter how little one might care about architecture's declarative potential.

Between present and past

Arrival at the Jewish Museum challenges the visitor staring at the entrance. There is, in fact, no entry, at least no obvious one. Entrance to Libeskind's Museum is through an eighteenth-century building a few paces north of it with no discernible link between the two structures, at least not in view anywhere from the street level; this absence of a link is another clue that something peculiar is going on here. After entering the older building, passing through airport style security checks, and making one's way into the hall, after purchasing a ticket, a search begins for how to access the Libeskind building itself. This search is at first increasingly uncertain, until one passes through the only promising portal, spied from the hall of the older building (the other possibilities lead to the restaurant, cloakroom or out again).

After one passes through the portal, Libeskind's building makes its first appearance in the interior, rising up into the older building from below as a concrete mass carefully opposed to its orthogonal arrangement. The top of a dark stairway now beckons downward into the ground, under the earth, as though descending into a tomb, recalling the catastrophic loss of European Jewry to exile and murder. Procession from entry to arrival at the exhibits is exquisitely delayed, giving the building ample time to emerge as its own constellation of stories, even for the most distracted visitor, who must, after all, make each of the preliminary steps necessary to arrive at the galleries.

Three routes, three axes

Arrival in the basement, which permits underground passage between the baroque entry building and Libeskind's, presents the visitor with three paths. The primary one is the Axis of Continuity, intersected by two others: the Axis of Exile, and the Axis of the Holocaust. The first leads to a long steep flight of stairs, the second to a Garden of Exile, and the third to the Holocaust Tower; all are paved with the same material as the stairway. The axes of Exile and the Holocaust are approximately the same

13.2
**Main entrance.
Jewish Museum
Berlin, 1989–1999.
Architect: Daniel
Libeskind**

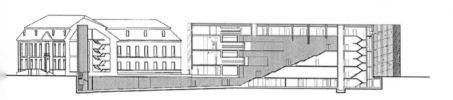

13.3
**Section (showing
connection
between entry
building and
Libeskind
building). Jewish
Museum Berlin,
1989–1999.
Architect:
Daniel Libeskind.
Drawing by
A. B. Dixon**

length. All of the paths are as funerary as they are institutional, characterized by a black floor, bright white wall and fluorescent lights above. Each of the axes has the feel of a long corridor to nowhere. Even so, each forms a part of Libeskind's ultimately hopeful story of continuity.

The Axis of Exile is something of an alternative to the Axis of Continuity, branching off it and crossing the Axis of the Holocaust on the way to the Garden of Exile. The Axis of the Holocaust cuts more violently across the other two Axes, leading almost perpendicularly in an opposite direction, ending at the Holocaust Tower. Both the axis of Exile and of the Holocaust are bound up with departure, in many ways nearly equally violent. One ends in the loss of a homeland, the other in death. Each axis leads to a setting analogous to the historical experiences associated with it, suffused by awareness that they cannot be represented, but only hinted at.

The longest path is the Axis of Continuity, which actually runs the full length of the basement, up a steep set of stairs, into the galleries, through them and back out of the Museum and into the city. Once inside the galleries, it is set aside for a while; the story of Berlin's Jews now begins to take over from the building's initial narrative.

13.4
Basement level plan. Jewish Museum Berlin, 1989–1999. Architect: Daniel Libeskind. Drawing by A. B. Dixon

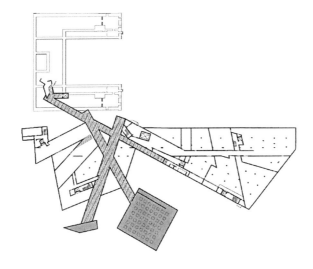

13.5
Axes. Jewish Museum Berlin, 1989–1999. Architect: Daniel Libeskind

As one moves through the galleries, past the various concrete voids and down again into the lobby, there is a constant vying for attention between the building's agenda, which exists apart from its specific museum function, and that function which now inhabits it. This is not so much a failing of either but a success; the tension between building and function is never fully resolved. The contents are

263

never fully assimilated into the container, which continuously asserts its own independent content. If attended to, this condition effectively analogizes the uneasiness appropriate to the multiple stories being told.

If Libeskind's Jewish Museum has a precursor, it is Claude Lanzman's film *Shoah* (1985). The film's incessant return to views of railroad tracks at the bottom of the screen, as if they were passing beneath the floor, is complemented by the accompanying sounds of cattle cars moving along the rails. Lanzman's film elicits a psychosomatic condition of dislocation and dread. Neither Lanzman nor Libeskind imagined that any art could possibly represent the Holocaust, any more than it can represent exile or continuity. Communication of this sort requires faith, confidence in the capacity of visual, formal and material expression to communicate experiences beyond the scope of words. When effective, a cognitive charge is induced producing responses in the mind and body simultaneously, in much the same way that the strongest poetry is felt meaning rather than intellectual understanding.

Axis of the Holocaust and the Holocaust Tower

The Axis of the Holocaust ends at the door to the Holocaust Tower, described as 'an empty vertical void' commemorating 'the many millions of holocaust victims'.[6] According to Libeskind, the tower is meant to analogize the experience of confinement 'before and during deportation and in the [concentration and death] camps themselves'.[7] Indeed, the experience of being inside the Tower is extremely unsettling; you are still in the world but during the moments spent within, the world is out of reach.

Certainly, the Holocaust Tower cannot analogize the experience of being hunted, captured, transported, selected and murdered. No architecture could. At such times, architecture fails, and eyewitness accounts, such as Primo Levi's '*Survival in Auschwitz*', are best consulted.[8] Nonetheless, even a modicum of willingness on the visitor's part reveals the Tower to be a place, set aside for reflection, where the mind will reasonably turn to thoughts of the disappeared inhabitants of this city, who happened to be Jewish.

Leaving the warm, well-lighted hall of the Holocaust Axes through a heavy door only to enter into the bottom of a cold dark shaft leaves one to wonder if the architect's declarations of how visitors to this room should receive it are at all necessary. What would be the response? Better yet, what could be the response, especially in a Jewish Museum in Berlin?

The sounds of the city, the banality of everyday life – a child yelling far above on the street; robbed of familiar occurrences, one lacks the comforts of normality. In death camps, the condemned were deprived of a life lived to its natural end. At the bottom of this shaft, one really needs no prompting on how to feel or respond – emptiness, outrage, disgust, or even hope.

The longer one remains in the shaft, the more unsettling the voices above become, but the more bright the slight shaft of light is as well. The light serves as a ray of hope: this is not a tomb, not yet at least. One can still hear the city – the traffic, children, planes and trains. Even those discomfiting voices out of reach far above seem to promise a return to comforting ordinariness. Maybe it is possible to climb out of the empty unheated shaft, which grows colder and colder the longer one remains.

Might it somehow be possible to jump high enough to grab hold of the ladder on the wall above but far out of reach? It would then be possible to climb through the darkness toward the light above, to somehow crawl across the ceiling toward the shaft of light, squeeze through the opening and escape this concrete pit; or, one could end the torment in an instant, move toward the door and grab the handle, which admits light and warmth from the hall beyond. Unlike in the death camps, here it is possible to quickly re-enter the bright illumination and heat of the Museum by pushing the oversized door back into it. Nevertheless, during those moments at the bottom of the Holocaust Tower, one could have thought, at least for a moment, that he or she was really trapped.

13.6
**Holocaust Void.
Jewish Museum
Berlin, 1989–1999.
Architect: Daniel
Libeskind**

The Axis of Exile and the Garden of Exile

At the end of the Axis of Exile, similarly to the Axis of Holocaust, there is a door. This time, however, it pushes outward to the exterior, toward the City and its sounds, into the Garden of Exile. Leaving the body of the Museum for the Garden of Exile is less unsettling than the tentative steps taken through the heavy door into the Holocaust Void. Here, a window permits initial access to what lies beyond. The sky above, the city around you, the trees, all recollect life in general. Yet, departing from the warmth of the well-lit museum for the Garden, especially in winter, confronts one with the cold.

The Garden of Exile is notable for its slanting ground and the forty-nine columns rising from it, each with a tree growing out of it. Forty-eight of the columns contain earth from Berlin, signifying 1948, the year Israel became an independent state. The forty-ninth column, at the centre, contains earth from Israel and represents Berlin. Awareness of these numbers and their intended significance comes from posted descriptions of the Garden, not because either is immediately perceived.

Nevertheless, in the Garden, Libeskind effectively analogizes strangeness through disorientation and containment, articulated with the forest of slanting columns that defines a difficult path of slanting pavements. Not surprisingly, moving through the Garden is unsettling, made even more disconcerting because although the city nearby can be heard, seen and smelled, it cannot be accessed from this location.

13.7
Exterior. Garden of Exile, Holocaust Void and Libeskind building. Jewish Museum Berlin, 1989–1999. Architect: Daniel Libeskind

Axis of Continuity and the steep stair

Before elevators and escalators replaced stairs as the primary means of accessing upper levels, stairways were often the most important symbolic element in a building. Achieving the goal of access, to the temple, courthouse or museum was made understandable to the body through the act of climbing. Upward climbs have correlates in the Bible as well, including in the story of Jacob's Ladder.

Up there is the enlightenment of wisdom but getting at it requires effort, which is what the Continuity Stairway at the Jewish Museum articulates through reference and experience. That it ends, at the top, in a blank wall signifies nothing more than that it could go on forever, all the way to Heaven, anything but a dead end. Climbing stairs requires effort, which involves all parts of the body from the feet to the head; ascent also alters one's breathing. A very long set of stairs, especially with risers just slightly taller than expected, makes the climb even more strenuous, and also rewarding.

The Axis of Continuity, the longest of the three paths at the basement level of the Museum, continues along a stair rising steeply upwards toward the start of the main exhibitions. The height of the risers and the length of the run increase the stress on the legs, making the body feel its ascension while climbing the stair upwards. Grated landings change the sound one hears, while variations in lighting, which enters the hall through slots in the ceiling, breaks up the climb. Although it is possible to descend these stairs, movement upwards is clearly the intention. By the time visitors make their way to and mount the Continuity Stairway, it is difficult to imagine how any of them could remain unstirred by the drama of delayed entry they have been enacting.

13.8
**Continuity
Stairway. Jewish
Museum Berlin,
1989–1999.
Architect: Daniel
Libeskind**

Exhibition spaces
When visitors finally enter the galleries displaying the permanent exhibition, habituation to the logic of the building is well underway, so the ensuing tension between it and the artefacts is not entirely unexpected.

It is fully appropriate for the building to nearly disappear behind the objects on display, which it can do momentarily without losing its impact. That the building permits such a negotiation without thwarting the exhibits or being thwarted by them makes the work even more effective. After all, the building was always intended to be a museum, a structure filled with objects on display to tell a story of Jewish life in Germany and its near destruction. Libeskind clearly wanted his building to be useable, to be engaged and to engage. Unworried by the burden of use, Libeskind's building is open to unforeseen appropriations.

Even though the exhibits at times almost completely obscure the interior spaces of the galleries, the strongest, most expressive and clearly defined architectural aspects of the Museum remain, not surprisingly, those free of artefacts or obvious use. This is especially so for the key linking and symbolic spaces of the building, which most effectively sustain Libeskind's vision throughout the less obvious parts of the Museum.

The entry stair downward from the old building, the three underground axes, the Holocaust Void, which is separate from the main building on the exterior, the Memory Void, which is the largest of the voids, and the stairway up from the basement axes to the galleries all effectively communicate their stories directly to the body. Equally evocative is the exterior, with its zinc cladding and eccentric windows, not to mention how the building sits on the site, cutting an unexpected zigzag across it to indicate its special purpose. By rejecting the convention of placing buildings orthogonally on city sites in adherence to the dominant grid of the development plot, the Jewish Museum is something like a permanent cut, or open wound, in Berlin. It is, though, a healing wound: only by periodically confronting its

13.9
Gallery. Jewish Museum Berlin, 1989–1999. Architect: Daniel Libeskind

13.10
Void plan, second floor. Jewish Museum Berlin, 1989–1999. Architect: Daniel Libeskind. Drawing by A. B. Dixon

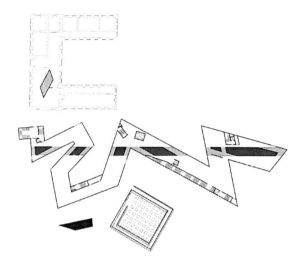

own dark past can Berlin hope to establish a good city to serve as the capital of a unified Germany.

In addition to the two stories told by the building and exhibits, a third asserts itself during progression through the galleries: a broken straight line of voids (hollow concrete towers) intersects the building's unique zigzag organization, which counterpoises functionally useable spaces to unusable ones. Most importantly, by reasserting the allegorical character of the building throughout, the voids primarily serve an important emotional function.

If the galleries extend the Axis of Continuity into an unknown horizon, the straight line of concrete towers, across which the path must be bridged, denies any possible exaggeration of the accident of survival into some kind of triumph of the human spirit over adversity. The towers materialize the absence of voided lives and the perils of forgetting.

Inscribing hope

In sum, Libeskind's Jewish Museum articulates the topography of Berlin's Jewish experience and the fate of Jews in Berlin. The building is a difficult, demanding and aggressive work that maps the trajectory of nearly unfathomable prejudice, betrayals and horrors, but also hope. Not surprisingly, in a number of important ways, it can also contain the concepts developed throughout this book. For example, the claims Libeskind makes for the forms and spaces of the building are neither arbitrary nor unexpected. Accordingly, the gap between the stories he tells and what is communicated to visitors is very narrow; disclosed through analogy, not melodrama.

Furthermore, direct presentations of meaning are experienced by the body at the moment of perception, articulated with great subtlety and eloquence, by forms disclosing a paradoxical preoccupation with articulating the unmeasurable and unrepresentable. Considering the nature of the stories the building tells, it has a surprising capacity for allowing the coexistence of apparent opposites, on a common ground, without requiring synthesis.

As with all of the projects examined here, the social dimension of architecture is central to Libeskind's thinking. His work voices the utopian dimension of architectural projection through a preoccupation with other possibilities, especially his belief 'that there is a relationship between the possible reality and the real possibility'.[9] Because of this, the work can tolerate appropriation without collapsing under uncertainty; the building has been able to receive the permanent exhibition even though at least some feared it could not.

Perhaps most profoundly, Libeskind, in a manner rarely experienced since Le Corbusier's Church at La Tourette, has comprehended the emotional power of concrete voids in three dimensions. In both the concrete Holocaust and Memory voids of the Museum, emptiness is a pregnant container. In this instance, emptiness carries a powerful emotional charge that these towers, which analogize the feelings they stir up, can ably hold, a notable achievement disclosing the extent of Libeskind's emotional and spiritual investment into his work on the Museum.

13.11
Church interior.
La Tourette,
1953–1960.
Architect:
Le Corbusier

Defying the Salk: Williams and Tsien in La Jolla

> We see architecture as an act of profound optimism. Its foundation lies in believing that it is possible to make places on the earth that can give a sense of grace to life – and in believing that that matters. It is what we have to give, and it is what we leave behind.[10]

At the risk of being reductive, it might be possible to argue that orthodox modern architecture was characterized by simple geometric diagrams, whereas an enriched modernism sought to render such diagrams more complex. After modernism, certainly during the last two decades, the diagram, in its most compact immediately perceptible form, increasingly disappears from view. By proposing an alternative perspective on the appropriate character of social settings, architectures of *situations* began, as early as with the immediate postwar period, to vie with architectures of rigidly defined programmatic events.

Accordingly, La Tourette, the Salk and Amsterdam Orphanage are transitional, articulating a territory somewhere between clear diagrams and something far more open-ended. More recently, projects such as the Neurosciences Institute, Jewish Museum and Tjibaou Cultural Centre elaborate on difficult diagrams that resist explanation by simple drawings showing the basic shape, layout or workings of the proposed settings.

Movement from simple squares to more complex shapes, leading toward the varied assemblages of some current architecture, demonstrates a developing transition from simplistic diagrammatic renderings of social life (by providing impoverished settings for it) toward a more comprehensive understanding of social life as varied. When responsive, architecture can contain the contradictory and spontaneous disposition of social life by establishing settings more able to receive it. In the present context, the Neurosciences Institute (NSI) is a particularly intriguing project, revealing correspondences with La Tourette, the Salk Institute and Amsterdam Orphanage. In common with these earlier projects, it materializes a vision of better conditions for the particular institution it now houses, disclosing an ethical dimension relevant to any problem of design.

In earlier chapters, I discussed how a monastic analogy overtly informed development of La Tourette and the Salk Institute; actually, such structures encouraged Le Corbusier and Kahn's understanding of architecture's ethical dimension as always bound up with defining relationships between individuals and between individuals and nature. Monasteries, as particularly concentrated examples of architecture's orientating potential, suffused both architects' thinking about the social

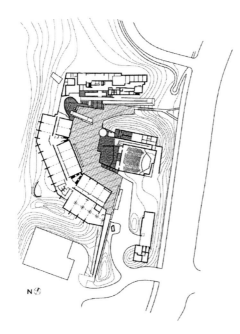

13.12
**Plan.
Neurosciences
Institute, La Jolla,
CA, 1992–1995.
Architects: Tod
Williams and Billie
Tsien Associates.
Drawing by A. B.
Dixon after
TWBTA**

N

life of individual institutions as well as of the city. The NSI elaborates on these ideas, motivated by the charge of its founding director, Gerald Edelman, that the architects invent a 'scientific monastery'.

If Le Corbusier's closed yet simultaneously open monastic enclosure for La Tourette analogized the Dominican's historically urban character, Kahn and Salk began with a desire to link scientific research to the broader society without sacrificing the undisturbed quiet researchers require to ponder big questions. The result, focused on its central plaza, deploys the laboratories as though they were the main institutions establishing the north and south edges of a representative civic square. Lime trees border its eastern edge and the canyon leading to the limit of the North American continent defines its western edge.

The arrangement of the Salk Institute is a grand sweeping gesture; equal, it seems, to the elation Salk must have experienced at perfecting a successful polio vaccine. Kahn's constructed fragment of his overall plan for the Salk could even appear as a monument, or temple, dedicated to Salk's one great discovery. Edelman, however, observes the temple-like character of the Salk as its major shortcoming. Tod Williams and Billie Tsien, the NSI's architects, concurred. Therefore, while they recognize the Salk as a monumental achievement of modern architecture, too close to the NSI to ignore it in terms of location as well as research agenda, the newer research institute gestures toward the earlier one while also significantly diverging from it.

It is at this point of divergence from the strongly axial arrangement of the Salk, that the NSI shows its affinity to the Amsterdam Orphanage, especially van Eyck's use of that project as an early exploration of what he called 'labyrinthine clarity'. Characteristically complex and demanding, labyrinthine clarity suggests corre-

13.13
General view from Theory Center toward auditorium and laboratory buildings. Neurosciences Institute, La Jolla, CA, 1992–1995. Architects: Tod Williams and Billie Tsien Associates

spondences between apparent opposites that come together across manifold associations to form an enriched whole, understandable as a unity made up of discernible diversity. The result is akin to a labyrinth in the sense of being made up of multiple, even criss-crossing, paths. Unlike in a labyrinth, though, rather than confusing, the setting is actually surprisingly comprehensible, especially in an emotional rather than rationalist way:

> Such clarity (ally of significant ambiguity) softens the edges of time and space and transcends visibility (allows spaces to enter each other and occasions to encounter each other in the mind's interior).
>
> It is kaleidoscopic. . . . Neither centralized nor decentralized but centred in every place and at every stage of multiplication, with the interior horizon of space as constant companion – that surely is our real home! It is also what Labyrinthian clarity can bring about – houses and city a bunch of places both.[11]

The kind of multiplicity van Eyck described would, if built, bring about settings ready to receive a full range of unexpected and spontaneous human inhabitation, much of which will contradict the architect's expectations. In more conventionally architectural terms, it suggests a reconciliation of specific but disparate architectural moments gathered within a recognizable overarching framework. Williams and Tsien's description of the NSI echoes just these aspirations:

> The whole evolved to become both the sum of its parts and greater – richer, more particular, more elusive, more memorable. The symphony of the spaces is both physical and intellectual. Wherever one is within the Neurosciences Institute, the experience is that of a place apart. One is always aware of the larger whole.[12]

The allusion to a 'symphony of spaces' is fitting; composition of the NSI is fugal, in much the same way that the Orphanage is. Both complexes state initial themes, subsequently repeated and varied with accompanying and strongly differentiated parts perceived simultaneously. However, occurrences of this sort are at once more explicit and subtler at the NSI than at the Orphanage.

Most explicitly, a curving, imperfect, ellipse-like form shows up in a number of places at the Institute. These places include the ceilings of the library, conference room and ground floor hallway, capped above by skylight structures reiterating the shape in three dimensions. All are located in the Theory Center. The shape is also found in the ceiling of a corridor in the Scientific Auditorium.

The curved concrete wall (or knuckle) linking the laboratories to the Theory Center takes the same form. Fragments of the shape recur in the landscape as well, most explicitly in the form of a berm facing the Theory Center, attached to the side of the Scientific Auditorium. It is discernible even in the water flow of the fountain located in the plaza. Material themes also work themselves across the three buildings or vary within the individual structures. Van Eyck described such qualities of building, site and city as harbouring 'bountiful qualities',

> [With] scope for what is small yet large – large yet small; near yet far –
> far yet near; open yet closed – closed yet open; different yet the same
> – the same yet different: scope for the right delay, the right release, the
> right certainty, the right suspense, the right surprise, the right security.
> And, withal, scope for multi-meaning.[13]

Both/and conditions such as van Eyck described, with the right balance of tension
and relief, dynamism and repose, action and reflection, would more realistically
analogize spatial experience as trajectories of intertwined intersecting movement,
walked through, akin to daily life. Pursuit of equilibrium infused van Eyck's thinking
much as it does Williams and Tsien's architecture. However, such balance need not
be static: rather, it can account for quite lively oppositions as part of whole
experiences:

> There is a kind of spatial appreciation which makes us envy birds in flight;
> there is also a kind that makes us recall the sheltered enclosure of our
> origin. Architecture will fail if it neglects either the one or the other kind
> . . . Labyrinthian clarity, at any rate, sings of both![14]

Whatever correspondences might be identifiable between van Eyck and Williams
and Tsien's ideas on the ethical function of architecture, the preceding is not intended
to suggest anything beyond discernibly associated habits of mind. Nevertheless, it
does seem that having Le Corbusier, Kahn and van Eyck's work at hand could soften
initial confrontation with Williams and Tsien's NSI, suggesting pathways toward
understanding the peculiarities of the complex.

13.14
Interior, Theory
Center.
Neurosciences
Institute, La Jolla,
CA, 1992–1995.
Architects: Tod
Williams and Billie
Tsien Associates

13.15
'Knuckle' between
Theory Center
and laboratory
buildings.
Neurosciences
Institute, La Jolla,
CA, 1992–1995.
Architects: Tod
Williams and Billie
Tsien Associates

Monastery, not temple

As our work matures, the perception of it is less and less understandable through photographs. One can only understand it by being there and moving and staying still. One reason is that we have been trying to integrate our buildings into the landscape. Thus, often the most important space is the empty space that is contained by the built forms. This empty space is the heart of the project at the Neurosciences Institute in La Jolla. It is the invisible magnet which holds together the separate buildings, and provides the coherence which makes the project feel whole. So what is not there is equally important. How does one photograph nothing? One experiences it.[15]

In this enigmatic description of their own work, Williams and Tsien reveal its utopian dimension. In an epoch characterized by ephemeral non-places best suited to a consumerist society of spectacle, hopelessly addicted to media-saturated over-stimulation, Williams and Tsien steadfastly go slow and stay small, committed to architecture as a material thing assembled, inflected by unique site conditions and experienced bodily. For them, speed forgets while slowness remembers.

We have written a mission statement for the office: whatever we design must be of use, but at the same time transcend its use. It must be rooted in time and site and client needs but it must transcend time and site and client needs. We do not want to develop a style or specialize in any project type. It is our hope to continue to work on only a few projects at a time, with intense personal involvement in all parts of the design and construction . . . We would like to be financially stable, but this will not outweigh artistic or ethical beliefs, which will always come first. The work should reflect optimism and love. The spiritual aspect of the work will emerge if the work is done well.[16]

Compared with the Salk, the NSI does seem more of a setting for private reflection and interactive exchange. There are two main reasons for this: first, the newer institute is a critical response to the earlier one, expressed in a distinctly less grand and directional arrangement. Second, the NSI responds to the symmetry and hierarchy of the Salk with an alternative kind of setting, intended to be conducive to chance encounters by encouraging lateral rather than axial movement. The physical forms these objectives take has as much to do with the personality of the architects and their clients as with the site of each complex. Both buildings are responsive to topographic conditions and include a plaza, but the Salk is sited perpendicularly to the Pacific coast within view of it, whereas the NSI is some distance from the ocean, horizontally sited, parallel to the eastern horizon.

Movement through the Salk follows a primarily east–west direction, through the court, following the water channel as much as the sun, toward the western horizon across the canyon to the ocean. Kahn's complex is inextricably bound to the canyon, which reveals the logic of the Salk's forceful directionality. The NSI began with a much less dramatic location – no procession across topographical features encourages its orientation except for the site's drop in elevation from the west to the east. If a strong directional orientation can be discerned, the Theory Center determines it, clearly pointing in an easterly direction, toward New York City, current home of the architects, former home of Edelman, and original home of the Neurosciences Institute.

13.16
Theory Center.
Neurosciences
Institute, La Jolla,
CA, 1992–1995.
Architects: Tod
Williams and Billie
Tsien Associates

Arguably, the civic character of the Salk's central court is out of step with what actually goes on in the complex: highly sensitive biological research. On the other hand, the NSI may be more in line with the character of the work carried out there: seclusion without distraction. Salk and Kahn certainly wanted the Institute to be a focal point of interest, a setting on people's minds, where science and the broader culture could come together, a desire significantly tempered at the NSI. The Salk was meant to be a monastery of the mind where Picasso would have felt welcome, but its grandeur arguably makes it more of a temple than a monastery.

Monasteries also provided the model for the NSI, but it is more reclusive than is the Salk. It is a place where Institute fellows and staff should feel welcome, and everyone else is a visitor. The space between the buildings, the nooks and crannies, are important to the overall social concept of the NSI; little places set apart lend themselves to spontaneous encounters between two or more scientists, simultaneously providing places of retreat for those wishing to be alone. Paradoxically, although when compared to the Salk the NSI is fragmented, it is also somewhat calmer and less intense. Likewise, unlike the Salk, the multivalent and elusive NSI is a decidedly non-monumental setting, not ruled by a single dominant axis. What is more, it is as if Kahn's tendency for trying to fix institutions at their moment of emergence is corrected at the NSI by van Eyck's desire to open them up to reveal not just the virtue of their beginnings but also the unimagined possibilities of their operation.

Kahn's hope was to provide society with a room by agreement, a piazza or agora, places for gathering where availabilities, assured by institutions, would be on offer to citizens. The central space of the Salk is the gathering place for Kahn's ideal city, a marketplace of availabilities. At the NSI, Williams and Tsien seem less convinced by the possibility of an operational commons, certainly not in La Jolla, where nearly everyone, no matter how far he or she must walk to the parking lot, arrives and leaves by car. Moreover, a scientific monastery dedicated to an unorthodox research programme, where investigators are given a free hand to pursue research agendas without having to worry about writing and receiving grants or publishing papers, is certainly not a place where the public, apart from on special occasions, should feel particularly comfortable visiting.

A scientific monastery[17]

Nobel Prize winner Dr Gerald Edelman, the founding director of the Neurosciences Institute, took advice from a selection committee on which architects should get the commission to design the new campus for his Institute. The committee foresaw that a large and famous firm would not be able to spare adequate time or energy to develop a project of the sort Edelman desired. Consequently, the committee recommended selecting a firm tried and tested enough to be able to manage a fairly large and complex project but not so established as to no longer be impassioned. The ideal firm would be on an upward trajectory, yet experienced enough to be trusted.

Edelman knew that he wanted something characterized by clarity and straightforwardness, like the Salk but different from it, with no sides or a front. When

Williams and Tsien asked him to describe what he envisioned, he returned to his desire for 'a scientific monastery'. Conceptualizing the not-yet designed Institute as monastic suggested not so much a particular historical architectural form (characterized by a structure closed to the outside world with rooms fronting on to a covered walk surrounding a cloister) as a degree of seclusion suited to introspection and exploration within a communal framework.

Even though, as it turned out, the NSI does have much in common with the character of a monastery, it achieves this without really looking like one. Nevertheless, Edelman's monastic analogy is key to an understanding of the resulting complex, particularly in relation to how he imagined the Institute would operate. He argues that all the major scientific breakthroughs of the last century have come out of small settings. His aim for the Institute, before selecting any architectural image or form, was to resurrect the character of past small settings that had encouraged significant research in the past. Toward this end, there are, at any given time, an absolute number of 40 non-permanent NSI fellows who circulate through the Institute after a maximum stay of up to ten years. Edelman saw these as the necessary first steps but wanted to go even further to establish a setting where the spectre of over-productivity would no longer haunt researchers, as is common in conventional research settings.

To function in the way he envisioned, the Institute would need to offer its fellows freedom to pursue their hunches, possible only if projects could be freely funded, which would be economically feasible in a setting kept manageably small. However, the virtue of smallness goes beyond the recollection of past research settings and economic imperatives alike; it permits diversity, which Edelman associates with youthfulness (unrelated to chronological age), while keeping diversity manageable.

For Edelman, a scientific monastery would operate according to a particular institutional ethos, which W. Einar Gall, Research Director of the Institute, describes as the 'semi-utopian goals of how to do research', ideas the completed complex would ideally 'inculcate'. Although, Edelman knew that he wanted the Institute to include three main functions, including settings for theory, wet science and an auditorium that could also function as a concert hall, he imagined the project as one job, with all functions embedded into a single building. He also knew that he wanted every view into and from the Institute to be beautiful, and if not beautiful then geometrically interesting.

As it turned out, Edelman went into the process envisioning one building; he wound up with three, which came as something of a surprise. In its present built form, each of the Institute's main functions (theory, laboratories and auditorium) is given its own building with a unique character, defining a court that unifies the entire complex.

Edelman, who is an accomplished violinist, could not be happier with the result. As he describes it, the complex is made up of musical-like statements of themes subsequently inverted, then repeated in other places and forms that do not get tiresome. His 'posterior reaction' to the constructed complex is that wherever one walks, the building reveals itself as fugal in every direction, vertically, horizontally

13.17
Detail, Theory
Center.
Neurosciences
Institute, La Jolla,
CA, 1992–1995.
Architects: Tod
Williams and Billie
Tsien Associates

and diagonally. Recurrent themes and variations of musical-like statements echo throughout the many parts of the project. As Edelman sees it, even though the same or similar things show themselves in the different structures of the Institute, the overall effect of this constant thematic repetition is never boring.

Embodying desire

The physical manifestation of Edelman's monastic analogy is reflected in the Institute's cloistered character, as much as in its attempts to establish a scientific community, for example by providing lunches in a refectory where all of the researchers come together at least once a day. Since it turns its back on the main road along its eastern edge, except for the Theory Center, which rises above it, the complex is effectively hidden from view, further protected by a very humble service building at the extreme south-eastern corner of the site. By making good use of the land's declivity, the Institute sits below and away from another main road above it to the west, shielded by a retaining wall along the upper walkway, which holds back a swathe of indigenous growth.[18]

Although the complex is open to main or access roads on all sides, the experience of being within its confines is similar in character to the quiet retreat of monastery cloisters, even without a continuous covered walkway built against the buildings surrounding a courtyard. However, there are some covered walkways and something like a courtyard. Indeed, its many architectural features provide numerous opportunities for walking around the complex, up and down ramps or stairs, or along the upper promenade on top of the laboratories (which receives the largest amount of non-Institute foot traffic), linked by a tunnel to other nearby research centres while offering passage to even more, as well as to parking lots.

Movement between the three main programmatic functions, the Theory Center, Laboratories and Scientific Auditorium, requires walking across the plaza but such movement is also clearly intended to be reflective: the colours, materials, planting in the plaza and its generally enclosed character encourage this. Moving in and out of the bright sun, into deep shadow, near a gently moving water element, past a crop of bamboo tress, all conspire to render the spaces between the buildings, as well as those linking them, as settings adapted to contemplative rambling, akin to a quiet walk around an ambulatory, though mostly in full sunlight here.

The most prominent ramp of the complex, to the south side of the Theory Center facing the plaza, leads from the upper walkway (and tunnel mentioned above) down to the plaza level and main reception point for the Institute in the lobby of the Theory Center. Although the ramp is necessary for accessibility, it also acts as an architectural promenade, bringing one up and through the complex as it unfolds visually and physically.

13.18
Plaza.
Neurosciences
Institute, La Jolla,
CA, 1992–1995.
Architects: Tod
Williams and Billie
Tsien Associates

13.19
Theory Center
ramp.
Neurosciences
Institute, La Jolla,
CA, 1992–1995.
Architects: Tod
Williams and Billie
Tsien Associates

Beginning with Edelman's powerful analogy associated with an architectural form (monasteries) but intended to express a particular way of conducting research and associating within an institutional community, the Neurosciences Institute is a compelling expression of how exemplary architecture requires a utopian dimension for its invention. Williams and Tsien's self-professed optimism, which they acknowledge as so necessary for the production of first-rate works of architecture, further reinforces this conclusion. Moreover, as a building designed and constructed during the 1990s, the NSI suggests that the ideas on architecture developed throughout this study are extrinsic to any particular form or even to a specific historical period of architectural production.

Elaborating on identity: Piano and the Building Workshop in Nouméa[19]

In a sense, the process of construction is never complete. I believe that buildings, like cities, are factories of the infinite and the unfinished. We must be careful not to fall into the trap of perfection: a work of architecture is a living creature that changes over time and with use. We live with these creatures of ours, linked to them by the umbilical cord of an adventure with no end.[20]

The Centre Culturel Tjibaou (Tjibaou Cultural Centre) in Nouméa, New Caledonia is worth examining not least because it is a building by a cosmopolitan Italian architect, funded by the French government, located in a colonial possession. What is more, it is dedicated to nurturing an indigenous culture and to the memory of a man who struggled for the colony's independence from the very government that paid for the project.

The Centre honours the life of Jean-Marie Tjibaou, who was, before his murder in 1989, a leader of the Kanak independence movement, Kanak being the name adopted by the indigenous people of this South Pacific island and smaller ones that surround it. New Caledonia is home to an exceptionally diverse group of aboriginal people, with an equally varied number of languages, loosely linked by shared traditions, myths and culture. Since 1864, when the French began sending convicts to the island, the Kanak have had to share their territory with settlers, who have taken more and more of it, slowly displacing the original population to a minority position in their own land.

Although the island is a last bastion of French colonialism in an epoch of post-colonialism, the struggle of its original inhabitants for self-rule, reparation for taken land and, ultimately, independence from France, has only come into more general view since Piano's building took shape on the outskirts of Nouméa, the traditionally white-French main city of New Caledonia.

The generalized visibility of the Tjibaou Cultural Centre simultaneously confirms its success as both a work of architecture and an embodiment of the aims envisioned for it. To say that these aims freight the project with a nearly impossible agenda is something of an understatement. Certainly no building on its own can change the world; nevertheless, it can perform a facilitating, even generative, role for taking the first tentative steps in the direction of transformation, an objective Piano acknowledges as the utopian dimension of architecture:

> Well architecture funnily enough is probably the most materialistic discipline you can think about, because it's really about physicality, it's about material. It's about fighting against gravity . . . So it's very much materialistic, but at the same time it's very idealistic, it's probably one of the most idealistic disciplines you can think about, because it's about people, it's about enjoyment, it's about utopia, it's about changing the world you know. And you do change the world in some way.[21]

Piano's negotiation of material and utopia as the main topics of architecture reveals just how well-suited his approach is to articulating a project as sensitive as the Tjibaou Cultural Centre. By arbitrating between imagined opposites, Piano recurrently identifies forums for investigating his preoccupation with the interdependence of concepts, which safeguards his work from absolutist tendencies. Moreover, in contradistinction to mainstream contemporary practice, he brings the same thoughtful comprehensiveness to the many relationships architecture finds itself in:

> Architecture is a complex practice because the expressive formal moment is . . . a moment of synthesis which grows out of all that is behind or before architecture: history, society, the real world of people, their emotions, hopes and desires; geography and anthropology, the climate, the culture of any country where one works; and also science and art [translation by author].[22]

13.20
**General view.
Tjibaou Cultural
Centre,
1991–1998.
Nouméa, New
Caledonia.
Architect: Renzo
Piano Building
Workshop**

Piano's architecture is a provocation; it challenges the propensity of banal and novel practices alike to reduce architecture's full complexity to some easily manageable bit of it, primarily by falling into an artificial argument between art and business. His resistance to such self-defeating oppositional thinking consistently wins his Building Workshop the enviable prize of being able to achieve great successes in art and business.

The most audacious characteristic of Piano's Cultural Centre is its active participation in ongoing articulations of Kanak identity. Its strongest symbolic feature is the 'cases', ten primarily wooden pods, arranged in three groupings, two of which have three well-serviced huts, and one that has four. Each of them shares the same character but varies in size and height. All ten shell-like structures open along a permeable corridor-path running from the north-east to the south-west of the complex; otherwise they are predominantly closed, taking advantage of the cooling effects of the prevailing winds, encouraged to push hot air upwards and outward. Most significantly, these distinctive structures carry discernible hints of traditional Kanak houses, something that caused Piano a good deal of anxiety:

> The dread of falling into the trap of folkloric imitation, of straying into the realm of kitsch and the picturesque, was a constant worry throughout this work. At a certain point I decided to tone down the resemblance between 'my' huts and those of local tradition.[23]
>
> [. . .]
>
> Moreover, it was not a tourist village that I had to build. I had to create a symbol: a cultural centre devoted to Kanak civilization, the place that would represent them to foreigners and that would pass on their memory to their grandchildren. Nothing could have been more loaded with symbolic expectations.[24]

As it turns out, the most perplexing problem confronting Piano was how to give flesh to a recollection of Kanak huts without producing an embarrassing representation of them. Alban Bensa, French anthropologist and specialist on New Caledonia and Kanak culture, who collaborated with Piano from the earliest stages of the project until its completion, suggests that the result of Piano's effort is a memory of Kanak huts that is utopian. It is utopian precisely because his very idea of bringing such an interpretation of traditional huts into the modern world was transgressive, requiring a daring mediation to make an effective transition between past and future. Piano, observes Bensa, was 'trying to bring an idea of [traditional] Kanak culture through [into] a modern idea of their culture'.[25]

In its realization, the Cultural Centre is an almost eerie embodiment of Jean-Marie Tjibaou's political vision. Less satisfyingly, its current management is not quite up to the challenge he laid out for it. In this instance, an unwelcoming organizational structure appears to frustrate the success of the building, on social as well as architectural levels. While the building is stately, the experience of moving through it is fragmented. What one is meant to get from a visit remains unclear even after many attempts to make contact with the institution.

However, this present condition may in fact disclose the utopian dimension of the whole enterprise. Tjibaou envisioned a degree of interdependence, between the Kanak, the French colonizers, more recent arrivals and among inhabitants of the South Pacific more generally, nearly incomprehensible in the aftermath of a long brutal experience with outsiders that is not yet concluded or resolved. Although the Cultural Centre is meant to be a gateway to dialogue, its present organization does not invite it. Consequently, although the negotiation between past and future accomplished by the complex may accurately embody Tjibaou's vision for renewed Kanak culture, the conditions for its realization are not yet in place. Nevertheless, the very presence of the complex, especially its far-reaching influence, suggests a way forward.

According to Jean-Marie Tjibaou, Kanak identity resides neither in some primordial archaeological past nor in a modern invention of tradition cynically constructed to justify minority privileges. If neither excavation nor fabrication promise to reveal Kanak identity, even less promising would be the non-critical embrace of Western agricultural, spatial, economic or political practices.[26]

Much as J.-M. Tjibaou envisioned charting a middle way between reactionary return to origins and assimilation into the excesses of consumer culture, Piano attempted to weave shadows of traditional Kanak culture through a modern articulation of it. In this way, the Centre does more than adequate justice to one of Tjibaou's most stirring and oft-quoted statements:

> The return to tradition is a myth. No people has ever done so. In the quest for identity, we must look forwards, never backwards. It is a process of constant redefinition. Our struggle is to build as much of our past and culture as we can into the future community . . . our identity lies before us.[27]

Whatever the shortcomings of the Centre's present operation, Tjibaou's utopian political project has found an apt and honourable setting in Piano's no less utopian architectural project.

Building character

The overall organization of the Centre is emphatically directional, organized around and focused onto an interior street or path. The linear organization of the building makes it very easy to navigate, also lending it an infinite quality; not much would keep it from being extended in either direction along the central spine. Although the main functions hang off this central spine, attention is also constantly directed outward, toward the land and the sea.

Exterior spaces of the Centre, beyond the building edge, and areas of paving at entry points, are extremely casual. Maybe this condition is exactly right, a significant part of the conciliation the building heralds by preceding it, this time with the land. Interestingly, the Kanak Path, a mythical, historical, agricultural introduction to the plant-based cosmology and traditions of Kanak life, bound to the land and the products from it they have long cultivated, actually seems more subversive than Piano's building. The Path is a path of discovery as much as of transformation,

13.21
**Site plan. Tjibaou
Cultural Centre,
1991–1998.
Nouméa, New
Caledonia.
Architect: Renzo
Piano Building
Workshop.
Drawing by
A. B. Dixon after
Renzo Piano
Building
Workshop**

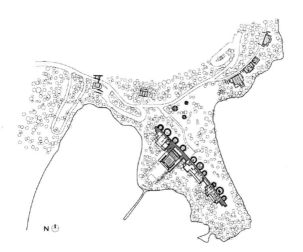

N

drawing even the casual visitor into Kanak cosmology almost imperceptively. The path is said to be more popular with Kanak visitors than are the interiors of the Centre proper.[28]

Wood is the predominant feature of the project, which, considering its size and structural virtuosity, make it substantially gentler. Glue-lam posts are the main construction material for the ten cases, interpreted huts that derive from traditional Kanak buildings without overtly copying them. Their red-orange colour in early photographs so over-emphasized them that the more humble character of the actual Centre comes as a surprise, especially now that the wood has weathered (as anticipated) to a mellow grey, similar in colour to the bark of the palm trees found on the island. Happily, the building is now less striking than it was when new. Rather than garishly sticking out of the landscape, it emerges organically from the land it inhabits as an integral part of it, while also calling attention to it.

The structure further echoes the character of the curving coconut palms and uprightness of the pine trees common to this part of the island. The verticality of the local pines, with equally vertical leaves, shows in the slats of the building. The bend of the palms shows in the curve of the cases. The relation of the pines and palms to the land clearly moved Piano, his subtle capturing of this important quality distinguished his original competition scheme from the other unsuccessful entries. These trees are also important to the Kanak: the chief is like the pine; woman is like the palm. By referring to local custom, landscape and materials, Piano explored nature and culture, or the correspondence of nature to culture as analogous to a rapprochement between tradition and modernity.

It is worth returning for a moment to the weathering of wood at the Centre: it might well symbolize a potentially premature reconciliation, as though independence was a foregone conclusion, even though at the detail level the building is more radical. Nevertheless, the only overtly anti-colonial room at the Centre is the one dedicated to Jean-Marie Tjibaou, as are many of the media resources available in the library, which are, naturally, less immediately visible to the casual visitor.

13.22
Case and trees.
Tjibaou Cultural
Centre,
1991–1998.
Nouméa, New
Caledonia.
Architect: Renzo
Piano Building
Workshop

13.23
Room dedicated
to Jean-Marie
Tjibaou. Tjibaou
Cultural Centre,
1991–1998.
Nouméa, New
Caledonia.
Architect: Renzo
Piano Building
Workshop

13.24
**Main entry.
Tjibaou Cultural
Centre, 1991–1998.
Nouméa, New
Caledonia.
Architect: Renzo
Piano Building
Workshop**

Again, this conciliatory gesturing may in fact be another aspect of the building's utopian content: presenting a not-yet condition as already operative in the present, no matter how far off its actualization might really lie. On the other hand, as one of François Mitterand's final *Grands Travaux présidentiels*, the building must carry within it a strong positively French component.

The fact of the building, its debt to the central government in Paris, which made the project possible in terms of organization, funds and will, begs the question: Is it a guilt offering, peace offering, or something else? It can be the third only if the government is genuinely pursuing a path toward decolonization leading, ultimately, to self-rule by the Kanak people of their own land, a prospect that, at least for the moment, seems exceptionally far off.

Articulating identity

The exhibits, paths, artefacts, archives and so on do certainly communicate something about the Kanak, but the experience when dealing with the administration is of a guarded bureaucracy. It is hard to get a sense at the Centre of just how ongoing Kanak traditions and habits of life really are. Does anything like traditional Kanak life actually exist? Alternatively, is past identity – a tradition – being invented to give an oppressed people some identity they can refer to in their quest for independence? Is Kanak cultural life an invented tradition propagated by the Centre as a means of assuring its own authority?

Continuity of tradition, when broken by occupation and oppression, is difficult if not impossible to rekindle. As J.-M. Tjibaou understood, 'in the quest for identity' a colonized people 'must look forwards never backwards'. Identity, then, even for a traditional society is not so much a matter of fact as one of interpretation, reinterpretation, redefinition and even of invention. If Kanak culture as ongoing and vitally operational does not jump out at you at the Cultural Centre, it is because the complex is honest, or even true, to J.-M. Tjibaou's profound understanding that identity, for individuals and groups, is dynamic, requiring negotiation and renegotiation on many fronts through time.

Beyond its few limitations, the Centre is most importantly a laboratory for experimenting on and with identity, to invent it out of remnants of past local traditions as well as out of encounters with the West and Asia. At its best, it is a workshop in whose spaces and grounds the project of enunciating a post-colonial identity is being carried out, even if that aspect of the Centre's project is neither overtly presented nor in particularly public view.

The secretive, subversive work of the Centre appears to be (or at least one hopes it is) the ongoing articulation of a Kanak national identity, cohesive enough to survive the conclusion of French occupation, even in its now somewhat more benign form. In that sense, the Centre is the first great civic monument of an (eventually) independent New Caledonia. It has already brought the Kanak a level of recognition nearly unthinkable before its existence. For all those who are drawn to the complex as a stop along some expanded modern grand tour, at least a few might develop empathy for the political struggle of the Kanak toward decolonization.

As one of the modalities of decolonization, the Centre is ideally located (perhaps culturally more than geographically) to become a focal point of its eventuality. Already, it is among the very first steps taken in the direction of a renewed Kanak society. In all likelihood, New Caledonian independence will parallel the Kanak community's emerging ability to occupy and manage the complex more effectively

13.25
Traditional Area. Tjibaou Cultural Centre, 1991–1998. Nouméa, New Caledonia. Architect: Renzo Piano Building Workshop

as an incubator of cultural identity. The status of the Centre as a first step is especially apparent in the Traditional Area and the Kanak Way (encircling the complex), which, in concert with Piano's building, points toward reformulating possession of the land and self-government of it.

Between anthropology and architecture

An anthropological approach obtains at the Centre, expertly guided by Bensa, whom Piano relied on to help him arrive at plastic correspondences between Kanak desire and tradition. Consequently, considering Bensa's long association with New Caledonia, support of the Kanak struggle, and relationship with Jean-Marie Tjibaou, the Cultural Centre happily elaborates on the long view rather than on the status quo. Future conditions are here eased into reality somewhat ahead of actualization, force-fully communicating Kanak difference, formal as well as cultural, while simultaneously capturing the fragility of Kanak habits and memory.

Although the Tjibaou Centre is meant to be a gateway to dialogue, its staff appears suspicious of outsiders, which is reasonable, especially in light of more than a century of, at times, brutally oppressive French colonial rule. After all, colonization displaced the Kanak, as it were, to islands within their own land, making them into statusless strangers in their own territory. Often enough, the very practice of traditional ways of life had to occur clandestinely, rendering typical forms of conduct subversive, at least as far as the dominating colonial power was concerned. Hence, the propensity seems, not surprisingly, for such doubly isolated island dwellers to be even more insular in their attitudes; suspiciousness seems quite reasonable. Can any single building ever hope to respond to such complex and entrenched conditions? Maybe, if only by example, at least for the present moment.

Piano's approach at the Tjibaou Cultural Centre is fully representative of his mode of thinking developed at least since the Pompidou Centre, Paris (1971–1977). All of his works demonstrate an awareness of the problems presented by conceptions of modernity as boundless progress. He is, though, equally aware that any meaningful contemporary cultural practice must, inevitably, include a willingness to embrace, albeit auto-critically, present conditions. His projects are formed, in large part, by what he observes as the consequences of the two profound revolutions of the twentieth century, which continue to confront individuals worldwide: global communication and techno-scientific advances that have wrought fundamentally changed conditions.

More precisely, the effects of globalization, especially in terms of global communication, including the unrestricted travel of individuals, data and culture, reveal the unavoidability of contact between richer and poorer nations and between traditional societies and modernity. In addition, the techno-scientific revolution has forever changed the character of materials, including the processes for manufacturing them as much as those required for engineering and assembling them.

Piano's inclusive approach occurs at a multitude of scales, from the organization of his office, to his engagement of specific communities and territories, to his openness to influences of a global nature, traditional as well as modern. It is at this intersection between professional organization and artistic approach that

Piano's requirement that the Tjibaou Cultural Centre should elaborate on an encounter between tradition and modernity discloses an attitude informing all of his project work. It is an approach that domesticates technology by not being enslaved to it, simultaneously extending its communicative potential by submitting it to the realities of place in a manner that, while promising quite evocative results, is also remarkably practical.

Modularized industrial building techniques are used to great effect by being harmonized with more traditional materials (especially wood) while indigenous materials and methods of construction are interpreted into a modern idiom. Initial elements and parts are small scale, seemingly graspable (something they have in common with those of the Pompidou). Soft, warm materials prevail; cold, hard materials (including metal connections, reinforcements and mullions) never over-whelm. The constant movement of air – modulated by automated as well as permanent openings (windows as well as grills) – softens the effect of the whole complex, as do the 'smart features' of the building, including automated windows, louvers and automatic doors.

As topographical as technological in approach, Piano's method of working depends on careful consideration of the character of a location, including its climate – qualities of light, prevailing winds, the cooling or warming effects of water, and the distribution of plant life and so on. It is also socio-anthropological, aware of historical conditions on the ground and of their effect on local society. As a result, the Tjibaou Cultural Centre is at once a fully serviced building that takes full advantage of the site's climatic characteristics for lighting and cooling, but also incorporates sensitive interpretations of indigenous building techniques and spatial practices.

13.26
Entry to Path. Tjibaou Cultural Centre, 1991–1998. Nouméa, New Caledonia. Architect: Renzo Piano Building Workshop

13.27
Interior path.
Tjibaou Cultural
Centre,
1991–1998.
Nouméa, New
Caledonia.
Architect: Renzo
Piano Building
Workshop

13.28 (below)
General view of
main gallery.
Tjibaou Cultural
Centre, 1991–1998.
Nouméa, New
Caledonia. Renzo
Piano Building
Workshop

Overall, the entire complex seems to emerge organically out of its site, as though it had grown there naturally, without ever betraying the degree to which it records a negotiation between indigenous building and global practices. As a modern technological building, given as a gift by France to a people long oppressed by its colonial rule of New Caledonia, the Centre stands symbolically at a crossroads between past and future. It is anything but the expression of a static society, conveying far more than a simple capture or representation of spent culture, nor does it engage in a calculating invention, or reinvention, of Kanak traditions. Rather, the aim of Piano's effort is to house identity in emergence, to offer a setting, a stage upon which Kanak identity can be elaborated on as prospective, while remaining faithful to memory just the same.

13.29
**Artists' area.
Tjibaou Cultural
Centre, 1991–1998.
Nouméa, New
Caledonia.
Architect: Renzo
Piano Building
Workshop**

Memory and tradition are acknowledged in the Centre while the uncertain condition of the present is carefully observed. However, the orientation of this work is toward the future, the *not-yet*. It effectively materializes the first steps in the direction of a new Kanak society able to cohesively endure beyond a time when the French government returns the island to its inhabitants for self-determination. How it will all turn out is not for the architect or the building to determine. The job of the first is now done; that of the second is just beginning, in no determining way except in as much as the structure is a setting open to possibility. It has already gone a long way toward manifesting a Kanak identity bound neither to France nor to the ossifying tendancies of heritage conservation.

The virtues of architecture

What unites the three newer projects examined in this chapter is that they are transformative, simultaneously projective and prospective. They are post-modern in the sense of extending the communicative potential of modernist architectural expression inherited from the post-World War II period, as well as in Vattimo's sense: appearing in an epoch when unquestionable confidence in progress is no more tenable than is an absolute conception of beauty. Nevertheless, none of them could be called stylistically post-modern; although the architectural expression of each alludes to near, more distant, or foreign pasts, decorated sheds are nowhere in view. Pastiche or the tacking-on of overt historical references is avoided in favour of analogy, introduced earlier, as the direct expression of meaning, which confidently explores the potentialities of form as content.

Material, structure and construction are the means by which architecture is re-imagined as having meaning, or better yet, as being meaningful. Each of these complexes touches emotion by way of architectural means in a direct way. In that sense, all are optimistic, expressing a faith in the possibility of accomplishing valid, even validating, cultural work despite being produced during an epoch characterized by a predisposition for the production of objects as easily consumed as they are disposed of. Between the extreme poles of self-defeating nostalgia for irrecoverable past conditions (better than they could ever have actually been) and the giddy embrace of a pathological present (characterized by spectacular overstimulation taken to extremes), each of these projects identifies not so much a common middle way as a uniquely alternative one.

Indeed, precisely these characteristics bind the Jewish Museum Berlin, Neurosciences Institute and Jean-Marie Tjibaou Cultural Centre to the habits of mind (explored throughout earlier chapters) that, even during the period of banal modern architecture's greatest success, could envision projects as strange and rebellious as La Tourette, the Salk Institute and the Amsterdam Orphanage.

Obviously enough, it is difficult to draw explicitly stylistic comparisons between the three projects built between 1955 and 1965, and the later three constructed during the 1990s. However, style is not the concern here; rather, an approach, mental tuning, or even an ethos is, although it is unlikely that Libeskind could see much of himself in Piano's approach, or vice versa. It is the attitude these six projects disclose toward the real potential for architecture to communicate that reveals correspondences between them. Although they may not share much in terms of appearance, beyond concrete figuring in each, architectural virtuousness is present in great abundance:

> In the main, we require from buildings, as from men, two kinds of goodness: first, the doing their practical duty well: then that they be graceful and pleasing in doing it; which is itself another form of duty.

> Then the practical duty divides itself into two branches, – acting and talking: – acting, as to defend us from weather or violence; talking, as the duty of monuments or tombs, to record facts and express feelings; or of churches, temples, public edifices, treated as books of history, to tell such history clearly and forcefully.

> We have thus, altogether, three great branches of architectural *virtue*, and we require it of any building.

1. That it act well, and do the things it was intended to do in the best way.
2. That it speak well, and say the things it was intended to say in the best words.
3. That it look well, and please us by its presence, whatever is has to say.[29]

In light of Ruskin's requirements of buildings, what associates the works examined here, apart from everything else that might separate them, is a conviction that form is content. It is a kind of meaning experienced directly by the body, revealed at the moment of contact simply by moving, with a modicum of mindfulness, through the settings invented by the architects as platforms and shelters for the occasions inflecting the forms housing them.

For all their correspondences, there are also certainly differences between each of the structures, as well as between the groupings of earlier and later works. It is worth noting that while La Tourette, the Salk Institute and the Amsterdam Orphanage rely on forcefully defined perimeters to establish a context for examining potential, and for reaching across their own edges toward the territory beyond, the Jewish Museum, Neurosciences Institute and Tjibaou Cultural Centre are each organized linearly along a path, none of which is arrow-straight. In the first, the line of movement is jagged, even broken. At the NSI, it is languid and relaxed, moving in and out from exterior to interior, up and down along ramps and steps, even under and through the earth. In the Tjibaou Cultural Centre, movement occurs along a gently arching double-loaded path following the contours of the land, which reasonably enough could be extended in either direction.

Significant in all this is that whereas a path is quite important at La Tourette and at the Amsterdam Orphanage, and the east–west axis at the Salk is probably its best-known feature, each is, for all its openness, a comparatively closed system, resistant to the possibility of extension (confirmed at least at the Salk, by the recent additions to it). When constructed, rescuing specificity from the generalizing abstractness of modern attitudes toward architecture and the city was necessary.

The discernible boundaries of La Tourette, the Salk Institute and Amsterdam Orphanage established compelling forms indicating something about the organization of the world as a grouping of communities. As expressed by these structures, open enough but defined edges suggested a way forward for a shaken postwar world living in the shadow of potential nuclear annihilation. The realities of contemporary megalopolises combined with generalized communication point out the unlikelihood of recovering compact traditional cities. Nonetheless, the horizontal, territorial and topographical character of the Jewish Museum, Neurosciences Institute and the Tjibaou Cultural Centre might each suggest avenues of investigation leading toward new urban conceptions capable of resisting self-defeating longings for irrecoverable earlier conditions on the one hand and surrender to the dislocating excesses of metropolitanism on the other.

Tradition, near and far, as well as very long ago and more recent, equally infuses the projects discussed here from 1955–1965 and the 1990s, but in somewhat different ways. La Tourette, the Salk Institute and Amsterdam Orphanage offer interpretations of neolithic, classical and early Christian architectural traditions. Each elaborates on architecture of the early twentieth century as well. Furthermore, the Salk Institute discloses an awareness of Islamic architecture, as does the Amsterdam Orphanage, which is also inflected by the sub-Saharan villages of the Dogon.

The Jewish Museum discloses the influence of Le Corbusier, but also of those following in his footsteps. It also courageously embraces the extreme edges of modern art, yet, even though it is something of an architect's architecture, potentially discernible only to critics and those in the know, the building displays such tremendous confidence in the lay public's sensitivity, it is no wonder that it touches the emotions in such a direct way. The Neurosciences Institute shows the influence of the Salk, even if only through disobedience to it, but La Tourette is here as well, albeit unfolded. Van Eyck's conviction that material is the first point of contact between building and occupant is everywhere in evidence as well. So also are the continuing potentialities of Le Corbusier's architectural promenade.

The Jean-Marie Tjibaou Cultural Centre is a beneficiary of architectural tradition in general, showing a remarkably sophisticated gathering of accumulated wisdom about the nature and purpose of buildings. More specifically, in this work Piano draws on traditions local to the territory of the project as much as on those native to him. Interestingly, there was a lot of anxiety about the use of indigenous building traditions in forming this project; he was afraid that he would veer off into folkloric kitsch when referencing foreign (at least to the architect), non-Western formal habits. Certainly, van Eyck did this with aplomb at the Orphanage, although he was inflecting modern Western architecture, his own native tradition, with distant borrowings, whereas Piano was attempting to animate an alien, fragile local tradition, from beyond his global turf, through an infusion of cosmopolitan modernism.

Perhaps Piano need not have been so worried about the dangers of such an operation, despite the strangeness of Kanak culture to him. After all, he has been interpreting traditions, albeit Western ones, whether Mediterranean, classical, indigenous, modern or technocratic, throughout his career, often with great success. What is strange, particularly in the context of the present discussion, is Piano's conviction that, as an architect, he could not be further from Kahn, even though he briefly worked with him in the 1960s. Actually, on closer analysis, he shares much with Kahn, especially his encounter with tradition informed by what he calls 'disobedience and curiosity', which permits him to interpret what comes his way as though it were something like Kahn's golden dust blown forward from the past or nearby from somewhere else. Because the past is irrecoverable as present fullness – as strange as some foreign country – operations with and on it are permitted great latitude.

Moreover, Piano's project has always been and remains inflected by just the same sorts of problems Kahn was trying to work out in his 1944 essay 'Monumentality':

> Standardization, prefabrication, controlled experiments and tests, and specialization are no monsters to be avoided by the delicate sensitivities of the artist. They are merely the modern means of controlling vast potentialities of materials for living, by chemistry, physics, engineering, production and assembly, which lead to the necessary knowledge the

artist must have to expel fear in their use, broaden his creative instinct, give him new courage and thereby lead him to the adventures of unexplored places. His work will then be part of his age and will afford delight and service for his contemporaries.[30]

Indeed, a survey of Piano's thoughts on architecture, modernity and progress reveals an unexpected commonality of themes between him and Kahn.[31] It is possible that, in his ability to consistently accomplish what Kahn strove for, Piano has surpassed but not escaped the earlier architect. For example, Piano's remarkable ability to bring technology within a realm of human emotional understanding, to gentle it without soft-pedalling it, is indeed a significant achievement, but its prehistory is persuasively outlined in the quote above.

Not to belabour the point, but what could be more revealing of Piano's endeavour than Kahn's convictions, expressed near the end of his life, that: 'The joint is the beginning of ornament. And that must be distinguished from decoration which is simply applied. Ornament is the adoration of the joint'.[32] Control of the construction process, while lavishing attention on how the myriad elements of any contemporary building assembly are fitted together at their individual points of contact, such as Piano does, goes a long way toward making an architecture at once modern and traditional. Modern in its embrace of the technological facts of the age, traditional in its reconceptualization of mechanized building industry as also making possible a craft-like love of production.

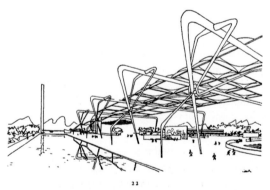

22

13.30
Monumentality Promenade. Sketch accompanying Louis I. Kahn's, *Monumentality in New Architecture and City Planning, A Symposium,* **P. Zucker (ed.), New York: Philosophical Library, 1944**
Source: Louis I. Kahn Collection, The Architectural Archives of the University of Pennsylvania

At any rate, Le Corbusier, Louis I. Kahn and Aldo van Eyck shared an attitude about working with tradition and modernity, as well as with the local and the distant that Daniel Libeskind, Tod Williams and Billie Tsien, and Renzo Piano have inherited, often enough disobediently.

That three such buildings, different as they are in character, could ever get built at all in Berlin, the US or New Caledonia, especially in a climate so enamoured of frivolous effervescences, conditioned by commodification and disposability, is proof enough of an uncanny optimism that only utopian perspectives could nourish.

Notes

Introduction: utopias and architectures?

1   Daniel Libeskind, *The Space of Encounter*, London: Thames and Hudson, 2001, p. 91.

2   CIAM, *Charter of Athens, Tenets* (1933), set out by Le Corbusier in the *Charter of Athens*, 1941, reprinted in *Programs and Manifestoes on 20th-Century Architecture*, Ulrich Conrads (ed.), Michael Bullock (trans.), Cambridge, MA: MIT Press, 1970, pp. 136–45.

3   *Optimistic* as I use it here draws upon Plato's assertion (particularly in *The Laws*) that the purpose of life is to strive for virtue, even if its ideal or perfect form is as unachievable by human beings as it is by states. Optimism tempered by a *tragic view* nonetheless requires maintenance of virtue as a target at which to aim. In the event, Plato's conception of the virtuous life and state suggest the possibility of an architecture that I am calling 'optimistic'.

1   Architecture and orientation

1   John Ruskin, 'Unto this Last' (1862), reprinted in *Unto this Last and Other Writings*, London: Penguin, 1985, p. 224.

2   *Ought* is employed here in much the way Ruskin intended it in his opposition of *ought* to *can*. *Can* is technically achievable but may be ethically questionable. Conversely, although *ought* may also be attainable, its achievement depends on a wider and deeper consideration of intent and consequences than the mere possibility of accomplishing some thing or another.

3   What I am calling the *orienting objective* of architecture has been informed by many writers including: Karsten Harries, *The Ethical Function of Architecture*, Cambridge: MIT Press, 1997, and Mircea Eliade, 'The World, The City, The House', in *Occultism, Witchcraft and Cultural Fashions: Essays in Comparative Religion*, Chicago: University of Chicago Press, 1976, pp. 18–31.

4   For further development of these ideas as they relate to architectural design see, Nathaniel Coleman, 'History, Theory, Design: A Pedagogy of Persuasion', in *Architectural Research Quarterly*, vol. 7, nos 3/4, 2003, pp. 353–60.

5   For an introduction to cognitive science and its relation to cognition and creativity, see John T. Bruer, *Schools For Thought: A Science of Learning in the Classroom*, Cambridge, MA: MIT Press, 1993.

6   Karl Popper, *The Poverty of Historicism* (1961), London: Routledge, 1994, and Karl Mannheim, *Ideology and Utopia: An Introduction to the Sociology of Knowledge* (1936), San Diego: Harcourt Brace & Company, 1985.

7   Leon Battista Alberti, *On the Art of Building in Ten Books*, J. Rykwert, N. Leach and R. Tavernor (trans), Cambridge, MA: MIT Press, 1988.

8   David Leatherbarrow, *The Roots of Architectural Invention*, Cambridge: Cambridge University Press, 1993.

9   Joseph Rykwert, *On Adam's House in Paradise* (1972), Cambridge, MA: MIT Press, 1981.

10   Robert Venturi, Denise Scott Brown and Steven Izenour, *Learning from Las Vegas*, revised edn, Cambridge, MA: MIT Press, 1977.

11   Joseph Rykwert, *The First Moderns*, Cambridge, MA: MIT Press, 1980.

12   Joseph Rykwert, *The Idea of a Town*, Cambridge, MA: MIT Press, 1988. See also, Joseph Rykwert, *The Seduction of Place, The City in the Twenty-First Century*, New York: Pantheon Books, 2000.

13 For an elaboration on these ideas, see Mary Douglas, *Natural Symbols, Explorations in Cosmology*, London: Routledge, 1996, pp. xxxii, xxxvi.

14 Marcus Vitruvius Pollio, *The Ten Books on Architecture (De architectura)*, Morris Hicky Morgan (trans.) (1914), New York: Dover Publications Inc., 1960, Book 1, chapter 2, pp. 13–16. See also, Joseph Rykwert, *The Dancing Column, On Order in Architecture*, Cambridge, MA: MIT Press, 1996.

15 Leon Battista Alberti, *On the Art of Building in Ten Books*, Book 9, chapter 5, pp. 302–03.

16 Sigfried Giedion, *Space, Time and Architecture*, 5th edn (1982), Cambridge, MA: Harvard University Press, 1967, p. xxxix.

17 *Ibid.*, p. xliii.

18 *Ibid.*, p. xliv.

19 *Ibid.*, p. 578.

20 Louis I. Kahn, 'How'm I doing Le Corbusier?' (1972), in *Writings, Lectures, Interviews*, Alessandra Latour (ed.), New York: Rizzoli, 1991, p. 307.

21 Louis I. Kahn, 'Talk at the Conclusion of the Otterlo Congress', in Oscar Newman, *New Frontiers in Architecture, CIAM '59 in Otterlo*, by order of Jacob B. Bakema for the Otterlo 1959 participants, Jürgen Joedicke (ed.), New York: Universe Books, 1961, p. 214.

22 Francis Strauven, *Aldo Van Eyck, The Shape of Relativity*, Victor J. Joseph (trans.), Amsterdam: Architectura and Natura, 1998, p. 353.

23 Guilliaume Jullian de la Fuente, quoted on the inside back cover of Francis Strauven, *Aldo van Eyck's Orphanage, A Modern Monument*, Netherlands: NAi Publishers, 1996.

24 To get a clearer sense of this contrast, compare the *Doorn Manifesto* (Bakema, van Eyck, van Ginkel, Hovens-Greve, Smithson, Voelker (29–31 January 1954), reprinted in *Architecture Culture 1943–1968*, compiled by Joan Ockman, New York: Columbia/Rizzoli, 1993, p. 183) to Robert Venturi's attempts to overcome the limitations of modernism (*Complexity and Contradiction in Architecture* (1966), New York: Museum of Modern Art, 1977, p. 16).

25 Peter Smithson, in Oscar Newman, *New Frontiers in Architecture, CIAM '59 in Otterlo*, pp. 94–97.

26 Jacob Bakema, in Oscar Newman, *New Frontiers in Architecture, CIAM '59 in Otterlo*, p. 97.

27 Jacob Bakema, 'Concluding Evaluation of the Otterlo Conference', in Oscar Newman, *New Frontiers in Architecture, CIAM '59 in Otterlo*, p. 221.

28 Geoffrey Scott, *The Architecture of Humanism, A Study in the History of Taste* (1914), (New York: W. W. Norton & Co. Inc., 1974, p. 157.

29 K. Michael Hays, 'The Textualization of Architecture, 1978–1986' (talk presented as plenary speaker at Text & Architecture, An International Word & Image Conference, Paris, 26–28 June 2003, organized by the University of Paris, 7 Denis-Diderot/College of the Holy Cross, Worcester, MA, 26 June 2003.

2 Situating utopias

1 Karl Mannheim, *Ideology and Utopia* (1936), Louis Wirth and Edward Shils (trans.), San Diego: Harcourt Brace and Company, 1985, pp. 262–63.

2 For an example of this, see Ruth Levitas's non-evaluative definition of utopia, which avoids offering anything particularly useful for analysing the relative merits of potential utopias. Also missing is an understanding of the slippage between imagination and 'reality' (Ruth Levitas, *The Concept of Utopia*, Syracuse, NY: Syracuse University Press, 1990).

3 Hesiod, 'Theogony', in *Hesiod, Homeric Hymns, Epic Cycle, Homerica* (1914), H. G. Evelyn-White (trans.), Cambridge, MA: Harvard University Press, 1995, pp. 87, 89.

4 Hesiod, 'Works and Days', in *Hesiod, Homeric Hymns, Epic Cycle, Homerica*, pp. 11, 15, 17.

5 *Ibid.*, p. 15.

6 *Ibid.*, pp. 15, 17.

7 Mircea Eliade, *Patterns of Comparative Religion* (1958), R. Sheed (trans.), Lincoln: University of Nebraska Press, 1996, p. 383.

8 *Oxford English Dictionary Online* indicates that use of the word *heimweh* (*heim* = *home* + *weh tun* = hurt or ache) originated with Swiss self-description of a desire to return home, especially from service in foreign lands. *Oxford English Dictionary Online*. Available at http://dictionary. oed.com/cgi/entry/0010427?query_type+fulltext&queryword=nostalgia (24 September 2000). Additionally, the *OED Online* defines home-sickness as 'at first a rendering of Ger. (Swiss) *heimweh*', which is 'a depressed state of mind and body caused by a longing for home during absence from it; nostalgia'. *Oxford English Dictionary Online*. Available at http://dictionary. oed.com/cgi/entry/00107422?query_type+fulltext&queryword=nostalgia (24 September 2000).

9 Mario Jacoby, *Longing for Paradise*, Myron B. Gubitz (trans.), Boston, MA: Sigo Press, 1985, p. 5.

10 Bachelard, for example, believed nostalgia for an ideal past infuses longing; thus the future is figured conservatively because, in his terms, we look backward toward it. Gaston Bachelard, 'The Oneiric House', reprinted in Joan Ockman, *Architecture Culture 1943–1968*, New York: CBA/Rizzoli, 1993, pp. 111–13).

11 For a detailed discussion of this transformation, see Jean Delumeau, *History of Paradise: The Garden of Eden in Myth and Tradition*, M. O'Connell (trans.), New York: Continuum, 1995, pp. 39–70. See also Manuel and Manuel, 'Sketch for a Natural History of Paradise', *Daedalus, Journal of the American Academy of Arts and Sciences*, 101, no. 1, Winter, 1972, pp. 83–128.

12 Henri Baudet defined utopia in terms of paradise, arguing that before Europeans turned their desire toward the New World, paradise and access to the age of gold were thought to reside in the East. However, once their gaze turned westward, Utopia emerged as a single concept linking paradise (thought to exist elsewhere in space), with an age of gold (thought to exist earlier in time). Identification of utopia with the New World rendered the search for the 'authentic paradise' obsolete because making an ideal society now seemed a real possibility. Henri Baudet, *Paradise on Earth: Some Thoughts on European Images of Non-European Man* (1965), Elizabeth Wentholt (trans.), Middletown, CT: Wesleyan University Press, (1988) 1959, p. 33.

13 Henri Baudet, *Paradise on Earth: Some Thoughts on European Images of Non-European Man*, p. 32.

14 E. M. Cioran, *History and Utopia*, Richard Howard (trans.), London: Quartet Books, 1987, 118.

15 *Ibid.*, p. 102.

16 *Ibid.*, p. 100.

17 *Ibid.*, p. 106.

18 *Ibid.*, p. 104.

19 Plato, 'Symposium' (189E–191E) in *The Great Dialogues of Plato*, W. H. D. Rouse (trans.), New York City: Mentor, 1984, pp. 87, 88.

20 Plato, 'Timaeus', in *Timaeus and Critias*, Desmond Lee (trans.), London: Penguin, 1977, pp. 40–41.

21 *Ibid*, p. 45.

22 Leon Battista Alberti, *On the Art of Building in Ten Books*, Joseph Rykwert, Neil Leach and Robert Tavernor (trans.), Cambridge, MA: MIT Press, 1998, (book 6, chapter 2, p 156).

23 *Ibid.*, p. 22 (1, 9).

24 *Ibid.*, p. 96 (4, 2).

25 Thomas More, *Utopia*, Robert M. Adams (trans.), 2nd edn, New York: Norton Critical Edition, 1992, p. 33.

26 *Ibid.*, p. 33.

27 Colin Rowe, 'The Architecture of Utopia' (1959), and 'Addendum' (1973), in *The Mathematics of the Ideal Villa and Other Essays*, Cambridge: MIT Press, 1976, p. 206.

28 Karl Mannheim, *op. cit.* (1936) 1985, p. 263.

29 *Ibid.*, p. 192.

30 *Ibid.*, p. 192.

31 *Ibid.*, p. 192.

32 *Ibid.*, p. 193.

33 *Ibid.*, p. 197.

34 *Ibid.*, p. 199.

35 *Ibid.*, p. 199.

36 For discussion of the chiliastic ideas of Anabaptists, see Bernard M. G. Reardon, *Religious Thought in the Reformation*, 2nd edn, London: Longman, 1995, pp. 194–221. See also, Norman Cohn, *The Pursuit of the Millennium*, revised and expanded, New York: Oxford University Press, 1970, pp. 234–61.

37 Karl Mannheim, *op. cit.* (1936) 1985, p. 249.

38 *Ibid.*, p. 212.

39 *Ibid.*, p. 211.

40 *Ibid.*, p. 253.

41 *Ibid.*, p. 255.

42 *Ibid.*, p. 256.

43 *Ibid.*, p. 256.

44 *Ibid.*, p. 255.

45 Paul Ricoeur, *Lectures on Ideology and Utopia*, G. H. Taylor (ed.), New York: Columbia University Press, 1986, p. 282.

46 Karl Mannheim, *op. cit.* (1936) 1985, p. 262.

47 Clive Wilmer (ed.), 'Introduction' John Ruskin, *Unto this Last and Other Writings*, London: Penguin, 1985, p. 21.

48 Jeremy Bentham coined Cacotopia in 1818 to describe the worst kind of place and government imaginable. For the full definition, see *Oxford English Dictionary Online*. Available at http://oed.library.upenn.edu/oedbin/oed-id?id=47307116 (29 January 2000).

49 John Stuart Mill in Hansard Commons, 12 March 1868, *Oxford English Dictionary Online*. Available at http://oed.library.upenn.edu/oedbin/oed-id?id=116696180 (29 January 2000).

50 John Ruskin, 'Preface', *Unto this Last* (1862) in *Unto this Last and Other Writings*, London: Penguin, 1985, p. 165.

51 Henri Lefebvre, 'The Right to the City' in *Writings on Cities* (1968), Eleonore Kofman and Elizabeth Lebas (trans.), Oxford: Blackwell, 1996, p. 151.

52 Henri Lefebvre, *The Sociology of Marx*, Norbert Guterman (trans.), New York: Vintage Books, 1968, p. 188.

53 *Ibid.*, pp. 87–88.

54 Guy Debord, 'Separation Perfected', Donald Nicholson-Smith (trans.), *Internationale Situationniste*, no. 11, October 1967. Online. Available at http://members.optusnet.com.au~rkeehan/si/perfected.html (19 August 2000).

55 See especially the contributions by Constant Nieuwenhuis to *Internationale Situationniste*, no. 2 (1958), some of which are available online at http://www.notbored.org.html. Other writing by Nieuwenhuis is available online at situationist international online – situationist.cjb.net.

3 Real fictions

1 Timothy Clark, Christopher Gray, Donald Nicholson-Smith and Charles Radcliffe, 'The Revolution of Modern Art', unpublished pamphlet by excluded English situationists, 1967. On-line. Available at http://members.optusnet.com.au~rkeehan/si/modernart.html (19 August 2000).

2 Gilles Ivain (Ivan Chtcheglov) 'Formulary for a New Urbanism' Kenn Knabb (trans.), *Internationale Situationniste*, no. 1, June 1958. On-line. Available at http://members.optusnet.com.au~rkeehan/presitu/formulary.html (19 August 2000).

3 In a manner quite similar to architectural representation, 'the utopia in its literary form engenders a kind of complicity of connivance on the part of the well-disposed reader. The reader is inclined to assume the utopia as a plausible hypothesis. It may be a part of the literary strategy of utopia to aim at persuading the reader by the rhetorical means of fiction. A literary fiction is an imaginative variation whose premises the reader assumes for a while.' Paul Ricoeur, *Lectures on Ideology and Utopia*, G. H. Taylor (ed.), New York: Columbia University Press, 1986, p. 270.

4 Italo Calvino, *Invisible Cities*, William Weaver (trans.), San Diego: Harcourt Brace, 1974, p. 35.

5 Robert Venturi, Denise Scott Brown and Steven Izenour, *Learning from Las Vegas*, revised edn, Cambridge, MA: MIT Press, 1977, p. 129.

6 Janine Chasseguet-Smirgel, 'The Archaic Matrix of the Oedipus Complex in Utopia', in *Sexuality and Mind, The Role of the Father and Mother in the Psyche*, Maisey Paget (trans.), London: Maresfield Library, Karnac, 1989, p. 92.

7 Plato, 'Timaeus', in *Timaeus and Critias*, Desmond Lee (trans.), London: Penguin, 1977, p. 45.

8 Colin Rowe, 'The Architecture of Utopia' (1959) and 'Addendum' (1973), in *The Mathematics of the Ideal Villa and Other Essays*, Cambridge: MIT Press, 1976, p. 207.

9 *Ibid.*, p. 207.

10 *Ibid.*, p. 208.

11 Robert Venturi, Denise Scott Brown and Steven Izenour, *Learning from Las Vegas*, p. 3.

12 Colin Rowe, *Mathematics of the Ideal Villa*, p. 212.

13 Janine Chasseguet-Smirgel, *Sexuality and Mind*, p. 100.

14 *Ibid.*, p. 102.

15 Manfredo Tafuri and Francesco Dal Co, *Modern Architecture*, Robert Erich Wolf (trans.), New York: Harry N. Abrams, 1976, p. 402.

16 *Ibid.*, p. 407.

17 Manfredo Tafuri, *Architecture and Utopia, Design and Capitalist Development*, Barbara Luigia La Penta (trans.), Cambridge MA: MIT Press, 1976, p. 37.

18 Henri Lefebvre, 'The Right to the City', in *Writings on Cities* (1968), Eleanore Kofman and Elizabeth Lebas (trans.), Oxford: Blackwell, 1996, p. 151.

19 *Ibid.*, p. 151.

20 Northrop Frye, for example, argued that the imagined promise of technology cannot be the main point of literary utopias: 'But while technology has advanced far beyond the wildest utopian dreams of the last century, the essential quality of human life has hardly improved to the point that it could be called utopian. The real strength and importance of the utopian imagination, both for literature and for life, if it has any at all, must lie elsewhere' (Northrop Frye, 'Varieties of Literary Utopia', in *Utopias and Utopian Thought*, F. E. Manuel (ed.), Boston, MA: Houghton Mifflin, 1966, p. 31). In defining social utopias (as opposed to technological ones), Frank E. Manuel argued 'neither specific reforms of a limited nature nor mere prognostications of the invention of new technological gadgetry need be admitted. Calendar reform as such would not qualify as utopian; but calendar reform that pretended to effect a basic transformation in the human condition might be' (Frank Manuel, 'Toward a Psychological History of Utopias', in *Utopias and Utopian Thought*, p. 70).

21 This idea of a utopia as an aim that guides but remains out of reach is present in Plato's *Republic* and *The Laws*, and in More's *Utopia*. In this regard, Frye noted: 'The implication seems clear that the ideal state to More, as to Plato, is not a future ideal but a hypothetical one, an informing power and not a goal of action' (Northrop Frye, 'Varieties of Literary Utopia', in *Utopias and Utopian Thought*, F. E. Manuel (ed.), Boston, MA: Houghton Mifflin, 1966, p. 36).

22 For further details, see Frank E. Manuel and Fritzie P. Manuel, 'Marx and Engels in the Landscape of Utopia', in *Utopian Thought in the Western World*, Cambridge MA: Belknap/Harvard, 1979, pp. 697–716. See also, Karl Marx, *The Communist Manifesto* (1888), Samuel Moore (trans.), Norton Critical Edition, New York: Norton, 1988. See as well, Friedrich Engels, 'Socialism: Utopian and Scientific', in *Marx & Engels, Basic Writings on Politics and Philosophy*, Lewis S. Feruer (trans. and ed.), New York: Anchor/Doubleday, 1959, pp. 68–111.

23 Sigfried Giedion, *Space, Time and Architecture: The Growth of a New Tradition*, 5th edn, Cambridge, MA: Harvard University Press, 1967, pp. 542–43.

24 Paul Ricoeur, *Lectures on Ideology and Utopia*, p. 1.

25 Paul Ricoeur 'Ideology and Utopia as Cultural Imagination', *Philosophic Exchange*, 2(2), 1976, p. 26.

26 *Ibid.*

27 For elaboration on this idea, see Paul Ricoeur, 'Ideology and Utopia as Cultural Imagination', p. 26, and Paul Ricoeur, *Lectures on Ideology and Utopia*, pp. 1–2, 296.

28 Paul Ricoeur, *Lectures on Ideology and Utopia*, p. 296.

29 Paul Ricoeur, 'Ideology and Utopia as Cultural Imagination', p. 26.

30 *Ibid.*

31 *Ibid.*

32 Ricoeur developed his conception of utopias through the course of many of his writings, including the following comprehensive definition of utopian possibility: 'What must be emphasized is the benefit of this kind of extra-territoriality for the social function of utopia. From this "no place", an exterior glance is cast on our reality, which suddenly looks strange, nothing more being taken for granted. The field of the possible is now opened up beyond that of the actual, a field for alternative ways of living. The question therefore is whether imagination could have any constitutive role without this leap outside. Utopia is the way in which we radically rethink [reality] . . . The fantasy of an alternative society and its topographical figuration "nowhere" works as the most formidable contestation of what is . . . [what may or ought to be] proceeds from the possible to the real, from fantasy to reality.' Paul Ricoeur, 'Ideology and Utopia as Cultural Imagination', p. 26.

33 Paul Ricoeur, 'Ideology and Utopia as Cultural Imagination', p. 24.

34 *Ibid.*, p. 27.

35 Paul Ricoeur, *Lectures on Ideology and Utopia*, p. 16.

36 *Ibid.*

37 Paul Ricoeur, 'Ideology and Utopia as Cultural Imagination', p. 24.

4 Varieties of architectural utopias

1 William Morris, 'News from Nowhere' (1890), in *News from Nowhere and Other Writings*, London: Penguin, 1993, p. 239.

2 Lewis Mumford, *The Story of Utopias* (1922), Gloucester, MA: Peter Smith, 1959, p. 15.

3 *Ibid.*, p. 25.

4 Colin Rowe, introduction to *Five Architects*, New York: Oxford University Press, 1975, p. 3.

5 Colin Rowe and Fred Koetter, *Collage City*, Cambridge MA: MIT Press, 1978, p. 48.

6 *Ibid.*, p. 149.

7 *Ibid.*

8 *Ibid.*, p. 151.

9 For an insight into some of the problems architects have had with the strategies advanced in *Collage City*, see William J. R. Curtis, *Modern Architecture Since 1900*, 3rd edn, London: Phaidon, 1996, p. 609.

10 Philip Johnson, *Philip Johnson's Writings*, New York: Oxford University Press, 1978, pp. 268, 270.

11 For details of the exhibition, see Terrence Riley, *The International Style: Exhibition 15 and The Museum of Modern Art*, New York: Rizzoli/Columbia, 1992.

12 Henry-Russell Hitchcock and Philip Johnson, *The International Style* (1932), New York: W. W. Norton, 1995.

13 Philip Johnson and Mark Wigley, *Deconstructivist Architecture*, New York: The Museum of Modern Art, 1988, p. 8.

14 Philip Johnson, 'Postscript', Eisenman, Graves, Gwathmey, Hejduk, Meier, *Five Architects* (1972), New York: Oxford University Press, 1975, p. 138.

15 Author unknown, contributors list in *Autonomy and Ideology: Positioning an Avant-Garde in America*, R. E. Somol (ed.), New York: Monacelli Press, 1997, p. 358.

16 Philip Johnson, 'A Conversation Around the Avant-Garde', in *Autonomy and Ideology: Positioning an Avant-Garde in America*, R. E. Somol (ed.), New York: Monacelli Press, 1997, pp. 42, 46, 47.

17 Manfredo Tafuri, *Architecture and Utopia, Design and Capitalist Development*, Barbara Luigia La Penta (trans.), Cambridge: MA, MIT Press, 1976, p. 63.

18 *Ibid.*, p. x.

19　Johnson describes this approach as follows: 'In short, my philosophy is *functional eclecticism* . . . I am a historian first and an architect only by accident, and it seems to me that there are no forms to cling to, but there is history . . . I am too far gone in my relativistic approach to the world really to care much about labels. I have no faith whatever in anything. . . . Where there is political passions, it is easier to have architectural passions. Since passion is absent, let us do what we please . . . Briefly, functional eclecticism amounts to being able to choose from history whatever forms, shapes or direction you want to, and using them as you please . . . I have no really expressible attitude on architecture, and if we are going to have chaos I feel we might as well have nice, juicy chaos . . . One should use the chaos, the very nihilism, the relativism of our architectural world to create whimsies.' Philip Johnson, 'Informal Talk, Architectural Association, November 28, 1960', reprinted in *Philip Johnson Writings*, New York: Oxford University Press, 1978, pp. 108–12.

20　Manfredo Tafuri, *Architecture and Utopia*, p. 38.

21　*Ibid.*, p. 41.

22　*Ibid.*, p. ix.

23　*Ibid.*, p. x.

24　Philip Johnson, 'Where are We At?', *Architectural Review*, CXXVII, September 1960, pp. 173–75, reprinted in *Philip Johnson Writings*, New York: Oxford University Press, 1978, p. 100.

25　Manfredo Tafuri, *Architecture and Utopia*, p. 181.

26　*Ibid.*, p.182.

27　Buckminster Fuller, 'Utopia or Oblivion', in *Utopia or Oblivion: the Prospects for Humanity*, New York: Bantam Books, 1969, p. 292.

28　Kenneth Frampton, *Modern Architecture, a Critical History*, 3rd edn, London: Thames and Hudson, 1992, p. 191.

29　William Morris, 'Review of Looking Backward' (1889) in *News From Nowhere and Other Writings*, p. 354.

30　On this subject, see, for example, William Morris, *News From Nowhere and Other Writings*, pp. 43–228, 233–54, 331–48, 353–58, 367–69, 373–75. Edward Bellamy, *Looking Backward* (1888), Cecelia Tichi (ed.), London: Penguin, 1986. Karl Marx and Friedrich Engels, in *Marx & Engels: Basic Writings on Politics and Philosophy*, Lewis S. Feuer (trans. and ed.), New York: Anchor/Doubleday, 1959, pp. 68–111, 112–32.

31　Edward Bellamy, *Looking Backward*, pp. 83, 117.

32　*Ibid.*, pp. 83, 117, 144.

33　Ibid, p. 234.

34　William Morris, 'Review of Looking Backward', in *News From Nowhere and Other Writings*, p. 357.

35　William Morris, 'Gothic Architecture' (1889), in *News From Nowhere and Other Writings*, p. 331.

36　Northrop Frye, 'The Meeting of Past and Future in William Morris'(1982) in *Myth and Metaphor*, R. D. Denham (ed.), Charlottesville: University Press of Virginia, 1990, pp. 337–38.

37　Frank E. Manuel, 'Toward a Psychological History of Utopias', in *Utopias and Utopian Thought*, Boston: MA, Houghton Mifflin, 1966, p. 70.

38　*Ibid.*, pp. 337–38.

39　Peter Cook, 'Some Notes on the Archigram Syndrome', *Perspecta*, Supplement 11, Yale 1967, reprinted in *A Guide to Archigram, 1961–1974*, London: Academy Editions, 1994, p. 29.

40　Peter Cook described the origins of Archigram as follows: 'In late 1960, in various flats in Hampstead, a loose group of people started to meet: to criticize projects, to concoct letters to the press, to combine to make competitions, and generally prop one another up against the boredom of working in London architectural offices . . . The title [of Archigram's magazine of the same name] came from the notion of a more urgent and simple item than a journal, like a "telegram" or "aerogramme", hence "archi(tecture)-gram".' Peter Cook, *ARCHIGRAM*, Peter Cook and Warren Chalk (eds), New York: Praeger, 1973, p. 8.

41　Reyner Banham, 'A Comment from Peter Reyner Banham', in *ARCHIGRAM*, p. 5.

42   Herbert Lachmayer, 'Archigram: The Final Avant-Garde of an Ageing modernism?', in *A Guide to Archigram, 1961–1974*, London: Academy Editions, 1994, pp. 420, 428.

43   David Greene, 'Archigram 1' (late 1960), reprinted in *ARCHIGRAM*, p. 8.

44   Peter Cook, 'Some Notes on the Archigram Syndrome', *Perspecta*, Supplement 11, Yale 1967, reprinted in *A Guide to Archigram, 1961–1974*, p. 25.

45   Warren Chalk, 'Housing as a Consumer Product' (1966) reprinted in, *ARCHIGRAM*, p. 17.

46   Katrina Heron interview with Rem Koolhaas, From Bauhaus to Koolhaas (WIRED) Online (July 1996). Available at http://www.wirednews.com/wired/archive/4.07/koolhaas_pr.html (29 August 2000).

47   Rem Koolhaas, 'Whatever Happened to Urbanism', in OMA, Rem Koolhaas and Bruc Mau, *S, M, L, XL*, New York: Monacelli Press, 1995, pp. 969, 971.

48   Rem Koolhaas, *Delirious New York* (1978), New York: Monacelli Press, 1994, pp. 207, 197.

49   *Ibid.*, p. 293.

50   Rem Koolhaas, *Conversations With Students* (1991), Architecture at Rice 30, 2nd edn, New York: Princeton Architectural Press, 1996, p. 65.

51   Rem Koolhaas, *Delirious New York*.

5   Postwar possibilities

1   Victor Turner, *The Ritual Process*, Chicago: Aldine Publishing Co., 1969, pp. 128–29.

2   Arnold van Gennep, *The Rites of Passage*, Monika B. Vizedom and Gabrielle L. Caffee (trans.), Chicago: University of Chicago Press, 1960.

3   The trajectory of this is revealed by the statements collected in Ulrich Conrads, *Programs and Manifestoes on 20th-Century Architecture* (1964), Cambridge, MA: MIT Press, 1971, and in the transitional and critical statements on modern architecture compiled in Joan Ockman, *Architecture Culture: 1943–1968*, New York, NY: Columbia/Rizzoli 1993.

4   Discussion of the development of this new condition for architectural theory and practice, which is the foundation for developments leading to the modern movement, is indebted to Joseph Rykwert's, *The First Moderns: The Architects of the Eighteenth Century*, Cambridge, MA: MIT Press, 1980.

5   For two versions of this story, see the following: Henry Russell Hitchcock, *Modern Architecture: Romanticism and Reintegration* (1929), New York, NY: De Capo, 1993, p. 17, and Kenneth Frampton, *Modern Architecture: A Critical History*, 3rd edn, London: Thames and Hudson: 1992, p. 8.

6   For an overview of Choay's ideas about the emergence of modern urbanism, see Françoise Choay, *The Modern City: Planning in the 19th Century*, Marguerite Hugo and George R. Collins (trans.), New York: George Braziller, 1969.

7   Le Corbusier evidences this in the following: 'A man is an exceptional phenomenon occurring at long intervals, perhaps by chance, perhaps in accordance with the pulsation of a cosmography not yet understood. Michel Angelo is the man of the last thousand years as Phidias was the man of the thousand years before.' Le Corbusier, *Towards a New Architecture* (1931), Frederick Etchells (trans.), New York: Dover Publications, Inc., 1986, pp. 165, 168.

8   Victor Turner, *The Ritual Process*, p. 94.

9   *Ibid.*, p. 94.

10   Antonio Sant'Elia, 'Futurist Architecture' (1914) reprinted in Ulrich Conrads, *Programs and Manifestoes on 20th-Century Architecture*, Cambridge, MA: MIT, 1971, p. 36.

11   Victor Turner, *The Ritual Process*, p. 94.

12   Henry van de Velde, 'Programme' (1903), reprinted in Ulrich Conrads, *Programs and Manifestoes*, p. 13.

13   Victor Turner, *The Ritual Process*, p. 97.

14   J. L. Sert, F. Léger, S. Giedion, 'Nine Points on Monumentality' (1943), reprinted in Joan Ockman, *Architecture Culture: 1943–1968*, New York, NY: Columbia/Rizzoli 1993, p. 29.

15 Victor Turner, *The Ritual Process*, p. 94.

16 Philip Johnson, preface, *Built in USA: Post War Architecture*, New York: Museum of Modern Art, 1952, p. 8.

17 Alfred Barr, then Director of the Museum of Modern Art in New York (MOMA), already saw modern architecture as having arrived: 'This book [*The International Style*] presents their [Hitchcock and Johnson's] conclusions, which seem to me of extraordinary, perhaps epoch-making, importance. For they have proven beyond a reasonable doubt, I believe, that there exists today a modern style as original, as consistent, as logical, and as widely distributed as any in the past. The authors have called it the International Style. Alfred Barr, preface, Hitchcock and Johnson, *The International Style* (1932), New York, NY: Norton, 1995, p. 27.

18 Manfredo Tafuri, *Architecture and Utopia: Design and Capitalist Development*, Barbara Luigia La Penta (trans.), Cambridge, MA: MIT Press, 1976, p. 181.

19 Louis I. Kahn, 'Monumentality' (1944), reprinted in Joan Ockman, *Architecture Culture: 1943–1968*, p. 48.

20 Leon Battista Alberti, *On the Art of Building in Ten Books*, Joseph Rykwert, Neil Leach and Robert Tavernor (trans.), Cambridge, MA: MIT Press, 1988, p. 156 (6, 2, 93–94).

21 Sigfried Giedion, *Space, Time and Architecture: The Growth of a New Tradition*, 5th edn, revised and enlarged, Cambridge, MA: Harvard University Press, 1967, p. 669.

22 Turner shows that during the liminal phase the neophyte enters what he called 'communitas', which is a period of relative undifferentiation. Turner uses the Latin to distinguish this state from 'Community', which he characterized as 'an area of common living', made up of differentiated relationships contained by and within structured society. (See Turner, *The Ritual Process*, pp. 94–130.) Turner also argued that 'ideological communitas . . . is a label one can apply to a variety of utopian models of societies based on existential communitas'. Turner, *The Ritual Process*, p. 132.

23 Giedion, *Space, Time and Architecture*, p. 669.

24 Victor Turner, *The Ritual Process*, p. 104.

25 Jean-François Lyotard, *The Postmodern Condition: A Report on Knowledge* (1979), G. Bennington and B. Massumi (trans.), Minnesota: University of Minnesota Press, 1984, pp. xxiv, 37.

26 Manfredo Tafuri, *Architecture and Utopia*, p. 24

27 Manfredo Tafuri, *The Sphere and the Labyrinth: Avant-Gardes and Architecture from Piranesi to the 1970s* (1980), P. d'Acierno and R. Connolly (trans.), Cambridge, MA: MIT Press, 1987, p. 267.

28 *Ibid.*, p. 267.

29 See especially, Martin Buber, *Paths in Utopia* (1949), Syracuse, NY: Syracuse University Press, 1996, pp. 29–138.

30 For an idea of how this might be resolved, see Joseph Rykwert, *The Idea of a Town: The Anthropology of Urban Form in Rome, Italy, and the Ancient World*, Cambridge, MA: MIT Press, 1988, p. 202.

31 According to Rykwert, in the past, architecture 'imitated culture. Monumental building reproduced the necessary forms of a rickety construction in permanent and noble materials. In so far as it came to imitating nature, it was the proportions of the human body which the architect abstracted in his measurements.' Joseph Rykwert, 'Ornament is no Crime' (1975), in *The Necessity of Artifice*, New York: Rizzoli, 1982, p. 92. For a sustained discussion of the body building metaphor, see Joseph Rykwert, *The Dancing Column: On Order in Architecture*, Cambridge, MA: MIT Press, 1996.

32 Mary Douglas, *Natural Symbols: Explorations in Cosmology*, London: Routledge, 1996, pp. xxxii, xxxvi. Douglas's book is an extended discussion of the body/system/social system analogy.

33 Le Corbusier, *Modulor* and *Modulor 2*, excerpts reprinted in Le Corbusier, Jacques Guiton (ed.), *The Ideas of Le Corbusier on Architecture and Planning*, Margaret Guiton (trans.), New York: George Braziller, 1981, pp. 67, 69.

34 Le Corbusier, *Towards a New Architecture* (1923), F. Etchells (trans.), New York, NY: Dover Publications, Inc., 1986, 7.

35   If correctly translated, the title of Le Corbusier's *Vers une Architecture* (1923) would read as *Towards an Architecture* (rather than as *Towards a New Architecture*, this would have highlighted his preoccupation with persisting problems of architecture rather than emphasizing newness above all else.

36   For a more detailed introduction to Le Corbusier's evolution, see Kenneth Frampton, *Modern Architecture: A Critical History*, 3rd edn, London: Thames and Hudson, 1992, pp. 149–60, 178–85, 224–30. See also, Kenneth Frampton, *Le Corbusier*, London: Thames and Hudson, 2001.

37   Le Corbusier, *Towards a New Architecture*, pp. 25–26, 29, 63.

38   Ibid., pp. 63–64, 72, 73.

39   Rudolf Wittkower, Architect's Yearbook, No. 5, 1953, quoted in Le Corbusier, *Modulor 2* (1955), P. de Francia and A. Bostock (trans.), Cambridge, MA: MIT Press, 1973, pp. 191–93.

40   Rudolf Wittkower, 'Le Corbusier's Modulor' (1961), reprinted in *In the Footsteps of Le Corbusier*, C. Palazzolo and R. Vio (ed.), New York, NY: Rizzoli, p. 19.

41   Le Corbusier quoted by Frampton, in *Modern Architecture: A Critical History*, 3rd edn, London: Thames and Hudson, 1992, pp. 271–72.

42   For more on Team X, see the *Team 10 Primer*, Alison Smithson (ed.), Cambridge, MA: MIT Press, 1968. See also, *Team 10 Meetings*, Alison Smithson (ed.), New York: Rizzoli, 1991.

43   Spiro Kostof, *A History of Architecture: Settings and Rituals*, 2nd edn, revised by G. Castillo, New York: Oxford University Press, 1995, p. 747.

44   Aldo van Eyck, 'Is Architecture Going to Reconcile Basic Values', in Oscar Newman, *New Frontiers in Architecture, CIAM '59 in Otterlo*, by order of Jacob B. Bakema for the Otterlo 1959 participants, Jürgen Joedicke (ed.), New York: Universe Books, 1961, p. 27.

45   Historian Carl Schorske, suggests that one of the fundamental commitments of history is 'to chart not only continuity, but change' and that anthropology is the social science 'most directly concerned with the mental world of culture, but traditionally least concerned with temporal transformation'. Carl Schorske, *Thinking with History: Explorations in the Passage to Modernism*, Princeton: Princeton University Press, 1998, pp. 229–30. The history of architecture, though, remains predominantly a taxonomy of styles outside of a theoretical frame. However, to reveal architecture as a collection of ongoing, and relatively stable, themes, architects would need to become more like anthropologists than historians, much as van Eyck attempted.

46   Giedion, *Space, Time and Architecture*, p. 578.

47   William Curtis, for example, remarks on the anthropological basis of van Eyck's work: 'Van Eyck's quest for these timeless qualities [of human existence, culture, and architecture] eventually took him far afield to Dogon mud communities in sub-Saharan Africa and into the field of linguistic anthropology. His approach to vernacular forms was mystical; he saw them as expressions of coherent spiritual mythologies'. William J. R. Curtis, *Modern Architecture Since 1900*, 3rd edn, London: Phaidon Press, 1996, p. 446.

48   Aldo van Eyck's best known building, the Amsterdam Orphanage, is the focus of Chapters 10 and 11 of the present book. For a brief description of how he put his theory into practice at the Orphanage, see, Kenneth Frampton, *Modern Architecture: A Critical History*, 3rd edn, London: Thames and Hudson, 1992, p. 276.

49   Robert Venturi, *Complexity and Contradiction in Architecture* (1966), New York, NY: Museum of Modern Art, 1977, pp. 13–14, 82.

50   For a discussion that sheds light upon how Venturi's pleasure seeking might be anti-structural (anti-cultural) see Victor Turner's discussion of existential or spontaneous communitas, in Turner, *The Ritual Process*, Chicago: Aldine publishing Co., 1969, pp. 134–40.

51   In *Learning from Las Vegas*, Venturi, Scott Brown and Izenour proposed buildings that accept a diminished role for architects by representing their role as exterior decorators of mute boxes prescribed by the building industry. In *Complexity and Contradiction*, Venturi called for an architecture of variety that is not exemplified by his work.

52   Robert Venturi, *Complexity and Contradiction in Architecture*, pp. 16, 17.

53 Aldo van Eyck, 'Steps Toward a Configurative Discipline' (1962), reprinted in Joan Ockman, *Architecture Culture 1943–1968*, pp. 348–49.

54 *Ibid.*, p. 349.

55 Along these lines, Turner wrote: 'There is a dialectic here, for the immediacy of communitas gives way to the mediacy of structure, while in *rites de passage*, men are released from structure into communitas only to return to structure revitalized by their experience of communitas. What is certain is that no society can function adequately without this dialectic . . . [S]tructural action swiftly becomes arid and mechanical if those involved are not periodically immersed in the regenerative abyss of communitas.' Victor Turner, *The Ritual Process*, pp. 129, 139.

6 Le Corbusier's monastic ideal

1   Le Corbusier, *Precisions On the Present State of Architecture and City Planning* (1930), Edith Schreiber Aujame (trans.), Cambridge: MA, MIT Press, 1991, p. 97.

2   H. Allen Brooks notes that Le Corbusier was familiar with a number of John Ruskin's books in French editions. These included *The Seven Lamps of Architecture* (1900), *The Bible of Amiens* (1904), *Sesame and Lillies* (1906), *Mornings in Florence* (1906), *The Stones of Venice* (1906), and excerpts from *Lectures on Architecure and Painting* (after 1910) (H. Allen Brooks, *Le Corbusier's Formative Years*, Chicago: University of Chicago Press, 1997, p. 68, n. 54 and p. 69). For additional details on Le Corbusier's early reading see Paul Venerable Turner, *The Education of Le Corbusier*, New York: Garland Publishing, Inc, 1971.

3   Kenneth Frampton, *Modern Architecture, A Critical History*, 3rd edn, London: Thames and Hudson, 1992, p. 10.

4   *Ibid.*

5   *Ibid.*

6   *Ibid.*

7   *Ibid.*

8   *Ibid.*

9   For an informative discussion of Ruskin and Morris's, see Clive Wilmer, 'Introduction', John Ruskin, *Unto this Last and Other Writings*, London: Penguin, 1985, pp. 7–44, and his introduction to *News From Nowhere and Other Writings* by William Morris, London: Penguin, 1993, pp. ix–xli.

10 Kenneth Frampton, *Modern Architecture*, p. 9.

11 *Ibid.*

12 For an overview of Le Corbusier's life and practice sympathetic to this reading see William J. R. Curtis, *Le Corbusier: Ideas and Forms*, London: Phaidon, 1986.

13 Le Corbusier, from a letter to his teacher L'Eplattenier, dated Sunday, 22 November 1908, reprinted in Jean Jenger, *Le Corbusier: Architect, Painter, Poet*, Caroline Beamish (trans.), New York: Harry N. Abrams, 1996, pp. 114–15.

14 Excerpt from *Entretien avec les étudiants des école d'architecture*, reprinted in Jean Jenger, *Le Corbusier: Architect, Painter, Poet*, pp. 118–19.

15 Claude Perrault, *Ordonnance For the Five Kinds of Columns After the Methods of The Ancients*, Indra Kagis McEwen (trans.), Santa Monica, CA: Getty Center, 1993.

16 For more details regarding Claude Perrault and his influence, see Joseph Rykwert, *The First Moderns. The Architects of the Eighteenth Century*, Cambridge, MA: MIT Press, 1980, and Alberto Pérez-Goméz, *Architecture and the Crisis of Modern Science*, Cambridge, MA: MIT Press, 1983. See also, Albérto Perez-Goméz, introduction to Claude Perrault, *Ordonnance for the Five Kinds of Columns After the Methods of the Ancients*, pp. 1–44, and Kenneth Frampton, *Modern Architecture*, 3rd edn, pp. 12–40.

17 For discussion and exemplification of this, see Joseph Rykwert, *The First Moderns. The Architects of the Eighteenth Century*, Cambridge, MA: MIT Press, 1980, pp. 415–70.

18 H. Allen Brooks, *Le Corbusier's Formative Years*, Chicago: University of Chicago Press, 1997.

19 Nikolaus Pevsner, *Pioneers of Modern Design: From William Morris to Walter Gropius*, revised

Notes

1975, London: Penguin, 1991. Nikolaus Pevsner, *The Sources of Modern Architecture and Design*, London: Thames and Hudson, 1968. Nikolaus Pevsner, 'William Morris and Architecture', Journal of the Royal Institute of British Architects, 3rd series, LXIV, 1957, reprinted in *Studies in Art, Architecture and Design: Victorian and After*, Princeton: Princeton University Press, 1968, pp. 108–117.

20 Paul Turner, 'Romanticism, Rationalism, and the Domino System', in *The Open Hand: Essays on Le Corbusier*, Russell Walden (ed.), Cambridge, MA: MIT Press, 1977, p. 23.

21 For a discussion of how Ruskin's *method* influenced Le Corbusier see Mary Patricia May Sekler, 'Ruskin, the Tree, and the Open Hand', in *The Open Hand: Essays on Le Corbusier*, pp. 42–95.

22 Le Corbusier *Modulor 2*, Peter de Francia and Anna Bostock (trans.), Cambridge, MA: MIT Press, 1958, p. 320.

23 Le Corbusier, 'Mise au Point (1966)' in *The Final Testament of Père Corbu*, Ivan Zanic (trans.), New Haven: Yale University Press, 1997, p. 92.

24 For a discussion of Ruskin and modern architecture, see Nikolaus Pevsner, *Pioneers of Modern Design: From William Morris to Walter Gropius*, revised 1975, London: Penguin, 1991; Sigfried Giedion, *Space, Time and Architecture: The Growth of a New Tradition* (1967), 5th edn, Cambridge, MA: Harvard, 1982, pp. 291–332, Mark Swenarton, 'Ruskin and the Moderns' in *Artisans and Architects: The Ruskinian Tradition in Architectural Thought*, New York: St. Martin's, 1989, pp. 189–220, and, William J. R. Curtis, *Modern Architecture Since 1900*, 3rd edn, London: Phaidon, 1996, pp. 21–159.

25 Le Corbusier, 'The Hour of Architecture', in *The Decorative Art of Today* (1925), James Dunnett (trans.), Cambridge, MA: MIT Press, 1987, p. 132. For a discussion of Le Corbusier's early education, including the influence of Ruskin, see H. Allen Brooks, *Le Corbusier's Formative Years*, Chicago: University of Chicago Press, 1997.

26 Le Corbusier's desire to integrate the machine is more an extension than a rejection of Ruskin's theory. For an alternative view, see Reyner Banham, *Theory and Design in the First Machine Age*, New York: Praeger, 1960, p. 12.

27 In this regard, see Roger Dixon and Stefan Muthesius, *Victorian Architecture*, London: Thames and Hudson, 1978, pp. 158–61, and John Maule McKean 'The First Industrial Age', in *Architecture of the Western World*, Michael Raeburn (ed.), New York: Rizzoli, 1980, pp. 218, 219.

28 Le Corbusier, 'The Hour of Architecture', in *The Decorative Art of Today* (1925), James Dunnett (trans.), Cambridge, MA: MIT Press, 1987, pp. 132, 133.

29 *Ibid.*, pp. 132, 133.

30 The essays in *Vers une Architecture*, as with those compiled in Le Corbusier's later *Decorative Art of Today* (1925), first appeared as individual essays in *L'Esprit Nouveau*.

31 Le Corbusier, *Towards a New Architecture* (1923), Frederick Etchells (trans.) (1931), New York, NY: Dover Publications, 1986, p. 271.

32 *Ibid.*, pp. 274, 275.

33 *Ibid.*, p. 275.

34 *Ibid.*, pp. 275–77, 288.

35 *Ibid.*, p. 288.

36 *Ibid.*, p. 276.

37 *Ibid.*, pp. 277, 278, 288.

38 *Ibid.*, p. 280.

39 David Leatherbarrow's reading of Le Corbusier' Salvation Army project suggests something of this conclusion. See D. Leatherbarrow, '*The Roots of Architectural Invention: Site, Enclosure, Materials*, Cambridge: Cambridge University Press, 1993, pp. 59–64.

40 Le Corbusier, *Towards a New Architecture*, pp. 288, 289.

41 In addition to Ruskin, Sitte's principles of city design, which were interpretations of his experiences of medieval cities, influenced Le Corbusier's early medievalism. For example, H. Allen Brooks has shown that Sitte's *Der Städtebau* (1889, French edition 1902), greatly influenced Le Corbusier's

early and unpublished *La Construction des Villes* (1910), H. Allen Brooks *Le Corbusier's Formative Years*, 1997, pp. 200–02. Augmentations to Brooks's research include Curtis's claim that Le Corbusier learned from Sitte to think of cities as wholes made up of intimate complexity (W. J. R. Curtis, *Le Corbusier: Ideas and Forms*, 1986, p. 30). Additionally, R. A. Etlin argues that Sitte's preoccupation with sequential spaces in cities as a fundamental aspect of their liveability persisted in Le Corbusier's *promenade architecturale*, long after Le Corbusier apparently rejected Sitte (Richard A. Etlin, *Frank Lloyd Wright and Le Corbusier: The Romantic Legacy*, Manchester, UK: Manchester University Press, 1994, pp. 106, 112, 113, 115). See also Stanislaus von Moos, 'Urbanism and Transcultural Changes, 1910–1935: A Survey', in *Le Corbusier*, H. Allen Brooks (ed.), Princeton, NJ: Princeton University Press, 1987, pp. 219, 220, 222. For Le Corbusier's more overtly negative view of Sitte, see Le Corbusier, *When the Cathedrals Were White* (1947), Francis E. Hyslop, Jr. (trans.), New York: McGraw-Hill, 1964, pp. 48, 49.

42 Le Corbusier, *Le Couvent Sainte Marie de La Tourette à Eveux*, Lyons: Lescuyer et Fils, 1971, p. 84.

43 Le Corbusier quoted, *Couvent Sainte Marie de la Tourette built by Le Corbusier*, L'Arbresle, photocopied pamphlet produced by the Dominican Convent of La Tourette, *c.* 1999, p. 1.

44 Alain Erlande-Brandenburg, *Three Cistercian Sisters of Provence: Sénanque, Silvacane, Le Thoronet*, Christopher Thierry (trans.), Paris: Le Éditions du Huitième Jour, 2000, p. 69.

45 Sigfried Giedion, *Space, Time and Architecture: The Growth of a New Tradition* (1967), 5th edn, Cambridge, MA: Harvard, 1982, p. 546.

46 John Ruskin, *The Stones of Venice* (1853) J. G. Links (ed.), New York: Da Capo Press, 1960, p. 29.

47 Ruskin is quite clear on this matter: 'Rudeness, and the love of change which we have insisted upon as the first elements of Gothic, are elements common to all healthy schools.' John Ruskin, 'The Nature of Gothic' (1853), in *Unto this Last and Other Writings*, p. 103.

48 *Ibid.*

49 *Ibid.*, p. 92.

50 Le Corbusier's attitude toward *beton brut*, rough concrete, should not be confused with the short-lived efforts of so-called *Brutalist* architects, who from the mid-1950s and throughout the 1960s employed materials, especially concrete, as found objects of industry. Because Le Corbusier's objective was to translate other construction methods into concrete, his use of it was interpretive in a way Brutalist architects claimed to eschew. For more on Brutalism, see Reyner Banham, *The New Brutalism* of 1966; John Fleming, Hugh Honour and Nikolaus Pevsner, *Dictionary of Architecture*, 4th edn, London: Penguin, 1991, p. 63; and Kenneth Frampton, *Modern Architecture, A Critical History*, 3rd edn, London: Thames and Hudson, 1992, pp. 262–68. See also William J. R. Curtis, *Modern Architecture Since 1900*, 3rd edn, London: Phaidon, 1996, pp. 443–45.

7 The life within

1 Le Corbusier, *Talks with Students* (1961), Pierre Chase (trans.), New York: Princeton Architectural Press, 1999, p. 31.

2 *Ibid.*, 44, 45, 47.

3 Le Corbusier would have read the following in French: 'If you will drive in the evening to the Chartreuse in Val d'Ema, . . . you may see some fading light and shade of monastic life, among which if you stay till the fireflies come out in the twilight . . . you will be better prepared for to-morrow morning's walk'. (John Ruskin, *The Mornings in Florence*, New York: John Wiley & Sons, 1876, p. 24).

4 For a list of books by Ruskin that Le Corbusier had with him in Florence, see H. Allen Brooks, *Le Corbusier's Formative Years*, Chicago: University of Chicago Press, 1997, p. 98.

5 The numerous mentions of Le Corbusier's trip to Ema include, Peter Serenyi, 'Le Corbusier, Fourier, and the Monastery of Ema (1967)' in *Le Corbusier in Perspective*, Peter Serenyi (ed.), New Jersey: Prentice Hall, 1975, pp. 103–16; Stanislaus von Moos, *Elements of a Synthesis*, Cambridge MA:

MIT Press, 1979. See also, H. Allen Brooks, *Le Corbusier's Formative Years*, pp. 105–07, 301–02; and William J. R. Curtis, *Le Corbusier, Ideas and Forms*, London: Phaidon, 1986, pp. 22, 62, 170, 181, 186.

6   Le Corbusier, reprinted in H. Allen Brooks, *Le Corbusier's Formative Years*, p. 49.

7   Le Corbusier, quoted in Jean Petit, *Le Corbusier lui-même*, p. 44, reprinted in Anthony Sutcliffe, 'A Vision of Utopia', in *The Open Hand, Essays on Le Corbusier*, Russell Walden (ed.), Cambridge, MA: MIT Press, 1977, p. 219.

8   *Ibid.*, p. 218.

9   Peter Serenyi, 'Le Corbusier, Fourier, and the Monastery of Ema', *Art Bulletin*, XLIX (1967), pp. 277–86.

10   Le Corbusier, *Precisions: On the Present State of Architecture and City Planning* (1930), Edith Schreiber Aujame (trans.), Cambridge, MA: MIT Press, 1991, p. 91.

11   Le Cobusier, originally quoted in Jean Petit, *Le Corbusier lui-même*, p. 44, Anthony Sutcliffe (trans.), reprinted in Anthony Sutcliffe, 'A Vision of Utopia', in *The Open Hand: Essays on Le Corbusier*, Russell Walden (ed.), Cambridge, MA: MIT Press, 1977, p. 218.

12   *Ibid.*, pp. 218, 219.

13   For Reyner Banham's confused reading of La Tourette see Reyner Banham, 'La Maison des hommes and La Misère des villes: Le Corbusier and the Architecture of Mass Housing', in *Le Corbusier*, H. Allen Brooks (ed.), New Jersey: Princeton University, 1987, pp. 107–16.

14   Reyner Banham, 'La Maison des hommes and La Misère des villes: Le Corbusier and the Architecture of Mass Housing', p. 115.

15   Much of what follows, as regards Carthusians, is drawn from Raymund Webster 'The Carthusian Order' in *The Catholic Encyclopedia*. Online. Available at http://www.newadvent.org/cathen/03388a.htm (31 March 2000). Ambrose Mougel 'Saint Bruno' in *The Catholic Encyclopedia*. Online. Available at http://www.newadvent.org/cathen/03014b.htm (31 March 2000). Much of what follows as regards Dominicans, draws upon conversations with a Dominican Friar at La Tourette as well as I. I. P. Mandonnet 'Order of Preachers', in *The Catholic Encyclopedia*. Online. Available at http://www.newadvent.org/cathen/12354c.htm (13 February 2000). John B. O'Conner 'Saint Dominic' in *The Catholic Encyclopedia*. Online. Available at http://www.newadvent.org/cathen/05106a (13 February 2000).

16   Reyner Banham, 'La Maison des hommes and La Misère des villes: Le Corbusier and the Architecture of Mass Housing', p. 115.

17   G. E. Kidder Smith, *The New Architecture of Europe*, Cleveland: Meridian Books, 1961, p. 100.

18   For Xenakis's description of his role in the design of La Tourette, see Iannis Xenakis, 'The Monastery of La Tourette', in *Le Corbusier*, H. Allen Brooks (ed.), New Jersey: Princeton University, 1987, pp. 143–61. Xenakis also contributed a description of his work on the facades of La Tourette to Le Corbusier's *Modulor 2*, see Le Corbusier, *Modulor 2* (1958), Peter de Francia and Anna Bostock (trans.), Cambridge, MA: MIT Press, 1973, pp. 326–31.

19   Iannis Xenakis, 'The Monastery of La Tourette', p. 146.

20   Iannis Xenakis quoted in Le Corbusier, *Modulor 2*, p. 326.

21   Iannis Xenakis, 'The Monastery of La Tourette', p. 145.

22   *Ibid.*, pp. 146, 147.

23   A familial resemblance identified by Robert Venturi, Vincent Scully and W. J. R. Curtis among others.

24   Colin Rowe, 'La Tourette' (1961), *Mathematics of the Ideal Villa and Other Essays*, Cambridge, MA: MIT Press, 1976, pp. 185–203.

25   The specifics of Dominican life in France and at La Tourette were shared with me by a brother resident at the convent.

26   See Martin Purdy, 'Le Corbusier and the Theological Program', in *The Open Hand, Essays on Le Corbusier*, Russell Walden (ed.), Cambridge, MA: MIT Press, 1977, pp. 292, 302, 303, 305.

27   Italo Calvino, *Invisible Cities*, William Weaver (trans.), San Diego: Harcourt Brace, 1974, p. 35.

8 Fairy tales and golden dust

1   Louis I. Kahn, *Conversations with Students*, Architecture at Rice 26, 2nd edn, New York: Princeton Architectural Press, 1998, p. 15.

2   These explanations of Kahn's crystallization are discussed in further detail in David B. Brownlee and David G. de Long, *Louis I. Kahn: In the Realm of Architecture*, New York: Rizzoli, 1991.

3   For further detail on Kahn's influences, see David B. Brownlee and David G. De Long, *Louis I. Kahn: In the Realm of Architecture*.

4   Louis I. Kahn, 'The Value and Aim of Sketching' (1931), *Writings, Lectures, Interviews*, Alessandra Latour (ed.), New York: Rizzoli, 1991, pp. 10, 11.

5   *Ibid.*, p. 11.

6   Kahn's use of *form* is reminiscent of *type*. Forms and Types are worked toward in the present, yet their origins lie in the past, which makes them models that future efforts could interpret. For more detail about *type*, see David Leatherbarrow, *The Roots of Architectural Invention, Site, Enclosure, Materials*, Cambridge: Cambridge University Press, 1993, pp. 70–83; see also Anthony Vidler, *The Writing on the Walls*, New York: Princeton Architectural Press, 1987, pp. 147–64.

7   Louis I. Kahn, *Conversations with Students*, p. 43.

8   Louis I. Kahn, in Richard Saul Wurman (ed.), *What Will Be Has Always Been, The Words of Louis I. Kahn*, New York: Access and Rizzoli, 1986, p. 142.

9   The following develops from an understanding of hermeneutics informed by various writings by Gianni Vattimo, Paul Ricoeur, Fredric Jameson and Martin Heidegger.

10 Louis I. Kahn, 'Silence and Light, an address to the Students at the School of Architecture, ETH, Zurich, Switzerland. 12 January 1969', in Richard Saul Wurman (ed.), *What Will Be Has Always Been, The Words of Louis I. Kahn*, p. 61.

11 Louis I. Kahn, 'Dedication, Temple Beth-El Chappaqua, New York, 5 May 1972', in Richard Saul Wurman (ed.), *What Will Be Has Always Been, The Words of Louis I. Kahn*, p. 260.

12 See for example Louis I. Kahn, *Conversations with Students*, and various writings throughout Richard Saul Wurman (ed.), *What Will Be Has Always Been, The Words of Louis I. Kahn*.

13 For more on the Yale Center for British Art, see Jules David Prown, *The Architecture of the Yale Center for British Art*, New Haven: Yale University, 1977. See also, Patricia Cummings Loud, 'Yale Center for British Art', in David B. Brownlee and David G. de Long, *Louis I. Kahn: In the Realm of Architecture*, pp. 410–13.

14 At the American Academy in Rome, Kahn was in contact with Frank E. Brown whose interpretation of Roman architecture does in words what Kahn attempts in buildings. Brown saw Roman architecture as a manifestation of Roman ritual; Kahn wanted to invent places where rituals could manifest themselves. See Frank E. Brown, *Roman Architecture*, New York: George Braziller, 1967, p. 9.

15 Louis I. Kahn, 'From a Conversation with Peter Blake, 20 July 1971', in Richard Saul Wurman (ed.), *What Will Be Has Always Been, The Words of Louis I. Kahn*, p. 131.

16 Such challenges to Kahn's work course through his interview with John W. Cook and Heinrich Klotz, in their book *Conversations with Architects*, New York: Praeger, 197, pp. 178–217.

17 Louis I. Kahn, 'Space and Inspirations', *L'Architecture d'Aujourd'hui*, vol. 142, February/March, 1969, reprinted in *Writings, Lectures, Interviews*, p. 226.

18 John W. Cook and Heinrich Klotz, 'Louis Kahn', in *Conversations with Architects*, p. 192.

19 Louis I. Kahn, 'Architecture and Human Agreement, A Tiffany Lecture, Philadelphia, PA. 10 October 1973', in Richard Saul Wurman (ed.), *What Will Be Has Always Been, The Words of Louis I. Kahn*, p. 215.

20 Bruno Bettelheim, *The Uses of Enchantment, The Meaning and Importance of Fairy Tales*, New York: Vintage Books, 1989, p. 10.

21 Louis I. Kahn, 'Lecture to Towne School of Civil and Mechanical Engineering, University of Pennsylvania, Philadelphia, Pennsylvania. 19 November 1968', in Richard Saul Wurman (ed.), *What Will Be Has Always Been, The Words of Louis I. Kahn*, p. 33.

22   Louis I. Kahn, 'Kimball Museum Dedication, Fort Worth Texas, Autumn 1972', in Richard Saul
     Wurman (ed.), *What Will Be Has Always Been, The Words of Louis I. Kahn*, p. 177.

23   Louis I. Kahn, 'Architecture and Human Agreement, Lecture at University of Virginia, Charlottesville,
     Virginia, April 1972', in Richard Saul Wurman (ed.), *What Will Be Has Always Been, The Words of
     Louis I. Kahn*,p. 135.

24   *Ibid.*, p. 135.

25   Kahn developed these ideas in his Otterlo Congress Address in 1959 published in Oscar Newman
     New Frontiers in Architecture, CIAM '59 in Otterlo, by order of Jacob B. Bakema for the Otterlo
     1959 participants, Jürgen Joedicke (ed.), New York: Universe Books, 1961, pp. 205–16. Kahn's
     Otterlo address has been reprinted in Louis I. Kahn, *Essential Texts*, Robert Twombly (ed.), New
     York: W. W. Norton and Co., 2003, pp. 37–61.

26   Louis I. Kahn, 'Iranian Panel, September 1970', in Richard Saul Wurman (ed.), *What Will Be Has
     Always Been, The Words of Louis I. Kahn*, p. 98.

27   Louis I. Kahn, 'A Verbal Autobiography, From a Conversation with Jamie Mehta, 22 October 1973',
     in Richard Saul Wurman (ed.), *What Will Be Has Always Been, The Words of Louis I. Kahn*, p. 228.

28   Louis I. Kahn, 'From Lecture and Walking Tour, Fort Wayne Art Center Dedication. Fort Wayne,
     Indiana 1974', in Richard Saul Wurman (ed.), *What Will Be Has Always Been, The Words of Louis
     I. Kahn*, p. 250.

29   For a fine introduction to fairy tales, see Bruno Bettelheim, *The Uses of Enchantment, The Meaning
     and Importance of Fairy Tales* (1975), New York: Vintage Books, 1989, pp. 3–40.

30   Louis I. Kahn, 'Silence and Light, Address to the Students at the School of Architecture, ETH,
     Zurich, Switzerland. 12 January 1969', in Richard Saul Wurman (ed.), *What Will Be Has Always
     Been, The Words of Louis I. Kahn*, p. 57.

31   Bruno Bettelheim, *The Uses of Enchantment, The Meaning and Importance of Fairy Tales*,
     p. 8.

32   Louis I. Kahn, *Conversations with Students*, p. 19.

33   Louis I. Kahn, 'Excerpts from an Interview with Patricia McLaughlin, *The Pennsylvania Gazette*,
     Philadelphia, Pennsylvania. December 1972', in Richard Saul Wurman (ed.), *What Will Be Has
     Always Been, The Words of Louis I. Kahn*, p. 176.

34   For more on this, see Marco Frascari, 'Tell-the-Tale Detail', *VIA7: The Building of Architecture*,
     1984. pp. 23–37, reprinted in *Theorizing a New Agenda for Architecture: An Anthology of
     Architectural Theory 1965–1995*, Kate Nesbitt (ed.), New York City: Princeton Architectural Press,
     1996, pp. 500–14.

35   For more on this, see Umberto Eco, 'Function and Sign: The Semiotics of Architecture', reprinted
     in Neil Leach (ed.), *Rethinking Architecture: A Reader in Cultural Theory*, London: Routledge, 1997,
     pp.183–202.

36   For more on this, see, Joseph Rykwert, *The Necessity of Artifice*, New York: Rizzoli, 1982. See
     also, Joseph Rykwert, *The Dancing Column: On Order in Architecture*, Cambridge, MA: MIT Press,
     1996.

37   See Adolf Loos, 'Vernacular Art' (1914), in *The Architecture of Adolf Loos*, London: An Arts Council
     Exhibition, 1985, p. 113. See also, David Leatherbarrow, *The Roots of Architectural Invention*,
     Cambridge: Cambridge University Press, 1993, p. 139. Leatherbarrow translation of Loos's words
     from the original is presented here. See also, Adolf Loos, 'Cultural Degeneration' (1908), in *The
     Architecture of Adolf Loos*, London: An Arts Council Exhibition, 1985, p. 98.

38   Many of the ideas elaborated on in the preceding four points can trace their origins to concepts
     developed by Piet Mondrian. See, for example, Piet Mondrian, *Abstract Reality and Natural Reality:
     An Essay in Trialogue Form, 1919–1920*, Martin S. James (trans.), New York: George Braziller,
     1995.

39   For details on the Mitchell/Guirgola buildings identified here, see John Andrew Gallery, General
     Editor, *Philadelphia Architecture: A Guide to the City*, 2nd edn, Philadelphia: The Foundation for
     Architecture, 1994.

40 For detail on Venturi, Scott Brown and Associates' Philadelphia buildings identified here, see John Andrew Gallery, General Editor, *Philadelphia Architecture: A Guide to the City*.

9 Kahn and Salk's challenge to dualistic thinking

1   Louis I. Kahn, 'Law and Rule in Architecture I' (1961) 'LIK Lectures 1969 [sic]' folder, Box LIK 53, Louis I. Kahn Collection University of Pennsylvania and Pennsylvania Historical and Museum Commission, Philadelphia, reprinted in Louis I. Kahn, *Essential Texts*, Robert Twombly (ed.), New York: W. W. Norton & Co., 2003, p. 132.

2   For further historical detail regarding the Salk Institute, see David B. Brownlee and David G. de Long, *Louis I. Kahn: In the Realm of Architecture*, New York: Rizzoli, 1991, pp. 94–102, 330–39.

3   See Michael Polanyi, *Science, Faith and Society*, Chicago: University of Chicago Press, 1946. See also Thomas S. Kuhn, *The Structure of Scientific Revolutions* (1962), Chicago: University of Chicago Press, 1996.

4   For an introduction to recent scholarship on this period, see Sarah Williams Goldhagen and Réjean Legault (eds), *Anxious Modernisms: Experimentation in Postwar Architectural Culture*, Montreal and Cambridge, MA: CCA and MIT Press, 2000.

5   For a brief introduction to the history of CIAM, see 'CIAM', in Vittorio Magnago Lampugnani, General Editor, *The Thames and Hudson Dictionary of 20th Century Architecture*, London: 1986, Thames and Hudson, pp. 68–70.

6   Louis I. Kahn, 'Talk at the Conclusion of the Otterlo Congress' (1959), in Oscar Newman, *New Frontiers in Architecture, CIAM '59 in Otterlo*, by order of Jacob B. Bakema for the Otterlo 1959 participants, Jürgen Joedicke (ed.), New York: Universe Books, 1961, p. 212.

7   *Ibid.*, p. 208.

8   For Kahn's development of these ideas, see his Otterlo Congress address from 1959 published in, Oscar Newman, *New Frontiers in Architecture, CIAM '59 in Otterlo*, pp. 205–16.

9   For further historical detail regarding the Richards Medical Laboratories, see David B. Brownlee and David G. de Long, *Louis I. Kahn: In the Realm of Architecture*, New York: Rizzoli, 1991, pp. 62–64, 324–29, and Wilder Green, *Louis I. Kahn Architect: Richards Medical Research Building*, Museum of Modern Art Bulletin, vol. 28, no. 1, 1961.

10 For more on the Larkin Building, see Dell Upton, *Architecture of the United States*, Oxford: Oxford University Press, 1998, pp. 159–60.

11 Louis I. Kahn, 'Talk at the Conclusion of the Otterlo Congress', p. 212.

12 Louis I. Kahn, 'Form and Design', from Vincent Scully Jr, *Louis I. Kahn*, New York: George Braziller, Inc. 1962, reprinted in *Writings, Lectures, Interviews*, Alessandra Latour (ed.), New York: Rizzoli, 1991, p. 118.

13 Louis I. Kahn, 'On Form and Design', *Journal of Architectural Education*, vol. XV, no. 3, Fall 1960, reprinted in *Writings, Lectures, Interviews*, Alessandra Latour (ed.), New York: Rizzoli, 1991, pp. 107–08.

14 Louis I Kahn, *Conversations with Students* (1968), Architecture at Rice 26, 2nd edn, New York: Princeton Architectural Press, 1998, 25.

15 John W. Cook and Heinrich Klotz, 'Louis Kahn', in *Conversations with Architects*, New York: Praeger 1973, p. 180.

16 Louis I. Kahn, 'Architecture and Human Agreement, A Tiffany Lecture, Philadelphia, PA. 10 October 1973', in Richard Saul Wurman (ed.), *What Will Be Has Always Been, The Words of Louis I. Kahn*, New York: Access and Rizzoli, 1986, p. 216.

17 Louis I. Kahn, 'On Form and Design', *Journal of Architectural Education*, vol. XV, no. 3, Fall 1960, reprinted in *Writings, Lectures, Interviews*, p. 107.

18 Louis I. Kahn, 'Form and Design', from Vincent Scully Jr, *Louis I. Kahn*, New York: George Braziller, Inc. 1962, reprinted in *Writings, Lectures, Interviews*, p. 118.

19 Louis I. Kahn, 'Spaces Order and Architecture', *The Royal Architectural Institute of Canada Journal*, vol. 34, no. 10, October 1957, reprinted in *Writings, Lectures, Interviews*, p. 77.

20   *Ibid.*, p. 77.

21   Louis I. Kahn, 'Talk at the Conclusion of the Otterlo Congress', pp. 206–07.

22   John W. Cook and Heinrich Klotz, 'Louis Kahn', in *Conversations with Architects*, p. 183.

23   Louis I. Kahn, 'The Invisible City, International Design Conference, Aspen. June 1972', in Richard Saul Wurman (ed.), *What Will Be Has Always Been, The Words of Louis I. Kahn*, p. 168.

24   Kenneth Frampton, *Modern Architecture, A Critical History*, 3rd edn, London, Thames and Hudson, 1992, p. 10.

25   *Ibid.*, p. 10.

26   For further detail regarding the monastic sources of the Salk Institute, see David B. Brownlee and David G. de Long, *Louis I. Kahn: In the Realm of Architecture*, 1991, pp. 94–96, 331, 333.

27   Norman L. Koonce, FAIA, President of AAF, 'Jonas Salk's Assisi Retreat', in *Human Experiences With Architecture*. Online. Washington, DC; The American Architecture Foundation, no date. Available at http://ameracrchfoundation.com/Salk.htm (24 May 2000).

28   Louis I. Kahn, 'Monumentality', *New Architecture and City Planning, A Symposium*, Paul Zucker (ed.), New York: Philosophical Library, 1944, reprinted in *Writings, Lectures, Interviews*, p. 18.

29   *Ibid.*, p. 18.

30   Headline, cover of *San Diego Magazine*, February 1962 for two articles by Mary Harrington Hall, 'Gift from the Sea' and 'The High Hopes of Jonas Salk' *San Diego Magazine*, February, 1962, pp. 41–45, 105, 106.

31   Louis I. Kahn, 'On Form and Design', *Journal of Architectural Education*, vol. XV, no. 3, Fall 1960, reprinted in *Writings, Lectures, Interviews*, p. 107.

32   Louis I. Kahn, quoted from typescript, 'Abstract of the Program for the Institute of Biology at Torrey Pines, La Jolla, San Diego' (no date), Box LIK 27, Louis I. Kahn Collection, University of Pennsylvania and Pennsylvania Historical and Museum Commission, Philadelphia.

33   For a description of this process, including Barragan's contribution, see David B. Brownlee and David G. de Long, *Louis I. Kahn: In the Realm of Architecture*, p. 334. See also Louis I. Kahn, 'Address' (1966), reprinted in *Writings, Lectures, Interviews*, pp. 209, 215–16; see also Louis I. Kahn, 'letter to Dr. Jonas Salk' (19 December 1966), Box LIK 27, Louis I. Kahn Collection, University of Pennsylvania and Pennsylvania Historical and Museum Commission, Philadelphia.

34   Louis I. Kahn, 'Silence' (1968), reprinted in *Writings, Lectures, Interviews*, pp. 232–33. See also Louis I. Kahn, 'Architecture: Silence and Light' (1970), reprinted in *Writings, Lectures, Interviews*, p. 256.

35   Kahn considered the water channel in the court to be 'like the fountains of Alhambra', quoted in Mary Harrington Hall, 'Gift from the Sea', *San Diego Magazine*, February 1962, p. 44.

36   For elaborations on the Solomonic and Paradisaical symbolism of Islamic courts, see Oleg Grabar, *The Alhambra*, Cambridge, MA: Harvard University Press, 1978, pp. 76–79, 115, 117–18, 127, 129. See also, Robert Hillenbrand, *Islamic Architecture*, New York: Columbia University Press, 1994, p. 4.

10   Aldo van Eyck's utopian discipline

1   Aldo van Eyck, 'Steps Toward a Configurative Discipline', *Forum 3*, August 1962, pp. 81–93, reprinted in Joan Ockman, *Architecture Culture: 1943–1968*, New York: Rizzoli and Columbia, 1993, p. 348.

2   Originally published in *Forum 3*, August 1962, pp. 81–93, 'Towards a Configurative Discipline' has been reprinted in Joan Ockman, *Architecture Culture: 1943–1968*, pp. 348–60.

3   CIAM, Charter of Athens: Tenets (CIAM VI, 1933, published 1941), excerpted in Ulrich Conrads, *Programs and Manifestoes on 20th-Century Architecture* (1964), Cambridge, MA: MIT Press, 1971, p. 137.

4   Aldo van Eyck, 'Steps Toward a Configurative Discipline', p. 348.

5   *Ibid.*, p. 349.

6   *Ibid.*

7   *Ibid.*

8   *Ibid.*, p. 348.
9   *Ibid.*
10 *Ibid.*, pp. 350, 351.
11 *Ibid.*, p. 353.
12 *Ibid.*, p. 349.
13 *Ibid.*, pp. 350, 351.
14 *Ibid.*, pp. 348, 349.
15 *Ibid.*, p. 348.
16 *Ibid.*, pp. 349, 350.
17 *Ibid.*, p. 350.
18 *Ibid.*, p. 351.
19 *Ibid.*, p. 354.
20 *Ibid.*, p. 360.
21 *Ibid.*
22 *Ibid.*
23 Aldo van Eyck, 'Otterlo Address' in Oscar Newman, *New Frontiers in Architecture, CIAM '59 in Otterlo*, by order of Jacob B. Bakema for the Otterlo 1959 participants, Jürgen Joedicke (ed.), New York: Universe Books Inc., 1961, pp. 33, 27.
24 *Ibid.*, p. 27.
25 Aldo van Eyck, 'Steps Toward a Configurative Discipline', p. 349.

11 Story of another idea

1   Aldo van Eyck, 'The Interior of Time', in *Meaning in Architecture*, Charles Jencks and George Baird (eds), New York: George Braziller, 1969, p. 171.
2   K. Michael Hays, 'The Textualization of Architecture, 1978–1986', talk presented as plenary speaker at Text & Architecture, An International Word & Image Conference, Paris, 26–28 June 2003, organized by the University of Paris, 7 Denis-Diderot/College of the Holy Cross, Worcester, MA, 26 June 2003. In his talk, Hays argued that the post-utopian architecture of practitioners including Rossi, Eisenman, Tschumi and Koolhaas, among others, shows that they are engaged in freeing 'architecture from the burden of utility' in an effort to realize the 'autonomy project', which turns on a 'recognition of the impossibility, or failure of meaning'. A position based on the conviction that architecture, in 'any traditional sense, such as van Eyck proposed', is irredeemably lost. For the opposite view, see Aldo van Eyck, 'Lured from His Den', Article of the Month, Archis, February 1998. Online. Available at http://www.archis.org/archis_old/english/archis_art_e_1998/archis_art_9802_ENG.html (17 December 2004).
3   Aldo van Eyck, 'Lured from His Den', Article of the Month, *Archis*, February 1998. Online. Available at http://www.archis.org/archis_old/english/archis_art_e_1998/archis_art_9802_ENG.html (17 December 2004).
4   Francis Strauven's exhaustive monograph on Aldo van Eyck's life and work was an invaluable resource for my research, see Francis Strauven, *Aldo van Eyck, The Shape of Relativity*, Victor J. Joseph (trans.), Amsterdam: Architectura and Natura, 1998.
5   Aldo van Eyck 'Lured from His Den'.
6   For further detail, see Francis Strauven, *Aldo van Eyck, The Shape of Relativity*, pp. 143–49.
7   For more on van Eyck's understanding of the Dogon, see Aldo van Eyck, 'The Interior of Time', and Aldo van Eyck, 'The Miracle of Moderation', Paul Parin, 'The Dogon People 1', and Fritz Morganthaler, 'The Dogon People 2', in *Meaning in Architecture*, Charles Jencks and George Baird (eds), London: Barrie & Rockliff, The Cresset Press, 1969, pp. 170–213.
8   Aldo van Eyck, 'The Interior of Time', in *Meaning in Architecture*.
9   Aldo van Eyck, 'The Interior of Time', p. 171.
10 For information on the brief and intentions for the Amsterdam Orphanage, see Francis Strauven, *Aldo van Eyck, The Shape of Relativity*, pp. 284–87; see also Francis Strauven, *Aldo van Eyck's*

Orphanage: A Modern Monument, John Kirkpatrick (trans.), Rotterdam: NAi, 1996, pp. 4–6. See also, Aldo van Eyck, *Works*, Vincent Ligtelijn (ed.), Basel: Birkhäuser Publishers, 1999, pp. 88–90.

11 Aldo van Eyck, 'Steps Toward a Configurative Discipline' (1962), in Joan Ockman *Architecture Culture: 1943–1968*, New York: Rizzoli and Columbia, 1993, p. 349.

12 Herman Hertzberger, *Space and the Architect: Lessons in Architecture* 2, Rotterdam: 010 Publishers, 2000, p. 199.

13 Herman Hertzberger, *Space and the Architect: Lessons in Architecture*, 2, p. 198.

14 For further detail, see Francis Strauven, *Aldo van Eyck, The Shape of Relativity*, p. 288–325; see also Francis Strauven, *A Modern Monument*, John Kirkpatrick (trans.), Rotterdam: NAi, 1996.

15 Herman Hertzberger, *Space and the Architect: Lessons in Architecture*, 2, p. 198.

16 Aldo van Eyck, *Works*, Vincent Ligtelijn (ed.), Basel: Birkhäuser Publishers, 1999, pp. 257–61.

17 Herman Hertzberger, *Space and the Architect: Lessons in Architecture*, 2, p. 198.

18 Leon Battista Alberti *On the Art of Building in Ten Books* (1486), Joseph Rykwert, Neil Leach and Robert Tavernor (trans.), Cambridge, MA: MIT Press, 1998, p. 156 (6.2.156).

19 Aldo van Eyck, 'Steps Toward a Configurative Discipline', p. 360.

20 See for example, Alberti, *On the Art of Building in Ten Books*, p. 23 (1.9.23).

21 Aldo van Eyck, 'The Medicine of Reciprocity Tentatively Illustrated', *Architects Yearbook*, no. 10, London, 1962, pp. 173–78, reprinted in Aldo van Eyck, *Works*, p. 89.

22 Sigfried Giedion, *Space, Time and Architecture: The Growth of a New Tradition*, 5th edn, Cambridge, MA: Harvard, 1967, pp. 542–43.

12 The unthinkability of utopia

1 Sir Thomas More, 'Utopia', in *Utopia: a revised translation, backgrounds, criticism*, 2nd edn, Robert M. Adams, (trans. and ed.) New York: W. W. Norton and Co., 1992, p. 85.

2 Hans-Georg Gadamer, 'What is Practice', in *Reason in the Age of Science*, Frederick G. Lawrence (trans.), Cambridge, MA: MIT Press, 1981, p. 80.

3 Paul Ricoeur, *Lectures on Ideology and Utopia*, G. H. Taylor (ed.), New York: Columbia University Press, 1986, p. 310.

4 Hans-Georg Gadamer, 'What is Practice', p. 81.

5 Colin Rowe and Fred Koetter, *Collage City*, Cambridge, MA: MIT Press, 1978, p. 149. Franco Borsi, *Architecture and Utopia*, Deke Dusinberre (trans.), Paris: Hazan, 1997, p. 10.

6 Rowe and Koetter, *Collage City*, p. 149.

7 Borsi, *Architecture and Utopia*, p. 10.

8 Manfredo Tafuri, *Architecture and Utopia, Design and Capitalist Development*, Barbara Luigia La Penta (trans.), Cambridge, MA: MIT Press, 1976, pp. 62–63.

9 Rowe and Koetter, *Collage City*, pp. 11–14.

10 Tafuri, *Architecture and Utopia*, p. 181.

11 Karsten Harries, *The Ethical Function of Architecture*, Cambridge, MA: MIT Press, 1997, p. 367.

12 *Ibid.*

13 David Leatherbarrow, *The Roots of Architectural Invention: Site, Enclosure, Materials*, Cambridge: Cambridge University Press, 1993, pp. 223–25.

14 *Ibid.*, p. 1.

15 *Ibid.*, pp. 118, 220, 224, 225.

16 Aldo van Eyck, 'Lured from his Den'. ARCHIS, February 1998. Online. Available http://www.archis.org/archis_old/english/archis_art_e_1998/archis_art_9802_ENG.html (17 September 2004).

17 *Ibid.*

18 *Ibid.*

19 *Ibid.*

20 Leon Battista Alberti, *On the Art of Building in Ten Books* (1486), Joseph Rykwert, Neil Leach and Robert Tavernor (trans.), Cambridge, MA: MIT Press, 1988, 6.2.155 (93–94v).

21 *Ibid.*, 6.2.156.

22 *Ibid.*

23 *Ibid.*

24 Aldo van Eyck, 'Steps Toward a Configurative Discipline' (1962), in *Architecture Culture 1943–1968*, compiled by Joan Ockman, New York: Rizzoli, 1993, p. 360.

25 *Ibid.*

26 *Ibid.*, p. 357.

27 Alberti, 1.2.8 (5v).

28 *Ibid.*, 6.6.163.

29 *Ibid.*, 6.2.156.

30 Aldo van Eyck, 'Steps Toward a Configurative Discipline', p. 360.

31 Alberti, 1.9.23.

32 *Ibid.*, 9.5.302–03.

33 Plato, 'The Republic', in *The Great Dialogues of Plato*, W. H. D. Rouse (trans.), New York: Mentor, 1984, 5.463b–465a, p. 263.

34 Alberti, 9.5, p. 302–03.

35 *Ibid.*, 9.5, p. 303.

36 *Ibid.*, 4.2, p. 96.

37 Gianni Vattimo, 'The End of Modernity, the End of the Project?', in *Rethinking Architecture, a Reader in Cultural Theory*, Neil Leach (ed.) London: Routledge, 1997, p. 154.

38 Martin Buber, *Paths in Utopia*, Syracuse, NY: Syracuse University Press, 1996.

39 Vattimo, 'The End of Modernity, the End of the Project?', p. 154.

40 Aldo van Eyck, *Hubertushuis – Hubertus House*, 2nd edn, Amsterdam: Stichting Wonen, 1986, p. 95.

41 Aldo van Eyck, (1966) quoted in *Team 10 Primer*, Alison Smithson (ed.), Cambridge, MA: MIT Press, 1968, p. 15.

42 Aldo van Eyck, 'Otterlo Address', in Oscar Newman, *New Frontiers in Architecture, CIAM '59 in Otterlo*, by order of Jacob B. Bakema for the Otterlo 1959 participants, Jürgen Joediche (ed.), New York: Universe Books Inc., 1961.

13 Into the present

1 Renzo Piano, *La responsibilità dell'architetto, Conversazione con Renzo Cassigoli*, Firenze-Antella, Passigli Editori, 2000, pp. 91, 92.

2 *Ibid.*, p. 34.

3 Daniel Libeskind, *Jewish Museum Berlin*, Germany: G + B Arts International, 1999, p. 10.

4 Janine Chasseguet-Smirgel, *Sexuality and Mind: The Role of the Father and the Mother in the Psyche*, London: H. Karnac Books Ltd, 1989, p. 767.

5 Daniel Libeskind, quoted in Bernhard Schneider, *Daniel Libeskind, Jewish Museum Berlin*, Munich: Prestel Verlag, 1999, p. 19.

6 Information panel, 'Holocaust Tower', Jewish Museum Berlin, Germany.

7 Statement attributed to Daniel Libeskind, Information panel, 'Holocaust Tower', Jewish Museum, Berlin, Germany.

8 Primo Levi, *Survival in Auschwitz* (1958), Stuart Woolf (trans.), New York: Touchstone, 1985.

9 Daniel Libeskind, *Jewish Museum Berlin*, p. 44.

10 Tod Williams and Billie Tsien, *Work Life*, Hadley Arnold (ed.), New York: Monacelli Press, 2000, p. 24

11 Aldo van Eyck (1962, 1965), reprinted in *Team 10 Primer*, Alison Smithson (ed.), Cambridge, MA: MIT Press, 1968, pp. 41, 104.

12 Tod Williams and Billie Tsien, *Work Life*, p. 78.

13 Aldo van Eyck (1962, 1965), reprinted in *Team 10 Primer*, 68, pp. 41, 43.

14 *Ibid.*, p. 43.

Notes

15 Tod Williams and Billie Tsien, 'Slowness', for Nexus in 2G, Issue 9, 1999. Online. Available at http://www.twbta.com/write/slowness.html#method (30 July 2004).

16 *Ibid.*

17 Much of the information in this section was drawn from interviews with Dr Gerald Edelman, Founding Director of the Neurosciences Institute and Dr W. Einer Gall, Research Director of the Institute. Dr Gerald Edelman, interview with author, La Jolla, California, 31 August 2004. Dr W. Einer Gall, interview with author, La Jolla, California, 1 September 2004.

18 For a compelling extended discussion of the relation of land to building at the Neurosciences Institute, see David Leatherbarrow, *Topographical Stories: Studies in Landscape and Architecture*, Philadelphia: University of Pennsylvania Press, 2004, pp. 17–58.

19 The reading of Piano's Tjibaou Cultural Centre elaborated derives from in situ investigation of the project, subsequently tested out in discussion with French anthropologist Alban Bensa, Paris, France, 14 October 2004.

20 Renzo Piano with the assistance of Roberto Brignolo, *Log Book*, New York: Monacelli Press, 1997, p. 14.

21 Renzo Piano, interview by John Tusa, radio broadcast transcript, May 2003, BBC Radio 3, Architecture on 3. Online. Available at http://www.bbc.co.uk/radio3/architecture/pa_piano.shtml (20 October 2004).

22 Renzo Piano, *La responsibilità dell'architetto*, pp. 17, 18.

23 Renzo Piano, *Log Book*, p. 180.

24 *Ibid.*, p. 174.

25 Alban Bensa, interview with author, digital recording, Paris, France, 14 October 2004. For much greater detail concerning Bensa's collaboration with Piano, see Alban Bensa, *Ethnologie & Architecture: Le Centre Culturel Tjibaou, une réalisation de Renzo Piano*, Paris: Adam Biro, 2000.

26 For a brief introduction to the unique character of Jean-Marie Tjibaou's social and political imagination, see, Jean-Marie Tjibaou, *Cibau Cibau*, Roy Benyon (trans.), Nouméa Nouvelle-Calédonie: Agence de dévelopment de la culture Kanak, 1998. This collection of excerpts in English translation are drawn from Alban Bensa and Eric Wittersheim, (eds), *La présence kanak. Écrits et dits de Jean-Marie Tjibaou*, Paris: Odile Jacob, 1996.

27 Jean-Marie Tjibaou, quoted in a display at the Centre Culturel Tjibaou, Nouméa, New Caledonia, as part of an exhibition dedicated to his life, a slightly different English translation of J.-M. Tjibaou's statement can be read in Eric Wittersheim, 'Melanesian Élites and Modern Politics in New Caledonia and Vanuatu', *State Society and Governance in Melanesia*, Australia National University: Research School of Pacific and Asian Studies, 03/1998, p. 6. Online. Available at http://rspas.anu.edu.au/melanesia/dplist.php?searchterm=1998 (28 October 2004).

28 Alban Bensa, interview with author, digital recording, Paris, France, 14 October 2004.

29 John Ruskin, *The Stones of Venice*, J. G. Links (ed.), New York: Da Capo Press, 1960, p. 29.

30 Louis I. Kann, 'Monumentality', *New Architecture and City Planning*, Paul Zucker, (ed.), New York: Philosophical Library: 1944, pp. 577–88, reprinted in *Architecture Culture 1943–1968: A Documentary Anthology* compiled by Joan Ockman with the collaboration of Edward Eigen, New York: Columbia/Rizzoli, 1993, p. 54.

31 See especially, Renzo Piano, *La responsibilità dell'architetto*, Conversazione con Renzo Cassigoli, Firenze-Antella, Passigli Editori, 2000, and Renzo Piano with the assistance of Roberto Brignolo, *Log Book*, New York: Monacelli Press, 1997.

32 Louis I. Kahn, *Light is the Theme*, Fort Worth: 1975, p. 43, quoted by Marco Frascari, 'The Tell-the-Tale Detail', *Via 7: the Building of Architecture* (1984), pp. 23–37, reprinted in *Theorizing a New Agenda for Architecture: An Anthology of Architectural Theory: 1965–1995*, Kate Nesbitt (ed.), New York: Princeton Architectural Press, 1996, p. 512.

Select bibliography

Adorno, Theodor, 'Functionalism Today', in *Rethinking Architecture*, NeiLeach (ed.), London and New York: Routledge, 1997, pp. 6–20.

Alberti, Leon Battista, *On the Art of Building in Ten Books* (1486), Joseph Rykwert, Neil Leach and Robert Tavernor (trans.), Cambridge, MA: MIT Press, 1988.

Andreotti, Libero and Costa, Xavier (eds), *Situationists, Art, Politics, Urbanism*, Barcelona: ACTAR, 1996.

Andreotti, Libero and Costa, Xavier (eds), *Theory of the Dérive and other Situationist Writings on the City*, Barcelona: ACTAR, 1996.

Archigram, *A Guide to Archigram, 1961–1974*, London: Academy Editions, 1994.

Arendt, Hanna, *Between Past and Future*, New York: Viking Press, 1968.

Armytage, Walter H. G., *Heavens Below: Utopian Experiments in England, 1560–1960*, London: Routledge and Kegan Paul, 1961.

Armytage, Walter H. G., *Yesterday's Tomorrows: A Historical Survey of Future Societies*, London: Routledge and Kegan Paul, 1968.

Banham, Reyner, *Theory and Design in the First Machine Age*, New York: Praeger Publishers, 1960.

Baudet, Henri, *Paradise on Earth: Some Thoughts on European Images of Non-European Man* (1965), Elizabeth Wentholt (trans.), Middletown, CT: Wesleyan University Press, 1988.

Bellamy, Edward, *Looking Backward* (1888), Cecelia Tichi (ed.) London: Penguin, 1986.

Benevolo, Leonardo, *The Origins of Modern City Planning* (1963), Judith Landry (trans.), Cambridge, MA: MIT Press, 1971.

Benjamin, Walter, *Illuminations*, Harry Zohn (ed.), New York: Shocken Books, 1969.

Benjamin, Walter, *Reflections*, Edmund Jephcott (trans.), New York: Shocken Books, 1986.

Bensa, Alban, *Ethnologie & Architecture: Le Centre Culturel Tjibaou, une réalisation de Renzo Piano*, Paris: Adam Biro, 2000.

Benson, Timothy O., *Expresssionist Utopias, Paradise, Metropolis, Architectural Fantasy*, Berkeley: University of California Press, 2001.

Bernieri, Marie Louise, *Journey Through Utopia*, London: Freedom Press, 1950.

Bettleheim, Bruno, *The Uses of Enchantment, the Meaning and Importance of Fairy Tales* (1975), New York: Vintage Books, 1989.

Bloch, Ernst, *The Utopian Function of Art and Literature, Selected Essays*, Jack Zipse and Frank Mecklenburg (trans.), Cambridge, MA: MIT Press, 1988.

Bloch, Ernst, *The Principle of Hope*, Three Volumes, Neville Plaice, Stephen Plaice and Paul Knight (trans.), Cambridge, MA: MIT Press, 1995.

Boullée, Etienne-Louis, 'Architecture: Essay on Art' in Helen Rosenau, *Boullée and Visionary Architecture*, New York: Harmony Books, 1976.

Boyer, M. Christine, *Dreaming the Rational City, The Myth of American City Planning*, Cambridge, MA: MIT, 1983.

Boyer, M. Christine, *The City of Collective Memory*, Cambridge, MA: MIT Press, 1994.

Braham, Allan, *The Architecture of the French Enlightenment*, Berkeley: University of California Press, 1980.

Select bibliography

Brooks, H. Allen, (ed.), *Le Corbusier*, Princeton, NJ: Princeton University Press, 1987.

Brownlee, David R. and de Long, David G., *Louis I. Kahn: In The Realm of Architecture*, New York: Rizzoli, 1991.

Buber, Martin, *Paths in Utopia*, R. F. C. Hull (trans.) (1949), Syracuse: Syracuse University Press, 1996.

Calvino, Italo, *Invisible Cities*, William Weaver (trans.), San Diego: Harcourt Brace, 1974.

Calvino, Italo, *The Uses of Literature*, P. Creagh (trans.), San Diego: Harcourt Brace, Jovanovich, 1986, pp. 213–55.

Certeau, Michel de, *The Practice of Everyday Life*, Steven Rendall (trans.), Berkeley: University of California Press, 1984.

Chermayeff, Serge and Alexander, Christopher, *Community and Privacy: Towards a New Architecture of Humanism*, New York: Doubleday, 1965.

Choay, Françoise, *Le Corbusier*, New York: George Braziller, Inc., 1960.

Choay, Françoise, *L'urbanisme: Utopies et Realities*, Paris: Éditions de Seuil, 1965.

Choay, Françoise, *The Modern City: Planning in the Nineteenth-Century*, New York: George Braziller Inc., 1969.

Choay, Françoise, *The Rule and the Model: On the Theory of Architecture and Urbanism*, D. Bratton (trans.), Cambridge, MA: MIT Press, 1996.

Cioran, E. M, *History and Utopia*, Richard Howard (trans.), London: Quartet Books, 1987.

Claeys, Gregory and Sargent, Lyman Tower (eds), *The Utopia Reader*, New York: New York University Press, 1999.

Cohn, Norman, *The Pursuit of the Millennium*, revised and expanded, New York: Oxford University Press, 1970.

Conrads, Ulrich, ed., *Programs and Manifestoes on 20th-Century Architecture* (1964), Michael Bullock (trans.), Cambridge, MA: MIT Press, 1971.

Cook, Peter and Chalk, Warren (eds), *ARCHIGRAM*, New York: Praeger, 1973.

Curtis, William J. R., *Le Corbusier, Ideas and Forms*, London: Phaidon, 1986.

Curtis, William J. R., *Modern Architecture, Mythical Landscapes and Ancient Ruins*, The Annual Soane Lecture, Sir John Soane's Museum, 1997.

Debord, Guy, *The Society of the Spectacle* (1967), Donald Nicholson-Smith (trans.), New York: Zone Books, 1994.

Delumeau, Jean, *History of Paradise: The Garden of Eden in Myth and Tradition*, M. O'Connell (trans.), New York: Continuum Press, 1995.

Dewey, John, *Art as Experience*, New York: Perigee, 1934.

Douglas, Mary, *Natural Symbols, Explorations in Cosmology*, London: Routledge, 1996.

Eagleton, Terry, *Ideology*, London, New York: Verso, 1991.

Eliade, Mircea, *The Myth of the Eternal Return, Or, Cosmos and History*, Willard R. Trask (trans.), Princeton, NJ: Princeton University Press, 1954.

Eliade, Mircea, 'Paradise and Utopia: Mythical Geography and Eschatology' in *The Quest: History and Meaning in Religion*, Chicago: University of Chicago Press, 1969.

Eliade, Mircea, 'The World, The City, The House', in *Occultism, Witchcraft, and Cultural Fashions*. Chicago: University of Chicago Press, 1976.

Filarete (Antonio di Piero Averlino), *Treatise on Architecture* (1461–1464), John R. Spencer (trans.), New Haven: Yale University Press, 1965.

Fishman, Robert, *Urban Utopias in the Twentieth Century: Ebenezer Howard, Frank Lloyd Wright, Le Corbusier*, Cambridge, MA: MIT Press, 1982.

Fourier, Charles, *The Utopian Vision of Charles Fourier: Selected Texts on Work, Love, and Passionate Attraction*, Jonathan Beecher and Richard Bienvenu (eds and trans.), Boston: Beacon Press, 1971.

Fourier, Charles, *Design for Utopia, Selected Writings*, Julia Franklin (trans.), New York: Shocken Books, 1971.

Fourier, Charles, *The Theory of the Four Movements* (1808), Ian Patterson (trans.), Cambridge, MA: Cambridge University Press, 1996.

Frampton, Kenneth, *Studies in Tectonic Culture*, Cambridge, MA: MIT Press, 1995.

Frampton, Kenneth, *Le Corbusier*, London: Thames and Hudson, 2001.

Frye, Northrop, 'Varieties of Literary Utopias', in *Utopias and Utopian Thought*, Frank E. Manuel (ed.), Boston, MA: Houghton Mifflin, 1966.

Frye, Northrop, *Myth and Metaphor*, R. D. Denham (ed.), Charlottesville, VA: University Press of Virginia, 1990.

Fuller, Buckminster, *Utopia or Oblivion: the Prospects for Humanity*, New York: Bantam Books, 1969.

Gadamer, Hans-Georg, *Reason in the Age of Science*, Frederick G. Lawrence (trans.), Cambridge, MA: MIT Press, 1981.

Garnier, Tony, *Une Cite Industrielle* (1918), New York: Princeton Architectural Press, 1989.

Gaunt, William, *The Aesthetic Adventure*, New York: Shocken Books, 1967.

Geogheghan, Vincent, *Utopianism and Marxism*, London: Methuen, 1987.

Giedion, Sigfried, *Space, Time and Architecture: The Growth of a New Tradition*, 5th edn, Cambridge, MA: Harvard University Press, 1967.

Goldhagen, Sarah Williams and Legault, Rejéan (eds), *Anxious Modernisms, Experimentation in Postwar Architectural Culture*, Montréal and Cambridge, MA: CCA and MIT Press, 2000.

Goodman, Paul, *Utopian Essays and Practical Proposals*, New York: Random House, 1962.

Goodman, Paul, and Goodman, Percival, *Communitas*, New York: Vintage, 1947.

Gregotti, Vittorio, *Inside Architecture*, P. Wong and F. Zaccheo (trans.), Cambridge, MA: MIT Press, 1996.

Gropius, Walter, *The New Architecture and the Bauhaus*, P. Morton Shand (trans.), Cambridge, MA: MIT Press, 1965.

Harries, Karsten, *The Ethical Function of Architecture*, Cambridge: MIT Press, 1997.

Heidegger, Martin, *Basic Writings* (1927–1964), David. F. Krell (ed.), New York: Harper and Row, 1977.

Herdeg, Klaus, *The Decorated Diagram, Harvard Architecture and the Failure of the Bauhaus Legacy*, Cambridge, MA: MIT Press, 1983.

Hermand, Jost, 'The Necessity of Utopian Thinking', *Soundings*, 58, Spring 1975.

Hertzberger, Herman, *Lessons for Students in Architecture*, Rotterdam: 010 Publishers, 1991.

Hertzberger, Herman, *Space and the Architect: Lessons in Architecture*, 2, Rotterdam: 010 Publishers, 2000.

Hesiod, 'Theogony', *Hesiod, Homeric Hymns, Epic Cycle, Homerica* (1914), H. G. Evelyn-White (trans.), Cambridge, MA: Harvard University Press, 1995.

Hesiod, 'Works and Days', *Hesiod, Homeric Hymns, Epic Cycle, Homerica* (1914), H. G. Evelyn-White (trans.), Cambridge, MA: Harvard University Press, 1995.

Hitchcock, Henry-Russell, and Johnson, Philip, *The International Style* (1932), New York: W. W. Norton, 1995.

Howard, Ebenezer, *Garden Cities of Tomorrow*, Cambridge, MA: MIT Press, 1965.

Huxley, Aldous, *Brave New World Revisted*, New York: Harper and Row, 1958.

Huxley, Aldous, *Brave New World* (1932), New York: Harper and Row, 1969.

Jacobs, Jane, *The Death and Life of Great American Cities*, New York: Vintage Books, 1961.

Jacoby, Mario A., *Longing for Paradise: Psychological Perspectives on an Archetype*, Boston: Sigo Press, 1985.

Jameson, Fredric, *Marxism and Form: Twentieth-Century Dialectical Theories of Literature*, Princeton, N.J.: Princeton University Press, 1971.

Jameson, Fredric, *The Cultural Turn: Selected Writings on the Postmodern, 1983–1998*, London, New York: Verso, 1998.

Kahn, Louis I., *What Will be Has Always Been, The Words of Louis I. Kahn*, Richard Saul Wurman (ed.), New York: Access and Rizzoli, 1986.

Kahn, Louis I., *Writings, Lectures, Interviews*, Alessandra Latour (ed.), New York, Rizzoli, 1991.

Select bibliography

Kahn, Louis I., *Conversations with Students*, Architecture at Rice 26, 2nd edn, New York: Princeton Architectural Press, 1998.

Kahn, Louis I., *Essential Texts*, Robert Twombly (ed.), New York: W. W. Norton and Co., 2003.

Klein, Florence, *Mwa Kaa, the Pathways of Kanak Tradition*, Stéphane Goiran (trans.), Nouméa, New Caledonia: ADCK, 2000.

Koolhaas, Rem, *Delirious New York* (1978)., New York: Monacelli Press, 1994.

Koolhaas, Rem, *Conversations With Students* (1991), Architecture at Rice 30, 2nd edn, New York: Princeton Architectural Press, 1996.

Lang, S., 'The Ideal City from Plato to Howard', *Architectural Review 112*, August 1952, pp. 91–101.

Lasdun, Denys, *Architecture in an Age of Scepticism*, New York: Oxford University Press, 1984.

Laugier, Marc-Antoine, *An Essay on Architecture* (1753), Wolfgang and Anni Herrman (trans.), Los Angeles: Henessay and Ingalls, 1977.

Leatherbarrow, David, *The Roots of Architectural Invention: Site, Enclosure, Materials*, Cambridge: Cambridge University Press, 1993.

Leatherbarrow, David, *Uncommon Ground: Architecture, Technology, and Topography*, Cambridge, MA: MIT Press, 2000.

Leatherbarrow, David, *Topographical Stories: Studies in Landscape and Architecture*, Philadelphia: University of Pennsylvania Press, 2004.

Le Corbusier, *When the Cathedrals were White* (1947), Francis E. Hyslop, Jr (trans.), New York: McGraw-Hill, 1964.

Le Corbusier, *The Sociology of Marx*, Norbert Guterman (trans.), New York: Vintage Books, 1968.

Le Corbusier, *Modulor 1 & 2*, Peter de Francia and Anna Bostock (trans.), Cambridge, MA: Harvard University Press, 1980.

Le Corbusier, *The Ideas of Le Corbusier On Architecture and Urban Planning*, Jacques Guiton (ed.), M. Guiton (trans.), New York: George Braziller Inc., 1981.

Le Corbusier, *Towards a New Architecture* (1931), Frederick Etchells (trans.), New York: Dover Publications, Inc., 1986.

Le Corbusier, *Journey to the East,* Ivan Zaknic (ed., ann., trans.), in collaboration with Nicole Pertuiset, Cambridge, MA: The MIT Press, 1987.

Le Corbusier, *The Decorative Art of Today*, James Dunnett (trans.), Cambridge, MA: MIT Press, 1987.

Le Corbusier, *The City of Tomorrow and its Planning* (1929), New York: Dover Publications, Inc., 1987.

Le Corbusier, *Precisions on the Present State of Architecture and City Planning* (1930), Edith Schreiber Aujame (trans.), Cambridge, MA: MIT Press, 1991.

Le Corbusier, 'Mise au Point', *The Final Testament of Père Corbu*, Ivan Zanic (trans.), New Haven: Yale University Press, 1997.

Le Corbusier, *Talks with Students* (1961), Pierre Chase (trans.), New York: Princeton Architectural Press, 1999.

Levitas, Ruth, *The Concept of Utopia*, Syracuse, NY: Syracuse University Press, 1990.

Lefebvre, Henri, 'The Right to the City', *Writings on Cities* (1968), Eleonore Kofman and Elizabeth Lebas (trans.), Oxford, England: Blackwell, 1996.

Libeskind, Daniel, *Countersign*, New York: Rizzoli, 1992.

Libeskind, Daniel, *radix-matrix*, Munich: Prestel-Verlag – New York and Daniel Libeskind, 1997.

Libeskind, Daniel, *Jewish Museum Berlin*, Gemany: G + B Arts International, 1999.

Libeskind, Daniel, *The Space of Encounter*, London: Thames and Hudson, 2001.

Libeskind, Daniel, 'Monument and Memory', in *Art in Society*, The Columbia Seminar on Art in Society, New York: Department of Art History and Archaeology of Columbia University, 22 September 2002, pp. 10–32.

Libeskind, Daniel, with Crichton, Sarah, *Breaking Ground, Adventures in Life and Architecture*, New York: Riverhead Books, 2004.

Livy, *The Early History of Rome, Books I–V*, Aubrey de Selincourt (trans.) London: Penguin Books, 1971.

Machiavelli, Niccolo, *The Prince* (1513), Daniel Donno (trans.), Toronto: Bantam Books, 1966.

Mannheim, Karl, *Ideology and Utopia* (1936), Louis Wirth and Edward Shils (trans.), San Diego: Harcourt Brace and Company, 1985.

Manuel, Frank E., *Prophets of Paris: Turgot, Condorcet, Saint-Simon, Fourier, Comte*, Cambridge, MA, Harvard University Press, 1962.

Manuel, Frank E. (ed.), *Utopias and Utopian Thought*, Boston, MA: Houghton Mifflin, 1966.

Manuel, Frank E. and Manuel, Fritzie P., *Utopian Thought in the Western World*, Cambridge, MA: Belknap/Harvard, 1979.

Manuel, Frank E. and Manuel, Fritzie P., 'Sketch for a Natural History of Paradise', *Daedalus, Journal of the American Academy of Arts and Sciences*, 101, Winter, 1972, p. 83–128.

Manuel, Frank E. and Manuel, Fritzie P., *French Utopias: An Anthology of Ideal Societies* (eds and trans.), New York: Free Press, 1966.

Martini, Francesco di Giorgio, *Trattati Di Architettura E Arte Militare*, A Cura di Corrado Maltese, Transcrizione di Lavia Maltese: Edizioni Il Polifilo, Milano, 1967.

McClung, William Alexander, *The Architecture of Paradise: Survivals of Eden and Jerusalem*, Berkeley: University of California Press, 1983.

Marx, Karl, *The Communist Manifesto* (1888), Samuel Moore (trans.), Norton Critical Edition, New York: Norton, 1988.

Marx, Karl and Engels, Friedrich, *Marx & Engels: Basic Writings on Politics and Philosophy*, Lewis S. Feuer (trans. and ed.), New York: Anchor/Doubleday, 1959.

More, Sir Thomas, *Utopia* (1516), Robert M. Adams (trans. and ed.), 2nd edn, New York: W. W. Norton and Co., 1992.

Morris, William, *News From Nowhere and Other Writings* (1890), Clive Wilmer (ed.), London: Penguin, 1993.

Morris, William, *Art and Society, Lectures and Essays by William Morris*, Gary Zabel (ed.), Medford, MA: Georges Hill, 1993.

Morton, A. L., *The English Utopia*, London: Lawrence and Wishart Ltd, 1978.

Mumford, Lewis, *The Story of Utopias* (1922), Gloucester, MA: Peter Smith, 1959.

Newman, Oscar, *New Frontiers in Architecture, CIAM '59 in Otterlo*, by order of Jacob B. Bakema for the Otterlo 1959 participants, Jürgen Joedicke (ed.), New York: Universe Books, 1961.

Office for Metropolitan Architecture, Rem Koolhaas and Bruce Mau, *Small, Medium, Large, Extra Large*, Jennifer Sigler (ed.), New York: Monacelli Press, 1995.

Onians, John, *Bearers of Meaning*, Princeton, NJ: Princeton University Press. 1988.

Ortega Y Gasset, José, *The Dehumanization of Art*, Princeton, NJ: Princeton Paperbacks, 1968.

Owen, Robert, *A New View of Society and Other Writings*, Gregory Claeys (ed.), London: Penguin, 1991.

Palazzolo, Carlo and Vio, Riccardo (eds), *In the Footsteps of Le Corbusier*, New York: Rizzoli, 1991.

Palladio, Andrea, *The Four Books of Architecture*, New York: Dover Publications, Inc., 1965.

Pérez-Goméz, Alberto, *Architecture and the Crisis of Modern Science* (1983), Cambridge, MA: MIT Press, 1992.

Perrault, Claude, *Ordonnance for the Five Kinds of Columns After the Methods of the Ancients*, Indra Kagis McEwen (trans.), Santa Monica, CA: Getty Center, 1993.

Petit, Jean (ed.), *Un Couvent de le Corbusier*, Paris: Les Editions de Minuit, 1961.

Pevsner, Nikolaus, *The Sources of Modern Architecture and Design*, London: Thames and Hudson, 1968.

Pevsner, Nikolaus, *Pioneers of Modern Design: from William Morris to Walter Gropius*, revised 1975, London: Penguin, 1991.

Piano, Renzo, *Renzo Piano 1987–1994*, with a contribution by Vittorio Magnaago Lampugnani, Basel: Birkhäuser, 1994.

Select bibliography

Piano, Renzo, *Renzo Piano Logbook*, New York: Monacelli Press, 1997.

Piano, Renzo, *La responsabilità dell'architetto*, Conversazione con Renzo Cassigoli, Firenze-Antella: Passigli Editori, 2000.

Plant, Sadie, *The Most Radical Gesture: The Situationist International in a Postmodern Age*, London, New York: Routledge, 1992.

Plato, *The Laws*, Trevor J. Saunders (trans.), London: Penguin Books, 1970.

Plato, *The Great Dialogues of Plato*, W. H. D. Rouse (trans.), New York City: Mentor, 1984.

Plato, *Timaeus and Critias*, Including an Appendix on Atlantis, Desmond Lee (trans.), London: Penguin Books, 1977.

Popper, Karl, *The Poverty of Historicism* (1961), London: Routledge, 1994.

Pugin, Augustus Welby Northmore, *Contrasts* (London, C. Dolman, 1841), 2nd edn, New York: Humanities, 1969.

Pugin, Augustus Welby Northmore, *The True Principles of Pointed, or Christian Architecture*, London: Academy Editions, 1973.

Rabelais, *The Works of Rabelais*, New York: Tudor Publishing Company, 1963.

Ricoeur, Paul, *The Conflict of Interpretation*, Don Ihde (ed.), Evaston: University of Chicago Press, 1974.

Ricoeur, Paul, *Ideology Utopia and Faith*, The Center for Hermeneutical Studies, 1976.

Ricoeur, Paul, 'Ideology and Utopia as Cultural Imagination', *Philosophic Exchange*, vol. 2, no. 2, 1976, pp. 17–28.

Ricoeur, Paul, *The Rule of Metaphor* (1975), Robert Czerny (trans.), Toronto: University of Toronto Press, 1981.

Ricoeur, Paul, *Lectures on Ideology and Utopia*, G. H. Taylor (ed.), New York: Columbia University Press, 1986.

Ricoeur, Paul, *From Text to Action*, K. Blamey and J. B. Thompson (trans.), Evanston, Illinois: Northwestern University Press, 1991.

Ricoeur, Paul, *Reflection and Imagination*, M. J. Valdé (ed.), Toronto and Buffalo: University of Toronto Press, 1991.

Riley, Terence, *The International Style: Exhibition 15 and the Museum of Modern Art*, New York: Rizzoli/Columbia, 1992.

Rosenau, Helen, *The Ideal City in its Architectural Evolution*, London: Routledge and Keegan Paul, 1959.

Rosenau, Helen, *Boullée and Visionary Architecture*, New York: Harmony Books, 1976.

Rossi, Aldo, *The Architecture of the City*, Diane Ghirardo and Joan Ockman (trans.), Cambridge, MA: MIT Press, 1982.

Rousseau, Jean-Jacques, 'Rousseau's Social Contract' in *Famous Utopias*, Charles M. Andrews (trans.), New York: Tudor Publishing Co., pp. 3–126.

Rowe, Colin, *Mathematics of the Ideal Villa and Other Essays*, Cambridge, MA: MIT Press, 1976.

Rowe, Colin and Koetter, Fred, *Collage City*, Cambridge, MA: MIT Press, 1978.

Ruskin, John, *The Stones of Venice* (1853), J. G. Links (ed.), New York: Da Capo Press, 1960.

Ruskin, John, *Unto this Last and Other Writings* (1862), Clive Wilmer (ed.), London: Penguin, 1985.

Ruskin, John, *The Seven Lamps of Architecture* (1880), New York: Dover Publications, Inc., 1989.

Rykwert, Joseph, *Church Building*, New York: Hawthorn, 1966.

Rykwert, Joseph, *The First Moderns: The Architects of the Eighteenth Century*, Cambridge, MA: MIT Press, 1980.

Rykwert, Joseph, *On Adam's House In Paradise: The Idea of the Primitive Hut in Architectural History* (1972) Cambridge, MA: MIT Press, 1981.

Rykwert, Joseph, *The Necessity of Artifice*, New York: Rizzoli, 1982.

Rykwert, Joseph, *The Idea of a Town: The Anthropology of Urban Form in Rome, Italy, and the Ancient World*, Cambridge, MA: MIT Press, 1988.

Rykwert, Joseph, *The Dancing Column: On Order in Architecture*, Cambridge, MA: MIT Press Inc., 1996.

Rykwert, Joseph, *The Seduction of Place, the City in the Twenty-First Century*, New York: Pantheon, 2000.

Sadler, Simon, *The Situationist City*, Cambridge, MA: The MIT Press, 1999.

St. Augustine, *City of God*, abridged, (various trans.), New York: Doubleday, 1958.

Schaer, Roland, Claeys, Gregory and Sargent, Lyman Tower (eds), *Utopia, the Search for the Ideal Society in the Western World*, New York/Oxford: New York Public Library/Oxford University Press, 2000.

Scott, Geoffrey, *The Architecture of Humanism, A Study in the History of Taste* (1914), New York: W. W. Norton and Co., 1974.

Segal, Howard P., *Technological Utopianism in American Culture*, Chicago: University of Chicago Press, 1985.

Semper, Gottfried, *The Four Elements of Architecture*, Mallgrave and Herrmann (trans.), Cambridge, MA: Cambridge University Press, 1989.

Serenyi, Peter (ed.), *Le Corbusier in Perspective*, Englewood Cliffs, New Jersey: Prentice Hall, 1975.

Serlio, Sebastiano, *The Five Books of Architecture*, New York: Dover Publications, Inc., 1982.

Sitte, Camillo. *The Art of Building Cities*, Charles T. Stewart (trans.), Westport, CT: Hyperion Press, Inc., 1845.

Skinner, B. F., *Walden Two* (1948), New York: Macmillan, 1970.

Smithson, Alison (ed.), *Team 10 Primer*, Cambridge, MA: MIT Press, 1968.

Smithson, Alison (ed.), *Team 10 Meetings*. New York: Rizzoli, 1991.

Soane, Sir John, *Lectures on Architecture*, London: Publications of Sir John Soane's Museum, No. 14, 1929.

Strauven, Francis, *Aldo van Eyck's Orphanage: A Modern Monument*, J. Kirkpatrick (trans.), Netherlands: NAi Publishers, 1996.

Strauven, Francis, *Aldo van Eyck, The Shape of Relativity*, Victor J. Joseph (trans.), Amsterdam: Architectura and Natura, 1998.

Sullivan, Louis H., *Kindergarten Chats and Other Writings* (1918), New York: Dover Publications, Inc. 1979.

Tafuri, Manfredo, *Architecture and Utopia, Design and Capitalist Development*, Barbara Luigia La Penta (trans.), Cambridge, MA: MIT Press, 1976.

Tafuri, Manfredo, *The Sphere and the Labyrinth: Avant-Gardes and Architecture from Piranesi to the 1970s* (1980), Pellegrino d'Acierno and Robert Connolly (trans.), Cambridge, MA: MIT Press, 1987.

Tafuri, Manfredo, and Francesco Dal Co, *Modern Architecture*, Robert Erich Wolf (trans.), New York: Harry N. Abrams, 1976.

Tjibaou, Jean-Marie, *Cibau Cibau*, Roy Benyon (trans.), Nouméa New Calédonie: Agence de dévelopment de la culture Kanak, 1998.

Turner, Paul Venerable, *The Education of Le Corbusier*, New York: Garland Publishing, Inc., 1971.

van Eyck, Aldo, 'The Interior of Time' (1966), in *Meaning in Architecture*, Charles Jencks and George Baird (eds), New York: George Braziller, Inc., 1969, pp. 161–215.

van Eyck, Aldo, *Aldo van Eyck, Projekten 1962–1976*, Uitgave: Johann van de Beek, 1983.

van Eyck, Aldo, 2nd edn, *Hubertus House*, Amsterdam: Stichting Wonen, 1986.

van Eyck, Aldo, 'Steps Toward a Configurative Discipline', *Forum 3*, August 1962, reprinted in *Architecture Culture 1943–1968*, compiled by Joan Ockman, New York: Rizzoli and Columbia, 1993, pp. 347–60.

van Eyck, Aldo, and Hannie van Eyck. *Built with Color: The Netherlands Court of Audit*, Rotterdam: 010 Publishers, 1999.

van Eyck, Aldo, *Works*, Vincent Ligtelijn (ed.), Basel: Birkhäuser, 1999.

Vattimo, Gianni, *The End of Modernity: Nihilism and Hermeneutics in Postmodern Culture*, Jon R. Snyder (trans.), Baltimore: Johns Hopkins University Press, 1992.

Vattimo, Gianni, *The Transparent Society*, David Webb (trans.), Baltimore: Johns Hopkins University, 1992.

Select bibliography

Vattimo, Gianni, *Belief*, Luca D'Isanto and David Webb (trans.), Stanford, CA: Stanford University Press, 1999.

Vattimo, Gianni, *Beyond Interpretation: The Meaning of Hermeneutics for Philosophy*, David Webb (trans.), Stanford, CA: Stanford University Press, 1997.

Vattimo, Gianni, 'The End of Modernity, The End of the Project?' in *Rethinking Architecture*, Neil Leach (ed.), London and New York: Routledge, 1997, pp. 148–60.

Venturi, Robert, *Complexity and Contradiction in Architecture* (1966), New York: Museum of Modern Art, 1977.

Venturi, Robert, Brown, Denise Scott and Izenour, Steven, *Learning from Las Vegas*, revised edn, Cambridge, MA: MIT Press, 1977.

Vico, Giambattista, *The New Science of Giambattista Vico* (1744), T. G. Bergin and M. H. Fisch (trans.), Ithaca: Cornell University Press, 1984.

Villari, Sergio, *J. N. L. Durand (1760–1834), Art and Science of Architecture*, Eli Gottlieb (trans.), New York: Rizzoli, 1990.

Viollet-Le-Duc, Eugène-Emmanuel, *Lectures on Architecture* (1863–1872), 2 vols, B. Bucknall (trans.), New York: Dover, 1987.

Viollet-Le-Duc, Eugène-Emmanuel, *The Foundations of Architecture: Selections from the Dictionnaire Raisonné* (1854), K. D. Whitehead (trans.), New York: George Braziller, Inc., 1990.

Vitruvius (Marcus V. Pollio), *The Ten Books on Architecture*, Morris Hicky Morgan (trans.) (1914), New York: Dover Publications Inc., 1960.

Voltaire (François-Marie Arouet), *Candide, Zadig and Selected Stories*, Donald M. Frame (trans.), New York: New American Library, 1961.

Walden, Russell (ed.), *The Open Hand: Essays on Le Corbusier*, Cambridge, MA: MIT Press, 1977.

Wilde, Oscar, *The Soul of Man Under Socialism* (1891), New York: Oriole Chapbooks, 1965.

Williams, Tod and Tsien, Billie, *Williams Tsien Works*, 2G International Architecture Review, Number 9, Spain 1999.

Williams, Tod and Tsien, Billie, *Work Life*, Hadley Arnold (ed.), New York, Monacelli Press, 2000.

Wittkower, Rudolf, *Architectural Principles in the Age of Humanism*, New York: Norton, 1971.

Wright, Frank Lloyd, 'The Living City' (1958), in *Frank Lloyd Wright Collected Writings, Vol. 5, 1949–1959*, New York: Rizzoli, 1995, pp. 251–344.

Young, James E., *At Memory's Edge: After Images of the Holocaust in Contemporary Art and Architecture*, New Haven: Yale University Press, 2000.

Index